Giant Book

of

Word Search Puzzles

Edited by Theresa Byrnes

Puzzles by Mark Danna, Francis Heaney,
Amy Goldstein, and Dave Tuller

STERLING INNOVATION
An imprint of Sterling Publishing Co., Inc.

New York / London
www.sterlingpublishing.com

D1402902

4 6 8 10 9 7 5 3

Published by Sterling Publishing Co., Inc.
387 Park Avenue South, New York, NY 10016

This book is composed of material from the following Sterling titles:
Sit & Solve® Word Search Puzzles © 2003 by Mark Danna
Sip & Solve™ Word Search Puzzles © 2005 by Francis Heaney
Sit & Solve® Commuter Word Search Puzzles © 2005 by Amy Goldstein
Sit & Solve® Travel Word Search Puzzles © 2007 by Amy Goldstein
Word Search Puzzles to Keep You Sharp © 2003 by Mark Danna
Wacky-Shaped Word Search Puzzles to Keep You Sharp © 2004 by Mark Danna
Super Tough Word Search Puzzles © 2002 by Dave Tuller

Distributed in Canada by Sterling Publishing
c/o Canadian Manda Group, 165 Dufferin Street
Toronto, Ontario, Canada M6K 3H6
Distributed in the United Kingdom by GMC Distribution Services
Castle Place, 166 High Street, Lewes, East Sussex, England BN7 1XU
Distributed in Australia by Capricorn Link (Australia) Pty. Ltd.
P.O. Box 704, Windsor, NSW 2756, Australia

Sterling ISBN-13: 978-1-4027-4998-8
ISBN-10: 1-4027-4998-8

Design by StarGraphics Studio

For information about custom editions, special sales, premium and
corporate purchases, please contact Sterling Special Sales
Department at 800-805-5489 or specialsales@sterlingpublishing.com.

Contents

Introduction

Studies have shown that solving word puzzles is a terrific way to keep the brain in fine working order. That's good news for everyone who enjoys puzzles, but it's especially so for older people who want to keep their minds sharp and stimulated. What's also great is that while we're solving puzzles, we're actually doing exercises for the brain without even thinking about it!

Now that's all well and good, but even if exercise is good for you, who wants to do it unless it's fun? Not me . . . and not you . . . which is why this book is geared not only to keep you sharp but to provide a whole lot of fun in the process!

USA TODAY Giant Book of Word Search Puzzles is very different from any other word search puzzle book you've ever seen. In fact, if variety is the spice of life, this book is downright spicy.

First off, there are two sections: the Quick Solve Word Search Puzzles and the Mind-Boggling Word Search Puzzles. The Quick Solve puzzles are smaller puzzles with fewer words to find. The shapes vary from your traditional square to puzzles with rounded edges. The Mind-Boggling puzzles are larger puzzles, with more words and more tricks. Let's start with the pictures. Many of the 177 puzzle grids in this section form distinctive pictures. For example, there's a galloping horse, a bouffant hairdo, a tennis racket, an engagement ring, a woman's boot, and lots of other lively shapes.

There's also a wide range of puzzle variations. In the rebus puzzles, a set of letters appears in the grid as a little drawing. For example, the consecutive letters CAR appear every time in one grid as a . In some other puzzles, it's up to you to fill in the letters that are purposely missing in the grid. And in a few cases, you'll need to uncover the word list from a set of clues.

As a big bonus, each and every puzzle contains a hidden message. Once you've found all the word-list entries in the grid, read the uncircled letters from left to right, top to bottom, to reveal a quip, fact, or quote appropriate to the puzzle's theme. Though the letters will be in order, you'll need to figure out how to break them into words and where to add punctuation . . . which makes this puzzle-within-a-puzzle a challenge.

If you prefer your word searches plain and simple, you'll find plenty of such puzzles here, too. And be assured: all the puzzles follow the traditional rules of word-search solving. That is, each puzzle consists of two main parts: the word list tells you what words and phrases are hidden in the grid; and the grid—which at first appears to be a meaningless jumble of letters—contains all of those words, which may run horizontally, vertically, or diagonally, but always in a straight line. (Actually, a few puzzles deviate from the straight line, but that will be explained in the particular puzzle directions). Remember to ignore all spacing, punctuation, and accent marks in the word list, as well as any words in brackets or in lowercase type.

To add to your enjoyment, we've picked puzzle titles that are playful and punny. And as a point of craftsmanship, with a few exceptions, we've made sure that all the words in every grid interconnect—an elegant detail that's all too rare in puzzles elsewhere.

We hope you'll have fun flexing your mental muscles straight through to the last puzzles.

Quick Solve Word Search Puzzles

1. Things To Do While Sitting

CHECK E-MAIL
DRIVE A CAR
EAT A MEAL
FLY A PLANE
HEAR A SERMON
KNIT
NOTHING
PLAY CARDS
PLAY PIANO
PUT BOOTS ON
READ A BOOK
RELAX
RIDE A BIKE
ROW A BOAT
SEE A MOVIE
TYPE
WATCH TV
WORK AT A DESK
WRITE A LETTER
YOGA

```
      I F L Y A P L A N E S
    H A X T E L L N U S I T H W E
  P L A Y P I A N O R T E O Y O G A
N A L N Y D O N F M F D B F O R R L G
T E D T A Y S A K R N R D O D K I E N
R A R E T T E L A E T I R W O A A A I
Y S O S A I D O W S N V E A M T L I H
K O O B A D A E R A C E E E A A S I T
R I D E A B I K E R T A K M N D W O O
O N D E R W L A N A D C E C H E A R N
  S E E A M O V I E E A H A C S T E
  R N O T I R N H L R A T L K O
    P L A Y C A R D S O V
```

ANSWER, PAGE 262

2. Famous Johns, Johnnys, and Jons

APPLESEED
BON JOVI
CLEESE
CUSACK
DENVER
DEPP
ELWAY
F. KENNEDY, JR.
GLENN
IRVING
LENNON
LOVITZ
MADDEN
MATHIS
MCENROE
PAYCHECK
PHILIP SOUSA
Q. PUBLIC
STAMOS
STEWART
TRAVOLTA
UNITAS
VOIGHT
WILKES BOOTH

```
      A C F E W O F T E H E
    R N L N W I L K E S B O O T H
  G L E N N O T E A B K L E R J O N
S H E D N N Y N S A C R B E C N O A S
T S R D E S N T R A V O L T A N E O T
E P N A W E E I S S N S C O N V M C A
W U A M D L S U L J E R I E V O S C M
A A S Y H M C E O I G L L L E I A A O
R R J A C B E V L N N C B H O G T N S
T R T W P H I L I P S O U S A H I Z H
  E S L P O E V T P P A P N I T N D
  C E O M R C E E L A Q S A T U
    E I L Y K D E N V E R
```

ANSWER, PAGE 262

3. Signs On Doors

BACK IN FIVE
   MINUTES
CLOSED
DO NOT DISTURB
EMPLOYEES
   ONLY
ENTER
GENTS
HOURS
IN USE
KEEP OUT
MAID SERVICE
MAIL

MANAGER
NO MENUS
OCCUPIED
OPEN
OUT TO LUNCH
PRINCIPAL
PRIVATE
PULL
PUSH
STEP UP
USE OTHER DOOR
VACANT
WOMEN

```
          A S I N G Y E N T E R
        M N T A C E K L E D O O N P T
      V A C A N T M O N T H O E U E D O
    S O I K H R D O N O T D I S T U R B O
    U F D E A C D W O S R G H U O B E D L
    N I S E T U N I M E V I F N I K C A B
    E S E P E A N U H E C E S I C H P O O
    M L R O C R V T L Y O C C U P I E D O
    O A V U L E O I A O D B A C C K I P N
    N F I T O E I V R L T M A N A G E R E
      M C L S H I N L P U T I S T N E G
      E U E T E U S M S R U I T S T
        D A P S T E P U P O Y
```

ANSWER, PAGE 262

4. Vowel Play

BLANDER
BLENDER
BLINDER
BLONDER
BLUNDER
DALLY
DELI
DILLY
DOLLY
DULLY
LAST
LEST

LIST
LOST
LUST
MASSES
MESSES
MISSES
MOSSES
MUSSES
PETTER
PITTER-PATTER
POTTER
PUTTER

```
          R S O M M R R E C O T
        M M E O N I W S E S S O M S O
      R I D T S S T H B D T A T C O I B
    N T A L T S M I L N N A T L T S E L L
    P I T T E R P A T T E R F U I V E O V
    O O W S P D N E S L L S E A P C H N U
    T B L I N D E R S S B M E Y L L O D D
    T S O N E C D S E R E D N U L B A E R
    E E U R S I E Q E S U S O I Y L A R F
    R A C L L E T I S S O U S L S O A U B
      C O L N A T E I N S E L N T S A D
      Y L A N S D U N C U O M P T L
        I M E T N T D A M R Y
```

ANSWER, PAGE 262

5. Car Pool

ACURA
AUDI
BUICK
CADILLAC
CHEVROLET
FERRARI
FORD
HONDA
INFINITI
JAGUAR
LAMBORGHINI
LEXUS
LINCOLN
MASERATI
MAZDA
MERCEDES-BENZ
NISSAN
PORSCHE
ROLLS-ROYCE
SAAB
SUBARU
TOYOTA
VOLKSWAGEN
VOLVO

```
            M H J M M I N F L P E
          O A R U C A P E L E F E A W M
        I Z A Y F R O G M X H O E M E E T
    T D N O S U B A R U E H C S R O P E O
    A L O I N G W U S C A C A C N R G L T
    A D N O H S E D I T A R E S A M A O T
    H O N V K G M I E S I D N C K D Y R O
    P R O L L S R O Y C E E I O P O L V I
    E D O O O A W O A S Y F S L T R O E M
    T V R V K C I U B H B E S A L I R H C
      A R O S T N E O M A O A L O A N C
        I N F I N I T I A G N G E T C
          C Z A R L S S L I C K
```

ANSWER, PAGE 263

6. Royal Flush

ALL-IN
ANTE
BAD BEAT
BLUFF
CALL
CARD ROOM
CHECK
DEALER
DRAW
FIVE CARD STUD
FOLD
FULL HOUSE
HIGH-LOW
HOLD 'EM
NO-LIMIT
PAIR
POKER
RAISE
SHOWDOWN
SHUFFLE
SIDE POT
STAKES
STRAIGHT
THREE OF A KIND

```
          A D S E D A S D M A T
        E S U O H L L U F T N H S H W
      A N D H A O S T W I O R B R A A C
    E S A N D F W T W O V E E A R A I G P
    W H N T F S D M I T E I S D I N I A O
    M O O U E D O S O O C F O B R G W S K
    R E L A E D W T F O A H A E T W H I E
    I B I H L D N A B K R L L A C U O T R
    A N M I G L K K C L D D H T F I L C K
    P O I K H I E E L D S W R F H E D N H
      E T L N W H S A S T S L A N T E H
        O D L C T I N T U E H E C B M
          A A T O P E D I S C K
```

ANSWER, PAGE 263

8

7. Off on a Cruise

"A FEW GOOD MEN"
"COCKTAIL"
"EYES WIDE SHUT"
"JERRY MAGUIRE"
KIDMAN
"LEGEND"
"MAGNOLIA"
"MISSION: IMPOSSIBLE"
"RAIN MAN"
"RISKY BUSINESS"
ROGERS
"TAPS"
"THE FIRM"
"TOP GUN"
VAMPIRE
"VANILLA SKY"

```
            T H O U G V A R H F I
        J E R R Y M A G U I R E L M S
      T A R T O M N C R U S L I S E H R
    A N S T H A I L I A T K C O C D O R A
    P A U H H L E N O M E Y N A N G L A M
    O M V G L E G E N D I B E C E G A I R
    E D E A P R F N E X T U T R O H A N I
    M I S S I O N I M P O S S I B L E M S
    S K M I R R T O R R H I E R I P M A V
    Y P E K E E P S A M P N I E C E O N F
      P A F E W G O O D M E N A P E R T
      H T U H S E D I W S E Y E A T
      R E A D S R E S L A X
```

ANSWER, PAGE 263

8. Things That Come in Pairs

ANIMALS ON NOAH'S ARK
ANTENNAE
ANTLERS
BALLROOM DANCERS
BOOKENDS
CONTACT LENSES
CUFF LINKS
CYMBALS
DICE
DRUMSTICKS
EARMUFFS
ICE SKATES
KNEEPADS
LOVEBIRDS
SHOES
SKIS
SOCKS
SPOUSES
TWINS
WINGS

```
            I F Y O C B U S K S I
        B A L L R O O M D A N C E R S
      C H O U L D O N F I N E I D R R O
    M U E A N C K E T Y S S E O W E E U S
    L F L A P E A N A T K A P N C T L D E
    P F W I N G S A C A C N A I S T T O S
    N L S D C N E M T O O R D E F A N L U
    N I S E D T E E L H S A S T F S A A O
    S N P A O I S T E R O F P A U B N T P
    S K R A S H A O N N O S L A M I N A S
      S I B Y A S L S A L A N Y R S H E
      R S D R I B E V O L C M A A N
      D R U M S T I C K S E
```

ANSWER, PAGE 263

9

9. Just Desserts

BABA AU RHUM
BABKA
BROWNIE
CANNOLI
CHEESECAKE
CHERRY COBBLER
COOKIE
CRÈME BRÛLÉE
CUSTARD
FUDGE
GELATI
ICE CREAM

JELL-O
KEY LIME PIE
MOUSSE
NAPOLEON
PARFAIT
POPSICLE
SHERBET
SPUMONI
SUNDAE
TAPIOCA
TART
TIRAMISU

```
            T R C E L C I S P O P
        B A B A A U R H U M O B A I N
      S O E N N R C H E E S E C A K E C
    T R U N I E S T O R N E W O U E B L D
    A H O A M N S P A R F A I T G Y V A U
    P L E E A B W S E Y E I P D N L E S B
    I T A L E G M O U C N T U O U I I C H
    O H D A R P P I R O E F E R L M K I F
    C H N E C D B E M B M J E N A E O S T
    A R U A E E L U R B E M E R C P O N D
      E S D C O P E N L A D I E S I C N
        S E I S H R L E T T I S L E A
        N S D O D R A T S U C
```

ANSWER, PAGE 264

10. Body Language

ARMCHAIR
BONE UP
BOOTLEG
BUTTERFINGERS
CHESTNUT
CHIN-UP
EARMARK
ELBOW GREASE
FOOTMAN
HANDOUT

HEARTTHROB
HIGHBROW
KNEE-SLAPPER
LIP SERVICE
NECKLACE
NOSEGAY
PALM TREE
PRIVATE EYE
SKIN DIVER
TOE SHOE

```
            L W O R B H G I H E T
        S F A K I T U N T S E H C C E
      I F T B A N O T D Y T P A B R T S
    E N S O H H O E T W U U P I O P N T G
    A O E C O R N S E L B O W G R E A S E
    R O M C F T E E R S V D E I H R T P L
    M R Y D K A M V F Y L N V P T H O U T
    A R A S E L S A I A P A L M T R E E O
    R N O S E G A Y N D T H P N R D S N O
    K T P U N I H C G E N H A P A T H O B
    S S E C I V R E S P I L A E Y O B
      I N G Q U Y R I T E K A H R E
        M O E U S T H F U S L
```

ANSWER, PAGE 264

10

11. Sitting on the Throne

ANASTASIA
CAESAR
CASTLE
CLEOPATRA
COAT OF ARMS
COLONIES
CORONATION
CZAR
EMPEROR
GUINEVERE
KING TUT
LEIA
MAJESTY

NERO
PALACE
PRINCE
  CHARMING
QUEEN
REALM
ROYAL HIGHNESS
SCEPTRE
TIARA
VERSAILLES
VICTORIA
"YES, MILORD"

```
            N O I T A N O R O C R
        T H V E P N R A T K R I O A T
      C E I I E A C A R A I T S O R Z N
  G O A L C S R M S E R N I C A T C C E
  E L O M T P S S E N H G I H L A Y O R
  C O I A O S M R A F O T A O C P E Q T
  A N S J R S A T C I H U E T L O U U P
  L I N E I E O C F T L T R O R E P M E
  A E H S A E U K S A N L T E E L I H C
  P S E T G U I N E V E R E N A C M A S
    G O Y D S A V E T H E E S Q L U E
      P R I N C E C H A R M I N G M
        Y E S M I L O R D E N
```

ANSWER, PAGE 264

12. The Doctor Is In

BEN CASEY
DEMENTO
DOLITTLE
EVIL
FAUSTUS
HAWKEYE PIERCE
HUXTABLE
JEKYLL
JOHN
JOYCE BROTHERS
KILDARE
LAURA

LIVINGSTON
MARK GREENE
PHIL
QUINN
RUTH
SEUSS
SPOCK
STRANGELOVE
SYDNEY HANSEN
WATSON
WELBY
ZHIVAGO

```
            M L I V I N G S T O N
        E R A D L I K S C S E U S S R
      E A U R T O B R Y O F V J U R A F
  S S R I K U C P E D O L I T T L E A A
  R A K A G S T R A N G E L O V E H U N
  L I H P R D T H V E C S E R M U I S C
  H L A E E L C R J Y I A C H X T O T N
  J O Y C E B R O T H E R S T N N I U Q
  G R B K N Z H I V A G O A E A D U S A
  T E L D E N F R O N M B H A Y R P V A
  R E D M J E D S S L W A T S O N C
    W H A W K E Y E P I E R C E H
      O D E M E N T O O K L
```

ANSWER, PAGE 264

13. There Is Superstition

AMULET
BLACK CAT
"BREAK A LEG"
BREAK A MIRROR
CHARM
"CROSS YOUR FINGERS"
CURSE
EVIL EYE
JINX
"KNOCK ON WOOD"
LUCK
MOJO
OUIJA BOARD
RABBIT'S FOOT
SEVEN
STEP ON A CRACK
TALISMAN
THIRTEEN
VOODOO
WALK UNDER A LADDER

```
            P U G E L A K A E R B
        T R N A M S I L A T P L R E H
      O H J R S C E S M H E A N E V E S
    E V I L E Y E H U O S E S C A A N D G
    R N R E D D A L A R E D N U K L A W E
    X E T N C L E O U R V E R S A C A R E
    S O E M E T L C U C M K Y C M H A A R
    O M E S T O V D R A O B A J I U O L F
    I J N N T O O F S T I B B A R D I N B
    C R O S S Y O U R F I N G E R S A L B
    O X M O F D T H A T C E R O E U A
    S T E P O N A C R A C K R C L
    D O O W N O K C O N K
```

ANSWER, PAGE 265

14. One for the $

"DOUBLE YOUR MONEY!"
EVEN MONEY
HUSH MONEY
IN THE MONEY
"IT'S ONLY MONEY"
MILK MONEY
MONEY BELT
"… MONEY CAN'T BUY ME LOVE"
"MONEY DOESN'T GROW ON TREES"
MONEY MARKET
MONEY ORDER
MONEY TO BURN
"MONEY'S NO OBJECT"
MONEYLENDER
"MONEYLINE"
MONEYMAKER
PIN MONEY
PRIZE MONEY
SEED MONEY
"SHOW ME THE MONEY!"
SPENDING MONEY
"THE MONEY PIT"
"TIME IS MONEY"
"WIN BEN STEIN'S MONEY"

```
          W $ E W T A N W N $ T
        Y O $ D U I T R O I G E H T Y
      E V O L E M Y U B T N A C $ S O U
    $ I R R $ E Z B D O U B L E Y O U R $
    S N W E I S O I R O T E K R A M $ H M
    R T I S D T T E R $ G N I D N E P S I
    H H $ P $ R D S O P T S H I S G R I L
    S E E R T N O W O R G T N S E O D $ K
    D $ C O E M E $ S T C E J B O O N S $
    $ B E L T K T H E $ P I T W I T H L A
    $ $ B A C A K $ Y L N O S T I I G
    $ E H T E M W O H S E V E N $
    U A R A $ N T $ E E E
```

ANSWER, PAGE 265

15. Things Found in the Bathroom

BATH MAT
BATHTUB
COMB
DRAIN
FAUCETS
FLOSS
HEAT LAMP
LOTION
LYSOL
MEDICINE
  CABINET
MILDEW
MIRROR
MOUTHWASH

Q-TIPS
RAZOR
READING
  MATERIAL
RUBBER DUCKY
SHAMPOO
SHAVING CREAM
SHOWER
  CURTAIN
SINK
SOAP
TOOTHBRUSH
TOWEL

```
        S O O P M A H S T L H
      E S H R S I C T H I S R O N G
    T O H O A L P M O U T H W A S H T
  Y L O R W D U A I R M F A L E Z Y M B
  F O R S E B U T H T A B V T E L O L A
  I I K W R E L Y T U Q O I F I W N R T
  M E D I C I N E C A B I N E T N O D H
  I Y K C U D R E B B U R G N T H I T M
  E B A T R S T H R O O M C I S O T S A
  T H E R T S I F A H S U R B H T O O T
    M R E A D I N G M A T E R I A L I
    L N I A R D K Y M E A M P B E
      N R H E A T L A M P S
```

ANSWER, PAGE 265

16. Road Trip

MAINE
BOSTON
TIMES SQUARE
PHILLY
WHITE HOUSE
ATLANTA
DISNEY WORLD
MARDI GRAS
ST. LOUIS
CHICAGO
MOUNT
  RUSHMORE

DODGE CITY
DALLAS
(THE) ALAMO
TAOS
ASPEN
YELLOWSTONE
LAS VEGAS
DEATH VALLEY
HOLLYWOOD

```
        D E A T H V A L L E Y
      A S F R N E W Y E A R S B A E
    C K A I A H O L L Y W O O D N G U
  Y N N A M U T E T D R O B M I A D E E
  A S I O X Q O L A S V E G A S T S Y S
  S E V S T S E L A N W D M A Y U R O A
  E R O M H S U R T N U O M A O Y D A L
  O A T R I E O P T S T O L H L S S E L
  T M E G A M M B E S A A E L T P A L A
  L M A R D I G R A S Y T I C E G D O D
  T H L I T R T Y M I H L N B Y S T
  O G A C I H C H P A D I U M S
    D L R O W Y E N S I D
```

ANSWER, PAGE 265

13

17. An Awarding Experience

BLUE RIBBON
CALDECOTT
CESAR
CLIO
EDGAR
EMMY
FELLOWSHIP
GOLD STAR
GOLDEN GLOBE
GRAMMY
GRANT
HONORARY
   DEGREE
MEDAL
MERIT BADGE
NOBEL
OBIE
OSCAR
PRITZKER
PULITZER
PURSE
ROTTEN TOMATO
TITLE
TONY
TROPHY

```
              P T T O C E D L A C T
          H E I C E S G A G P R I C S M
        T B T H H E F R R R P U R S E E N
    G O L D S T A R M C A H V L R E S R S
    I E U O W N R E T O M N F I I T H A E
    O S E C O A D O T A M O T N E T T O R
    R R R B L A N O P T Y B T E N T Z O M
    L A I T L Y O E S H A P R I T Z K E R
    A E B R E E R G E D Y R A R O N O H R
    E G B I F V E A G N M T O A T H C E W
      O O O R S T E G M M O V C I L E S
      N O N F T H E D E Y E S I A R
      E B O L G N E D L O G
```

ANSWER, PAGE 266

18. Things with Strings

APRON
BAGGAGE TAGS
BALLOON
BANJO
BOLO TIE
CAT'S CRADLE
FISHING POLE
GUITAR
KITE
MACRAMÉ
MANDOLIN
MARIONETTE
MASKS
MITTENS
MOBILE
PIANO
PLUMB LINE
PULL TOY
PURSE
SOME DEALS
TENNIS RACKET
VIOLIN
XMAS TREE
   LIGHTS
YO-YO

```
              D P O E L I B O M V N
          T P L U M B L I N E A B I C C
        E M C P L A T A A D E A A L O S F
    M R A O A L M F I S H I N G P O L E O
    A K R A L T G P R A T I U G U Y A I J
    C Y I O W O S H N O S M A A Y O E S N
    R H O T E Y L C O L S A E G L Y D L A
    A N N T E K C A R S I N N E T Y E O B
    M U E H I S P H P A A D R T P W M I S
    E I T O L O B U A T D O H A N O O K S
    T T X M A S T R E E L I G H T S R
    E I N G S A T S T I E S A A C
    H E M I T T E N S D M
```

ANSWER, PAGE 266

19. I'd Like to Be a Rich and Famous ...

ACTOR
AUTHOR
CHEF
COMEDIAN
DANCER
DESIGNER
DOCTOR
GENERAL
GOLFER
INVENTOR

LAWYER
MERCHANT
NEWS ANCHOR
PAINTER
PUBLISHER
ROCK STAR
SCIENTIST
SUPERMODEL
TALK SHOW HOST
WORLD LEADER

```
        D S I A D Y O T L U E
    V E R N U N E W S A N C H O R
  O T I C T E P T H R L A T T R H R
E O L D H S R A E E Y K I N O R G O I
D D G O L F E R N R T S I T N E I C S
R A R A T H N E E E M H C R B H E K R
I N C O H T G H A Y N O F A A S M S O
U C R E T N I A P W D W D C S I I T S
U E H S U N S A L A L H T E Y L S A A
I R R E D A E L D L R O W D L B B R Y
  P E O F P D V L E R S W H O U A R
    M E R C H A N T E T N E I P T
      H E R N A I D E M O C
```

ANSWER, PAGE 266

20. W.C.

WAR CHEST
WEBCAM
WEST COAST
WHEAT CHEX
WHITECAP
WHITE-COLLAR
"WHO CARES?"
WILD CARD
WILL-CALL

WILT
  CHAMBERLAIN
WIND CHILL
WINE CELLAR
WINSTON
  CHURCHILL
WIRE CUTTER
WOLF CUB
WORST-CASE

```
        W I N E C E L L A R A
    C W I R E C U T T E R A C O R
  W W D I N G W T O S S P L O P U L
A O R O L E H G E E E N A L D T H E W
A R T L L I H C R U H C N O T S N I W
E S R C T F L A O S C E T C C O R I W
C T F E O R C S H O R R T E W T N A S
M C C I N O V U E N A T E T D D S B Y
A A P L H U M B B E W R N I C A M E E
P S C W N I A L R E B M A H C T L I W
E D B T H D R A C D L I W O M A S
W H E A T C H E X L C R A P P
  E W L L A C L L I W R
```

ANSWER, PAGE 266

21. "& So It Goes ..."

ANDY ROONEY
BANDANNA
BANDWIDTH
CANDLELIGHT
COTTON CANDY
DANDELION
GANDALF
GRAND CANYON
HAND-TO-HAND
  COMBAT
"I CAN'T STAND
  IT!"
IN DEMAND
"... LAND OF THE
  FREE ..."
MARLON
  BRANDO
MEANDER
NEANDERTHAL
ORGANDY
PANDAS
PROPAGANDA
SCANDINAVIA
SPANDEX
TANDEM
  BICYCLE
UGANDA
VERANDA
ZINFANDEL

```
        &  Y  R  O  O  N  E  Y  L  I  F
     &  C  Y  G  X  &  N  A  H  R  C  E  I  H  A
  S  &  U  O  E  E  R  F  E  H  T  F  O  &  L  A  T
B  C  G  M  &  T  A  B  R  B  &  R  D  T  A  F  N  H  S
T  &  R  P  E  E  T  N  I  G  S  E  O  I  &  W  N  G  A
A  I  S  P  L  &  G  O  K  R  E  H  R  &  W  D  A  I  H
&  N  &  I  N  &  E  L  N  &  &  H  N  T  &  &  &  L  Z
W  A  &  G  A  P  O  R  P  C  O  U  O  S  H  L  B  E  D
S  V  I  L  &  T  C  A  O  A  &  A  I  T  U  A  S  L  Y
E  I  F  A  R  S  C  M  &  N  A  Y  L  N  L  O  L  &  R
   A  T  &  E  M  B  I  C  Y  C  L  E  A  J  U  G  C
      S  T  V  A  B  E  J  O  I  M  &  C  D  R  &
         T  &  M  E  D  N  I  Y  D  I  O
```

ANSWER, PAGE 267

22. Wooden It Be Nice?

BALSA
BARN
BOOKCASE
CABINET
CANE
CHAIR
DOWEL
HANDRAIL
KINDLING
KNOTHOLE
LOG CABIN
LUMBER
MAST
MOLDING
PANELING
PLYWOOD
RAFTER
SAWDUST
STILT
TABLE
TIMBER
TOTEM POLE
TWO-BY-FOUR
WOODEN SHOE

```
        K  N  O  T  H  O  L  E  P  P  A
     C  P  E  T  R  K  O  I  S  T  A  B  L  E  N
  O  R  H  M  E  I  A  L  T  L  N  Y  M  D  A  N  D
E  F  R  O  A  N  W  O  O  D  E  N  S  H  O  E  M  A  W
O  M  O  L  D  I  N  G  O  L  D  M  B  A  O  T  U  T  C
T  T  O  L  S  B  R  A  I  V  U  E  P  T  W  R  E  L  E
S  T  I  I  T  A  O  N  T  S  A  M  C  O  Y  D  O  I  U
L  N  I  B  A  C  G  O  L  D  A  L  B  S  L  O  U  T  A
G  B  N  M  E  M  A  D  K  E  F  Y  R  E  P  E  O  S  M
C  O  R  T  B  T  O  N  F  C  F  L  W  A  R  X  L  A  T
   R  A  F  T  E  R  N  D  O  A  O  E  V  E  A  N  B
      B  A  N  A  R  N  U  A  D  S  S  T  B  A  L
         L  I  A  R  D  N  A  H  E  K  S
```

ANSWER, PAGE 267

23. #1 Or #2?

JANUARY
ALPHA
AMAZON
COKE
HYDROGEN
HANK AARON
GENESIS
TORTOISE
JUPITER
VANILLA
GOLD
GEORGE
   WASHINGTON

FEBRUARY
BETA
NILE
PEPSI
HELIUM
BABE RUTH
EXODUS
HARE
SATURN
CHOCOLATE
SILVER
JOHN ADAMS

```
            F  E  U  C  A  L  L  O  F  G  F
      E  A  B  L  K  H  Y  D  R  O  G  E  N  E  S
   S  L  A  N  D  P  O  G  O  O  D  A  N  X  D  M  V
J  I  I  C  E  L  S  C  C  A  R  E  T  E  S  O  A  O  P
H  A  N  K  A  A  R  O  N  Y  E  O  O  S  N  C  D  E  S
E  A  N  I  T  H  D  L  R  A  V  B  R  I  E  L  A  U  I
L  C  O  U  N  T  T  A  E  N  L  T  T  S  O  W  N  I  S
I  T  R  H  A  U  U  T  M  Y  I  L  O  G  O  U  H  R  P
U  N  G  E  O  R  G  E  W  A  S  H  I  N  G  T  O  N  E
M  L  O  T  B  E  Y  O  A  N  Z  E  S  N  C  H  J  A  P
   N  N  E  O  B  T  T  B  E  F  O  E  I  A  R  S  T
      F  I  N  A  E  E  V  E  R  Y  N  R  T  V  H
         I  B  N  J  U  P  I  T  E  R  G
```

ANSWER, PAGE 267

24. Go for the Green

BIG BERTHA
BIRDIE
BOGEY
CADDIE
CART
DIVOT
FAIRWAY
FLAGSTICK
"FORE!"
HOLE-IN-ONE
LINKS
LPGA
MATCH PLAY

MULLIGAN
NINETEENTH
   HOLE
PEBBLE BEACH
PRO-AM
PUTTER
ROUGH
SAND TRAP
SLICE
ST. ANDREWS
STANCE
TIGER WOODS

```
            Y  A  L  P  H  C  T  A  M  C  S
      M  T  H  S  E  R  A  E  P  S  A  A  J  K  O
   K  A  E  T  P  D  H  A  R  U  R  T  G  O  S  N  B
E  N  O  N  I  E  L  O  H  H  T  N  E  E  T  E  N  I  N
L  L  R  F  I  B  S  R  O  L  T  D  I  A  K  E  T  G  L
A  X  P  E  O  B  S  O  Y  W  E  O  N  Y  U  D  R  B  I
V  N  A  G  I  L  L  U  M  E  R  D  C  A  D  D  I  E  A
S  H  E  A  A  E  R  G  D  A  R  E  S  W  S  R  Y  R  O
U  Y  C  C  R  B  A  H  N  E  T  O  G  R  D  G  E  T  T
T  O  T  O  N  E  H  E  W  C  G  R  E  I  E  N  O  H  O
   N  F  F  L  A  G  S  T  I  C  K  E  A  T  V  L  A
      Y  T  O  C  T  E  N  L  D  U  P  F  I  I  N
         T  H  H  S  E  S  H  O  L  D  E
```

ANSWER, PAGE 267

25. With Ease

BEECH TREE
CHEEK TO CHEEK
DEEP FREEZE
"FEEL FREE!"
FIDDLE-DEE-DEE
FLEET STREET
GREENS FEE
GREENSLEEVES
HEEBIE-JEEBIES
JEEPERS
  CREEPERS
KNEE-DEEP

LEE VAN CLEEF
PEEWEE
QUEEN BEE
REEL-TO-REEL
SQUEEGEE
SWEET SIXTEEN
TEE-HEE
TEENSY-WEENSY
TEEPEE
THREE
  MUSKETEERS

```
S H S R E P E E R C S R E P E E J E D
E T T S A R E L B L R I E N E S F E T
H A E T H O L S E E D E D A S H E I P
K E E H C O T K E E H C E S S P E A E
N I N L S I E L C V F T E B F H L E E
E Y S A R E T E H A E L D R N O F O G
E S Y E P O E T T N H E E E S E R R E
D P W E R H I H R C P E L I S O E U E
E T E E O F C O E L Z N D S T E E U U
E T E E R T S T E E L F D R N O L H Q
P L N E W N C N E E T X I S T E E W S
E T S H R E E E S F H E F E T S E T O
T H Y E H E E B I E J E E B I E S R W
I T H R E E M U S K E T E E R S N D G
```

ANSWER, PAGE 268

26. A Quick Workout

AEROBICS CLASS
BARBELLS
CHIN-UP BAR
EXERCYCLE
HEADBAND
HOT TUB
IPOD
LOCKERS
PERSONAL
  TRAINER
SAUNA
SCALE
SHOWERS
SNEAKERS

SPOTTERS
STAIRMASTER
STEAM ROOM
SWEAT PANTS
SWIMMING POOL
TOWEL
TRACK
TREADMILL
VITAMINS
WATER
  FOUNTAIN
WEIGHTS
YOGA MAT

```
I R A B P U N I H C S H A L V E N E V
R E R E T S A K E N N A L O C K E R S
E N Y E R H H X S E I I P O D R E C T
T A M A G O Y I S C M E E P X C X E N
S P T S T W B L E D A E P G I N E G A
A A N T R E N I A R T L A N O S R E P
M D U S R R E E C S I T E I I N C B T
R B G R A S R N D S V W I M N E Y A A
I S R E T T O P S V C E E M R L C R E
A I N K R T E A N D T L O I E T L B W
T N I A T N U O F R E T A W G A E E S
S K C E E N A Y M A R O S K H T L W
A K D N A B D A E H I T N A S T T L A
G E S S E V E N T M O O R M A E T S Y
```

ANSWER, PAGE 268

27. Careful!

BABY ON BOARD
BEWARE OF DOG
CAUTION
DANGER, HIGH
   VOLTAGE
DO NOT DISTURB
DO NOT ENTER
KEEP OFF THE
   GRASS
KEEP OUT
LANE ENDS
MERGE
NO OUTLET

NO PARKING
NO SMOKING
NO U-TURN
ONE WAY
RR CROSSING
SLIPPERY WHEN
   WET
STOP
TOWAWAY ZONE
WET PAINT
WRONG WAY
YIELD

```
T S L I P P E R Y W H E N W E T R E A
P P G I S T O M O N N O P A R K I N G
N O O U T L E T K S S T A K E A D O B
R V D O W O F S S M I L Y E N R C Z R
R E F Y A W G N O R W I B U A T T Y U
C H O I C L S K D K E E P O U T Y A T
R W E T P A I N T L O T B E S A N W S
O T R M E N U A D N T N N H W E Y A I
S S A R G E H T F F O P E E K D O W D
S N W T C E O M I Y M U N N T I C O T
I A E T G N E T B O H O E Y U O S T O
N E B R S D I A G N N O U T U R N L N
G A E N G S B U A G E I N S T E A O O
D M E G A T L O V H G I H R E G N A D
```

ANSWER, PAGE 268

28. That's About the Size of It

BIG DEAL
BROAD-
   SHOULDERED
FAT CHANCE
HEAVY METAL
LEAN-TOS
LITTLE LEAGUE
LONG SHOT
NARROW-
   MINDED
PEE WEE REESE
PINT OF STOUT

SAN FRANCISCO
   GIANTS
SHORT SHRIFT
SLIM JIM
SMALL POTATOES
SPARE TIRE
TALL ORDER
THIN EXCUSE
TINY DANCER
U.S.S. TITANIC
WIDE-EYED

```
T H E L D E R E D L U O H S D A O R B
S A N F R A N C I S C O G I A N T S A
M R A G T U O T S F O T N I P E S D F
A T R L I V L T I H N G T H I N E G A
L O R N E A I A R R E C N A D Y N I T
L T O L I T T L E L E A G U E H I E C
P S W A A O G L I D M A V E N T U R H
O N M N D H E O R G G I D Y R O L I A
T F I R H S T R O H S I J U M E N T N
A C N D F G U D N G W U B M A E S E C
T T D H A N T E S U C X E N I H T R E
O C E O V O E R R S M O T R E L T A H
E A D N T L W O T H O O U S A N S P L
S P E E W E E R E E S E D A C R E S S
```

ANSWER, PAGE 268

29. In Fashion

ANNA SUI
BOUDICCA
CHANEL
CHLOE
DIESEL
DIOR
DKNY
ETRO
GAULTIER
GIANNI VERSACE
GUCCI
HALSTON
HERMES
ISSEY MIYAKE
JIL SANDER
KARL LAGERFELD
KENNETH COLE
LACOSTE
MICHAEL KORS
MIU MIU
MOSCHINO
PERRY ELLIS
PRADA
SEAN JOHN
TOMMY HILFIGER
VERA WANG

```
F H A E S H R I R O N I S S G U C C I
K A R L L A G E R F E L D O M H E S S
S L T H E O I I G N G B A R A B S E R
I S A T R T C O J I L S A N D E R A O
L T R D L U S H F O F R E I Y T P N K
L O K U E R O D T U C L E M S I N J L
E N A N S O V B A E G T I I C H L O E
Y G E O E E O N W I N Y T H H O U H A
R T T M I U M I U S A N N A Y R E N H
R A S R D S P R O K W N E A N M D I C
E M O I O I R T E A A T I K O N M W I
P I C T H I A O U H R O N I H C S O M
T C A B E N D E F I E T G S A N T A T
A Y L A E C A S R E V I N N A I G N A
```

ANSWER, PAGE 269

30. Spy Game

ALDRICH AMES
ALIAS
AUSTIN POWERS
CIPHER
CLOAK-AND-
    DAGGER
CODES
COUNTERSPY
DISCREET
ESPIONAGE
GEORGE SMILEY
GET SMART
HIT MEN
INTERPOL
JAMES BOND
MATA HARI
MOLES
NAPOLEON SOLO
QUISLING
SAFE HOUSE
SMERSH
THE CIA
"THE COMPANY"
THE KGB
UNDERCOVER
    AGENTS
WIRETAP

```
S E M A H C I R D L A L O V Q E I N S
W A H A S T I T E D V E R U Y O U A C
A G I E N H S P T I I W I R E T A P L
L E L L L E B E H Y P S R E T N U O C
T O R A A C Y B E E L T C R A Y P L Y
M R A L C I S A G I R N J R B R O E N
A G C L O A K A N D D A G G E R G O A
T E N O L Y N G F H M A K T P E E N P
A S P E D O N I F E Y E N O U L T S M
H M O V I E E F S R H I T M E N S O O
A I O P M A S B P T E O R F E C M L C
R L S R E W O P N I T S U A T S A O E
I E P Y B N Y L E C A R R S M E R S H
E Y U N D E R C O V E R A G E N T S T
```

ANSWER, PAGE 269

31. Sound Effects

BLEEP
BOING BOING
CLACKITY-CLACK
CLANK
CLOMP
COCK-A-
  DOODLE-DOO
CRUNCH
GURGLE
KABOOM
KERPLUNK
OINK
OOMPAH
PLOP PLOP, FIZZ
  FIZZ
QUACK

RAT-A-TAT-TAT
RATTLE
SCREECH
SPLASH
SQUEAK
SWOOSH
TANTARA
THUD
THUMP
THWACK
TU-WHIT
  TU-WHOO
TWEET
WHAM
WHOOSH
YADA YADA

```
F O C L E Y A R K A E U Q S T I S T S
W H O O S H C K R H E K E R P L U N K
K A C T K C A L C Y T I K C A L C E S
A N K O U G N E D A E F F C D E A C T
B S A F C U E O L R W R A A A D I S O
O A D L N R D M F T I H R L Y U M F H
O O O R C G R A T A T A T T A T Q E A
M M O S X L A H M W T A P L D E S H P
P H D A K E U W I N E N R G A M C S M
E T L A K M L S A H E E E D Y N T O O
B L E E P N S T U W H I T T U W H O O
T O D M A K I E T H E S O R U H N W D
O B O I N G B O I N G F C T H U T S N
P L O P P L O P F I Z Z F I Z Z D E R
```

ANSWER, PAGE 269

32. Look Out Above!

ACORNS
ANVILS
BIRD DROPPINGS
BOMBS
BUNGEE
  JUMPERS
CLIFF DIVERS
COCONUTS
HAILSTONES
ICICLES
LEAVES

METEORITES
PARACHUTERS
PIANOS
PIECES OF
  SKYLAB
RAINDROPS
RIPE APPLES
SLEET
SNOWFLAKES
TICKER TAPE
VOLCANIC ASH

```
B F R O G S S H A R S V E B E E N K S
A N V I L S G P A R A C H U T E R S R
L N O W I N T N E O F I A L L O B U E
Y T V O F C R V I T H E N S K M Y T P
K S H O E M I A O P S T L D O I K E M
S N L Y L D P C E X P C S B R P L E U
F O A N F C E O L A T O I O N O T I J
O W S F T H A R A E N C R T T E P H E
S F I S E Y P N H A S O A D O V E S E
E L B E L E P S I N E N C R D A U G G
C A H T U E L P P C V U I I N R A W N
E K A T E R E S E P A T R E K C I T U
I E H A I L S T O N E S P O U T A B B
P S N D B L O W N S L F H A R A W A Y
```

ANSWER, PAGE 269

33. Why?

BABY BUGGY
BILLY BARTY
BLOODY MARY
BOTANY BAY
BOY TOY
BY CRACKY
DANNY BOY
EASY MONEY
GARY BUSEY
GRAY LADY
HAPPY FAMILY
KENTUCKY
  DERBY

LIKELY STORY
MILKY WAY
MY GUY
MY WAY
OY VEY
PETTY LARCENY
PLAY HOOKY
RAINY DAY
RICKY JAY
STAY AWAY
VERY SHY
WINDY CITY

```
Y T H L I K E L Y S T O R Y E Y T H R
B T B O W T A S H E B A L L I H Y I Y
R T I O I T S T T H G A R Y B U S E Y
E E P C Y Y Y H I A T T N H G E V B L
D A L L Y T M L I C Y E A Y T Y Y C I
Y R A M Y D O O L B C A M H O T H B M
K I Y I A T N Y Y R W I W R R L S A A
C C H L B I E I A E Y K C A R C Y B F
U K O M Y A Y L W M Y S B I Y A R Y Y
T Y O L N I Y A Y O B Y N N A D E B P
N J K S A T T W K H L E S Y A Y V U P
E A Y H T E A Y L L K I D D O N H G A
K Y I E O Y S S I E C R E A T T O G H
S U P C B C E B M S G R A Y L A D Y S
```

ANSWER, PAGE 270

34. Keeping a Clear Head

Andre AGASSI
Stone Cold Steve
  AUSTIN
Charles BARKLEY
Yul BRYNNER
Michael CHIKLIS
Winston
  CHURCHILL
Sean CONNERY
Billy CORGAN
Danny DEVITO
Vin DIESEL
Michael Clarke
  DUNCAN
Fred DURST
Robert DUVALL
Kevin EUBANKS

Ed HARRIS
Samuel JACKSON
Michael JORDAN
G. Gordon LIDDY
Mark MESSIER
MOBY
Sinead O'CONNOR
Pablo PICASSO
Ving RHAMES
Telly SAVALAS
Paul SHAFFER
Patrick STEWART
Michael STIPE
Stanley TUCCI
Jesse VENTURA
Damon WAYANS
Montel WILLIAMS
Bruce WILLIS

```
T I M E M T R O T U R N Y T S R U D B
A D I E S E L A C K A N R R Y D R D E
S U S J F C S E S K N A B U E N E D D
T H S F A E S S T A W I R H L N N U W
I T A T H C A B I E A L A D K S N P O
T H G R I I K N T E T R H E R C Y O M
S M A I O N V S D D R L E N A G R O C
A T O F S N E M O I Y H A N B I B R T
V H U E S M N D S N A Y A W Y Y W I L
A L S C A A T O U Y H D E V I T O O E
L L I H C R U H C V R D W H I L S H P
A A R I I I R R I O A I S G R O L W I
S I N G P T A H J W I L L I A M S I T
I N B Y T S E L C H I K L I S I O T S
```

ANSWER, PAGE 270

35. Not Keeping a Clear Head

BEANIE
BERET
BOATER
BONNET
CLOCHE
COONSKIN CAP
COWL
CROWN
DEERSTALKER
DERBY
FEDORA
HEADDRESS
HOMBURG
MORTARBOARD
OPERA HAT

PILLBOX
PITH HELMET
PORKPIE HAT
SHAKO
SKI MASK
SNOOD
STETSON
STOVEPIPE HAT
STRAW HAT
TAM O'SHANTER
TEN-GALLON HAT
TIARA
TOP HAT
TRILBY
YARMULKE

```
H E W A B C L O C H E S I M P A T I P
R E N T E T O W O P E R A H A T F T I
E T S H A K O T O O P C O A E T S A T
T A D D N H A N N C K D H R D A T H H
N H S E I P E R S E S S E R D D A E H
A P F R E E A P K R R B A I N R G I E
H O M B U R G T I O B O R M A E T P L
S T E Y O X S P N P B O E I I E S K M
O T E D D E B T C R E W T Y N K H R E
M D E K L U M R A Y I V A N B T S O T
A F O T E W O T P L R X O B L L I P I
T T I O S W R N G A K B B T B O I U T
J T A H N O L L A G N E T O S H N R F
K E N N M S N E D Y S T R A W H A T T
```

ANSWER, PAGE 270

36. Doubling Up

BAZAAR
CARIBBEAN
SOCCER
CODDLE
UMPTEEN
JEFFERSON
EGGHEAD
WITHHOLDING
HAWAIIAN
HAJJ
JACKKNIFE
BULLHEADED
GLIMMER

CEZANNE
MONGOOSES
SNIPPY
IQ QUIZ
UEBERROTH
DISTRESS
HIT THE HAY
CONTINUUM
DIVVYING UP
YOU-KNOW-WHO
EXXON
"HEY, YOU!"
JAZZY

```
D O J A C K K N I F E U Y B L E C I N
D E M A N I T Y P A U P T B A Z A A R
E N N A Z E C H U O P E R J I A R M B
E S M Y C Z A O G I I N G U L I I K U
J E D A T H Y E N P N S Q G L O B E L
E J R H T Y O S I T A Q S T H W B I L
F S A E E T U S Y I I N T E H E E E H
F M O H C M K V V I I N E S R O A M E
E U C T P C N C V H A H U R E T N D A
R E S T A I O D I H W E O U M D S H D
S A E I V D W S D E A T U S M E D I E
O E T H D H W I T H H O L D I N G E D
N M I L F H H E D T H O U G L H T O F
T H E E X X O N E S E S O O G N O M M
```

ANSWER, PAGE 270

37. Let's Stick Together

BRASS FASTENER
CAULKING
C-CLAMP
CEMENT
DUCT TAPE
ELMER'S GLUE
EPOXY
JOINT
  COMPOUND
MORTAR
MUCILAGE
NAILS
NUTS AND BOLTS
PAPER CLIP
PASTE
PLASTER OF
  PARIS
PUTTY
RIVETS
ROPE
RUBBER BAND
SCOTCH TAPE
SCREWS
SOLDER
STAPLES
THUMBTACK
TWINE
VISE GRIPS

```
I B E B R A S S F A S T E N E R L I E
S R U B B E R B A N D V E T H P A S K
T M T T S T L O B D N A S T U N O C R
A U U T H E I S C S U T H M E G A R L
P I L C R E P A P U O S E T O T H E E
L M A T I H U A O L P L D S B R G W L
E O A S V L E R T I M D D M N M T S M
S E N L K T A T R H O O U E G E Y A E
T H E I C R F G R O C H Y C R T M P R
R E N A S C E M E N T T X E T S A P S
I G D N E S N T G E N R O U A T L D G
S T E V I R R F O R I D P C S I A N L
A U G V S I R A P F O R E T S A L P U
U R A T I O N S P E J E C H T W I N E
```

ANSWER, PAGE 271

38. Springfield Is in the Air

BARNEY GUMBLE
BART
CLETUS
COMIC BOOK
  GUY
DISCO STU
DR. HIBBERT
FAT TONY
FLANDERS
HOMER
ITCHY AND
  SCRATCHY
KRUSTY
LISA
MAGGIE
MARGE
MARTIN
MAYOR QUIMBY
MILHOUSE
MOE SZYSLAK
MR. BURNS
MRS. KRABAPPEL
OFFICER
  WIGGUM
OTTO
PATTY AND
  SELMA
SIDESHOW BOB
SMITHERS
WILLIE

```
M M A Y O R Q U I M B Y T H T D S E A
S A S I M P E L B M U G Y E N R A B M
M S R O N A S M A G G I E A E H A R L
I S Y T S U R K K E N A M D G I E B E
T D I I I B A O F T E Y N E R B R M S
H A L D U N O T T S T A N G A B R O D
E D E R E B N T U I L N H O M E R G N
R I N S C S F O A F M I L Y T R E X A
S S L I T C H Y A N D S C R A T C H Y
C C M L E L P O T F O R B L A R A T T
W O F F I C E R W I G G U M E H O F T
C S S M E W N A M B E I S A N T A N A
A T K A L S Y Z S E O M G R A M U O P
F U B R A M R S K R A B A P P E L S T
```

ANSWER, PAGE 271

39. Musical Numbers

BLINK 182
EVE 6
4 NON BLONDES
FRONT 242
HAIRCUT 100
HEAVEN 17
JACKSON 5
JURASSIC 5
LEVEL 42
MAROON 5
MATCHBOX 20
1910 FRUITGUM CO.

OLD 97'S
STARS ON 45
10,000 MANIACS
THE 5TH DIMENSION
THE B-52'S
.38 SPECIAL
TIMBUK3
2 LIVE CREW
2PAC
UB40

```
I F Y O 6 1 0 2 X O B H C T A M U S A
S N G E 9 9 8 9 B U 3 O E T T L E S O
E L V F 1 1 B E B E 8 R M A R O O N 5
D E O N K 0 T 4 H E S W A L V W L A O
N V N N F F 0 D C O P U N T E E D 0 L
O E I 5 A R L 0 T H E B 5 2 S R N 0 D
L L J L C U O T 0 H C E N U M C B 1 9
B 4 A N O I S N E M I D H T 5 E H T 7
N 2 C E R T S S T M A E N T I V O U S
O N K E D G T S H 2 L N R O U I G C H
N O S U T U T H A E 4 E I N T L I R R
4 E O S O M N G I R T 2 C A P 2 W I O
U L N D A C T I M B U K 3 D C D U A P
T O 5 4 N O S R A T S J 1 4 8 S 5 H 0
```

ANSWER, PAGE 271

40. Foul Play

BALK
BODY CHECK
CHARGING
CLIPPING
CROSS-CHECKING
DELAY OF GAME
DOUBLE DRIBBLE
ELBOWING
FACE MASK
FALSE START

GOALTENDING
HIGH-STICKING
HOLDING
ICING
INTERFERENCE
OFFSIDES
SLASHING
SPEARING
TRAVELING
TRIPPING

```
F O O D O U B L E D R I B B L E T G B
A G L C L C O M B M N H I N E S T N T
G N I R A E P S H T A I E T W O R I W
O I B O D Y C H E C K G N I G R A H C
R W S S T T H R I N G H F S A B T S O
U O T S O F F S I D E S A O M T S A E
R B I C C E A A I T I T S V Y R E L I
O L L H R E C L I P P I N G N A S S G
C E E P U E N C T U C A T E V L D N
I B N C Y C M O M B M K I T T E A E I
E C E K M E A E A T I I N G S L F P D
E O I I L I S L T I G N I P P I R T L
C A L N P U K N D I T G G E O N R G O
E W I G G O A L T E N D I N G G L L H
```

ANSWER, PAGE 271

41. Some Stuff

SALISBURY STEAK
SAN SIMEON
SAY SOMETHING
SEESAW
SETTING SAIL
SEVEN SEAS
SILLY STRING
"SI, SI"
SIXTH SENSE
SOB STORY
SOFT SPOT
"SO SORRY!"
SOY SAUCE

SPACE SUIT
STAGE SET
STEVEN
   SPIELBERG
STOP SIGNS
STRAWBERRY
   SODA
SUMMER
   SOLSTICE
SUNFLOWER
   SEEDS
SWEET SIXTEEN

```
T G H L I A S G N I T T E S E W R I E
S N I S T E D R I S S E O I T H S E C
N I R O W A P O R O A C T P I I C I I
G R E B L E I P S N E V E T S N G R T
I T E S C L E O U Y S E S O R T A D S
S S S T E L R T I N R Q E E U I F A L
P Y E O N R E T S G U R V I E U N O O
O L L R Y S T G N I H T E M O S Y A S
T L R Y E S I D D E X N N B I E A O R
S I N G E O A R B O T T S M W C H W E
U S A L I S B U R Y S T E A K A S U M
A T L L Y B O T C H S O A E U P R S M
S I X T H S E N S E N A S N N S S T U
O N T A G S U N F L O W E R S E E D S
```

42. Let's Dance

BOSSA NOVA
BUNNY HOP
CHA-CHA
CHARLESTON
CONGA LINE
FANDANGO
FLAMENCO
FOXTROT
GAVOTTE
HULA
HUSTLE
JITTERBUG
LAMBADA
LIMBO
LINDY

MAMBO
MERENGUE
MINUET
PAS DE DEUX
POLKA
RUMBA
SALSA
SAMBA
SOFT SHOE
SQUARE DANCE
TANGO
TAP DANCE
TWIST
TWO-STEP
WALTZ

```
W A L T Z L I S D O F B N T W A N T T
E H T W P I O A B N O T S E L R A H C
N E U O T M H M E S X B O L D P E U S
I T L S P B P B S E T R M F D O R L M
L K E T T O V A G E R C H A C H A A R
A I N E C L N A S P O T N I M V J I B
G S T P Y O E I D D T C O N T I W A U
N N L T V C T U O L E O H S T F O S N
O G N A D N A F G O O D K T L A M I N
C K E A S E L I T N T T E L L I N D Y
E O L R U M B A D W E R M U N A N G H
A D A B M A L D I A B R N U X C I N O
G O U T T L H S Q U A R E D A N C E P
E R E F R F T E G D A T S M T A I R E
```

43. Secret Identities

BATMAN — Bruce WAYNE
CAPTAIN AMERICA — Steve ROGERS
CAPTAIN MARVEL — Billy BATSON
CATWOMAN — Selina KYLE
DAREDEVIL — Matt MURDOCK
IRON MAN — Tony STARK
SPIDER-MAN — Peter PARKER
SUPERMAN — Clark KENT
THE HULK — Bruce BANNER
THE SHADOW — Lamont CRANSTON
UNDERDOG — SHOESHINE BOY
WONDER WOMAN — Diana PRINCE
ZORRO — Don Diego DE LA VEGA

```
S U A P E R Y O B E N I H S E O H S R
M A C N E H L A S B S E U E W L N I N
N V I K O L E C N I R P V E A D Y U A
D A R E D E V I L W E I I T Y H N K M
F A E I O U R R W R G O M D N D M E O
P N M L R A A E M N O A U L E C A D W
N C A T W O M A N G R L R R O R I E R
S L N A N N E L N Y L D A L A M L E
B E I R O R I M O L A O O A N N D A D
L A A S O R A I A L G B C R E S M V N
A R T K R A T S I N S A K M R T E E O
R A P M M A P N T H E S H A D O W G W
B I A D A W A H E A T S W I T N Z A H
T H C E L N C S D K L U H E H T U D E
```

ANSWER, PAGE 272

44. Rare Antonyms

ADVERTENT
BEKNOWNST
CHALANT
CHOATE
COGNITO
COMBOBULATED
COMMUNICADO
CONSOLATE
CORRIGIBLE
DEFATIGABLE
DESCRIPT
DOMITABLE
EVITABLE
FLAPPABLE
GAINLY
GRUNTLED
MACULATE
NOMER
PAREIL
PECCABLE
PECUNIOUS
PETUOUS
PLUSSED
PROMPTU
RULY
SHEVELED
SIPID
TERMINABLE
WIELDY

```
P I T S O U E L B A P P A L F R E X D
E L B A T I M O D E F A T I G A B L E
C P E E T A O H C E Y D L E I W R L T
C O K I Y E D U N O C E T R H S B A A
A D N T P L N V O L R I P A I A T C L
B E O S I I U D E S C R I P T C H A U
L S W N O M E R L R O L I I E A A D B
E S N U E L T R S M T D V G L D O N O
T U S A E L A W P A Y E S A I M E T B
A L T V D E L T N U R G N N T B I H M
E P E T U O U S E O P T P T O N L S O
I H T E O F C W H Y L N I A G A T E C
S T H E O D A C I N U M M O C Y S A Y
E L B A N I M R E T A B C B A E B A N
```

ANSWER, PAGE 272

45. Aye, 'Tis a Word Search About Pirates, It Is

AHOY
ANCHOR
AVAST
BLACKBEARD
BOOTY
CANNONS
CAPTAIN
CORSAIR
EYEPATCH
FIRST MATE
FLAG
GROG
HOOK
JOLLY ROGER
KEELHAUL

LANDLUBBER
LONG JOHN
   SILVER
MAINSAIL
PARROT
PEGLEG
PIECES OF EIGHT
PISTOL
SCURVY DOG
SWORD
TORTUGA
TREASURE MAP
WALK THE
   PLANK
"YARRRRRR!"

ANSWER, PAGE 273

```
J P O H N N W A L K T H E P L A N K Y
P I D H S N O N N A C E P B O O T Y N
I S P B O A Y G S T N O E D H I R S I
E T A E P O I R A A T D R E S O E F A
C O G T H R K P T L H E L S A V A S T
E L U A H L E E K C F M A U A R S I P
S B T M B Y P G E A N C A H B I U A A
O W R T E A R L O A G C T I A B R E C
F R O S R R O E N R K E I T N H E R I
E C T R H R A G O D Y V R U C S M R R
I D O I D R S G W H O L P L H A A Y E
G T D F D R A E B K C A L B O H P I I
H S F A T R H E R I N T H O R E S E L
T Q U E L R E V L I S N H O J G N O L
```

46. Hot ...

AND BOTHERED
BLOODED
BUTTERED RUM
BUTTON ISSUE
CEREAL
CHOCOLATE
COMMODITY
CROSS BUN
DATE
DIGGITY
FLASHES
FUDGE
OFF THE PRESS
PEPPER
PLATE

POCKETS
POTATO
PURSUIT
SAUCE
SPRINGS
STREAK
TAMALES
TEMPERED
TICKET
TO TROT
UNDER THE
   COLLAR
WATER
WIRE

ANSWER, PAGE 273

```
I M D L I T K E D T P O C K E T S O S
U D U N D E R T H E C O L L A R P W I
E I T R H M M Y P B R A T B B E R I W
S G Y T D P O P N I O E G A U H R B T
S G D R E E E F I L S L H T T H L T E
E I C U U R R P U R S U I T T O P S S
R T W S F E I E T H B M Y B O A B P Y
P Y A E T D O N T I U S G D N B H R T
E B U L A E R E C T N T E I I A D I I
H E N A O T K U P T U D O H S M Y N W
T B T M D C A B Y T O B N I S G H G A
F T C A I T O R T O T A E C U A S S T
F U T T L S E H I T S T O O E D L A E
O E R N H P O T C O M M O D I T Y F R
```

28

47. Higher Education

AMHERST
BARD
BARNARD
BATES
BAYLOR
BROWN
BRYN MAWR
CALTECH
COLBY
COLUMBIA
CORNELL
DARTMOUTH
DEPAUL
DREXEL
DUKE
EMORY
FORDHAM
HARVARD
LEHIGH
LOYOLA
MOUNT HOLYOKE
NOTRE DAME
OBERLIN
PENN STATE
POMONA
PRINCETON
PURDUE
RHODES
RICE
RUTGERS
SMITH
STANFORD
SWARTHMORE
TEMPLE
TUFTS
TULANE
VASSAR
VILLANOVA
WELLESLEY
WESLEYAN
WILLIAM AND MARY
YALE

```
Y R A M D N A M A I L L I W R E D U C
W E S L E Y A N T E M P L E H I G H M
A E T I O O S T A N F O R D S N C C O
I S L T H Y E N V A E R T R Y A L E U
V I L L A N O V A S O M E A F M P T N
N C S U E M A L S T H G O N B K U L T
I O E A O S H I S F T N D R A V R A H
L L T P G M L E A U U A Y A Y L D C O
R U A E M A D E R T O N N B L L U E L
E M B D C R T H Y S M I T H O E E T Y
B B I P E N N S T A T E C A R N L G O
O I A X K E I S W A R T H M O R E O K
R A E R U F O R D H A M G N W O R B E
H L S E D O H R P E D Y B L O C G E L
```

ANSWER, PAGE 273

48. Wild Kingdom

BEAR MARKET
BUSY BEE
CATNAPS
CLAMS UP
CLOTHES HORSE
CRAB APPLES
DOG-TIRED
FISH STORY
FOR THE BIRDS
FOXGLOVES
FROG IN ONE'S
  THROAT
GO APE
LION-HEARTED
MONKEY
  AROUND
MOTHER GOOSE
NIGHT OWL
PAPER TIGER
PIG OUT
POOL SHARK
RATS ON
SEX KITTEN
SWAN DIVE
WHOLE HOG
WOLF WHISTLE

```
A F R O G I N O N E S T H R O A T E L
L C E A S E X K I T T E N N P I S W E
D R V M A D L S E X S C V E O R H P L
E A I L T N R M A P P N K O O O N O T
R B D W W U T I A H A U T H L T H E S
I A N E P O R N B Y I N S E S G K T I
T P A P E R T I G E R E H M H R X U H
G P W C I A P H A L H O B U A S I O W
O L S N C Y E S G T G T T M R L S G F
D E T R A E H N O I L O R S K F C I L
L S I F E K I L A S N A T O H O E P O
R A T S O N C N P J E O Y I F S T A W
U T H O R O S E E B Y S U B A M I U E
L B U T L M O T H E R G O O S E E F R
```

ANSWER, PAGE 273

49. Wilder Kingdom

ABOMINABLE
  SNOWMAN
BASILISK
BEHEMOTH
CENTAUR
CERBERUS
CHIMERA
COCKATRICE
DRAGON
GRYPHON
HARPY
HIPPOGRIFF
HOOP SNAKE
HOUYHNHNM
HYDRA

JACKALOPE
LEVIATHAN
LOCH NESS
  MONSTER
MANTICORE
MERMAID
PEGASUS
PHOENIX
SATYR
SEA SERPENT
SPHINX
UNICORN
WEREWOLF
WYVERN
YETI

```
M W J H A T C A C H M I M E R A T H E
N N N A M W O N S E L B A N I M O B A
H H E I C S C E R B E R U S M A N W H
N T R A T K K M A N N N C O Y P R A H
H O O P S N A K E V A O E E L T N T I
Y M C Y X I T L U W H H X I N E O H P
U E I A D N R N O T A P T E M T G S P
O H T O N S I T E P R Y P A W H A A O
H E N I T C C H I M E R A W I T R U G
A B A A O C E O P N E G T R Y V D A R
D I M R C T I O N S W H A R A V E T I
A P N D R O D B A S I L I S K I E L F
G Y B Y W E R E W O L F P A U S C R F
L O C H N E S S M O N S T E R S A L N
```

ANSWER, PAGE 274

50. The Things We Carried

ADDRESS BOOK
ASPIRIN
BALLPOINT PENS
BEEPER
BUSINESS CARD
CALENDAR
CELL PHONE
CHANGE PURSE
CHEWING GUM
DIGITAL CAMERA
DRIVER'S
  LICENSE
GAMEBOY

HEADPHONES
HOUSE KEYS
IPOD
LAPTOP
  COMPUTER
LIP BALM
NOTEPAD
PAGER
PALM PILOT
SUBWAY PASS
WALKMAN
WALLET
WORK ID

```
B N U T W C H A N G E P U R S E D H A
T I H A H S A D R A C S S E N I S U B
D R I V E R S L I C E N S E G I N S A
T I G O A T M I E N I T A I S P O S L
O P R C D K U E T N W T T M S E T A L
H S E O P A G E R O D A S E K H E P P
O A P N H O G T R M L A B P I L P Y O
U I E S O T N K R C I I R N G P A A I
S R E E N C I I A O U S P B W U D W N
E T B N E D W M O Y O B E M A G T B T
K O O B S S E R D D A N O T L H I U P
E N G G O R H L L U M F R O L A M S E
Y T H E A H C E L L P H O N E O P B N
S B I L A P T O P C O M P U T E R T S
```

ANSWER, PAGE 274

51. Rise and Shine

BRUSH TEETH
COMB HAIR
DO MAKEUP
DRESS
DRIVE
EAT
EXERCISE
FIND KEYS
FLUSH
GARGLE

GET PAPER
GET UP
LOCK DOOR
ROLL OVER
SHAMPOO
SHAVE
SHOWER
WALK DOG
WASH FACE
YAWN

```
O C I N D R O L L O V E R
Y O C D R I V E O R A E W F Y
O R P O D O N S E C A F H S A W
R C E M S A H I S T K D E V W A
I E N A A O I D I O G D N T N L
A W G K W H A K C A E S O U P K
H T E E T H S U R B L H O O O D
B S R U T K I G E T P A P E R O
M N U P G U L L X I K V E E C G
O I N L D E P Y E C R E S A W
C F O R F I N D K E Y S D
```

ANSWER, PAGE 274

52. On the Train and Bus

BACKPACK
BAGEL
BOOK
BRIEFCASE
CELL YELL
COAT
COFFEE
DELAY
DONUT
EXPRESS
IPOD
"IS THIS SEAT
    TAKEN?"

LAPTOP
NEWSPAPER
OVERHEAD RACK
PDA
PEAK PERIOD
PRETZELS
PURSE
SLEEP
SODA
STANDEES
STATION
TICKET

```
N B T K C A P K C A B W H
E E O E D E L A Y E S A R L E
S X W O K D O P B R E O G L K P
A P S S K C A R D A E H R E V O
C R S E P C I E R A D S S Y L T
F E T I O A T T D O N U T L O P
E S A A N A P Z T R A A I L E A
I S T H I S S E A T T A K E N L
R P I N T H E L R S S T L C O C
B C O F F E E S K C E S R U P
A R N D O I R E P K A E P
```

ANSWER, PAGE 274

53. Java Jive

AROMA
BEANS
BLACK
BREW
CAFFEINE
CAPPUCCINO
CINNAMON
CREAM
CUP O' JOE
DECAF
ESPRESSO
FILTER
FRENCH ROAST
GRIND
HAZELNUT
JOLT
LATTE
MOCHA
PERK
SCOOP
STIRRER
STRONG
SUGAR
TRAVEL MUG

```
T E O J O P U C G E L C F
G N O R T S D D R Y R A G U S
R L S O N O S E I V C F T E L T
T T S A O R H C N E R F D T R U
B B E E D M A M D X W E E L E S
K B R L H N O M A N N I C O T C
C A P P U C C I N O U N S I L O
A R S E H E G O B O D E R T I O
L O E A R O T H E R L R A S F P
B M T A D K R H A Z E L N U T
O A G U M L E V A R T W P
```

ANSWER, PAGE 275

54. The Beatles' "A Day in the Life"

WOKE
FELL
OUT
BED
DRAGGED
COMB
ACROSS
HEAD
FOUND
WAY
DOWNSTAIRS
DRANK
CUP
LOOKING
NOTICED
LATE
COAT
HAT
MADE
BUS
SECONDS
FLAT
UPSTAIRS
SMOKE
SPOKE
DREAM

```
T D H E S S O R C A M M A
S S N P E I V U E H A T F D F
I N O U C A P L N D O E T E E O
H K F N O T I C E D T K K G L H
E E Y S N F O G N G B O T G O L
A O A K D T H N R E M W E A D P
D O W N S T A I R S O I A R N O
S R A L N A D K L A C S E D T S
C O A T O L V O S R I A T S P U
E T R N F F U O O R M T U Y S
E E C O K T N L D D E B S
```

ANSWER, PAGE 275

55. Work, Work, Work

BUSINESS
CAREER
DAILY GRIND
EMPLOYMENT
FIELD
GIG
JOB
LABOR
LIVELIHOOD
LIVING

METIER
OCCUPATION
POSITION
POST
PROFESSION
RAT RACE
SPHERE
TOIL
TRADE
VOCATION

```
H A N O I T A P U C C O B
R D D E W O R N O I T A C O V
K A G R N E V P R E S R R K J R
L I V E L I H O O D S I D E L A
G L L H E D B S A N E Y L B E T
O Y D P Y A B I U L N T E W H R
T G Y S L T T G N I V I L E A
P R O F E S S I O N S O F I A C
K I A E A C O O H A U N T C E E
E N D D G A P N R B B E E R G
E D T N E M Y O L P M E N
```

ANSWER, PAGE 275

56. All the News That Fits

ABOVE THE
   FOLD
ADS
ARTS
CAPTION
COLUMNS
COMICS
CROSSWORD
FRONT PAGE
HEADLINE
HOROSCOPE
LOCAL

"MAN BITES
   DOG"
METRO
NATIONAL
OBITS
OP-ED
PHOTO
REPORT
SECTION
SPORTS
STORY
STYLE

```
T H E H O R O S C O P E F
A E L Y T S T F I R S H R T L
R N C D L O F E H T E V O B A R
T I O S R N S W O R D W N T N A
S L S Y S O I N T S E C T I O N
N D H E T I W R N E W Y P L I O
M A N B I T E S D O G R A K T W
U E O R B P L D S D I C G D A N
L H T N O A I A N O O E E T N E
O E N R T C H I R L R P T E E
C S T R O P S C I M O C N
```

ANSWER, PAGE 275

57. Car Talk

BACKUP
BUMPER TO
   BUMPER
CARPOOL
COFFEE MUG
DETOUR
DRIVE TIME
EXIT
HIGHWAY
HONK
HOV LANE

KEYS
MERGE
RADAR
RADIO
ROAD HOG
RUBBERNECK
RUSH HOUR
STOP AND GO
TRAFFIC
TRUCK

```
T H R T E M I T E V I R D
K A I F F I O C R N S I A G N
C X K G A L G S I A A R A D A R
E N C B H N D E W K F L Y O I U
N R U A K W N A R N E F V J U O
R S R C R O A D H O G T I O R T
E O T K U P P Y G H H G U C H E
B I D U E C O F F E E M U G G D
B U M P E R T O B U M P E R L I
U N E S L E S T L T E K E Y S
R U O H H S U R R M A M N
```

ANSWER, PAGE 276

58. Think "Inc."

BRAINCHILD
CHINCHILLA
CINCH
GRINCH
INCENSE
IN CODE
INCOGNITO
INCOME
INSTINCT
LINCOLN
LOINCLOTH

MINCE
NINCOMPOOP
PRINCE
PRINCIPAL
QUINCE
TIN CAN
TRAIN CAR
TWIN CITIES
VITAMIN C
WINCH
ZINC

```
T I A L L I H C N I H C N
R C A L I C P S Q O L C M E A
A P R I N C E R U N O T N M S E
I N G I C D S E I T I C N I W T
N N R R O A N V N N N E D N W B
C G S C L Y E F C H C N I C R E
A O N T N M C A E T L I H E M E
R I C N I Z N I N C O M P O O P
D L I H C N I A R B T W C A O R
O T I N G O C N I D H N I N L
C I S E D V I T A M I N C
```

ANSWER, PAGE 276

59. Working Scripts

BABY BOOM
CLERKS
DESK SET
GUNG HO
MATEWAN
MODERN
   TIMES
NINE TO FIVE
NORMA RAE

ON THE
   WATERFRONT
ROGER AND ME
THE FIRM
THE TEMP
TIN MEN
TOOTSIE
WALL STREET
WORKING GIRL

```
W O R K I N G G I R L I C
A A N S O H G N U G I T A N B
L D D N I N E T O F I V E A S M
L P O N O T I H H R I N B G K A
S E M I T N R E D O M Y A S R T
T G O E M O I F D A B A S A E E
R N Y E T S O I N O E C R S L W
E L N O T E C R O K W A K A C A
E T C O H E H M R S Q S U O E N
T N O R F R E T A W E H T N O
T T R O G E R A N D M E E
```

ANSWER, PAGE 276

60. Bagel Break

BINS
BUTTER
CINNAMON
   RAISIN
CREAM CHEESE
DELI
DOZEN
EVERYTHING
FRESH
GARLIC
KNIFE
LOX
MARBLE

MINI-BAGEL
ONION
PLAIN
POPPY
PUMPERNICKEL
SANDWICH
SESAME
SHMEAR
SLICED
SPREAD
TOASTED
WHEAT

```
P P U M P E R N I C K E L
M R E L B R A M O I S N I B T
S I A E C O T X O L Y O I U D R
A I N G N I H T Y R E V E F A A
N I S I A R N O M A N N I C E E
D R O B B A G A E G L T S P R M
W N D U T A L S S E S A M E P H
I P O P P Y G T O X O E N T S S
C L Z H E C R E A M C H E E S E
H R E T T U B D L M S W R H O
P S N D E C I L S I G F N
```

ANSWER, PAGE 276

61. At the Train Station

"ALL ABOARD!"
BENCH
CLOCK
CONCOURSE
DELAY
DELI
MUZAK
NEWSSTAND
PASSENGER
PLATFORM
REDCAP
SHOESHINE
SIGN
STAIRS
TICKET WINDOW
TRACK
TRAIN
TRASH CAN
WAITING ROOM
"WATCH THE GAP"

```
W O D N I W T E K C I T E
A V K A K E R Y B E D A D N Y
T P K C H S H O E S H I N E A L
C F A H O A M M N R R I L W L S
H R Z S L L R I C U O I N S P I
T E U A S O C O H O P L A S E G
H R M R F E P P A C D E R T Y N
E A A T S S N T H N R O U A S G
G W A I T I N G R O O M L N H G
A L R A N N D C E C E E N D T
P R A L L A B O A R D A L
```

ANSWER, PAGE 277

62. Why We Do It

ALMIGHTY
   DOLLAR
BREAD
BUCKS
CASH
CLAMS
CURRENCY
DO-RE-MI
DOUGH
GELT
GREENBACKS
INCOME
JACK
LEGAL TENDER
LETTUCE
LUCRE
MAZUMA
MONEY
MOOLAH
SCRATCH
SIMOLEONS
SPECIE
WAMPUM

```
R U E N S C R A T C H W F
G O R M N D Y O U K C A J R L
R A L L O D Y T H G I M L A I C
E F E U E C F R S O S P M O A L
E N G E L T N Y A K M U I A O A
N H N R O W T I C H A M U Z A M
B O T C M E C U R R E N C Y O S
A R L U I L B S C R Y O U N T H
C A E L S T M O O E I C E P S N
K E Y A I S E D V I L Y R A N
S D R E D N E T L A G E L
```

ANSWER, PAGE 277

63. RR Crossings

RABBIT, RUN
RAG RUG
RAH RAH
RAT RACE
RAY ROMANO
REC ROOM
RED ROVER
RENE RUSSO
RIB ROAST
ROAD RULES

ROB ROY
ROLLS-ROYCE
RONALD REAGAN
ROOT ROT
ROSE RED
ROUGH RIDERS
ROY ROGERS
RUBY RED
RUG RAT
RUN RIOT

```
E C Y O R S L L O R S R E
O X R N E E R O A D R U L E S
S D T A R G U R M E E P L R T Y
S A Y M H E B D V O G R I M O O
U Y R O A A Y O B R O B E E R R
R C K R U N R I O T R R I S T B
E A N Y R D E H I O Y D C G O O
N A G A E R D L A N O R E E O R
E C A R T A R S P R R R E S R E
R X C N U R T I B B A R H A N
G E R O U G H R I D E R S
```

ANSWER, PAGE 277

64. "Sorry I'm Late"

CAR DIED
CHECKUP
CONSTRUCTION
DETOUR
FLAT TIRE
FLOOD
FOG
HANGOVER
LEAK
LOST KEYS

MIGRAINE
MISSED BUS
OVERSLEPT
POWER OUT
SICK KID
SLEET
SNOW
STORM
TRAFFIC
TRAIN DELAY

```
T P E L S R E V O N E T A
R T E X N C R S U R E S E T T
A H E S O M I S S E D B U S U D
I P O Y W C T G L V A T K E O M
N Y U E K K T S D O O L F A R E
D Y S K S W A M I G R A I N E E
E E I T C A L R E N O H I T W L
L D T S O E F T R A F F I C O C
A H H O I R H K I H N G T O P T
Y H E L U V M C A R D I E D E
C O N S T R U C T I O N T
```

ANSWER, PAGE 277

65. TV Working Stiffs

(Lennie) BRISCOE
(Al) BUNDY
(Archie) BUNKER
(Drew) CAREY
(Cliff) CLAVIN
(Roseanne)
   CONNER
(Laverne)
   DEFAZIO
(Louie) DE
   PALMA
(Shirley) FEENEY
(Barney) FIFE
(Fred)
   FLINTSTONE

(Hank) HILL
(Ralph)
   KRAMDEN
(Sam) MALONE
(Rhoda)
   MORGENSTERN
(Ed) NORTON
(Alex) RIEGER
(Jim) ROCKFORD
(Fred) SANFORD
(Dwayne)
   SCHNEIDER
(Homer)
   SIMPSON
(Andy) SIPOWICZ

```
T D S C H N E I D E R V D
U E D W I D E O R K N I N G H
C P S V T R I D S I P O W I C Z
R A A R F O F S M H A N L D J B
O L R F E F I M B A O L N A R U
C M R E K N U B E R R L O I M N
K A U E Y A N S T I H K S I A D
F L I N T S T O N E N C P D M Y
O I I E C H N A C G O E M L K E
R A F Y O I Z A F E D T I O N
D N R E T S N E G R O M S
```

ANSWER, PAGE 278

66. Subway Stop

CROWDED
FARE
JOSTLING
LINE
METRO
PLATFORM
POLE
RAPID TRANSIT
RIDE
SEAT
STATION

STRAPHANGER
"TAKE THE A
   TRAIN"
THIRD RAIL
TOKEN
TRACK
TRANSFER
TUBE
TURNSTILE
UNDERGROUND

```
E A J O S T L I N G B F A
L P L A T F O R M B Y B A C O
I R N O A O N T E H E L T R U B
T A K E T H E A T R A I N O E E
S E W U I A S L R N A A M W E D
N T B H O D N U O R G R E D N U
R E F S N A R T L P E D L E M K
U I E A U R S I U L A R B D C E
T A D T I S N A R T D I P A R A
T T R E I E C E E L E H R A N
O R R E G N A H P A R T S
```

ANSWER, PAGE 278

67. Office Seeking

BOSS
CIRCULAR FILE
CLOCK-WATCHER
COFFEE ROOM
COMPUTER
COPIER
CUBICLE
DESK
FAX
HUMP DAY
I.D. BADGE
IN-BOX
LUNCH HOUR
MAILROOM
MEETING
MEMO
PHONE
TGIF
VOICEMAIL
WATERCOOLER

```
R E L O O C R E T A W D I
U L B M E R F T C U B I C L E
O S E E A L I A M E C I O V Y M
H M S G E F V E X R Y Y F T H E
H P I D C I R C U L A R F I L E
C H N A G G C A N D B D E E F T
N O I B L T E D P U N D E E R I
U N P D M C O M P U T E R S N N
L E I I S C U E L L S S O B K G
A N E R E H C T A W K C O L C
O M A I L R O O M U S X M
```

ANSWER, PAGE 278

68. Time Sheet

BIG HAND
CALENDAR
CENTURY
CLOCK
DAY
DECADE
EPOCH
FOURTH
  DIMENSION
FUTURE
HOUR
MIDNIGHT
MILLENNIUM
MINUTE
MOMENT
MONTH
NOON
PAST
PRESENT
SECOND
SUNDIAL
TICK-TOCK
WATCH
WEEK
YEAR

```
M U I N N E L L I M S Y E
I A O R M T F U T U R E H I S
D O S T I L O W I N G A C S O L
N O I S N E M I D H T R U O F A
I L E A U A T P N W N Y E W N I
G A C P T N R C A L E N D A R D
H W O L E N T B H E S E N T E N
T C H M O N T H G E E E K C D U
K C O T K C I T I E R D A H E S
O M U P N S K F B R P D A Y O
M N R O E Y R U T N E C W
```

ANSWER, PAGE 278

39

69. Cell Out Crowd

ANSWER
ANYTIME
  MINUTES
BELT CLIP
CALL
"CAN YOU HEAR
  ME NOW?"
CHARGER
DIAL
FEATURES
FLIP
HANDS-FREE
LOW BATTERY
PLAN
RING TONES
ROAMING
SEND
SIGNAL
TALK
TEXTING
VIBRATE
"YOU'RE
  BREAKING UP"

```
L T H A N D S F R E E D R
O H E F N I R S S T R C I E L
W O N E M R A E H U O Y N A C C
B L S V I B R A T E A C G A L H
A K S E T U N I M E M I T Y N A
T C L N T L L W A P I S O M A R
T D A A E T E X T I N G N T E G
E B E L T C L I P L G O E W T E
R F H P L E I N V F E N S T O R
Y O U R E B R E A K I N G U P
R S R I V A S I G N A L L
```

ANSWER, PAGE 279

70. "Bus" Depot

AMBUSH
BABUSHKA
BUSBOY
BUSHEL
BUSHES
BUSINESS
BUSTER BROWN
BUSTLE
BUSTS
BUSY
COLUMBUS
DEBUSSY
E PLURIBUS
  UNUM
GARY BUSEY
GHOSTBUSTERS
INCUBUS
NIMBUS
REBUS
ROBUST
SYLLABUS

```
H B O Y E S U B Y R A G P
B U E Y S O U S A R R E G O I
U S R E T S U B T S O H G N G I
S H G A N B U S T E R B R O W N
I E G B A U U B S T S E U R R C
N S E L T S U B E S T O E S L U
E I L A M B U S H D S B N E T B
S Y M T C O L U M B U S H H I U
S S C B O Y M M U S B S T E R S
O M U N U S U B I R U L P E M
N I A K H S U B A B B U S
```

ANSWER, PAGE 279

71. The Fortune 100

ALCOA
ALLSTATE
AMERICAN
  EXPRESS
BANK ONE
BEST BUY
BOEING
COMCAST
CVS
DELL
DISNEY
EXXON MOBIL
FEDEX

FORD
GENERAL
  ELECTRIC
IBM
INTEL
J.C. PENNEY
LOWE'S
MICROSOFT
PFIZER
SPRINT
TARGET
UPS
WAL-MART

```
L  I  B  O  M  N  O  X  X  E  D  E  F
S  B  A  M  L  W  A  D  I  S  N  E  Y  L  A
T  M  O  O  N  M  I  C  R  O  S  O  F  T  O  B
S  A  W  A  L  M  A  R  T  Y  I  T  K  D  C  E
T  E  C  A  U  P  I  G  E  T  A  A  L  N  L  S
S  S  E  R  P  X  E  N  A  C  I  R  E  M  A  T
A  P  D  I  S  S  N  I  L  N  T  G  S  I  C  B
C  I  R  T  C  E  L  E  L  A  R  E  N  E  G  U
M  A  O  I  P  V  R  O  E  C  E  T  V  I  S  Y
O  I  F  C  N  O  S  B  D  R  E  Z  I  F  P
C  N  J  I  E  T  A  T  S  L  L  A  S
```

ANSWER, PAGE 279

72. I've Been Working on the Railroad

WORKING
RAILROAD
LIVELONG
DAY
JUST
PASS
TIME
AWAY
WHISTLE
BLOWING
RISE
EARLY

MORN
HEAR
CAPTAIN
SHOUTING
DINAH
HORN
SOMEONE
KITCHEN
KNOW
STRUMMING
OLD
BANJO

```
S  O  K  I  T  C  H  E  N  M  E  H  T
R  H  Y  S  I  O  N  O  K  Y  L  R  A  E  D
A  I  U  A  N  J  A  H  R  I  S  A  B  N  T  R
I  J  G  A  W  N  I  N  G  N  O  L  E  V  I  L
L  N  N  N  I  A  T  P  A  C  O  O  N  T  A  D
R  W  I  O  I  B  M  A  N  W  T  W  O  N  K  A
O  H  T  E  N  K  W  H  I  S  T  L  E  A  M  Y
A  M  U  I  E  M  R  N  E  I  G  S  M  H  P  T
D  L  O  E  M  V  G  O  E  A  I  N  O  A  C  O
M  E  H  R  F  E  R  O  W  R  R  M  S  D  I
N  E  S  G  N  I  M  M  U  R  T  S  R
```

ANSWER, PAGE 279

73. The Telecommute

BROWSER
CHAT
DIAL-UP
DOT-COM
DOWNLOAD
E-MAIL
FLAME
GOOGLE
HOME PAGE
HOST
INSTANT
  MESSAGE
INTRANET

LINK
MENU
NETIQUETTE
POST
ROUTER
SCROLL
SEARCH
SPAM
SURF
URL
WEB SITE
WIRELESS

```
I D A O L N W O D F I A T
E L L I N K G S O N R S R A E
T I A W M N V C T E O N D W H T
T M R E S W O R B H U O E I D C
E T N B H U A O H E T I N R T E
U U D S R N R L N C E E T E E M
Q I I I E N V L O E R N M L T A
I N S T A N T M E S S A G E E P
T D U E S L P E L L O E S O S
E C R H E C U K Q F O U A S Y
N L F H O M E P A G E E T
```

ANSWER, PAGE 280

74. Weekend Planner

CARWASH
CLEANING
DINNER
ERRANDS
FAMILY VISIT
GARDENING
GOLF
MOVIE
MUSEUM
NIGHTCLUB

PARTY
POKER
READING
RESTAURANT
SHOPPING
SOCCER
TENNIS
THEATER
TRAVEL
VIDEO

```
T I S I V Y L I M A F O N
L T Y I R O G B U I N L S O N
S H D C S M N R S U S P O K E R
H E O E O I I R E C C O S G G H
O A A V D E N R U V A E R N Y P
P T I T H I E N M N R G I I D A
P E R R A N D S E O W N N D E R
I R B A N Y R E S T A U R A N T
N F R I V I A D A E S Y S E P Y
G E D A K E G E L R H U N R K
N O W N B U L C T H G I N
```

ANSWER, PAGE 280

75. Welcome Aboard

AHOY
BONJOUR
BUENOS DIAS
BUON GIORNO
CIAO
DZIEN DOBRY
G'DAY
GOD DAG
GOOD MORNING
GREETINGS
GUTEN TAG
HAIL

HELLO
HEY
HI THERE
HOLA
HOWDY
JAMBO
KALIMERA
KONNICHIWA
SALAAM
SALUTATIONS
SALVE
SHALOM

```
O T H D O M O L A H S M A S Y D W O H E
B D I Z S L C O L N A I G N T A R O D M
M U U I L C I I E D I A H G E L D L O A
A K O E A B A G O O D M O R N I N G S A
J A H N T H O H E D S E R E H T I H T L
E L L D G E P N O H O O N E E G R E E A
T I I O N I A G J S N O I T A T U L A S
G M A B L H O E X O E A N I D E A R A G
H E Y R O R A R H G U T E N T A G L A M
B R E Y L L S A N I B R D G A H V O O Y
I A W I H C I N N O K N S S T E E A D H
```

ANSWER, PAGE 280

76. "Bon" Voyage

BLUE BONNET
BONE UP
BONFIRE
BONGOS
BONIER
BON JOVI
BONK
BONNIE RAITT
BONNY
BONSAI
BONUS
BOURBON
CARBONARA
CINNABON
DEBONAIR

DO A JOB ON
EBONY
GIBBON
HERRINGBONE
JAMES BOND
LISBON
RIBBON
RIBONUCLEIC
  ACID
T-BONE
TROMBONE
VAGABOND
WISHBONE
ZAMBONI

```
D I S N I D O D N O B A G A V C U R E E
B V O O T N A F Z N O B S I L A I N D N
J O E B G S R I A N O B E D B R O P B O
A J O R O N U N M M T E N N O B E U L B
M N O U T B O N B E S B B O M O O E N G
E O D O A J O B O N R A O O N N Z N B N
S B Y B K A D N N B R I R N I A V O O I
B O N N I E R A I T T T F E S R Y B N R
O O O U O T R U L E Y C I N N A B O N R
N B E N O B H S I W R B O N O I I K Y E
D I C A C I E L C U N O B I R B E R S H
```

ANSWER, PAGE 280

77. I Packed My Suitcase ...

ADAPTER
BATTERIES
CAMERA
CLOTHES
COMFORTABLE
  SHOES
DRAMAMINE
FANNY PACK
HAT
IPOD
ITINERARY
MAPS
MONEY BELT

NOVEL
PASSPORT
PENS
PURSE
SUNSCREEN
TICKETS
TOILETRIES
TOTE BAG
TRAVELERS'
  CHECKS
TUMS
VISA
WALLET

```
T S T E K C I T S H E A W O D O P I R K
L D O S A L O N E G P A S S P O R T E C
S T T M B D S E I R T E L I O T A I E A
G G E A S G A E R L S M O S V V S N E P
I R B P N G S P E Y S E T M E M I E A Y
A T A K W U A B T L T A H U A M L R U N
L M G M P A Y U T E R S A T A I R A P N
S E O H S E L B A T R O F M O C P R U A
O R V T N R U L B N S O A V E L R Y R F
T W E O T R A V E L E R S C H E C K S N
T Y M M N I L E S T D S U N S C R E E N
```

ANSWER, PAGE 281

78. Leaving on a Jet Plane

BAGS
PACKED
READY
STANDING
OUTSIDE
DOOR
HATE
WAKE
GOODBYE
DAWN
BREAKIN'
EARLY
MORN
TAXI'S
BLOWIN'
HORN
LONESOME

CRY
KISS
SMILE
TELL
WAIT
HOLD
NEVER
LEAVIN'
JET
PLANE
DON'T
KNOW
WHEN
BACK
AGAIN
BABE

```
J K C A B O S G A B H N D Y L R A E E O
M N V A E S M R O W R O R T E T K H U E
S O B L O W I N O O N C E G R A B T U T
I E R T O N L X B E D C A A W E S M E A
D A W N H I E T A F O B D R N I V A E L
O P K I E T E H A T E R Y P D A U E L A
N N D A M E A R W Y I B R E A K I N N T
T W A G N I D N A T S S T T H I E T R H
I E O A S R O N L I Y S E M O S E N O L
O N L G D O O R T A O J C L I S M L B T
O P N L U M B H E W R P A C K E D O N E
```

ANSWER, PAGE 281

79. Anchors Aweigh!

AMISTAD
ARIZONA
BEAGLE
BISMARCK
BONHOMME
 RICHARD
BOUNTY
CONSTITUTION
ENDURANCE
GOLDEN HIND
HALF MOON
LUSITANIA

MAINE
MAYFLOWER
MISSOURI
MONITOR
NINA
PINTA
PUEBLO
RAINBOW
 WARRIOR
SANTA MARIA
TITANIC
VICTORY

```
A R O I R R A W W O B N I A R T W O T I
I T A N I R E W O L F Y A M N C S L U R
R V Y R O T C I V I V O M C O O R U S M
A G O L D E N H I N D W I H O O Z S A K
M O W E A R A E B I N N S F M L A I N C
A O T S M W R O H E A N S I F B N T R R
T T N O I T U T I T S N O C L E S A A A
N A N I S N D K I A R E U L A U I N V M
A P I N T A N T I N G A R T H P I I T S
S H I Y A O E L G A E B I S W N R A I I
T I N G D D R A H C I R E M M O H N O B
```

ANSWER, PAGE 281

80. Travel Log

BUSHWHACK
CRUISE
EXPLORE
FLIT
GAD ABOUT
GALLIVANT
GLOBETROT
HIKE
HIT THE ROAD
JOURNEY
MEANDER
MIGRATE
MOSEY
PEREGRINATE

RAMBLE
RANGE
RELOCATE
ROAM
SAUNTER
SCHLEP
SEE THE WORLD
SIGHTSEE
TOUR
TRAIPSE
TREK
VACATION
VOYAGE
WANDER

```
T R A M B L E H D A O R E H T T I H E S
K W O E I R R D S T R E S I U R C A V E
C E K A A G L I I E S T F R O M E T R E
A I A N P E R E G R I N A T E T V K A T
H I G D L P S A H E R A H M A A P J U H
W E S E B P Y E T C A V A C A T I O N E
H A U R I O S T S E E I O T R O B U T W
S A N A V V E I E R O L P X E A R R O O
U L R D S C H L E P E L U S D E D N U R
B T T O E B E F S R O A S A U N T E R L
H A R T O R T E B O L G G M O S E Y D D
```

ANSWER, PAGE 281

81. Wise Guides

ACCESS
BAEDEKER
BEST PLACES
BLUE GUIDES
CADOGAN
EYEWITNESS
FIELDING
FODOR'S
FOOTPRINT
FROMMER'S
INSIDER'S

INSIGHT
KNOPF
LET'S GO
LONELY PLANET
MICHELIN
MOON
   HANDBOOKS
OPEN ROAD
RICK STEVE'S
ROUGH GUIDES

```
I  T  H  E  F  I  L  S  E  V  E  T  S  K  C  I  R  R  S  T
N  R  E  D  G  U  E  I  Y  D  E  B  Y  F  M  I  E  C  H  G
S  E  C  A  L  P  T  S  E  B  E  L  I  O  N  O  K  N  N  A
I  A  L  O  C  H  S  A  W  T  I  K  N  O  P  F  E  I  C  N
D  R  O  U  G  H  G  U  I  D  E  S  O  T  N  O  D  C  U  I
E  T  F  I  S  I  O  D  T  E  N  A  L  P  Y  L  E  N  O  L
R  E  S  O  E  O  P  E  N  R  O  A  D  R  E  S  A  U  R  E
S  N  S  E  D  I  U  G  E  U  L  B  O  I  S  P  B  E  I  H
I  S  T  H  E  O  N  E  S  W  G  U  F  N  A  G  O  D  A  C
F  R  O  M  M  E  R  S  S  I  D  E  T  T  O  N  E  W  Y  I
O  R  K  C  I  T  Y  S  K  O  O  B  D  N  A  H  N  O  O  M
```

ANSWER, PAGE 282

82. Cruise Control

ATRIUM
BERTH
BINGO
BUFFET
CABIN
CAPTAIN'S TABLE
CASINO
CREW
CRUISE DIRECTOR
DECK CHAIRS
DOCK
HELM

KIDS' CLUB
POOLSIDE BAR
PORT OF CALL
PURSER
RAILING
SAIL TIME
SHUFFLEBOARD
STATEROOM
STEWARD
SUNGLASSES
SUNSET
TOUR

```
M  D  R  A  O  B  E  L  F  F  U  H  S  L  S  O  M  M  E  L
O  U  X  U  E  R  Y  K  C  T  R  U  I  L  S  E  S  U  S  D
O  H  I  R  R  P  S  I  S  E  O  L  S  A  I  L  T  I  M  E
R  O  T  C  E  R  I  D  E  S  I  U  R  C  L  C  E  R  O  C
E  H  N  D  S  O  S  S  T  H  O  S  R  F  U  P  W  T  E  K
T  R  R  I  R  S  C  C  E  B  I  N  G  O  H  P  A  A  C  C
A  E  E  S  U  N  G  L  A  S  S  E  S  T  N  O  R  O  P  H
T  L  F  N  P  E  M  U  W  B  H  O  W  R  A  I  D  N  W  A
S  T  S  F  T  R  A  B  E  D  I  S  L  O  O  P  S  E  O  I
L  E  I  V  U  E  R  A  I  L  I  N  G  P  O  N  R  A  B  R
T  O  A  E  L  B  A  T  S  N  I  A  T  P  A  C  R  D  C  S
```

ANSWER, PAGE 282

83. Island Hopping

ALCATRAZ
BAFFIN
BLOCK
CHRISTMAS
CONEY
DEVIL'S
EASTER
ELLIS
FIRE
GILLIGAN'S
KODIAK
PARRIS
PITCAIRN
PRINCE EDWARD
RHODE
RIKER'S
ROANOKE
ROCK
SANIBEL
SKULL
STATEN
TEMPTATION
THREE-MILE
TREASURE
VICTORIA
WAKE

```
W S H E K O N A O R E E R U S A E R T N
S K K C U R E V I E V N O R W A S K E S
N A O U S L E C W A L O A R N E W Y A O
R L K D L E D O H R G I L L I G A N S W
B C E I I L R N C A R T M R T K I O T S
S A S O V A N E S O H A O E B B E W E I
E T D A E N K Y T I M T A L E A S R R R
D R A W D E E C N I R P V L O R F T S R
I A N T R G I T O H E M U N I C H F O A
R Z N I E V O F F R T E N R I A C T I P
H E F I S N C H R I S T M A S L A N D N
```

ANSWER, PAGE 282

84. Circling at the Airport

AGENT
ARRIVALS
BAGGAGE CLAIM
BAR
BOARDING PASS
CAR RENTAL
COFFEE
COURTESY
  PHONE
CUSTOMS
DELAYS
DEPARTURES
DUTY FREE
ESCALATOR
E-TICKET
GATES
HARD SEATS
LAYOVER
LIMO
LINES
LOUNGE
LUGGAGE TAG
PARKING
PLANES
RUNWAY
SKYCAP
STANDBY
TAXI
TERMINAL

```
L S T E H E S S A P G N I D R A O B M S
A E A T S K R O T A L A C S E T N W E C
N N H I Y H A R D S E A T S O N I T E A
I A N C A S P L S I E R P E E E A D F R
M L A K L T M I A L C E G A G G A B F R
R P H E E E X N T A A N R E R A R M O E
E U I T D A N E A Y U V L F L K G S C N
T T N B T C U S T O M S I I Y L I G L T
L I V W A E S A L V T D M R E T G N U A
A D E P A R T U R E S U O L R L U E G L
E N O H P Y S E T R U O C S T A N D B Y
```

ANSWER, PAGE 282

85. Travelers of Yore

AMUNDSEN
BALBOA
BYRD
CABOT
CHAMPLAIN
CLARK
COLUMBUS
COOK
CORONADO
CORTES
DA GAMA
DE SOTO
DRAKE
ERICSON

HUDSON
LA SALLE
LEWIS
MAGELLAN
PEARY
PIZARRO
POLO
PONCE DE LEON
RALEIGH
SCOTT
SHACKLETON
STANLEY
TASMAN
VESPUCCI

```
V P S C O T T O N O D A N O R O C C E S
E D E L K L E S O R N W A T N S R E A I
S B Y R D L O A H R L Y N O O A T L S W
P O A C H A M P L A I N O S S K M T I E
U L M H N A G E F Z C O R E L L A S A L
C T U H G H E A F I O K T D U N G N A T
C A N A U I I R N P O R L F L Y E O K T
I U D D T H E Y W P O N C E D E L E O N
H E S U B M U L O C N H Y E T D L B O I
S O E C O V E K A R D B A L B O A E C R
N E N D N O S C I R E F L O R C N I D A
```

ANSWER, PAGE 283

86. Fictional Millionaires

(Montgomery)
   BURNS
(Blake) CARRINGTON
(Jed) CLAMPETT
(Cruella) DE VIL
(Philip) DRUMMOND
(J.R.) EWING
(Jay) GATSBY
(Gordon) GEKKO
(Auric) GOLDFINGER
(Jonathan) HART

(Thurston) HOWELL
(Charles Foster) KANE
(Tracy) LORD
(Lex) LUTHOR
(Scrooge) MCDUCK
(Mr.) POTTER
(Richie) RICH
(Oliver "Daddy")
   WARBUCKS
(Bruce) WAYNE
(Willie) WONKA

```
T H G A T S B Y E M O D N
O P N O N O T G N I R R A C L
Y G I U K Y D S N A B U R N S M
D E W K W A E S C L A M P E T T
R R E I C H V U N C L M E P K E
N G O L D F I N G E R O N Y C L
A B A L G H L S W A Y N E B U U
T K I E S A N H O W O D F T D F
I A N W A R B U C K S C H I C A
L N L O Y T M R M I O O N O M
P E O H W P O T T E R L Y
```

ANSWER, PAGE 283

87. Berlitz Blitz

AIRPORT
BANK
BATHROOM
BILL
BREAKFAST
COFFEE
DO YOU SPEAK
ENGLISH?
DOLLARS
EXCUSE ME
GOODBYE
HELLO
HELP
HOTEL
HOW DO YOU
SAY ...

HOW MUCH?
LOST
MENU
MUSEUM
PLEASE
POSTCARD
REPEAT
SORRY
STOP, THIEF!
TAXI
TELEPHONE
TICKET
TRAIN
WAITER
WHAT
WHERE

```
A C E M E S U C X E T B A N K T Y U A D
H L E U S I G G M N A R T I A T A H W R
C N B S A N O C O F F E E H R G S X K A
U O H E L L O Y O K N A D O R P U Y I C
M C L U E A D N R O E K R T L S O D R T
W O P M W O B Y H R O F U E R T Y R R S
O A N O L H Y P T U O A A L L S O E T O
H S I L G N E K A E P S U O Y O D R L P
S H A T E L R R B E E T S F O R W B L E
S R R T E R E F E I H T P O T S O E I S
S U T T L R E P E A T E K C I T H T B S
```

ANSWER, PAGE 283

88. Amtrak Meet

ADIRONDACK
BLUE WATER
CARDINAL
CLOCKER
COAST
STARLIGHT
CRESCENT
DOWNEASTER
EMPIRE BUILDER
HEARTLAND
FLYER

HIAWATHA
KEYSTONE
PALMETTO
PERE
MARQUETTE
PIEDMONT
SILVER STAR
STATE HOUSE
VERMONTER
WOLVERINE

```
R E Y L F D N A L T R A E H T H E R F C
E I K R E T S A E N W O D N R O A S T L
T P H C A S N S E N G E R T O T R A W O
A I I N A I T H G I L R A T S T S A O C
W T A O D D O F F E R F U R L E S L L K
E V W R I E N C R E S C E N T M W Y V E
U D A R E T N O M R E V O M E L C A E R
L C T R S W A S R T L H E C A A L I R K
B F H O R R E D L I U B E R I P M E I N
S T A T E H O U S E D I P I E D M O N T
A Z E P H Y P E R E M A R Q U E T T E R
```

ANSWER, PAGE 283

89. Get a Room

BELLHOP
BIBLE
CHECKOUT
CLERK
CONCIERGE
CONTINENTAL
  BREAKFAST
COT
"DO NOT
  DISTURB"
DOUBLE
FLOORS
FOUR STARS
FRONT DESK
GUEST

KEY CARD
LINENS
LOBBY
LOUNGE
MAID
MINIBAR
MINT
POOL
RATES
ROOM SERVICE
SUITE
TURNDOWN
  SERVICE
WAKE-UP CALL

```
B R U T S I D T O N O D F D S L A S D V
E E G U R A B I N I M A L S R I R S O H
G O I M S E T O T I S I O X A A T E U E
R T N D O N F S T H M E O T T W C E B T
E E C I V R E S M O O R R E S N T Y L U
I G Y A T U R N D O W N S E R V I C E O
C L N M G A B R I L L A C P U E K A W K
N L G U E S I T H L O T P L O B B Y E C
O L E S O I B E L L H O P N F T H T E E
C W O R R L L L F R O N T D E S K D O H
T S A F K A E R B L A T N E N I T N O C
```

ANSWER, PAGE 284

90. Currency Exchange

To complete this word list chain, start at the top with DEN. Take the letter that must be "exchanged" to give you the name of a currency—the D in this case, to give you YEN—and find a spot in the next word (RANK) where it can be exchanged with a letter to give you a new currency name. Write that currency in the blank and continue down the chain, using in the next word the letter in RANK that was exchanged. All 24 words can then be found in the grid, so you can work back and forth to complete the chain. See page 252 for a word list.

YEN	DEN
————	RANK
————	PRONE
————	ROUND
————	MASK
————	LUCRE
————	REAR
————	DINAH
————	BART
————	LISA
————	CHILLING
————	FRANZ

```
T F H E K N A R P R E P T S F A
S R E R R E I R E E S O O R F R
G A O S I Y O X C A E U A O A I
N N S F R N D I N A R N R N O B
E Z I M E S O D M A C D D L D L
I A S L A A D E L L U I N T I H
M E U S L H G N I L L I H S N M
A A C I P I E S U O F F A A A M
O U R S B A H T E O L E C S H T
R A E K I C G C U I R T K A R S
```

ANSWER, PAGE 284

91. Shipping Department

ARK
BARGE
BRIGANTINE
CANOE
CATAMARAN
CIGARETTE BOAT
CORACLE
DINGHY
DORY
FERRY
GALLEON
GONDOLA
JUNK
KAYAK
KETCH

OCEAN LINER
PUNT
SAMPAN
SCHOONER
SCOW
SKIFF
SKIPJACK
SLOOP
STEAMSHIP
TANKER
TRAWLER
TUGBOAT
UMIAK
WINDJAMMER
YACHT

```
T P I H S M A E T S H P E F E R R Y W O
R L Y D C T G O N D O L A S L C A H R P
G A E R H S T S H O I N O E L L A G U S
T P R C O R A C L E A S I S S A T N K A
A N A K O D K S K R R E K N A T T I O R
O Y R E N I L N A E C O A I M E F D R E
B T H T E A T M Y C A R I R P F I E S L
G A H C R A A L A F R E M M A J D N I W
U A R H M T I L K L I O U N N U A T O A
T C I G A R E T T E B O A T O N N C S R
O F O C E N I T N A G I R B I K S L K T
```

ANSWER, PAGE 284

92. Plane Speaking

AISLE
ARMREST
BARF BAG
BEVERAGES
CABIN
CARRY-ON
COACH
COCKPIT
CREW
CRUISING
   ALTITUDE
EXIT ROW
FIRST CLASS
FLIGHT
   ATTENDANT

IN-FLIGHT
   MOVIE
LEGROOM
MEAL
OVERHEAD BIN
PILLOW
PILOT
SEAT BELT SIGN
SLEEP
TAXIING
TOUCH DOWN
TRAY
TURBULENCE
WINGS

```
O M T E C N E L U B R U T Y H N T E S S
V M O O T N A D N E T T A T H G I L F S
E A A O L C L E S T X R L J E T P B P A
R C L A R M R E S T T I G A A N K E A L
H S I E N G I S T L E B T A E S C N T C
E G W B E V E R A G E S A R B M O H A T
A N E W O S R L L D I S X P O F C R J S
D I N F L I G H T M O V I E U W R S T R
B W S E T W E L W O L L I P V Y E A F I
I E E L T O U C H D O W N E O T L O B F
N P N G E D U T I T L A G N I S I U R C
```

ANSWER, PAGE 284

51

93. Lost: The Trip from Hell

ANA-LUCIA
BOONE
CHARLIE
CLAIRE
CRASH
DHARMA
   INITIATIVE
DRIVE SHAFT
FLASHBACKS
"FRECKLES"
FUSELAGE
HATCH
HURLEY
ISLAND
JACK
JIN
JUNGLE
KATE

LOCKE
LOS ANGELES
MICHAEL
MR. EKO
MYSTERY
NUMBERS
OCEANIC
   AIRLINES
PLANE
RADIO
RAFT
SAWYER
SAYID
SHANNON
SUN
SYDNEY
THE OTHERS
WALT

```
S T F A H S E V I R D T H S A W Y E R E
D H O S R R I C G S K C A B H S A L F I
A I A E N E K H A L L O S A N G E L E S
I R Y N S H A A S Y D N E Y C H R I T R
C A L A N T T R P T H I L D A C A T D E
U D E L S O E L G N U J K T N L F J A B
L I A P S E N I L R I A C I N A E C O M
A O H K C H Y E L R U H E K R I L O D U
N I C E E T A M Y S T E R Y R R N S U N
A A I K L E G A L E S U F M R E K O I Y
J O M N E V I T A I T I N I A M R A H D
```

ANSWER, PAGE 285

94. Wonders of the World— Natural Department

ALPS
AMAZON
ANDES
ANGEL FALLS
AYERS ROCK
CRATER LAKE
DEAD SEA
DENALI
GOBI
GRAND CANYON
GREAT BARRIER
   REEF
GREAT LAKES

KILAUEA
LOIRE
MAUNA LOA
MOJAVE
MT. ETNA
MT. EVEREST
NIAGARA FALLS
NILE
OLD FAITHFUL
RIVIERA
ROCKIES
SAHARA

```
T H E E L I N O Y N A C D N A R G O D O
A R O C K I E S R E R O E D O S S E V S
E E K L T N A A M E C R A T E R L A K E
U D C G L U F H T I A F D L O N L D E K
A A O L A N U A M N V I S A L S A T O A
L B R W L O I R E O E R E T N H F L E L
I C S E O U N A T Z J R A A Y T L S I T
K S R N I A G A R A F A L L S F E I R A
T S E R E V E T M M S P V T N D G T A E
T I Y O N A I L M A S O N E N U N M M R
E N A T F E E R R E I R R A B T A E R G
```

ANSWER, PAGE 285

95. Wonders of the World— Man-Made Department

ALAMO
ALHAMBRA
ANGKOR WAT
ARC DE
   TRIOMPHE
BIG BEN
COLOSSEUM
EIFFEL
   TOWER
GREAT WALL
KREMLIN

LEANING TOWER
   OF PISA
PARTHENON
PENTAGON
PYRAMIDS
SPHINX
STATUE OF
   LIBERTY
STONEHENGE
TAJ MAHAL
VERSAILLES

```
Y T R E B I L F O E U T A T S T H E S E
N S M P I B R E S T A N A T E C B E X U
O T S D I M A R Y P I O L W D O L I N G
G O N G G S K T I L L N H A R L S Z I R
A N B O E P R A R C D E T R I O M P H E
T E P E M L E I N M O H O A R S K I P A
N H A L H A M B R A N T S G G S E G S T
E E I F F E L T O W E R A R T E H O N W
P N U G H T I A H E E A I D E U A N E A
V G E R W O N R K V E P T A J M A H A L
D E A S I P F O R E W O T G N I N A E L
```

ANSWER, PAGE 285

96. Road Trip

BACK ROAD
BILLBOARDS
BRIDGE
CAR GAME
CONVENIENCE
   STORE
COWS
DETOUR
DINER
EXIT
GAS STATION
HITCHHIKER
LIGHTS
LITTER

MAP
MERGE
MOTEL
RADIO
RAMP
REST AREA
ROADSIDE
   STAND
RUMBLE STRIP
SCENIC ROUTE
SEMI
SHORTCUT
SPEED TRAP
TRUCK STOP

```
T H E P I R T S E L B M U R L O N N G L
P E M S S H O R T C U T T I M N O T I C
A A P O T S K C U R T E L T R O I T S A
R T A B A S T E O R E K I H H C T I H R
T I E S R I E I R N I X G N E E A E T G
D Y R R U I D M C N E N H P R I T N L A
E E A R O A D S I D E S T A N D S G B M
E E T T R I W G N E W E S M N S S E E E
P A S O N T T L E O B I L L B O A R D S
S E E E U A B A C K R O A D N D G B O S
T O R N E R O T S E C N E I N E V N O C
```

ANSWER, PAGE 285

97. Frame-Up Job

BRITISH MUSEUM
CLUNY
FRICK
GARDNER
GETTY
GUGGENHEIM
HERMITAGE
L'ORANGERIE
LOUVRE
MADAME
    TUSSAUD'S
METROPOLITAN
MOMA
PRADO
RIJKSMUSEUM
SMITHSONIAN
TATE
TUILERIES
UFFIZI
VICTORIA AND
    ALBERT
WHITNEY

```
M U E S U M H S I T I R B A U T H E O H
I R P E Y T E M U E S U M S K J I R R E
E R G D E E V R I T E S O N S R C E S R
H E A E N I S D U A S S U T E M A D A M
N N D M T U R A L T S I N G I R E Y S I
E D S M I T H S O N I A N T R A N U R T
G R A N H T Y S A P A A R E E U O N A A
G A V P W A R M E T R O P O L I T A N G
U G W U I T O H T O H A K C I R F E F E
G O O D O M I N L M U S D E U F F I Z I
U T R E B L A D N A A I R O T C I V M S
```

ANSWER, PAGE 286

98. S.S. Wordloop

SAD SACK
SAM SPADE
SAY SO
SEA SALT
SEA SERPENT
SECRET SANTA
SESAME STREET
SET SAIL
SILVER SCREEN
SISSY SPACEK
SIXTH SENSE
SLAP SHOT
SMART SET
SOB SISTER
SODA SHOP
SO SAD
SOY SAUCE
SPACE SUIT
SPUN SUGAR
STOP SIGN
SUNSET STRIP
SWIZZLE STICK

```
S T R K O N G S E S A M E S T R E E T P
S S S E E A A O R T I U S E C A P S C I
I H M C S M O Y L L V E R A S G S S U R
X R E A S O B S I S T E R L D U O Y S T
T N E P R E S A E S S O I D E S D S O S
H L A S T T S U S T O P S I G N A H E T
S D A Y P T S C P E S D S Y T U S C I E
E C K S E C R E T S A N T A A P H Y K S
N S I S A T U A T T D I O N A S O S S N
S I M I N E E R C S R E V L I S P P L U
E Y S S A I S D K C I T S E L Z Z I W S
```

ANSWER, PAGE 286

99. Jet Set

AER LINGUS
AEROFLOT
AIR CANADA
AIR FRANCE
ALITALIA
ALOHA
AMERICAN
AVIANCA
BRITISH
  AIRWAYS
CONTINENTAL
DELTA
EL AL

IBERIA
JETBLUE
KLM
LUFTHANSA
OLYMPIC
PAN AM
QANTAS
SOUTHWEST
SPIRIT
UNITED
VARIG
VIRGIN
  ATLANTIC

```
L W H S Y A W R I A H S I T I R B E N O
A S H A O A W M I N L G R A S I N M L K
T M A I I N S M A O S O T A U I R Y L E
N I N R E E O S E N X N H C G E M P A C
E Q E C U L U F T H A N S A N P T Q V N
N B A A L A T N G C N P A L I T A L I A
I T A N B S H T I R I P S C L C U T A R
T R A A T Y W R R T O L F O R E A T N F
N S A D E A E Y A I E N G Q E A L N C R
O T A A J M S S V I S D S A A E F A A I
C I T N A L T A N I G R I V D E S T L A
```

ANSWER, PAGE 286

100. Souvenir Shop

BASEBALL CAP
BELT
BUMPER STICKER
CALENDAR
DECALS
DECK OF CARDS
FLAG
FRAME
GLASSES
KEYCHAIN
LAPEL PIN
MUG
NECKTIE
NOTEPAD

PENCIL
PLATE
POSTCARD
POSTER
SNOWGLOBE
SOCKS
SPOON
STUFFED ANIMAL
TOTE BAG
TOWEL
TOY CAR
T-SHIRT
VISOR
WALLET

```
R E K C I T S R E P M U B T T H E S O G
D E M A R F F A F I C L E O L P F D T L
R H E I T L O D N I A H C Y E K L R S A
A A H N O E G N E P L D E S B C V A O S
C S U N W T L E E S L A C E D I Y C T S
T B A S E B A L L C A P C P S O R F O E
S N E R L F P A A A K E B O L G W O N S
O P E N C I L C C W M T R S T U A K O L
P L O Y N H A A S U A O I T T O Y C A R
S O T O T E B A G U V N E E N I K E R S
L A M I N A D E F F U T S R T S O D R E
```

ANSWER, PAGE 286

101. "Oh, Heavens!"

ANDROMEDA
BIG DIPPER
CANIS MAJOR
CASSIOPEIA
CONSTELLATIONS
DRACO
GALAXY
GEMINI
HALLEY'S COMET
HYDRA
JUPITER
METEORS
MILKY WAY
MOON
NEBULA
ORION
PEGASUS
PISCES
SATURN
SCORPIO
SUPERNOVA
TAURUS
VENUS
VIRGO

```
        W A P V V I R G O N T
      C O N S T E L L A T I O N S T
      T A A O E F N G L Y Y P T C E O B
  N E N V S C E U R A L A R N M A D I T
  N O I R O S H S W V S M O O N G R G A
  R E S N J I I Y T O A U C K E E T D H
  U E M S U P K O E N T S S M C O E I N
  T D A S P L T Y P R Y A I A R M T P O
  A T J H I E R X I E A N U G O H T P A
  S N O M T D S A L P I R S R O E T E M
    T R N E B U L A U R A D A U I G R
    H T R O A A N S T N I Y L S L
    M H O G R N A I N G H
```

ANSWER, PAGE 287

102. Rave Reviews

"A-ONE!"
"AMAZING!"
"AWESOME!"
"BOFFO!"
"BRILLIANT!"
"DANDY!"
"FABULOUS!"
"FANTASTIC!"
"FAR-OUT!"
"FIRST-RATE!"
"GLORIOUS!"
"GREAT!"
"INCREDIBLE!"
"MAGNIFICENT!"
"MARVELOUS!"
"NOT TO BE
    MISSED!"
"PHENOMENAL!"
"STUNNING!"
"SUPERB!"
"THE BEST!"

```
        M A G N I F I C E N T
      W O I N C R E D I B L E S S W
    T T H I A E T W A S R T O U T A O
  L M N Z L Y N M I N D E S O O B O F G
  G L A N E M O N E H P P L T I L A F I
  D M I R N G A G T A B U S O R R L O U
  A T L E V L R Y A H B S S T O A O B E
  N U L N D E I N G A E T R U L U T M L
  D Y I S A E L N F S A B T T G I O E O
  Y N R T A L N O T T O B E M I S S E D
  U B G N I N N U T S H H S E U H B
  U T W A S I T S A N Y W T G O
    O C I T S A T N A F D
```

ANSWER, PAGE 287

103. Electronic Marvels

AM-FM RADIO
ATMS
CAMCORDER
CD-ROM
DIGITAL WATCH
DVDS
ELECTRIC
  BLANKET
E-MAIL
FAX MACHINE
GAME BOY
HALOGEN LAMP
INTERNET

LAPTOP
LASER
MICROWAVE
MODEM
PAGER
REMOTE
SONAR
STEREO
TELEVISION
VCRS
WALKMAN
XBOX

```
        E T O M E R H W Y I S
      R H L H E A E L C L A O M A F
    E V A W O R C I M T D K L B E A E
  L E S L N C E N T R A I R O K E X C I
  M E D O M O T L T Y W I I O S M M P O
  R C H G E E S A A P L D L T M V A A H
  A T O E R X N L Y P A T H E R G C N G
  T E K N A L B C I R T C E L E I H R C
  H C E L A N A O M F I O F R O R I D S
  T T S A O B U F X R G N P D C A N N D
    L E M S T M H N O I S I V E L E T
      O P T A M A S A D E D D I S O
        C A M C O R D E R S N
```

ANSWER, PAGE 287

104. Nature Calls

BEAR HUG
BOOKWORM
CLAM UP
DOG-TIRED
EAGER BEAVER
EAT CROW
FOX TROT
GO APE
HORSE AROUND
LEAPFROG
LION'S SHARE

LOAN SHARK
MONKEY
  BUSINESS
NIGHT OWL
PIG LATIN
RAT RACE
ROAD HOG
SCAPEGOAT
SNAKEBIT
TOADSTOOL

```
        D O N M T K B E A B G
      D N U O R A E S R O H I R O D
    B R A I O G O R F P A E L N I A F
  L Y O U W H L I O N S S H A R E A P B
  M O N K E Y B U S I N E S S V E E S E
  T O O M A K S N A K E B I T N C C E A
  T O R T X O F I E A G E R B E A V E R
  B A B E S E L G O H D A O R P R O C H
  I N E F O D R H T H E A N E S T L L U
  W E R S A E A T C R O W G N D A Y O G
    D E R I T G O D U L O L B M R E T
      H E C A T W T S A P A U J A M
        P I G L A T I N P A S
```

ANSWER, PAGE 287

105. Down Under

ABORIGINE
AMERICA'S CUP
AYERS ROCK
BONDI BEACH
BOOMERANG
"CROCODILE"
    DUNDEE
"G'DAY"
GREAT BARRIER
    REEF
KANGAROO
KOALA

MATE
MEL GIBSON
MELBOURNE
OLYMPICS
OUTBACK
RUGBY
SHEEP
SYDNEY
VEGEMITE
"WALTZING
    MATILDA"

```
        H C A E B I D N O B A
      V U S S I O E S L O V E T Y N
    O K E K C O R S R E Y A E S O A A
  R T A V G M E O L Y M P I C S H G D E
  M U N F E E R R E I R R A B T A E R G
  I T G R E A M Y E Y A S I T B A T E E
  K C A B T U O I X T E G R O A L A C P
  T N R T Y H E Y T L L N R L S A M P R
  G E O E E D N U D E L I D O C O R C A
  D O O N B R E A M D G A N Y D K O T H
  E R P U C S A C I R E M A S F O O
    W A L T Z I N G M A T I L D A
        D S M E L B O U R N E
```

ANSWER, PAGE 288

106. Broadway Blockbusters

AIDA
ANNIE
CABARET
CAMELOT
CATS
CHICAGO
(A) CHORUS LINE
EVITA
FIDDLER ON THE
    ROOF
GREASE
GYPSY
HAIRSPRAY
(THE) KING AND I

LES MIZ
(THE) LION KING
MAME
MAMMA MIA!
(THE) MUSIC
    MAN
MY FAIR LADY
OKLAHOMA!
PETER PAN
PIPPIN
(THE)
    PRODUCERS
RENT

```
      I N C V E E S A T G I
    N G I A Z N A B N D R R E O A
  M A M M A M I A D W I N E V I T A
A L Y E Y S D H M O W A L A I S N S O
R I L M F N I N H S M S K S R Y T N G
H O K L A H O M A C E E O E U P D D A
T N S G I M O F I P R L C E I R C O C
U K N P R I E S R N R U G P T O O A I
N I E S L M U O S N D E P E N Y B H H
K N A R A M E O P O S I T N E A L Y C
G F I D D L E R O N T H E R O O F
  A B Y O U P A T O N A E P E I
    N Y S P Y G T E T C N
```

ANSWER, PAGE 288

107. Weather or Not

BREEZY
BRISK
CLOUDY
COLDER
EL NINO
FLURRIES
FORECAST
HUMIDITY
HURRICANE
LIGHTNING
MILDER
OZONE

PATCHY FOG
PRECIPITATION
RAINY
RECORD HIGH
SHOWERS
SMAZE
SNOW
STORM WATCH
SUNSET
TEMPERATURE
THUNDER
TWISTER

```
            S  I  G  O  F  Y  H  C  T  A  P
      N  M  U  E  H  P  O  C  O  R  R  I  R  C  H
   A  A  R  N  E  R  U  T  A  R  E  P  M  E  T  S  D
R  Z  S  O  S  A  R  A  M  L  M  A  N  M  C  E  A  C  C
E  B  Z  E  E  E  W  G  N  I  N  T  H  G  I  L  N  F  O
D  O  T  R  T  M  N  A  N  K  D  Y  L  R  P  L  I  Y  L
N  N  S  S  R  A  I  A  S  D  N  I  R  S  I  O  D  Z  D
U  M  I  O  A  E  A  N  C  I  R  U  T  Y  T  E  W  E  E
H  W  T  E  A  C  O  T  A  I  L  H  D  Y  A  E  K  E  R
T  S  S  H  O  W  E  R  S  F  R  U  R  W  T  S  I  R  S
   E  S  O  M  E  A  R  E  C  O  R  D  H  I  G  H  B
   R  E  L  N  I  N  O  L  E  O  U  R  O  T  H
   E  R  W  I  C  F  S  E  B  H  N
```

ANSWER, PAGE 288

108. Gardener's Delight

APHIDS
BASKETS
BULB
BURPEE
CARROTS
COMPOST
FLOWERS
GREENHOUSE
HERBS
MULCH
PESTICIDE
PLANTERS

PRUNERS
ROCK
SPREADER
SPRINKLER
STAKES
TOMATOES
TRELLIS
TROWEL
WATERING CAN
WEED
WINDOW BOX
WORMS

```
            T  E  O  K  E  S  D  I  H  P  A
         S  R  E  T  N  A  L  P  R  E  P  B  B  A  N
      P  M  P  B  I  L  I  E  R  K  E  E  A  L  K  A  N
   I  R  R  M  R  B  A  S  K  E  T  S  W  M  U  L  C  H  W
   A  U  L  S  O  I  T  U  T  A  O  F  X  O  B  T  G  O  O
   B  N  S  H  E  I  N  G  A  D  R  D  O  E  L  N  N  T  R
   H  E  E  T  C  R  E  K  S  E  T  A  B  B  R  F  I  T  M
   A  R  N  I  O  D  S  O  L  R  F  R  W  E  P  E  R  L  S
   D  S  D  L  M  R  B  E  O  E  S  U  O  H  N  E  E  R  G
   E  E  N  T  P  S  R  W  K  P  R  R  D  A  L  Y  T  C  A
   L  E  L  O  E  E  A  D  A  N  O  N  L  T  T  A  O
   N  W  S  L  H  I  C  G  T  H  I  T  D  E  W
      T  O  M  A  T  O  E  S  W  E  R
```

ANSWER, PAGE 288

109. Cup o' Joe

BIDEN
BOLOGNA
COCKER
CONRAD
COTTEN
DIMAGGIO
FIENNES
FRAZIER
JACKSON
LIEBERMAN
LOUIS
MCCARTHY
MONTANA
NAMATH
ORTON
PANTOLIANO
PAPP
PATERNO
PESCI
PISCOPO
ROGAN
STALIN
TORRE
WALSH

```
P J O O N A I L O T N A P
P A T E R N O E W Y U I L E J
A E D R R E I Z A R F A L N D O
P I S P T O G E L M O N T A N A
B D T C F H G D S R E N P M T C
O A M E I M A A H E N I I A O S
L I E B E R M A N K S O C T K E
O O Y R N O I M C C A R T H Y O
G N U O N E D Y O O A E R R O T
N F C I E T E P R C N F A M O
A E H I S N O S K C A J T
```

ANSWER, PAGE 289

110. Business Trip

BAGS
CALL HOME
CAR RENTAL
CARRY-ON
CLIENT
FLIGHT
FREQUENT FLYER
HOTEL
LAPTOP
LAYOVER
MINIBAR
NOTES
RECEIPTS
REDEYE
ROOM SERVICE
SALES
SHUTTLE
SUIT
TAXI
TICKETS
TIPS
WAKE-UP CALL

```
S L A T N E R R A C A M E
T R A I E C A C A L L H O M E
P X N A L I P R R L S E I N E C
I S S E T O N H E A T D T T H A
E B E F T E C I V R E S M O O R
C I A P U H R S O T K F S R H R
E L A G H E G Q Y T C U A E E Y
R L I N S S T I A F I L L D Y O
W A K E U P C A L L T U E E R N
R A B I N I M M I F L Y S E S
R E Y L F T N E U Q E R F
```

ANSWER, PAGE 289

111. The S&P

SAFETY PIN
SAO PAULO
SEAN PENN
SHOT PUT
SILENT PARTNER
SILLY PUTTY
SKI POLE
SNAKE PIT

SNOW PEA
SOLE PROPRIETOR
SPACE PROBE
SPORTS PAGE
SPY PLANE
STAMP PAD
STAY PUT
STOCK PRICE

```
S  S  E  G  A  P  S  T  R  O  P  S  Q
T  S  C  U  A  N  I  P  Y  T  E  F  A  S  T
A  P  I  R  O  E  P  E  Y  U  G  S  S  E  I  N
M  A  R  W  S  I  L  L  Y  P  U  T  T  Y  P  S
P  C  P  S  T  A  Y  P  U  T  L  T  P  A  E  C
P  E  K  K  I  N  G  S  O  H  A  O  A  K  U
A  P  C  L  D  I  N  T  P  H  O  O  N  H  A  P
D  R  O  L  U  A  P  O  A  S  O  P  O  E  N  H
R  O  T  E  I  R  P  O  R  P  E  L  O  S  S  S
E  B  S  V  E  R  A  N  L  N  C  E  P  A  Y
R  E  N  T  R  A  P  T  N  E  L  I  S
```

ANSWER, PAGE 289

112. Working Dogs

AKITA
BOXER
BRIARD
COLLIE
CORGI
DOBERMAN
GERMAN
  SHEPHERD
GREAT DANE
HUSKY
KOMONDOR

KUVASZ
MALAMUTE
MASTIFF
NEWFOUNDLAND
PULI
SAMOYED
SCHNAUZER
ST. BERNARD

```
D  D  C  O  M  G  K  U  V  A  S  Z  I
R  S  A  O  A  R  E  O  C  O  L  G  O  L  R
A  B  L  I  L  N  D  S  M  H  R  O  G  U  U  I
N  M  D  N  A  L  D  N  U  O  F  W  E  N  D  P
R  A  E  D  M  O  I  S  C  H  N  A  U  Z  E  R
E  S  M  G  U  S  K  E  L  O  O  D  K  A  T  T
B  T  R  R  T  Y  A  B  O  X  E  R  O  F  F  I
T  I  D  R  E  H  P  E  H  S  N  A  M  R  E  G
S  F  C  R  A  B  T  H  E  A  K  I  T  A  R  T
H  F  A  D  E  Y  O  M  A  S  N  R  L  I  G
H  T  G  R  E  A  T  D  A  N  E  B  S
```

ANSWER, PAGE 289

113. Happy Hour

BARTENDER
BOTTLE
CARAFE
CHIPS
COASTER
DRINKS
LADIES' NIGHT
LEMON
MARGARITA
MARTINI
MICROBREW
NAPKIN
NOISE
NUTS
ON TAP
ON THE ROCKS
PITCHER
PUB
STOOL
SWIZZLE STICK
TAVERN
TIPS
TWIST
WINE

```
W  T  B  U  P  S  S  H  N  T  C  E  M
E  Z  O  A  B  O  K  M  B  A  I  A  A  E  W
R  E  T  S  A  O  C  N  A  V  P  S  R  I  N  W
B  N  T  V  R  E  O  N  I  E  T  K  T  A  E  I
O  D  L  A  T  I  R  A  G  R  A  M  I  T  F  N
R  N  E  O  E  B  E  E  A  N  D  T  N  N  C  E
C  U  O  S  N  T  H  G  I  N  S  E  I  D  A  L
I  H  I  M  D  R  T  E  T  I  P  S  N  F  O  O
M  O  I  R  E  H  N  A  W  N  G  O  U  O  V  E
N  R  S  P  R  L  O  T  R  E  H  C  T  I  P
K  C  I  T  S  E  L  Z  Z  I  W  S  S
```

ANSWER, PAGE 290

114. Rails in America

BOXCAR
CASEY JONES
COACH
COAL
CREW
DEPOT
ENGINE
FREIGHT
GANDY DANCER
GOLDEN SPIKE
HANDCAR
HOBO
IRON HORSE
JOHN HENRY
PULLMAN
RAILS
SIGNAL
SMOKE
STEAM
STEEL
SWITCH
UNION PACIFIC
WHISTLE
YARD

```
E  T  W  H  R  A  C  D  N  A  H  S  L
K  N  H  A  E  C  R  E  W  B  H  E  O  A  J
I  C  I  F  I  C  A  P  N  O  I  N  U  S  O  T
P  L  S  G  B  O  U  O  W  X  O  O  R  I  H  C
S  L  T  D  N  L  I  T  N  C  T  J  H  G  N  E
N  L  L  I  L  E  S  T  E  A  M  Y  I  N  H  R
E  S  E  M  L  A  M  H  C  R  N  E  G  A  E  W
D  D  A  E  I  R  O  N  H  O  R  S  E  L  N  A
L  N  R  S  T  B  K  H  O  F  A  A  B  O  R  H
O  E  M  A  O  S  E  S  W  I  T  C  H  I  Y
G  A  N  D  Y  D  A  N  C  E  R  A  H
```

ANSWER, PAGE 290

115. The Great Outdoors

BACKPACK
BINOCULARS
BOTTLED WATER
BUG REPELLENT
CAN OPENER
CANTEEN
COMPASS
FIREWOOD
FIRST AID
FLASHLIGHTS
FOAM PAD
GHOST STORIES
GLOVES
GORP
HIKING BOOTS

ICE CHEST
MATCHES
MESS KIT
MOUNTAIN
  BIKE
PICNIC TABLE
PILLOW
SLEEPING BAG
S'MORES
SUNSCREEN
SWISS ARMY
  KNIFE
TENT
THERMOS
TRAIL MIX

```
B C B A M W G P H I K I N G B O O T S
U M I A O N G A X I D I A T S R I F W
G S E L C E K I B N I A T N U O M N I
R H L S A K M T I G U E R E N S W A S
E I O S S L P Y N O N F D F S P P R S
P O M S I K O A O T T I A I C N R M A
E L B A T C I N C I P R P G R T O N R
L H R P E S M T U K O E M E E R G E M
L T T M B O T T L E D W A T E R G E Y
E E L O B M U O A S I O O S N L N T K
N E S C S R H U R M O O F R O W S N N
T S E H C E C I S I R D I V T E R A I
D M A T C H E S A R E N E P O N A C F
V E B A S T H G I L H S A L F R R Y E
```

ANSWER, PAGE 290

116. Department of Redundancy Department

ASCENDED UP
ATM MACHINE
EXACT REPLICA
FREE GIFT
FROZEN TUNDRA
HE-MAN
MADE OUT OF
MERGE
  TOGETHER
NEW RECRUIT
OLD CUSTOM
PASSING FAD

PIN NUMBER
PLAN AHEAD
PLEASE RSVP
RAM MEMORY
REFER BACK
SAFE HAVEN
SUM TOTAL
THE HOI POLLOI
TINY SPECK
TIRED CLICHE
UPC CODE

```
F F O T U O E D A M P I N N U M B E R
N O O P T M B A L V O L I F S A T N I
D E N C U R E E S D I T R B L E I G D
A X W Y A D M R E S O O S M E T R I A
E A M R E S E I G T Z S S U O I E N F
H C C O E S R D E E D U P C C O D E G
A T M M A C H I N E T I B L E D C I N
N R T E S U R T H E H O I P O L L O I
A E L M N B U U E L C I G E V A I O S
L P B M N N L T I N Y S P E C K C E S
P L F A D A A M E T D D A A T L H L A
A I S R S U M T O T A L C O A H E C P
K C A B R E F E R H T T F I G E E R F
O A M L N E V A H E F A S A N D R R Y
```

ANSWER, PAGE 290

117. The Periodical Table

ALLURE
BON APPETIT
COSMOPOLITAN
DETAILS
DISCOVER
EBONY
ENTERTAINMENT
  WEEKLY
ESQUIRE
FORBES
FORTUNE
GOURMET
HARPER'S
HOT ROD
JANE
MAXIM
MOTOR TREND
NEWSWEEK
NEW YORKER
PEOPLE
PREMIERE
REAL SIMPLE
ROLLING STONE
SHAPE
SPIN
TEEN VOGUE
TIME
TV GUIDE
VANITY FAIR
VIBE

```
E N T E R T A I N M E N T W E E K L Y
T U H E B Y D I D P N R D N N T E W T
A N G F T O I T A E O G I O I N E O I
M D T O H E N H W Y T W A U A P W N T
O T M R V E S Y D G S A V J Q I S T E
T W I B E N O D O N G A I E E S W R P
O S X E D R E U A Y N R R L O D E B P
R E A S K R R E T I I U H P S I N E A
T I M E I M N A T I L O P O M S O C N
R N R L E E I Y N L L O N E W C R I O
E N U T R O F T A I O N R P G O S C B
N I F I F A O R H A R P E R S V P U L
D P E D I U G V T M A G A Z I E B I V
N E S R E A L S I M P L E D O R T O H
```

ANSWER, PAGE 291

118. Word Ladders

The words below can be transformed into each other by changing one letter at a time (like CAT, COT, COG, DOG). There are many ways of getting from one word to the other, but the words we used for the transformations (50 total—the starting and ending words below are not in the grid) have been hidden in the accompanying word search. Can you find them all?

STALE to BREAD (in 11 steps)
WHITE to PAGES (in 18 steps)
GRASS to STAIN (in 24 steps)

For a list of the words to be found, see page 252.

ANSWER, PAGE 291

```
S E L A B R U S H A L L E W S Y O U W
R L I R L T R I C K L S E E T W H A T
A I A T W I S E C R U S T A R E I L A
T S S I D I C R A C K R B E B R S L B
S P L A N T U T O G I O N E E D E E L
C L I O W E N T T L H T I A L P A H E
C R E E L U S R L O C I A A L T R S L
T L A O P R A N K A P A L E S D S D E
C R H N K C I H C T T C P C E H A L N
H W T O K C H L R I S M H B P L A N K
O I T W H O S E E F R E O O M I I C A
S L I G S H A R E U C L A C R U S H A
E R O H S D R B K K C I H T Y E A L W
B E R T C A B A L L S M U S S H A L E
```

64

119. A Concerted Effort

AMPLIFIER
"ARE YOU READY TO ROCK?"
BACKSTAGE
BASS
BOUNCER
CORDS
CROWD SURFING
DRUM KIT
ELECTRIC GUITAR
ENCORE
FANS
GROUPIES
LIVE CD
MANAGER
MICROPHONE
MOSH PIT
OPENING ACT
ROADIES
SET LIST
SOUND CHECK
STAGE DIVE
SYNTHESIZER
TEENS
TICKET STUB
TOUR VAN
T-SHIRTS

ANSWER, PAGE 291

```
W H A R E Y O U R E A D Y T O R O C K
B E N F I L W A N S C T W E O E B N T
R A Y A I C E O S E O U L A D G U N T
E I S N M A H C V E V I D E G A T S G
I I N S E P S I T T T I I L L N S D O
F I N D O G L T H R E L I E S A T A T
I T G R O U P I E S I H I I R M E R T
L T C O P E N I N G A C T S S O K Y S
P I I C I A R E P A U L G M T C C C A
M P R K V T E C R O W D S U R F I N G
A H N R M T E Y O N A G I N I G T A E
N S U D R U O C R E Z I S E H T N Y S
B O U N C E R K A N B A C K S T A G E
T M K C E H C D N U O S D R T O L R L
```

120. Form Letters

ANY DAY
ARABIAN NIGHTS
"ARE YOU BEING SERVED?"
ARTIE SHAW
CAGEY CHARACTER
CUE CARD
CUTIE PIE
DEVIOUS PLAN
EIGHTY-SIX
ELLEN BARKIN
EMMY AWARD
ENERGY CRISIS
ESSAY TEST
FOR A WHILE
ICY COLD
"I DON'T ENVY YOU!"
IVY LEAGUE
KATIE HOLMES
KEWPIE DOLL
LINGERING EFFECTS
OPIUM DEN
OVER EASY
PRISON ESCAPEE
RADIOACTIVE DECAY
RUNNING ON EMPTY
SEA ANEMONE
SEEDY BAR
SWORN ENEMY
VERY TEDIOUS
WRETCHED EXCESS
YOUR EXCELLENCY

ANSWER, PAGE 291

```
D A W N S I S I R C G R N O M A N S B
E E S I T L O W V Y O U R X L N C E R
V D L K R A D I O A C T I V E D K O A
R E R R T U T D E R E R S A B R V K B
E U G A E L V I I E N E D A Y E A G N
S L N B C S W N P A Y N R T R S W C N
G R D N P Q I K T H O L M E S L T H I
N T M L I E S N Q N V T Z E Y E O A G
I N A T O N E D M P O E W A H S T R H
E N H E O C G M A N D D R S H S E A T
B I S S B E C O T R A O I Y I Y I C S
U L I N G E R I N G F X L X T N G T L
R R A D R A W A E M W R E L N D C E E
P D U R R E L W R E T C H E D X S R L
```

121. Um ... Um ...

ALUMINUM
CRUMB BUM
DUMB AND
   DUMBER
DUMDUM
HARUM-SCARUM
HUMDRUM
HUMPTY
   DUMPTY
LUMP SUM
MUMBO-JUMBO

OMNIUM-
   GATHERUM
QUANTUM JUMP
STUMBLEBUM
SUMMA CUM
   LAUDE
SUMP PUMP
"WHY SO GLUM,
   CHUM?"
YUM-YUM

ANSWER, PAGE 292

```
I  T  C  M  U  R  E  H  T  A  G  M  U  I  N  M  O  Y  S
E  T  S  R  H  M  E  S  M  Q  A  L  L  D  O  B  U  T  B
T  D  T  S  U  O  F  T  S  U  M  P  P  U  M  P  I  P  M
I  D  U  Y  S  M  O  U  A  A  L  S  T  U  H  H  A  M  M
T  A  M  A  C  C  B  L  O  N  M  P  J  L  A  I  S  U  H
T  U  B  H  L  E  U  B  I  T  R  O  R  U  R  I  S  D  N
Y  I  L  T  S  M  T  M  U  U  B  H  E  N  U  P  A  Y  R
R  O  E  W  I  V  U  I  S  M  I  O  N  T  M  H  E  T  F
E  A  B  N  R  R  A  C  U  J  N  D  D  U  S  T  R  P  E
M  B  U  L  D  I  N  M  A  U  U  G  L  H  C  E  S  M  I
T  M  M  M  A  T  R  E  B  M  U  D  D  N  A  B  M  U  D
I  O  U  N  T  H  A  T  D  P  M  C  O  N  R  S  T  H  I
W  H  Y  S  O  G  L  U  M  C  H  U  M  T  U  U  T  E  D
E  F  E  A  T  A  M  M  A  C  D  O  S  U  M  G  A  L  L
```

122. Vacation Reading

(Peter) BENCHLEY
(Tom) CLANCY
(Mary Higgins)
   CLARK
(Jackie) COLLINS
(Michael)
   CRICHTON
(Clive) CUSSLER
(E.L.) DOCTOROW
(Janet)
   EVANOVICH
(Ken) FOLLETT
(Frederick)
   FORSYTH
(Sue) GRAFTON
(John) GRISHAM
(P.D.) JAMES
(Stephen) KING
(Dean) KOONTZ

(Judith) KRANTZ
(Louis) L'AMOUR
(John) LE CARRE
(Robert) LUDLUM
(Colleen)
   MCCULLOUGH
(Terry) MCMILLAN
(James)
   MICHENER
(Mario) PUZO
(Anne) RICE
(Sidney)
   SHELDON
(Danielle) STEEL
(Jacqueline)
   SUSANN
(Scott) TUROW
(Leon) URIS
(Gore) VIDAL

ANSWER, PAGE 292

```
T  L  H  E  S  V  C  R  I  C  H  T  O  N  A  K  R  A  L  C
L  E  L  E  H  E  Y  O  D  F  R  Z  T  T  H  S  I  E  S  D
O  C  M  L  C  L  S  O  K  I  U  I  Y  E  L  H  C  N  E  B
N  A  L  L  I  M  C  M  R  P  S  W  C  N  L  E  I  I  G  D
J  R  E  L  V  T  G  R  A  F  T  O  N  E  Y  L  T  H  O  H
U  R  G  H  O  U  T  T  N  H  O  A  A  Z  L  D  O  B  E  T
T  E  H  R  N  E  R  S  T  B  S  V  L  O  T  O  E  F  U  Y
R  U  O  M  A  L  T  I  Z  U  M  I  C  H  E  N  E  R  S  S
T  W  S  E  V  E  L  L  S  I  N  D  R  G  N  O  O  V  E  R
L  O  F  R  E  L  S  S  U  C  A  A  L  G  L  W  T  O  I  O
L  U  D  L  U  M  M  H  G  U  O  L  L  U  C  C  M  E  K  F
```

123. Avast Conspiracy

ANCHOR
BEAM
BOOM
BOWSPRIT
BRIDGE
BULKHEAD
BULWARK
COMPANIONWAY
CROW'S NEST
FORECASTLE
GANGPLANK
GUNWALES
HATCH
HELM
HOLD
HULL

JIB
KEEL
MIZZENMAST
PORTHOLE
PROW
QUARTERDECK
RIGGING
RUDDER
SAIL
SCUPPER
SPAR
STEM
STERN
TILLER
WINCH
YARDARM

```
T K T S E N S W O R C H M R I G G I N G
E N P C L I A S S C L L U H U U T F T L
E A Q U A R T E R D E C K R B N P O U T
R L T P H E W Y A H S O B U L W A R K R
I P E P M O G A N C H O R D I A N E O B
A G L E L Y L R A S W H I D I L P C E W
H N S R K B W D A S T E D E N E R A C I
Y A W N O I N A P M O C G R A S M S S N
K G T O T J H R M I Z Z E N M A S T E C
W A M C T E I M R C O T I L L E R L O H
L E L O H T R O P E S R B U L K H E A D
```

ANSWER, PAGE 292

124. The Inn Crowd

ALGONQUIN
BEST WESTERN
BILTMORE
CLARION
DAYS INN
DRAKE
ECONOLODGE
FOUR SEASONS
HILTON
HOLIDAY INN
HOWARD
    JOHNSON'S

HYATT
MARRIOTT
OMNI
PLAZA
RADISSON
RAMADA
RITZ
SAVOY
SHERATON
WALDORF-
    ASTORIA
WESTIN

```
T H E R N R E T S E W T S E B P E A R R
E R E R R K A L N I U Q N O G L A I H O
T H O W A R D J O H N S O N S A T E N L
S T C R M D O N S S S T I R U Z C T N E
D T D O A F I H A H S C N N O A W A I N
H O D W D I Y S E C B I L T M O R E S E
T I H E A A A R S T A R E A R O E B Y S
U R L S T I A I R O T S A F R O D L A W
L R T T E T V E U R N Y Y E A I R V D A
F A T I O E R T O E G D O L O N O C E H
E M Y N M N E L F H O L I D A Y I N N T
```

ANSWER, PAGE 292

125. The Love Boat

EXCITING
NEW
EXPECTING
YOU
SWEETEST
REWARD
FLOW
FLOATS
BACK
LOVE
BOAT
MAKING
ANOTHER
RUN
PROMISES
SOMETHING
EVERYONE
COURSE
ADVENTURE
MIND
ROMANCE
WON'T
HURT
ANYMORE
OPEN
SMILE
FRIENDLY
SHORE
WELCOME
ABOARD

```
G H D E N E P O S P G N I T C E P X E P
N E U R S N A T E R H O U S R E W W I E
I F D R A O B A E O T E R O I H G A E C
T T U C T Y H S O M E T H I N G N E R N
I O S T A R W R T I B S E F D M I N D A
C S M I L E E H E S R A L C A R K E N M
X E R A E V S W A E M O C L E W A Y S O
E R U T N E V D A S W W I K B N M G I R
N V E G U O Y D A R N O C A N O T H E R
I S O N R G L O Y L D N E I R F A V E B
T O F L O A T S A T M T E E R M A T I D
```

ANSWER, PAGE 293

126. Round Trip

BAGEL
BASKETBALL
CLICK WHEEL
COIN
COMPASS
DONUT
DVD
EGGO WAFFLE
FERRIS WHEEL
FRISBEE
GLOBE
GUMBALL
HULA HOOP
LIFESAVER
MANHOLE COVER
MARBLE
MEDAL
MOON
ORANGE
OREO
PANCAKE
PEARL
PERIOD
PIE CHART
PIZZA
RING
SAUCER
SMILEY FACE
THE LETTER O
TIDDLYWINK

```
T R D B A T O L E E H W S I R R E F X I
I V I N U Z G R I F N E G S S K C A D M
D R P N E O Z P R F F L I C A I L O A O
D L O E G S M I L E Y F A C E U I L I O
L D O Y L E S E P S V F N Q U R C A R N
Y R H E B B U C O M P A S S E O K E O T
W W A E E O R H L R P W S P R E W O R B
I R L E I L G A R E V O C E L O H N A M
N I U N P G D R M A L G O L F Y E G N C
K T H E L E T T E R O G I R C I E U G L
L L A B M U G B A S K E T B A L L A E R
```

ANSWER, PAGE 293

127. Touchdown!

BARAJAS
BEN-GURION
BRADLEY
CHARLES DE
   GAULLE
DULLES
FRANKFURT
GATWICK
HARTSFIELD
HEATHROW
KENNEDY
LAGUARDIA

LOGAN
MALPENSA
MCCARRAN
MIDWAY
NARITA
NEWARK
O'HARE
ORLY
REAGAN
SHANNON
SHEREMETYEVO

```
O A I R S H E R E M E T Y E V O P G L A
N H E T R A A N V I E L I M S N A A A T
H E A T H R O W E D S A J A R A B T U N
R E S R S T W R A W K Y S L O F I W M A
A B H K E S I N L A A E G P Y R O I U R
F R A N K F U R T Y L R N E A L O C O R
K A N L I I K E Y L O U K N R P A K E A
S D N S P E L L U A G E D S E L R A H C
O L O R T L P D H O T O R A E D G M A C
R E N A I D R A U G A L K F R A Y O M M
A Y L G L O G A N O I R U G N E B O R E
```

ANSWER, PAGE 293

128. Travel and Vacation Flicks

AIRPLANE!
AIRPORT
BOUNCE
CITY SLICKERS
CON AIR
DIRTY DANCING
EASY RIDER
GIDGET
KALIFORNIA
MIDNIGHT RUN
POSEIDON

RAIN MAN
ROAD TO BALI
SIDEWAYS
SOME LIKE IT
   HOT
STARMAN
THE TERMINAL
THE TRIP TO
   BOUNTIFUL
TITANIC
TWINS

```
R P G N I C N A D Y T R I D L A N E S N
E T R A I A N T H E T E R M I N A L S U
D A S O M E L I K E I T H O T N B E D R
I R Y R A U T T O T R O P R I A O N I T
R O A D T O B A L I E O M O B I U A L H
Y T W I E S I N S S S G A I D T N L O G
S B E E N S T I E E V E D M A O C P R I
A N D T I M N C I T Y S L I C K E R S N
E S I F A V A D O R I T E O G F H I I D
S F S W I L O N M A I N R O F I L A K I
L U F I T N U O B O T P I R T E H T S M
```

ANSWER, PAGE 293

129. Captains Courageous

AHAB
AMERICA
BEEFHEART
BLIGH
BLOOD
CAVEMAN
COOK
FURILLO
HASTINGS
HOOK
HOWDY
JACK AUBREY
JACK SPARROW
JOHN SMITH
KANGAROO
KIDD
KIRK
LOU ALBANO
MARVEL
MIDNIGHT
MORGAN
NEMO
PICARD
QUEEG
SPAULDING
STUBING
UNDERPANTS
VIDEO

```
Y N M C A P K T T R A E H F E E B N A S
E H A S T I N G S K I N K K A N E A G T
R A R M R R P O O O J O H N S M I T H N
B A V K E N I O D T O H E M O I C G K A
U E E A Y V C M O H F U M B S G I E E P
A C L N O N A B L A U O L D L N L E U R
K B B G O T R C H H R A O E D I V U D E
C S P A U L D I N G I O T I H B G Q E D
A M E R I C A I A R L T M V D U E H D N
J B U O T S O N N B L T H E S T A I M U
E D H O W D Y A Y W O R R A P S K C A J
```

ANSWER, PAGE 294

130. It's Good to Be Home

CLEAN CLOTHES
COMPUTER
DOLLARS
DRIVE ON
  RIGHT
FAMILY
FRIDGE
FRIENDS
FULL WARDROBE
GOOD COFFEE
HOME-COOKED
  MEAL
HOT SHOWER
MAIL
NEWSPAPER
PETS
SIGNS IN ENGLISH
TIVO
TWO-PLY
YOUR OWN BED

```
T T H G I R N O E V I R D H E H U S M O
R R I S T G E G O R G E E F A D R E O N
E E F F O C D O O G C E B S R A A I D R
P T H E S I G N S I N E N G L I S H T E
A T I M R E T Y O E N J W L O Y E A E W
P U I F R C L E A N C L O T H E S N O O
S P E V A P N T M R I D R P I S P A D H
W B E B O R D R A W L L U F O U E T T S
E H R W E E W E I E K C O M P U T E R T
N S T A F A M I L Y F T Y E R U S N P O
A C K I N G L A E M D E K O O C E M O H
```

ANSWER, PAGE 294

Mind-Boggling Word Search Puzzles

131. Rarin' to Go

```
G W H E Z R E I P U D E P M U P S H A L
S U P E R E N T H U S I A S T I C L I O
T B S E G S A I N L Y O S U R M A J H E
U S T H P Y T L E F F U S I V E H G T R
O E W I I H I T O T E R I A B B N I U E
B T R A S N M K F U L L O F G U S T O A
A E E D B E G E G P S I N N G A T T B D
D E H E A S U O R U T P A R B E I G A Y
E N I T N F N I V D N G T T H E N K G T
Z A E I N E O B S E S S E D W I T H N O
A M G S A R I D N R R G A R A V E E I G
R O B R E V O G N I L B B U B X N B V E
C R E U L I Y A N F P D O G C O S U A T
O E N T O D I L L L Y U U I O U E L R S
C D E H C Y S P Y L L A T O T O M L E T
D W T O T R A H R A H E H H E E N I N A
D I T H E N S N T O D P A L G I C E E R
I T B N F A N A T I C A L W O U D N N T
D H E A R L O T N I Y L L A E R A T A E
N T N A R E B U X E D C I T A T S C E D
```

ALL FIRED UP	EFFUSIVE	GUSHING OVER	RAH-RAH
ARDENT	ENAMORED WITH	INSPIRED	RAPTUROUS
BUBBLING OVER	EXCITED	INTENSE	RAVING ABOUT
BUOYANT	EXUBERANT	"LET ME AT 'EM!"	READY TO GET STARTED
CAUGHT UP IN	FANATICAL	OBSESSED WITH	REALLY INTO
CRAZED ABOUT	FERVID	PASSIONATE ABOUT	SUPER-ENTHUSIASTIC
EBULLIENT	FULL OF GUSTO	PUMPED UP	TOTALLY PSYCHED
ECSTATIC	GUNG-HO	RABID	ZEALOUS

ANSWER, PAGE 295

132. So How Sharp Are You?

```
I  P  F  T  Y  O  S  U  R  S  E  K  E  F  I  N  K  K  A  E  T  S  E
E  U  U  E  G  N  J  A  G  G  E  D  E  D  G  E  E  L  Y  H  O  K  D
S  S  B  S  E  N  R  V  B  A  R  W  N  T  H  N  I  L  U  G  I  H  A
K  H  T  F  C  B  A  R  B  E  D  W  I  R  E  R  L  M  K  P  N  Y  L
E  P  S  I  A  H  R  F  G  C  R  A  S  N  T  U  B  M  S  C  C  L  B
W  I  T  S  N  I  A  G  C  S  V  E  I  R  G  T  Y  A  F  A  I  S  H
E  N  H  H  I  G  A  I  C  O  N  P  A  B  A  N  L  C  E  U  S  S  C
R  K  A  H  G  D  E  I  N  N  S  E  E  C  D  I  E  H  Q  G  O  G  T
O  I  O  O  D  I  S  R  W  S  L  I  K  N  B  P  T  E  H  U  R  A  I
S  N  R  O  H  S  L  L  U  B  A  S  G  A  C  R  N  T  D  I  S  U  W
N  G  N  K  O  Y  O  T  O  U  R  W  Y  S  E  I  A  E  S  L  C  H  S
O  S  H  R  P  A  C  W  H  R  P  O  E  R  P  A  L  Y  E  L  E  A  D
L  H  S  L  I  A  N  R  E  G  N  I  F  U  S  H  H  P  E  O  A  T  R
A  E  B  P  C  T  O  O  N  E  I  G  C  P  U  E  D  A  O  T  S  C  H
T  A  A  E  K  Z  R  P  T  D  R  R  E  S  S  S  T  E  R  I  W  H  H
O  R  S  S  A  L  G  N  E  K  O  R  B  S  A  S  S  H  A  N  N  E  R
P  S  S  R  X  K  H  O  O  P  I  T  C  H  F  O  R  K  T  E  E  T  R
```

BARBED WIRE	ELBOW	PENCIL POINT	SICKLE
BAYONET	FANG	PICKAX	SKEWER
BEAK	FINGERNAILS	PINKING SHEARS	SPIKE
BRIGHT LIGHT	FISHHOOK	PITCHFORK	SPURS
BROKEN GLASS	GUILLOTINE	PORCUPINE QUILL	STEAK KNIFE
BULL'S HORNS	HAIRPIN TURN	PUSHPIN	STINGER
CACTUS SPINE	HATCHET	RAZOR	SWITCHBLADE
CHAIN SAW	INCISORS	SABER	TALONS
CLEATS	JAGGED EDGE	SCISSORS	THUMBTACKS
DAGGER	MACHETE	SEWING NEEDLE	TUSK

ANSWER, PAGE 295

133. Off and Running

Shaped like a galloping horse, the grid below contains references to horse racing.

```
        I
      S B S E
    T N S H D F
  E T I R O V A F
  O L E N W A H E O
O K N R U T R A F L E R
S S       E E H C T E R T S E H T N W O D
          S T E B E H Y A D T B F T E J E
          O O C N C T T E O D I U G N O L R U F
          N H A O N S N N H N O A M E C     B I T     C A
          S L M A S E M I T T S O P K       Y L L I F
          G P E T E I S N E D A E T E
          N F A S N H H A     N X L Y
          O B A I K         F A P
      A L     D A         C S
      E       T E         T R
      F R     I R     V     R A
      E I   P I H W   A C
          S           C E
        K
```

"AND THEY'RE OFF!"   FAR TURN   LONG SHOT   REINS
BETS   FAVORITE   NOSE   SHOW
BUMP   FILLY   ODDS   SILKS
DERBY   FINISH   PLACE   SIRE
DISTANCE   FURLONG   POST TIMES   STABLE
"DOWN THE STRETCH!"   GATE   PREAKNESS   TRACK
EXACTA   IN THE LEAD   RACE   WHIP
FADE   JOCKEY

ANSWER, PAGE 296

134. Gossip Columns

```
P  A  P  A  R  A  Z  Z  I  P  S  H  T  E  L  R  A  T  S  O  W  M  S
E  U  L  U  G  O  M  S  H  O  L  G  M  J  B  E  S  N  U  B  S  B  T
S  O  B  N  E  A  W  O  L  H  O  A  O  U  N  U  E  P  L  V  E  E  O
L  O  R  L  N  G  L  L  W  A  R  B  S  S  O  L  L  A  L  L  E  T  P
A  S  T  S  I  L  D  E  S  S  E  R  D  T  S  E  B  C  E  I  S  I  S
I  P  I  O  Y  C  S  A  L  L  T  D  A  F  I  I  N  C  T  D  T  I  T
T  O  S  W  H  L  I  K  L  A  S  E  E  R  H  C  P  O  S  H  N  W  O
N  Y  O  O  P  U  S  S  I  I  O  J  I  T  M  S  E  E  O  G  R  H
E  O  C  M  O  N  E  W  T  T  H  N  O  E  V  A  I  U  C  S  O  I  S
D  Y  I  R  E  D  C  A  R  P  E  T  E  N  T  O  B  O  R  M  N  W  N
I  L  A  N  O  I  T  A  T  U  P  E  R  D  T  A  M  L  U  G  H  I  O
F  N  L  C  M  T  E  R  E  N  S  T  E  S  D  M  V  R  O  O  E  I  O
N  N  I  E  H  R  E  H  T  E  G  O  T  N  E  E  S  I  S  I  P  R  C
O  E  T  O  P  T  L  E  W  R  S  C  A  N  D  A  L  I  R  A  D  L  Y
C  I  E  X  P  O  S  E  T  P  D  A  T  I  N  G  N  E  R  P  S  S  T
```

BEST DRESSED LIST	ITEM	PHOTOS	SNUBS
BRAWL	"JUST FRIENDS"	PLASTIC SURGERY	SOCIALITE
CELEBS	LEAK	PRENUPTIALS	"SOURCES TELL US ..."
CONFIDENTIAL	LIMO	PRIVATE JET	SPLIT
DATING	MANSION	PUBLICIST	STARLET
DENIAL	MOGUL	RED CARPET	TABLOIDS
EXPOSÉ	MOVIE DEAL	REPUTATION	TELL-ALL
GOSSIP	NIGHTCLUB	RUMOR	TYCOONS
HOLLYWOOD	"NO COMMENT"	SCANDAL	WHO'S IN
HOT SPOTS	PAPARAZZI	SEEN TOGETHER	YACHTS

ANSWER, PAGE 296

135. It's in the Cards

Shaped like a spade in a deck of cards, the grid below contains references to cards and card games.

BLACKJACK
CANASTA
CASINO
CHEAT
CHEMIN DE FER
CLUBS
CRAZY EIGHTS
CRIBBAGE
CROUPIER
DEAD MAN'S HAND
DECK
DIAMOND
DRAW
DUPLICATE BRIDGE
EUCHRE
FAN-TAN
FOLD
FULL HOUSE
GO FISH
HEARTS
HOYLE
JOKER
MISDEALS
NO TRUMP
OLD MAID
PINOCHLE
QUEEN
RAISE
ROYAL FLUSH
SHOOT THE MOON
SHUFFLE
SLOUGH
SOLITAIRE
SPADE
STRAIGHT
STUD POKER
TRICKS
UNDERBID
WHIST
WILD CARD

```
                            A
                          A   S   F
                      S   B   T   L   O
                  E   U   I   U   S   G   L
              S   L   O   L   D   M   A   I   D
              C   T   T   H   P   T   O   N   F
          F   H   R   R   J   O   K   E   R   A   A
          C   I   N   D   A   K   A   R   T   N   C
      I   C   R   A   Z   Y   E   I   G   H   T   S   S
      K   S   T   O   W   S   R   H   H   G   A   O   R
  S   E   R   H   C   U   E   E   L   I   O   N   K   O   E
  N   S   T   O   O   P   P   R   L   A   F   Y   H   Y   I
S O   E   L   H   C   O   N   I   P   C   I   D   R   A   W   O
A T   E   L   Y   O   H   T   A   E   C   S   R   D   L   S   N
D R   L   C   F   L   O   S   T   R   R   H   L   D   F   B   I
Q U   E   E   N   F   T   S   I   H   W   E   N   O   L   T   S
F M   P   S   O   T   U   B   L   H   E   O   E   A   U   V   A
E P   S   L   I   T   B   H   O   M   M   M   C   A   S   G   C
Y T   H   G   I   A   R   T   S   A   I   K   O   N   H   H   H
  A   S   N   G   C   R   A   I   P   J   U   H   O   E   A
  V   E   E   D   E   A   D   M   A   N   S   H   A   N   D
      A   N   A           T   C   D           T   C   E
                          K   E   U
                      P   R   S   B   H
                      B   I   P   S   R
                  I   S   L   A   E   K   I
              D   W   I   L   D   C   A   R   D
          E   M   I   S   D   E   A   L   S   V   G
      E   R   E   F   E   D   N   I   M   E   H   C   E
```

ANSWER, PAGE 297

76

136. Bad Ideas for Movie Sequels

This grid contains titles of movie sequels that—thank goodness!—were never made. It's up to you to determine what those titles are. To do so, use the list of clues below, which give hints to the titles of the original movies. (To help, we've put these originals in alphabetical order: ignore the "The" at the start of any titles.) If you want the word list, you'll find it on page 252.

```
H T N E E T R U O F E H T Y A D I R F O U R T H M A N A S M
N H D B E S U R S T N E M D N A M M O C N E V E L E E E E A
N I N E A N D T H R E E Q U A R T E R S W E E K S Y V V L G
O R U L M E I G H T Y E A R I T C H T I S S X T W E O L D N
F T L A E W O V E G R S R H E N I N Y T R O F I N T T E N I
S E V E N D A Y S E I G H T N I G H T S H E C T S U U W A F
P E C S T N E M E L E H T X I S K O H F O S H N E O S T C I
E N T H F O U R C O I N K S I N T H I E O S F O U N T S N C
T A N T T W O E Y E D J A C K S T A R I E U N S N E O N E E
S N T H R E E F O R T H E R O A D W D N W H R I T M E A E N
Y G A G N D T H E E I G H T D L W A S R F S A A N E D E T T
T R S I X E A S Y P I E C E S A C E T R O U N D M N T C N E
R Y H E V E F O S E C A F R U O F O R E W O R L D I I O E I
O M N E I S E I B A B O W T D N A N E M R U O F G N G H V G
F E T C B E N O D N A N O I L L I M E N O Y O N E D A O E H
Y N S F I V E W E D D I N G S A N D T W O F U N E R A L S T
```

1988 John Cusack; baseball
1997 Bruce Willis; sci-fi
1970 Jack Nicholson
1982 Nick Nolte, Eddie Murphy
1933 Ruby Keeler; backstage musical
1994 Hugh Grant, Andie MacDowell
1980 First of a horror series
1960 Yul Brynner, Steve McQueen; western

1986 Mickey Rourke, Kim Basinger
1980 Jane Fonda, Lily Tomlin, Dolly Parton
1960 (original) Frank Sinatra, Dean Martin
1961 Marlon Brando; western
1940 Victor Mature; cavemen (1966 remake with Raquel Welch)
1957 Director: Ingmar Bergman

1955 Marilyn Monroe, Tom Ewell
1998 Harrison Ford, Anne Heche
1984 Molly Ringwald
1999 Bruce Willis, Haley Joel Osment
1956 Charlton Heston; Bible epic
1949 Orson Welles; espionage
1935 Director: Alfred Hitchcock

1986 Steve Martin, Chevy Chase, Martin Short
1957 Joanne Woodward, Joanne Woodward, Joanne Woodward
1987 Tom Selleck, Steve Guttenberg, Ted Danson
1957 Henry Fonda, Lee J. Cobb
1949 Gregory Peck, Dean Jagger; WWII flyers
1967 Audrey Hepburn, Albert Finney

ANSWER, PAGE 297

137. Give Me a Break!

The mug-shaped grid below contains words and phrases associated with coffee.

```
R P T V A C U U M P A C K E D H
E I M O R R A V A J N M F I N D
H C C E G C U F P D O R O F E E
C K A H S C C O F F E E G R O W E R
S M O B T P F F E E P I H A E E A S
T E A L N A R E Z X I W E H I R       L T A
A U R A S A S E G R I N D E R B       L T
L P R C O I D T S O G N E I T H       I A
K B F K N R O U E S R T T I T S       N F
E L W A I H I C C O S H T H E         S E
E A I E C S T A R B U C K S F R       T T
F E D M C E H F L R N P N C S F       A G
F O C O U N D E O R D P O U R S       N E
O V H E P N N A I N S L G F G C       O T
C U I P P D O U F T O A E B J A   C R A
M O C H A H N L N M R P E R C O L A T E
O T O D C B S A B E E A T X P A E S
E C R T E B O I L I N G H O T D
T I Y O R E A T R S P R O T G D
P U P L A N T A T I O N E C E O
```

AROMA	COFFEE KLATSCH	GROUNDS	RICH TASTE
BEANS	COLOMBIAN	INSTANT	STARBUCKS
BLACK	CREAM	IRISH	STEEPED
BLEND	CUP OF JOE	JAVA	STIRRER
BOILING HOT	DECAF	LATTE	STRONG
CAFÉ AU LAIT	DRIP	MILK	SUGAR
CAFFEINE	ESPRESSO	MOCHA	TO-GO
CAPPUCCINOS	FILTER	PERCOLATE	TURKISH
CHICORY	FREEZE-DRIED	PICK-ME-UP	VACUUM-PACKED
COFFEE GROWER	FRESH-BREWED	PLANTATION	WIRED
	GRINDER	POURS	

ANSWER, PAGE 298

138. Car Pool

In the car-shaped grid below, every item in the word list contains the letters CAR in consecutive order. When these letters appear in the grid, they have been replaced by a 🚗. So take 🚗E when solving.

```
              D 🚗 R E T S A M D I
            🚗 S A S Y D K E 🚗 D 🚗 A
        A D O S F O E T A N O B 🚗 I B
      🚗 I F 🚗 E R E R E I E N E U D P G
    T A C Y D E 🚗 S E 🚗 I D E M T H R A N 🚗
  O F W 🚗 A O F Y S Y M T E I E A N B E D I N
O L E N N U T L A P 🚗 Y I O U P X 🚗 N M R T B A E P L
T O T M Q A T W E E V Y J O 🚗 U 🚗 O A R A H O T T E L 🚗 S
🚗 🚗 R S A T A I H R E S 🚗 G O T Y T I E S S U R M P 🚗 🚗 A S
H N E E S 🚗 N T A E S P A I O R D E E D N I 🚗 A G U A C 🚗
V C H I L I C O N 🚗 N E H E O 🚗 D I N A L N B 🚗 A R Y O C I D
T I M V P P O N E D S L N T H R E E 🚗 D M O N T E R I D V
    A P 🚗 R I                         I X B V E
      L A E                         🚗 E 🚗
      M                               D
```

APOTHECARY	CARBURETOR	CARTWHEEL	NICARAGUA
APPLECART	CARDINAL	CHILI CON CARNE	PLACARD
BETA-CAROTENE	CAREEN	ESCARGOT	SCAREDY-CAT
BICARBONATE OF SODA	CARESS	I.D. CARD	SCARLETT O'HARA
BOX CAR	CARIBOU	JIM CARREY	SCARVES
CAPTAIN PICARD	CARNIVAL	MACARONI	SCORECARD
CARAFE	CARPAL TUNNEL	MACAROON	SHAG CARPET
CARAMEL	CARPE DIEM	MASCARA	SQUAD CAR
CARAWAY SEEDS	CARRY-ON BAG	MASTERCARD	THREE-CARD MONTE
CARBON DIOXIDE	CARTOON	MEDICARE	VICARS

ANSWER, PAGE 298

139. Let's Celebrate

The birthday cake–shaped grid below contains causes for and means of celebration.

```
            J           I           F
            U           L           G
            B           L           N
            I           A           I
            L           B           M
  S O Y N E M E H T E A S T E R O H I T
  N G R E E E A O S M Y P I Q A S R A H
  S P A I D W E E C U E K T U W O N P G
  F I S A C A J D K T E W B I E U O N I
  A P R I L F O O L S D A Y N S T I O N
  Y A E B G O U W B O C N A O U M N I G
  P N V T R H C N A C V Z E X O P U N N
  A N I B A R M I T Z V A H C H A E U I
  G E N Y D O L B N U R C E M A Y R M N
  E E N K U U I E A C N M A E D R G M E
  A W A E A R F A T I O R Y T R A P O P
  N O T U T T I O O H D D D O L I E C O
  T L S H I W E D D I N G E A T S O H A
  T L D M O E S A G N N O T M H E I S N
  G A E I N S T R E W O H S L A D I R B
  Y H E N V Y A D S R E H T O M Y E R E
    A S T S E F R E B O T K O Y O
```

ANNIVERSARY	COSTUME BALL	HOUSEWARMING	OPENING NIGHT
APRIL FOOLS' DAY	EASTER	JUBILEE	PAGEANT
BAPTISM	EQUINOX	KWANZA	PARADE
BAR MITZVAH	FIESTA	LENT	PARTY
BIRTHDAY	GALA	LUAU	PAY RAISE
BRIDAL SHOWER	GRADUATION	MARDI GRAS	PROM
BRIS	HALLOWEEN	MOTHER'S DAY	REUNION
CINCO DE MAYO	HOEDOWN	NEW JOB	SOIREE
COMMUNION	HOMECOMING	OKTOBERFEST	WEDDING

ANSWER, PAGE 299

140. White on Schedule

```
N W L I G H T N I N G Y R E N O I T A T S I M
R U T E H T N C O S R K L N N O Y W K I N A S
I T R N Y E H E O F E L L V A N I L L A R A W
A M A S H E D P O T A T O E S O A C I B I R E
H W E E T P C A B T S T L E H T H L L E S A
S K B I L S O A G D W O G O C N E E O O N O T
N L R A E P S N R W H N N P N E E R R O U S S
O A A E S U O H E T I H W E H T S X I D I D O
S D L T O P U H O I T S M G U U E S S C T B C
R S O D G O R N B E E S T U N D E R W E A R K
E W P N R O C I N U S O R I R E Y E V L E E S
P R I Y T H R I V E H N F G Y N N U B L L A L
D P T R I C E U H O A O R N O K N I G H T D U
L T A L H L A C O R R E C T I O N F L U I D W
O H S N O W M A N M K Y I T M O B Y D I C K E
```

ALBINO
BIRCH
BLOOD CELL
BREAD
BUNNY
CHALK
CHESSMEN
CLOUD
CORRECTION FLUID
COTTON

ENVELOPE
EYE PART
GREAT WHITE SHARK
IVORY
KLEENEX
KNIGHT
LIGHTNING
LILY
LINEN
MARBLE

MASHED POTATOES
MOBY DICK
NOISE
NURSE'S SHOES
OLD PERSON'S HAIR
PEARL
PING-PONG BALL
POLAR BEAR
RICE
SAILOR'S UNIFORM

SNOWMAN
SOUR CREAM
STATIONERY
SWAN
SWEAT SOCKS
TEETH
THE WHITE HOUSE
UNDERWEAR
UNICORN
VANILLA

ANSWER, PAGE 299

141. Start the Music

Shaped like a CD, the grid below contains a compilation of many kinds of music plus words relating to compact discs.

```
              M G M O T O W N
            B U S A I E C C I K S Y
          F L I O N A V U E L R K J N
        D O U W N G N A E E D C X E Z P
      E O I E N G S R R Z I O Y W W I Z R
      E N E S E K T P M G R N A Z E C P A
    Y I H E R C Y A E I K O G U R L O T G J
    R D C L A H M R T N R E N R U B D C T O
    T L E R A U G A U D H A T S E O C S I D
    N O T O Y T L P N     S T B O X U N M R
    U N P W P A E A R     Y I I S D S O E M
    O E I F U E B M E F Y L O U O T D M O N
    C D T D O G R C Y S L I N E R N O T E S
    G L I L I R I A A V V S E U I O A T I P
      O T B W O T L L N A T M F D T C L O
      G S O U L S Y P O S E N U T W O H S
        M P E A W P D O N N H S U T P O
          F E Y I S C T O I U I R I H
            O L N O A R N N P O H A
              G L R K E G R N
```

BEBOP	EASY LISTENING	JAZZ	RAVE
BIG BAND	FUNK	JEWEL BOX	REGGAE
BLUES	FUSION	KLEZMER	SALSA
CALYPSO	GANGSTA RAP	LINER NOTES	SHOW TUNES
CD BURNER	GOLDEN OLDIE	MOOD	SOUL
CD PLAYER	GOSPEL	MOTOWN	SWING
COUNTRY	HEAVY METAL	NEW AGE	TECHNO
DIGITAL AUDIO	HIP-HOP	OPERA	TOP FORTY
DISCMAN	INSPIRATIONAL	PUNK ROCK	TRACKS
DISCO	INSTRUMENTAL	RAGTIME	ZYDECO

ANSWER, PAGE 300

142. Black Hole #1

In this puzzle, the letters in the center of the grid are missing. It's up to you to write them in by figuring out which words in the list are missing some of their letters in the grid. When you've completed the puzzle, the missing letters will spell out a quip about a certain activity. The uncircled letters will reveal two other quips—plus their authors—on the same theme. (Note: Many, but not all, of the words on the list also are also associated with the theme.)

```
T  S  L  C  O  U  N  T  I  N  G  S  H  E  E  P  E  E  T  N  P  I  N  R
O  G  S  I  D  E  B  O  T  O  G  B  S  N  Z  O  M  H  E  W  W  A  E  E
S  N  A  N  A  R  T  F  E  U  O  A  R  F  I  O  E  I  T  O  S  A  S  B
S  A  K  P  O  M  A  E  R  D  O  N  A  E  M  M  O  O  N  D  L  C  Y  M
E  R  N  E  M  R  U  S  U  T  S  D  T  A  E  Y  A  N  N  E  W  A  A  U
D  E  E  P  B  R  E  A  ■  ■  ■  ■  ■  ■  ■  E  S  S  I  D  T  K  L
A  S  E  A  L  L  D  T  ■  ■  ■  ■  ■  ■  ■  A  T  Y  L  G  C  N  G
N  T  S  O  T  I  U  Q  ■  ■  ■  ■  ■  ■  ■  A  T  N  A  F  H  I  N
D  L  P  E  T  Z  S  C  ■  ■  ■  ■  ■  ■  ■  H  M  I  E  L  S  T  I
T  E  T  A  L  L  I  C  ■  ■  ■  ■  ■  ■  ■  E  G  N  A  R  O  I  W
U  S  F  E  N  I  A  S  S  O  E  E  M  E  M  C  T  H  R  U  I  M  N  A
R  S  E  Y  E  T  U  H  S  I  G  E  I  T  A  O  L  D  U  O  G  E  W  S
N  H  E  N  C  Y  A  O  S  U  C  H  A  D  C  N  T  E  T  G  E  Z  T  T
E  G  N  I  Z  O  D  C  O  S  L  C  E  E  O  P  L  D  R  O  W  S  Y  E
D  B  T  O  W  I  T  Y  T  R  A  P  A  M  A  J  A  P  E  K  A  W  A  Z
```

APNEA	DOZING	LIE DOWN	SIESTA
AWAKE	DREAM	MOSQUITOS	SNOOZE
B AND B	DROWSY	NIGHT	SNORE
CAMEO	FADERS	ORANGE PEELS	SUTURE
CATCH SOME Z'S	FANTASIA	OSCILLATE	THEME SONG
CATNAP	FILE CLERK	PAJAMA PARTY	TIC-TAC-TOE
CHEESE	GO TO BED	REAL ESTATE	TIRED OUT
COUNTING SHEEP	GUNMAN	RESTLESS	TOSSED AND TURNED
DEEP BREATH	ITEMIZE	SAWING LUMBER	TURN IN
DISSECTS	JODIE FOSTER	SHUTEYE	YAWN

ANSWER, PAGE 300

143. It's a Shoe Thing

Shaped like a half-boot, the grid below contains words and phrases relating to footwear.

```
                        D  R  E  P  P  I  L  S  Z  I
                        O  P  J  A  Z  Z  S  H  O  E
                        C  A  R  L  T  P  S  O  R  I
                        K  T  S  I  I  I  M  E  I  C
                        S  E  P  K  L  F  F  H  L
                        I  N  E  O  O  A  T  O
                        D  T  P  S  O  S  G  R
                     I  E  L  S  L  I  P  O  N
                     B  R  E  L  P  A  E  T  O
                  T  O  B  A  S  B  M  T  E  W  E
                  L  S  S  T  A  P  S  U  F  M  T  P
               L  L  A  L  H  D  R  H  E  P  O  S  L
               S  N  A  K  E  S  K  I  N  O  C  R  I
            F  N  D  E  E  C  R  E  G  N  B  E  C  E  M
         F  E  A  D  S  L  S  E  D  H  Y        A  T  S
      U  A  L  R  E  D  O  U  E  S  O           S  S  O
   C  K  I  O  A  N  C  S  W  M  B              I  I  L
H  S  E  E  F  P  I  T  G  N  I  W              N  L  L
A  R  P  X  C  O  R  N  S  I  O                 S  B  S
S  N  O  I  N  U  B  S  H  C                    O  E  S
```

BLISTERS	JAZZ SHOE	PLIMSOLLS	SLIPPER
BUNIONS	LACES	POLISH	SNAKESKIN
CLOG	LIFT	PUMPS	SNEAKERS
CORNS	LOAFER	SABOT	SPATS
COWBOY BOOT	MOCCASINS	SANDAL	SPIKE
DOCKSIDER	MULES	SCUFF	STRAP
FLATS	OXFORD	SHINY	WEDGIE
HEELS	PATENT LEATHER	SHOEHORN	WINGTIP
INSOLE	PLATFORM	SLIP-ON	ZORI

ANSWER, PAGE 301

144. Give It the Old College Try

The pennant-shaped grid below contains words and phrases about college.

```
S  I  N
T  H  E  S  I  S
G  E  R  R  T  P  S  E  T
P  E  B  O  C  U  M  L  A  U  D  E
H  S  E  O  P  E  D  G  A  M  O  L  P  I  D
I  E  R  M  O  K  A  E  R  B  G  N  I  R  P  S  S  E
B  A  A  M  I  K  D  O  N  E  B  D  U  O  E  C  F  F  E  A  M
E  C  T  A  I  O  S  Q  N  T  S  S  I  J  S  M  R  W  H  R  E  N  Y  C
T  N  O  T  E  S  U  T  O  U  C  R  E  A  A  A  E  D  O  A  G  T  S  L  R  H  E
A  Y  F  E  E  A  I  S  N  H  H  E  E  M  T  R  S  D  L  I  B  E  R  A  L  A  R  T  S
K  R  P  F  D  R  I  I  O  N  O  T  N  E  U  E  H  U  X  P  N  E  D  S  R  I  M
A  A  O  F  I  N  A  L  S  Y  O  E  R  T  N  E  M  N  G  I  S  S  A  S
P  R  N  I  N  C  A  S  E  D  L  N  C  I  E  N  A  S  O  W  H
P  B  O  A  N  R  T  N  Y  U  I  E  O  U  I  R  N  R
A  I  I  G  S  U  E  A  Y  T  L  U  C  A  F
T  L  T  H  W  H  J  E  Y  S  E  N
S  E  I  T  R  A  P  D  Y
O  P  U  U  D  O
N  T  T
```

ALUMNI	DEAN'S LIST	LECTURE	QUAD
ASSIGNMENT	DEGREE	LIBERAL ARTS	ROOMMATE
BOOKS	DIPLOMA	LIBRARY	SCHOLARSHIP
B-SCHOOL	DORM	MAJOR	SENIOR
CAMPUS	FACULTY	NOTES	SPRING BREAK
CLASS	FINALS	PARTIES	STUDENT CENTER
COED	FRATERNITY	PHI BETA KAPPA	STUDY
CRAM	FRESHMAN	PREMED	THESIS
CUM LAUDE	JUNIOR	PROFESSOR	TUITION

ANSWER, PAGE 301

145. Just Add Water

The hidden message explains the theme.

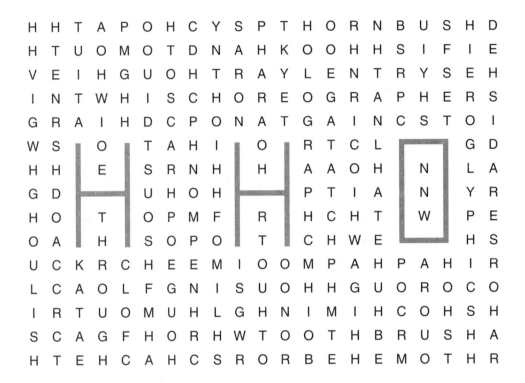

```
H H T A P O H C Y S P T H O R N B U S H D
H T U O M O T D N A H K O O H H S I F I E
V E I H G U O H T R A Y L E N T R Y S E H
I N T W H I S C H O R E O G R A P H E R S
G R A I H D C P O N A T G A I N C S T O I
W S O T A H I O R T C L G D
H H E S R N H H A A O H N L A
G D H U H O H P T I A N Y R
H O T O P M F R H C H T W P E
O A H S O P O T C H W E H S
U C K R C H E E M I O O M P A H P A H I R
L C A O L F G N I S U O H H G U O R O C O
I R T U O M U H L G H N I M I H C O H S H
S C A G F H O R H W T O O T H B R U S H A
H T E H C A H C S R O R B E H E M O T H R
```

BEHEMOTH	HICCOUGH	HORSERADISH	THORNBUSH
CHOREOGRAPHERS	HIEROGLYPHICS	OOMPAH-PAH	THOUGH
DISHCLOTH	HO CHI MINH	PHARAOH	THROUGH
FISHHOOK	HOGWASH	PHNOM PENH	TOOTHBRUSH
FORTHWITH	HOLOGRAPH	PSYCHOPATH	UH-OH
GHOULISH	HOOKAH	RORSCHACH	WHOOSH
HAND-TO-MOUTH	HOPSCOTCH	ROUGHHOUSING	

ANSWER, PAGE 302

146. Smell It Like It Is

```
T H N S L L A B H T O M L I E M P E T F O O D O G V
I E E P O L E Y E S T E E R N O R S I G Y R E K A B
I N W O O P M A H S S A M L L C E Y C R L R A M S E
O U L T S C E N T E D S O A P R E I D N O B A C O N
C O Y I D O R A W H S M N A O M A N G I O M M G L F
H O M E M A D E B R E A D F E R U T S A P W O C I I
E C O K I B R N W H A R E I E A O D C E D H A S N C
R U W D C I U E N C A N E B L S C T E O E U H L E D
R E N E H S E R F R I A B H S M E L T G T M L C V B
Y A G R O I O U G P R U S S B A D B R E A T H I O U
B N R O C P O P D E R E T T U B T O H R N B D L O S
L R A S O I O N M G R T G Y M S O C K S I E R R H E
O E S B L R M U N F S C O V I E K E B Y R U G A S X
S I S T A N F I G A S C H R A T T U C H O A N G G H
S D N N T R N S L C O F F E E B E A N S L N I F S A
O I G F E R N O C A R D S A E T N O T K H E D M O U
M E M P U E O D R A C F F I N S D N A H C T A R C S
R U B B I N G A L C O H O L N T E C I R O C I L S T
```

AIR FRESHENER	COFFEE BEANS	LEATHER	PINE FOREST
BACON	COW PASTURE	LEMON	ROTTEN EGGS
BAD BREATH	FISH MARKET	LICORICE	RUBBING ALCOHOL
BAKERY	FRESH LAUNDRY	LIMBURGER CHEESE	SALOON
BARN	GARBAGE DUMP	MINT	SCENTED SOAP
BURNING RUBBER	GARLIC	MOTHBALLS	SCRATCH-AND-SNIFF CARD
BUS EXHAUST	GASOLINE	NEWLY MOWN GRASS	SEA AIR
CHERRY BLOSSOM	GYM SOCKS	ORANGE	SEWER
CHLORINATED POOL	HOMEMADE BREAD	PERFUME	SHAMPOO
CHOCOLATE	HOT BUTTERED POPCORN	PET FOOD	SKUNK
CIGAR	INCENSE		

ANSWER, PAGE 302

147. Tennis, Anyone?

Shaped like a tennis racket, the grid contains words and phrases about tennis.

ACES
AD IN
ALLEY
BACKHAND
BALL BOY
BASELINE
CHAMPION
CLAY
COURT
DEUCE
DINK
DOUBLES
DROP SHOT
FOOT FAULT
FOREHAND
GAME
GRASS
GROUND STROKE
LINESMAN
LOBS

LONG
LOVE
MATCH
NET JUDGE
ON SERVE
PASSING SHOT
POINT
RACKET
RETURN
ROLAND GARROS
SETS
SLICE
SMASH
TIE-BREAKER
TOPSPIN
TOURNAMENT
U.S. OPEN
VOLLEY
WIMBLEDON
WINNERS

```
                K A D I N
              W I N N E R S
            N O A D H C T A M
          W W H H N O Y I Y C E
        T Y E L L A O U E U S K L
        D R O P S H O T B H O O E
      U O F U C L K D G R L B R N T
      F T O L O L C R G E S E T S O
      O O O U P C A H S A M S S T N
      W N T I A S B Y T K D H D T S
      G A F T S E N A N E W E N N E
      A N A M S E N I L R I E U V R
      M I U N I S D S P L M L O C V
      E A L E N I L E S A B L R Y E
        E T P G R T I N O L O G H
        N I O S M L R C E E O Y P
          R S H V U E Y E D M O
            U O O E A N S O I
            T O P S P I N
            E           T
            N R       N S
            O         E
            L C       T
            A H       J
            N A       U
            D M       D
            G P       G
            A I       E
            R O       O
            R N       T
            O H       I
            S N       G
```

ANSWER, PAGE 303

148. What a Beast!

The grid below is filled with words and phrases that contain the names of animals. To determine those entries, fill in the blanks surrounding the listed animals by using the crossword-style clues next to them. When properly completed, the list will appear in alphabetical order. That list can be found in full on page 253.

```
T V H E J E D S E S W R A T H S H A R E S I R
E I T O E A L E A V E I T T O B E A V E R T C
A D K T E M Y A Y E S R O H W A S E S D Y I O
C E A I N O I L E D N A D H O T D O G B R N M
T O G I P S I I E E I S N S P H E S R H E A M
G T P S N L T N H N P E A A G I R R T S T E A
E A A T R E G S R O T M F B N E E I O T A N
R P T E D U R W E R E U G O W G H G L I O C D
H E G D E K R A H S L O O P B S N I S W L L E
T I T I D N D X V E G K R U G U A C A M O L E
T I S T R E H E T E W S F M P I L L A A N B R
E X C L A M A T I O N P O I N T W L F N M R O
M A N G E C I M R A T O R T X O F L E A T S D
O C L T B O S M R W I L U L C I A M L T O E S
L E E C R O W N J E W E L S Y L F F I T S R R
```

MULE Talisman

BAT_ _ _ _ _ _ _ _ Swimwear

BEAR_ _ _ Having chin hair

_ _ _ _ WORM Bibliophage

OWL _ Tenpins player

BULL_ _ Revolver ammo

ANT _ Horse's gait

_ _ _ _ _ _ DEER Seize for military purposes

CROW_ _ _ _ _ _ _ Royal British gems

_ _ _ _ LION Yellow weed

_ _CLAM_ _ _ _ _ _ _ _ _ Punctuation mark

LAMB Served on fire

FOX _ _ _ _ Ballroom dance

FROG_ _ _ Navy diver

GOAT_ _ Chin growth

_ _ _ _ MOLE Avocado dip

_ _ -BEE_ Passé celebrity

_ _ _ DOG Frankfurter

_ _ RAVEN_ _ Type of hospital hook-up

JAY _ _ _ _ Late-night host

_ _ _ _ _ _ _ _ _ BEAVER Old TV show

OTTER Keno's cousin

_ _ _ _ SHARK Hustler

_ _ HORSE Carpenter's frame for cutting wood

CAT _ _ Disperse

COW Show displeasure

SEAL_ _ _ _ _ _ Material once used to secure envelopes

HARE Fair portions

_ _GN U_ Enroll

PIG _ Faucet

_ _ _ _ _ _ -EAGLE Sprawled

_ _ _ FLY Rigidly

TIGER _ _ _ _ Orange flower

TOAD_ _ _ _ _ Mushroom

_ _ _ _ _ APE Use a home camera

RAT Deep anger

ANSWER, PAGE 303

149. Up in the Air

The blimp-shaped grid below contains items that are seen in the air or sky.

```
                    W K C O C E L T T U H S
                A I R P L A N E N A M R E P U S K H E
              W F L Y I N G F I S H N R I T C U O R M E S     H D S
          T O O O P L N R E D I C T A I I R N S G R O C K E T R T E
        H E W B E A O U T H G I E L S S A T N A S H E W L R E A A I
      N O O M N T N S E G E E M F S T I S H T G P A T I E D T G
      S H U E I B L S E K A L F W O N S K I K E E L C I I R L O
      H D S O A P B U B B L E S O D O D Y K T P F O O L S E I N
      F U L R A N E Y Y F M S R O R E W E I C P N G M T A S F
        L O C U S T E S N O O L L A B R I A T O H O J A V E L I N
            L T B E N B I P N T G R P I I E G E K H C R T I Y S C
              C O M O P S M L E H A T T R E L E Y U P S
                H C T I W G N I D I R M O O R B
                    L R I N T H N
                    B E F A I R G
```

AIRPLANE	FIREWORKS	KITE	SANTA'S SLEIGH
BLIMP	FLARE	LOCUST	SEA GULL
BROOM-RIDING WITCH	FLYING FISH	MOON	SHUTTLECOCK
CANNONBALL	FRISBEE	MOTH	SKYWRITING
CLOUDS	GLIDERS	PEGASUS	SMOKE
CONFETTI	HELICOPTER	PETER PAN	SNOWFLAKES
DRAGONFLY	HONEYBEE	RAINBOW	SOAP BUBBLES
DUMBO	HOT-AIR BALLOONS	RAINDROPS	STARS
EAGLE	JAVELIN	ROCKET	SUPERMAN

ANSWER, PAGE 304

150. Think Big

```
S  O  I  Y  D  F  T  H  U  N  E  A  O  C  C  A  S  I  O  N  F  G  O
V  M  T  N  I  A  T  N  U  O  M  M  E  R  N  M  E  N  T  O  A  I  S
S  I  I  B  P  I  I  G  C  I  E  A  T  N  E  M  E  V  O  R  P  M  I
C  L  N  L  P  V  O  U  H  T  N  Z  G  H  W  T  O  T  G  I  I  V  E
I  H  E  R  E  L  T  S  E  R  W  O  M  U  S  O  B  Y  O  P  H  U  E
P  C  C  R  R  L  V  E  E  O  R  N  Y  I  Y  A  R  T  A  H  S  L  I
M  T  S  O  N  G  E  Y  S  P  O  U  D  N  L  C  O  L  I  S  E  U  M
Y  E  W  A  N  N  T  P  E  I  T  E  A  L  A  I  A  S  D  A  S  B  E
L  R  C  A  S  T  L  E  H  T  A  I  L  O  G  C  I  G  G  C  I  E  T
O  T  N  O  E  P  I  D  U  A  G  I  L  H  E  T  D  U  O  T  U  A  I
K  S  E  N  L  C  O  N  V  E  N  T  I  O  N  C  E  N  T  E  R  P  T
L  A  W  A  A  A  Y  A  E  E  E  T  Z  V  E  S  S  E  A  R  C  R  E
Y  A  N  T  H  E  H  B  M  N  I  N  D  G  K  A  E  R  B  R  A  Y  P
O  S  E  U  W  H  C  E  A  V  T  E  O  G  E  F  R  R  A  E  G  L  P
T  B  E  D  L  A  N  O  I  T  A  N  G  D  F  O  T  O  H  S  R  D  A
```

AMAZON	CRUISE SHIP	HEART	PALACE
APPETITE	DEAL	IDEA	PLANS
BAND	DESERT	IMPROVEMENT	PORTION
BREAK	DIPPER	LEAGUES	SHOT
CASTLE	ELEPHANT	MOUNTAIN	SMILE
CHEESE	FEET	NAME	STRETCH LIMO
CITY	FOOTBALL LINEMEN	NATIONAL DEBT	SUMO WRESTLER
COLISEUM	GODZILLA	OCCASION	UNIVERSE
CONTINENT	GOLIATH	OCEAN	WHALE
CONVENTION CENTER	GRAND CANYON	OLYMPICS	WORLD CUP

ANSWER, PAGE 304

151. Gridlock and Key

In the lock-shaped grid below, every item in the word list contains either the letters LOCK or KEY in consecutive order. When these letters appear in the grid, they have been replaced by a  or respectively. So that's the to solving. Good !

A CHIP OFF THE OLD
    BLOCK
ALICIA KEYS
BIOLOGICAL CLOCK
BLOCKADE
BLOCKHEAD
COMBINATION LOCK
CUCKOO CLOCK
DOOHICKEY
DREADLOCKS
FIELD HOCKEY
GLOCKENSPIEL
GRIDLOCK
HAMMERLOCK
HAWKEYE
HEMLOCK
HOKEY-POKEY
JOCKEY
JOHN MAYNARD
    KEYNES
KEYBOARD
KEY GRIP

KEY LARGO
KEY LIME PIE
KEYNOTE SPEAKER
KEYSTROKE
KEY TO MY HEART
LANDLOCKED
LATCHKEY CHILD
LOCKER ROOM
LOCKHEED
LOCK HORNS
LOCKSMITH
MALARKEY
MICKEY MOUSE
MONKEY BARS
OKEY-DOKEY
SHERLOCK HOLMES
TURKEY TROT
UNDER LOCK AND
    KEY
VAPOR LOCK
WHISKEY

ANSWER, PAGE 305

152. Don't Touch Me!

```
S I H W N L A C D L O C E H T N I T U O E A S
L L C I W O O P D O N T T O U C H M E R I F T
D U U T S N O D A N T D I S O L A T E D N L A
D N O H H E E E D R L E N F I S T D E E D E N
E L T N A W L N I E T H W F W I T H L N E S D
T I F O S O E I S S P C O O A R A G S W P E O
C N O T T L E O C U N A S T E S N S E A E N F
E K T I N F A J R L O T E U W I E O C R N O F
N E U E R L D S E C S T N H S H T I L D D Y I
N D O S O N T I T E H A O S E E O G U H E B S
O R I O D C O D E R N N N N E R M C D T N F H
C T F D I S T I N C T U O W I M E T E I T F H
S E A W A Y F R O M I T A L L I R A D W C O H
I D E R E T S E U Q E S O T H T E C U T O F F
D D I S T A N T E N O L A E B O T T N A W I R
```

ALOOF
APART
AWAY FROM IT ALL
CUT OFF
DISCONNECTED
DISCRETE
DISJOINED
DISTANT

DISTINCT
"DON'T TOUCH ME!"
HERMIT
INDEPENDENT
ISOLATED
"I WANT TO BE ALONE"
LONE WOLF
OFF BY ONESELF

ON ONE'S OWN
OUT IN THE COLD
OUT OF TOUCH
RECLUSE
REMOTE
SECLUDED
SEQUESTERED

SHUT OFF
SINGLE
STANDOFFISH
UNATTACHED
UNLINKED
WITHDRAWN
WITH NO TIES

ANSWER, PAGE 305

153. Hair Apparent

Shaped like a bouffant hairdo, the grid below contains references to hair and hairstyles.

```
                    H A I R D O
                  O N T U C W E R C C
                I T N S C L A O K S E I O K
              B A R B E R S H O P A N A C L S
            G B U D A Y H E A H A I E I D A O R
            S B A D H A I R D A Y S L P L L A R
          M U L O N N N T D Y N H W T O S A O E S
          A P T W D G B E A E C O R N R O W S C S
        T R O S D H O S U V J C T L T I E N O E K G
        O C N R I U A T A S O D Y O B E G A P D O S
        P E Y O F E N W O L B D N I W D R S K I I F
        K L T F T O T                 R E G O N U W
        N O A R D N                   P H U G P T
        O N I E E O                   U C C H S P
        T A L N S R                   M O H A W K
          I A C G I                   P I X I E
        N T M H H O G                 A F T R E L H
      S D R A S T S N                   I F D L P E B H
      P E E U A W N I K               C B U I I N R T O
      P L R L D I A L A               O B R U N E T T E
      B A Y Y S R R G                 M O E A E N E T
        T I N T L U O                 B E E H I V E
        M T O S C                     R R O W D
```

AUBURN	COLORS	HENNA	SNARLS
BAD HAIR DAY	COMB	MARCEL	STREAK
BANGS	CONK	MOHAWK	STYLED
BARBER SHOP	CORNROWS	PAGEBOY	TEASED
BEEHIVE	COWLICK	PERMANENT WAVE	TINT
BLEACHED BLONDE	CREW CUT	PIXIE	TOPKNOT
BOUFFANT	CURLING IRON	PLAIT	UPSWEEP
BRAID	DREADLOCKS	PONYTAIL	WASH-AND-DRY
BRUNETTE	DYE JOB	RECEDING HAIRLINE	WIDOW'S PEAK
BRUSH	FRENCH TWIST	SALON	WINDBLOWN
COIFFURE	HAIRDO		

ANSWER, PAGE 306

154. On a Roll

The grid below contains things that roll or can be rolled.

```
L R B E L L Y D A N C E R S B E L L Y N O C O
K I E N G L C O U D T T U O P N H O E A A N T
R B T D L H E O F U I T C U L A R W E I L I U
E O C O N U O U I L R C D N N L S O S T S C M
L A D N T U G U R N E Y E D O P A S D A E H B
L T P E I T H G I B S F M I A T O W W I S S L
O S E T R H E T A S H O P P I N G C A R T K E
R I D A L E R L E G W I E K E U T H E Y M A W
M N I L C A L Y S E E R S Y O T L L U P B T E
A A I P C A E L R T Y P I S T S C H A I R E E
E S R F S R R S O K I P P I I T J W U T S B D
T T L B U T K T A R E E W H E E L B A R R O W
S O P O L S R Y O L T A B O R C A N L V U A I
G R Y N G E A A L O N S G C H U K R C G E R H
I M R O C K S I N A N A V A L A N C H E L D L
```

ACROBAT	DOUGH	PLATEN	TANK
BELLY DANCER'S BELLY	GOLF CART	PULL TOY	TEACART
BOATS IN A STORM	GURNEY	ROCKS IN AN AVALANCHE	THUNDER
BOCCE BALL	HAND MOWER	ROLLAWAY BED	TIRES
CAISSON	HEADS	SHOPPING CART	TUMBLEWEED
CLAY	KAYAK	SKATEBOARD	TYPIST'S CHAIR
COINS	LUGGAGE	STEAMROLLER	WAVE
DICE	MARBLES	STROLLER	WHEELBARROW
DOLLY	NEWSPAPER	STUNT PLANE	YOUR EYES

ANSWER, PAGE 306

95

155. What's on TV

Shaped like a TV set, the grid below contains references to television watching.

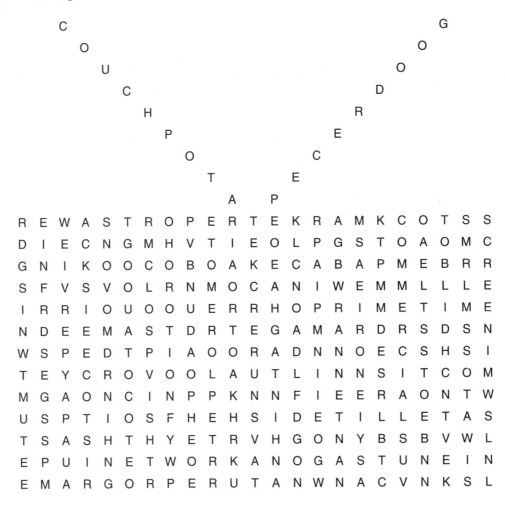

R	E	W	A	S	T	R	O	P	E	R	T	E	K	R	A	M	K	C	O	T	S	S
D	I	E	C	N	G	M	H	V	T	I	E	O	L	P	G	S	T	O	A	O	M	C
G	N	I	K	O	O	C	O	B	O	A	K	E	C	A	B	A	P	M	E	B	R	R
S	F	V	S	V	O	L	R	N	M	O	C	A	N	I	W	E	M	M	L	L	E
I	R	R	I	O	U	O	O	U	E	R	R	H	O	P	R	I	M	E	T	I	M	E
N	D	E	E	M	A	S	T	D	R	T	E	G	A	M	A	R	D	R	S	D	S	N
W	S	P	E	D	T	P	I	A	O	O	R	A	D	N	N	O	E	C	S	H	S	I
T	E	Y	C	R	O	V	O	O	L	A	U	T	L	I	N	N	S	I	T	C	O	M
M	G	A	O	N	C	I	N	P	P	K	N	N	F	I	E	E	R	A	O	N	T	W
U	S	P	T	I	O	S	F	H	E	H	S	I	D	E	T	I	L	L	E	T	A	S
T	S	A	S	H	T	H	Y	E	T	R	V	H	G	O	N	Y	B	S	B	V	W	L
E	P	U	I	N	E	T	W	O	R	K	A	N	O	G	A	S	T	U	N	E	I	N
E	M	A	R	G	O	R	P	E	R	U	T	A	N	W	N	A	C	V	N	K	S	L

ANTENNA	DRAMA	NEWS	SCREEN
BIOGRAPHY	GAME SHOW	ON TAPE	SITCOM
BROADCAST	GOOD RECEPTION	PAY-PER-VIEW	SOAP OPERA
CABLE	LIVE	PRIME TIME	SPORTS
CARTOONS	MOVIES	REALITY TV	STOCK MARKET REPORTS
CHANNELS	MUSIC VIDEO	REMOTE	TALK SHOW
COMMERCIALS	MUTE	RERUNS	TUNE IN
COOKING	NATURE PROGRAM	SATELLITE DISH	VOLUME
COUCH POTATO	NETWORK	SCI-FI	WEATHER

ANSWER, PAGE 307

156. Black Hole #2

In this puzzle, the letters in the center of the grid are missing. It's up to you to write them in by figuring out which words in the list are missing some of their letters in the grid. When you've completed the puzzle, the missing letters will spell out one quote while the uncircled letters, as usual, will reveal another quote plus the source and author of both quotes. (Note: A few of the items in the word list relate to the theme.)

```
L  K  H  S  U  R  B  T  N  I  A  P  E  O  X  P  P  C
L  A  T  N  O  Z  I  R  O  H  E  B  I  E  E  R  R  R
I  N  R  E  N  A  C  E  N  I  G  R  A  N  S  O  T  H
E  G  D  O  R  I  A  N  G  R  A  Y  G  C  W  O  N  A
P  A  M  T  M  E  E  V  R  N  T  U  E  S  K  F  R  D
Y  R  R  O  N  M  E  G  E  I  I  V  F  E  N  R  S  N
T  O  I  O  V  T  ▓  ▓  ▓  ▓  ▓  ▓  D  O  M  E  U  A
P  O  H  N  I  N  ▓  ▓  ▓  ▓  ▓  ▓  D  E  I  A  R  B
M  C  A  R  C  H  ▓  ▓  ▓  ▓  ▓  ▓  I  I  S  D  T  S
J  O  U  S  T  I  ▓  ▓  ▓  ▓  ▓  ▓  L  L  E  N  T  U
N  U  A  K  O  E  ▓  ▓  ▓  ▓  ▓  ▓  S  F  L  R  O  H
O  R  M  T  R  S  ▓  ▓  ▓  ▓  ▓  ▓  B  R  E  A  K  L
I  T  H  E  I  S  P  G  L  T  M  L  A  Y  L  P  G  A
T  A  H  D  A  Y  W  T  B  I  E  E  N  D  U  E  R  E
A  T  S  E  N  R  A  E  D  E  N  I  Z  E  N  S  M  D
X  E  R  R  L  E  L  A  S  F  T  A  D  O  N  B  Y  I
I  A  O  S  A  L  O  M  E  S  U  A  C  A  N  R  W  N
F  I  L  D  Y  N  O  I  T  A  M  A  F  E  D  E  E  A
```

"AN IDEAL HUSBAND"
ARCHERY
BACKRUB
CROW'S FEET
DEFAMATION
DENIZENS
DORIAN GRAY
EARNEST
EXCELLENT

FAR EAST
FIXATION
HERITAGE
HORIZONTAL
IMMORAL
INSIST
JOUSTING
KANGAROO COURT
MADE-UP

MODERN
MOMENTUM
"NO DICE!"
NONGREASY
OTHELLO
PAINTBRUSH
PENGUINS
PORTRAIT
POTBELLY

PRINCIPAL
PROOFREAD
"SALOME"
SCENARIO
STATION BREAK
TAG TEAM
TIME ZONE
VICTORIAN
VILLAGE

ANSWER, PAGE 307

157. It's a Shore Thing

The seashell-shaped grid below contains references to a day at the beach.

```
                    B W F H S H E
                  P U B L I C B E A C H
                N Y R A O O C N A U A U S W E
              L E N Y A S T A O B B M S S A B H
            D O O W T F I R D C R B A A H T E U L
          L S W A O N T H I E L R A U N D E R T O W
          E L T S A C D N A S E S H L D A R L O B Y
          R C I E A S I D R L V E B Y A O W L L U G
          H U D M O K E R L S O H O A L R I A E S T
            S E H I A W A T C H T H E S U N S E T
              I B D W T O B T S H W H E K G S Y
                F A Y S B R R L P A E E S S G
                  R R A F T J E R V T E A G
                  A A R S E K E E H L U
                    T U L T R E Z G B
                    S L S O L N E
                    S K N U N
                    I S U
                    D
```

BASK	CORAL	RAFT	STARFISH
"BAYWATCH"	DRIFTWOOD	SANDALS	SUNGLASSES
BIKINI	DUNE BUGGY	SANDCASTLE	SURFBOARD
BLANKET	FLOAT	SEA BREEZE	SWIM
BOATS	GULL	SEASHELLS	UMBRELLA
BUOY	JET SKI	"SHARK!"	UNDERTOW
BURN	LOW TIDE	SHOVEL	WATCH THE SUNSET
CABANA	PUBLIC BEACH	SLEEP	WATER WINGS
CONCH	RADIO	SNORKEL	WAVE

ANSWER, PAGE 308

158. We're in the Money

Shaped like a dollar sign, the grid below contains references to money and finance.

BANKRUPT
BORROW
"CAN YOU SPARE A DIME?"
C-NOTE
COUNTERFEIT
DEBT
DOLLAR
"E PLURIBUS UNUM"
EQUITY
EURO
FROZEN ASSETS
FUND
GOLD
HIGH FINANCE
LIRA
LOAN
LOOSE CHANGE
MEGABUCKS
MILLIONAIRE
MOOLA
NEST EGG
NICKEL
PAY STUB
PERSONAL CHECKS
PESO
PIGGY BANK
POCKET MONEY
PRIME RATE
PURSE
RAND
RIAL
RUBLE
RUPEE
SAFE-DEPOSIT BOX
SAVINGS BOND
SAWBUCK
SHEKEL
SOLVENT
STOCKS
T-BILL
TAXES
TREASURY
U.S. MINT
WALLET
WAMPUM

```
    B S P       M I S
    V A E       U G E
    Y V N       N O X
  T T D P S E I S K C U B A G E M O N
O M U N T U C N H G R S H T M U O S N E
Y I T U E K R G E C O U N T E R F E I T
D L B F E V O S K L A B P S S O T P M
E L F L     L B E     I B T
O I O R     T O L     R O O
H O E G     R N S     U R C
D N A R     C D E     L R K
S A T O F S A F E D E P O S I T B O X
H I G H F I N A N C E E W M Y L W L I T
F R K N A B Y G G I P R I M E R A T E R
  E E J F R O Z E N A S S E T S L I U E
    U S E     O T A     L I R A
    S S P     N L O     E N M S
    P G U     A E A     T U S U
    A E R     L I S     P B T R
  D O L L A R L T P O C K E T M O N E Y
E G N A H C E S O O L H C D A E I O N D
E Q U I T Y A R T O N E U W H M G A V E
  T O B U B D U Y A M C B A S N Y G T
    I B O     K W U
    M L H     S A I
    E E L     N S G
```

ANSWER, PAGE 308

159. Cover Letter

```
Y  S  O  F  A  N  M  A  I  L  E  S  U  I  D
M  I  S  S  I  V  E  N  O  N  S  V  T  N  W
U  N  N  O  I  T  A  D  N  E  M  M  O  C  R
N  C  I  T  A  B  E  B  N  E  C  A  U  L  E
A  E  S  D  O  T  P  I  R  C  S  T  S  O  P
N  R  E  T  Y  C  S  O  U  W  E  A  N  S  I
S  E  T  O  N  U  O  Y  K  N  A  H  T  I  S
W  L  T  W  B  T  O  P  S  A  L  Y  Y  N  T
E  Y  S  H  O  M  C  E  Y  T  E  L  T  G  L
R  H  F  O  L  L  O  W  U  P  D  I  H  B  E
E  Y  N  M  G  Y  N  O  U  N  W  W  G  E  R
D  R  I  I  T  E  D  B  O  R  I  E  I  S  C
L  E  T  T  E  R  O  F  I  N  T  E  N  T  A
U  N  C  M  S  E  L  T  Y  O  H  U  R  R  C
M  O  V  A  S  S  E  R  D  D  A  E  E  E  E
A  I  G  Y  P  S  N  O  R  T  K  C  V  G  R
I  T  S  C  O  S  C  M  O  I  I  M  O  A  T
L  A  N  O  S  R  E  P  E  P  S  T  H  R  I
B  T  N  N  I  M  S  L  I  N  S  R  E  D  F
O  S  G  C  O  T  O  E  B  S  A  P  A  S  I
X  Y  F  E  I  T  N  Z  G  U  L  E  R  E  E
Y  O  U  R  S  T  R  U  L  Y  O  A  L  D  D
S  I  G  N  A  T  U  R  E  R  E  D  N  E  S
```

ADDRESS	DOUBLE-SPACED	MAILBOX	SENDER
BEST REGARDS	EPISTLE	MEMO	SIGNATURE
BUSINESS	FAN MAIL	MISSIVE	SINCERELY
CERTIFIED	FOLLOW-UP	OVERNIGHT	STATIONERY
COMMENDATION	FONDLY	PERSONAL	THANK-YOU NOTE
CONDOLENCES	IN A BOTTLE	POSTSCRIPT	TO WHOM IT MAY CONCERN
COPY	IN CLOSING	RECIPIENT	UNANSWERED
DATE	LETTER OF INTENT	REPLY	WRITE SOON
DEAR SIR	LOVE	SEALED WITH A KISS	YOURS TRULY

ANSWER, PAGE 309

160. Today's To-Do List

The house-shaped grid below contains the names of common around-the-house/everyday activities. The hidden message contains two quotes: the first unattributed, the second by American journalist Don Marquis.

```
                        R  R
                  V  N  E  E
            T  V  S  S  A  R  E  G  O  T  O  O  F  F  I  C  E  R  P
         H  U  H  T  T  D  N  E  I  R  F  A  H  T  I  W  H  C  N  U  L
      C  D  A        O  N  F  F  N  D  T  E  E  F  F  O  C  K  N  I  R  D
   T  D  V  E        O  E  T  O  U  N  M  S  L  L  I  B  Y  A  P  P  L  M  O
   A  R  E  R  O  B  W  W  W  A  S  H  D  I  S  H  E  S  H  A  R  O  T  O  N  Y  I
W  O  H  S  A  C  T  E  G  S  T  U  C  A  N  D  F  P  U  T  O  H  D  M  F  F  O  R  T
A  O  T  S  G  H  E  D  K  P  E  L  Z  Z  U  P  E  V  L  O  S  A  E  N  P  L  Y  O  A
T  A  K  E  O  U  T  T  R  A  S  H  E  M  O  H  E  V  I  R  D  N  F  T  U  I  E  N  G
E  R  T  R           P  M  T  A           D  O  A  M  O           Y  A  O  C  R
R  U  R  D           E  O  W  T           K  P  R  H  O           D  M  L  L  G
P  C  R  T           R  A  S  S           I  T  P  M  I           I  P  N  O  A
L  E  T  E           W  I  H  N           D  F  O  N  U           T  U  D  T  D
A  I  E  G           S  O  T  A           S  H  L  E  C  U  A  R  T  K  O  H  F
N  W  A  L  W  O  M  K  E  W  E  R  C     S  R  O  O  D  K  C  O  L  C  P  E  I
T  N  G  U  S  T  A  K  E  N  A  P  K     P  W  O  I  S  T  H  A  Y  I  E  S  S
S  E  I  R  E  C  O  R  G  Y  U  B  T     E  K  A  B  E  S  W  R  V  P  D  A  Y
```

BAKE	GET CASH	MOW LAWN	SOLVE PUZZLE
BUY GROCERIES	GET DRESSED	PAY BILLS	TAKE NAP
COOK	GET UP	PHONE MOM	TAKE OUT TRASH
DO LAUNDRY	GO ONLINE	PICK UP MAIL	TIDY UP
DRINK COFFEE	GO TO OFFICE	READ NEWSPAPER	VACUUM
DRIVE HOME	HAVE DINNER	REST	WALK DOG
DUST	IRON CLOTHES	SHAVE	WASH DISHES
EAT SNACK	LOCK DOORS	SHOP	WATCH TV
FEED KIDS	LUNCH WITH A FRIEND	SHOWER	WATER PLANTS
FLOSS	MAKE BED	SLEEP	WORK

ANSWER, PAGE 309

161. At the Pharmacy

```
V R X S S T A P U R Y S H G U O C N Y D S F O
A R F T Y H E L R A S T I N N S P O R D E Y E
P I L L B O T T L E S S I W O R D F H O N R R
O E C O U I T P G G S K G M N O S E S P R A Y
R E C T S M O N U A S C A U I O A P R P E S C
I P A I N R E L I E V E R S R T I C R H I P T
Z G M O I Z P D L O R N I I I D A N T A C I D
E A E N O R S O I C A R E N P C I P T R I S L
R U R L A E M D E C O N G E S T A N T M C P A
F Z A E O R M R I X I P I N A G I I N A E O X
N E F O R P U B I B A N D A G E S O G C B N A
R P I E D T A I Y D E M E R D L O C N I A G T
E A L G N I R O L O C R I A H N T S T S G E I
O D M E M A C O S M E T I C S N I M A T I V V
K S D I A P E R S L I O H T A B E A D R U G E
```

ANTACID	DECONGESTANT	HEATING PAD	PAIN RELIEVERS
ASPIRIN	DENTURE CREAM	IBUPROFEN	PHARMACIST
BANDAGES	DIAPERS	ICE BAG	PILL BOTTLES
BATH OILS	DRUGS	LAXATIVE	PRESCRIPTIONS
CAMERA FILM	EARPLUGS	LOTION	SOAP
CANDY	EYE DROPS	LOZENGES	SPONGE
COLD REMEDY	FLU MEDICINE	MOLESKIN	TOYS
COSMETICS	GAUZE PADS	NOSE SPRAY	VAPORIZER
COUGH SYRUP	HAIR COLORING	OINTMENT	VITAMINS

ANSWER, PAGE 310

162. Wordy Gurdy

A Wordy Gurdy is a two-word rhyming phrase such as SMALL BALL or OCEAN MOTION. We've hidden 32 such rhymes in the grid, but first you'll have to discover them by using the clues below. The number after each definition gives the number of syllables in each word, and the rhymes are in alphabetical order. Should you need it, the complete list can be found on page 253.

```
J A G G E R S D A G G E R S M X A E K E M P Y
P L F E T P T E P R B E E T T A E R U O O R G
T E I R I V E D S E H C T E K S S E H C T E F
R M E N E Y L E R S E S O T O X Z R P E W N Y
Y G P R L E O A U I R J Y L A A N O Z D O E Q
I I D H F I T R N L A L P P L W T I O S B U N
N E R E F E R E N C E P R E F E R E N C E C C
G A R A Y E A A A E E E D E P C O I E R T L
S I W T H A N R G E T S D R S K W W N I T E A
P I N S G B T E N T E G D E A U T S O M A K W
Y E U U N B A S Y V E R Y A S R J E W L O I L
I R S I E O A C D A N E D Y N E L L A F L L A
N O I T A C I D N I N O I T A C I D N I V E W
G O U E C T O M A M A I T N A R E H E Y M E Y
C G R A Y D A Y R D I M S E O F E S O H C M E
```

1. Everyone collapses (1)
2. Lousy commercial (1)
3. Picked enemies (1)
4. Bear hand statute (1)
5. Loved hearing organ (1)
6. Looks at a reward (1)
7. Gets quick drawings (2)
8. Gratis hot beverage (1)
9. Obtain volleyball court separator (1)
10. Gloomy 24 hours (1)
11. Warm up connected hotel rooms (1)
12. Yours truly fibs (1)
13. Singer Mick's knives (2)
14. Retain an army car (1)
15. Cyclist Armstrong's waltzes (2)
16. Servant didn't go (1)
17. Unused billiard stick (1)
18. Zero winter flakes (1)
19. Atop "ugly duckling" (1)
20. Jury member dread (1)
21. Lovely urban center (2)
22. Hive leader's Levi's (1)
23. Scarce twosome (1)
24. One's choice of a dictionary, e.g. (3)
25. Whirl a needle's cousin (1)
26. Highest-ranking policeman, for short (1)
27. Attempting activity of agent 007 (2)
28. One who hurries a theater seater (2)
29. Sign that points to the clearing of one's name (4)
30. Band instrument made of candle material (1)
31. Banana-colored string instrument (2)
32. Animal house personnel (1)

ANSWER, PAGE 310

163. Give Me a Ring

Shaped like an engagement ring, the grid below contains things with rings.

```
        E O G H C T A M G N I X O B R T H H
        N R A R C H E R Y T A R G E T K
        C O L L A R P E O M I W L D I M
          O H L F O O A C D N E N N Y
          M O P T C P O E N C A G I R
            M I E L I E M A A E S B
            N S T L S P R A L I I T
              T R E E B M A G E F
              O I B M T N Y H I T
              A N O R O C H E L O C S
        M S S A                 O U I A
        L U H                   L S A
      C I C                     D E N
      R J R                     R C R
      L U I                     A E U
      O G C                     O O T
      O G F                     B D A
      L L O                     T O S
        E A L                 W R R
        R V E I             D D A F
          H A N D G R E N A D E D
          I N B U T H T A B N
            G R A I N G
```

ARCHERY TARGET	CIRCUS	GYMNAST	OLYMPIC FLAG
AUDI LOGO	COLLAR	HALO	OPERA HOUSE
BATHTUB	CORONA	HAND GRENADE	PISTONS
BELL	DARTBOARDS	JUGGLER	POPE
BINDER	EARS	KING	SATURN
BOXING MATCH	FIANCÉE	MAGICIAN	TELEPHONE
BRIDE	FRODO	NAVEL	TREE
CHARM BRACELET	GROOM		

ANSWER, PAGE 311

164. In the Papers

```
E D I T O R I A L S C N E A H
P O L P E O E N B O C N B E O
O N E P A S E H R R I I G P R
A D R T E N T R T L I A M H O
E S A P I R E R D A P D I O S
N M U L O C S A O T E D G M C
C F Y O T L E O N P R W U E O
L B R I H H I O N O E S T D P
A I O D L A R T S A A R S E E
S N E N N F A E I W L S D L R
S P A P D A U E R C E S A I E
I P T H E A T E R S S A S V S
F U A N R N I S E M T O E E T
I Z B R O O B L S E A N L R A
E Z L T H I O O Y W T B A Y U
D L O F E H T W O L E B S E R
S E I F A S E I I S E N A E A
K R D E L A D S D T E V V H N
O E S A T F T N P E A I A T T
O H M O H I U S A O E N V R S
B U S I N E S S D W R T B O T
A Y O G R P I S S O G T A N M
E T S T O C K Q U O T E S L S
```

ARTS
BELOW THE FOLD
BOOKS
BRIDGE
BUSINESS
BYLINE
CLASSIFIEDS
COLUMN
COMICS
CORRECTIONS

CRIME
DAILY
EDITORIALS
EVENT LISTINGS
FASHION
FRONT PAGE
GOSSIP
HEADLINE
HEALTH
HOME DELIVERY

HOROSCOPE
LATE EDITION
MOVIES
NEWSSTAND
OBITUARIES
OP-ED
PERSONALS
POLITICS
PUZZLE
REAL ESTATE

REPORTS
RESTAURANTS
REVIEWS
SALES ADS
SPORTS
STOCK QUOTES
TABLOIDS
THEATER
TRAVEL
WEATHER

ANSWER, PAGE 311

165. Solar Eclipse

It's a bright idea to consider the title when searching the sun-shaped grid below.

```
                                    E
                                  W N H
          K                         E I S                              N
                C T E           N T H T H              E M Y
                B E A M           O A S E O          N D S I
                M S D N M I D E R S T A N D I N G
                  T E H L E E S U E T S T D B N
                    G F L O W E R H E D E A U
                    D B R N T O G T R O K Y M
                N R U B E I O I B O F E N S G I A
          T N E R F S D F L O O T D A N C E K I D K
        C L H S I T P A S U E H N T Y O H S C R E E N
        U T E A O V A L L E Y I D A H O T C N O U
          Y A H L E D S S E F A E K O R T S
              L V S T Y H I F T S P L R
              A S R P D G A O F S O E A
            R R E O E M L R E H T A B M I
          D O E R G R F A N D A S T U L R D
          A T C L     I S L I U       N W O D
          S H U       S S E R D       N B C
      L                 E E O                    K
                        S C S
                          K
```

ASUNDER	SUNBURST	SUNKEN TREASURE	SUNSHADE
"GESUNDHEIT!"	SUNDANCE KID	SUNLAMPS	SUNSHINE
HOT FUDGE SUNDAE	SUNDAY SCHOOL	SUNLIGHT	SUN SPOT
MISUNDERSTANDING	SUN DECK	SUNNY SIDE OF THE	SUNSTROKE
RIDE OFF INTO THE SUNSET	SUNDIAL	STREET	SUNTAN LOTION
SUNBAKED	SUNDOWN	SUN PORCH	SUN VALLEY, IDAHO
SUNBATHER	SUNDRESS	SUNROOF	SUN YAT-SEN
SUNBEAM	SUNFLOWER	SUNSCREEN	"THE SUN ALSO RISES"
SUNBLOCK	SUNGLASSES	"SUNSET BOULEVARD"	TSUNAMI
SUNBURN			

ANSWER, PAGE 312

166. Picture Perfect

```
S O M E P W Y T R E P O R P L A N O S R E P E
P I E D P I P E R O E E L A O L K E N O E W P
N P P P S A K R W P R N E I L L I P P E P P E
P I E P L A T E E A M O B N L O O O R Y P R T
I P C D A S R A S P A H S T O L I P M L A P E
P A O P A P R E P N P I P P S R P O E C L R
I R I L A L L T A A E Y P O R E E S P N S L P
C K E C A Y P R P P N A A T S T A Y T P Y I R
K P K N P E C U A U T P K S G E L C P O E M I
P L T T E E R S S P P U I P K E H H T O R N
O A A V L P O R K H R R Y P C I G O A P N D C
C C E P A T E N T P E N D I N G T L M I I H I
K E O E N P I N K I S R R P A N T O H E E T P
E S P E T E R P A N S P S G N O P G N I P R L
T P I A N O P L A Y E R E P O O P Y T R A P E
```

PAINT POT

PALM PILOT

PARCEL POST

PARK PLACE

PARTY POOPER

PATENT PENDING

PAY PHONE

PEACH PIT

PEA PLANT

PEDAL PUSHERS

PEER PRESSURE

PEN PAL

PEP PILL

PERMANENT PRESS

PERSONAL PROPERTY

PETER PAN

PETER PRINCIPLE

PET PEEVE

PIANO PLAYER

PICKPOCKET

PIED PIPER

PIE PLATE

PIKES PEAK

PING-PONG

PLAYPEN

POLO PONY

POMPOM

POP PSYCHOLOGY

POT PIE

POWER PACK

PRICKLY PEAR

PUSHPIN

ANSWER, PAGE 312

167. Changing Direction

Shaped like a light bulb, the grid below contains things that change or are changed.

ADDRESSES
ATTITUDE
BEHAVIOR
BOYS' VOICES
CHANNELS
CLOTHES
[THE] COURSE OF
   HISTORY
DIAPERS
DIET
DIRECTION
ELEVATION
FASHION
HAIRSTYLES
HEALTH
JOBS
LANES
LIGHT BULB
LOCKS
LUCK
MENU

MONEY
MOOD
MUSICAL KEYS
NEIGHBORHOOD
OIL FILTER
OPINIONS
PLACES
PLANS
PRINCE INTO A TOAD
ROUTINE
SCHEDULE
SCHOOLS
SEATS
SHEETS
SHOES
SPEEDS
TIRES
TRAINS
YOUR MIND
YOUR TUNE

```
              S   I   F   D   L   I   K   M
          S   N   E   D   N   I   M   R   U   O   Y   S
      M   A   R   A   D   D   R   E   S   S   E   S   K   O
      L   S   P   E   T   P   E   I   D   E   O   P   C   L
  P   E   Y   R   O   P   U   C   L   D   U   O   J   O   B   S
  N   L   T   I   S   E   A   T   S   U   L   T   I   L   E   I
  H   K   A   N   E   L   Y   I   C   H   D   L   I   N   A   B
  A   L   U   C   K   N   G   O   D   E   F   E   A   T   L   E
  I   E   C   E   E   H   A   N   U   I   N   L   H   U   T   H
  R   N   Y   I   G   S   S   E   L   R   Y   I   B   C   O   A
  S   S   U   N   R   C   A   T   T   T   T   T   I   S   V
  T   T   N   T   H   M   E   N   U   U   H   U   D   U   E   I
  Y   D   O   O   H   R   O   B   H   G   I   E   N   A   O   O
  L   B   O   A   I   O   U   T   I   C   H   F   A   E   N   R
  E   L   G   T   E   N   A   L   S   N   I   A   R   T   N   D
  S   Y   R   O   T   S   I   H   F   O   E   S   R   U   O   C
      P   Y   A   S   H   O   P   O   I   U   H   M   I   H
          E   D   G   E   H   T   O   T   E   I   N   A
          E   S   E   H   J   O   A   Y   O   N
              D   T   T   B   V   C   N
              H   S   L   A   O   E   E   N
                  Y   A   G   Y   L   E
                  F   E   O   S   E   C
                  H   N   V   R
                  M   O   O   D
                  A   S   I   M
                  C   E   C   H
                  T   R   E   A
                  N   I   S   G
                  T   E
```

ANSWER, PAGE 313

168. Things You Make

The hidden message is made up of two quotes: the first is a New England saying; the second is from a speech by a U.S. diplomat.

```
F  U  S  F  E  Y  I  Y  T  U  P  D  F  W  C  E  S  A  P  E  A  C  E
I  R  U  I  A  E  W  A  V  E  S  T  I  G  O  O  D  S  A  L  A  R  Y
R  S  O  U  P  N  T  D  M  A  G  K  R  F  F  E  N  I  T  T  A  A  D
S  F  O  O  L  O  F  Y  O  U  R  S  E  L  F  O  E  T  F  R  W  N  E
T  O  O  R  A  M  E  M  A  D  A  N  O  W  E  E  I  D  A  A  I  T  S
M  H  M  L  Y  O  N  U  R  M  D  T  T  D  E  H  R  E  T  C  C  M  R
O  O  O  E  F  A  O  E  N  S  E  N  S  E  W  A  F  E  H  K  T  E  O
V  V  O  O  M  N  A  M  K  N  N  E  C  W  S  G  N  N  S  O  M  W
E  I  B  R  R  N  I  E  S  T  U  E  D  I  B  K  E  S  U  C  X  E  S
G  A  E  K  I  M  E  R  R  Y  T  E  N  S  C  I  S  D  O  E  E  S  R
N  N  L  D  O  T  L  H  T  S  R  G  U  I  T  H  G  I  L  F  S  U  E
L  L  I  H  E  L  O  M  A  F  O  T  U  O  N  I  A  T  N  U  O  M  T
L  U  E  V  A  L  H  H  L  P  F  Q  Y  N  M  A  K  E  I  T  A  E  T
I  N  V  Y  I  T  H  I  P  O  P  C  O  R  N  N  G  P  E  M  A  H  A
W  E  E  L  E  L  B  U  O  R  T  Y  O  U  R  B  E  D  P  M  E  S  M
```

AMENDS	[AN] EXCUSE	HASTE	POPCORN
A PLAY FOR	[A] FACE	[A] HOLE-IN-ONE	[A] QUICK GETAWAY
BELIEVE	[A] FIRE	[A] LIVING	ROOM
[THE] BIG TIME	[THE] FIRST MOVE	LOVE	SENSE
COFFEE	[A] FLIGHT	MATTERS WORSE	SOMEONE HAPPY
CONTACT	[A] FOOL OF YOURSELF	MERRY	[THE] TEAM
[A] DECISION	[A] FORTUNE	MONEY	TRACKS
[A] DETOUR	FRIENDS	[A] MOUNTAIN OUT OF A	TROUBLE
[A] DIFFERENCE	[A] FUSS	MOLEHILL	WAVES
DINNER	[A] GOOD	MY DAY	[A] WILL
[A] DRAWING	SALARY	PEACE	YOUR BED
ENDS MEET	[THE] GRADE	PLANS	

ANSWER, PAGE 313

169. Road Signs

Shaped like a stop sign, the grid below contains inscriptions on signs commonly seen on U.S. streets and highways.

```
            W H I Y L E Y D
            P N O P A S S I N G
          O C R I V W I N E G I G
        T S I A S C H O O L Z O N E
      S W A F S I G G N T D H A I T S
    A I I D F A L L I N G R O C K S T T
  E N G Y E A A S R H D E T O U R S A F T
  Y L N O S R A C T D T H E S A A M E E L
  O C A A T T E W N E H W Y R E P P I L S
  I L L O T Y A P O D E N N O W O M K E O
  S T A B U A S G A I R P O R T N R I G N
  E A H S S W E S N V W O H U L O D B R E
  P D E R N O T H G I R O N I W R O U E D
  O F A R T W H A F D X T A T L C B U M P
    H D I A T E U V E M D A E N L T B O
    N E X T E X I T O N E M I L E N
      U T L S T H I E S W P A S E
      A R L E O M A D C R E W
        W O N R U T U O N A
        W R O N G W A Y
```

AIRPORT	MEN AT WORK	ONE-WAY	SLOW
BUMP	MERGE LEFT	PAY TOLL	STEEP HILL
CARS ONLY	NEXT EXIT ONE MILE	PED XING	STOP
DETOUR	NO PARKING	REST AREA	TWO-WAY TRAFFIC
DIVIDED HIGHWAY	NO PASSING	SCHOOL ZONE	WRONG WAY
FALLING ROCKS	NO RIGHT ON RED	SIGNAL AHEAD	YIELD
FUEL	NO U-TURN	SLIPPERY WHEN WET	

ANSWER, PAGE 314

In this puzzle, the letters in the center of the grid are missing. It's up to you to write them in by figuring out which words in the list are missing some of their letters in the grid. When you've completed the puzzle, the missing letters will spell out a humorous question. (You may consider whether any of the items on the list answer it.) The uncircled letters, as usual, will reveal another quote that relates to the theme.

```
E  I  N  T  E  L  E  V  I  S  I  O  N  R  V  E  N  T
Z  I  I  R  E  N  G  I  S  P  A  P  E  X  R  A  Y  S
N  S  T  E  N  G  A  M  C  U  A  H  U  O  M  R  B  S
O  I  H  T  N  A  T  I  O  M  S  P  N  L  E  O  F  E
R  W  B  S  S  C  I  T  S  A  L  P  E  T  L  E  R  R
B  A  R  A  P  I  I  N  W  N  S  A  T  R  T  E  N  P
W  D  O  O  M  A  ■  ■  ■  ■  ■  ■  L  T  Z  A  Y  G
I  T  T  T  E  R  ■  ■  ■  ■  ■  E  R  I  R  A  N
N  I  O  L  R  I  ■  ■  ■  ■  ■  K  P  A  D  S  I
D  L  M  S  D  T  ■  ■  ■  ■  H  M  E  M  E  T
M  A  C  H  I  N  ■  ■  ■  ■  I  O  R  E  N  N
I  O  I  B  I  R  ■  ■  ■  ■  ■  O  U  T  S  A  I
L  A  R  H  I  N  O  A  S  L  S  A  R  Y  O  R  L  R
L  U  T  C  U  S  M  T  E  D  T  S  H  O  E  E  P  P
S  O  C  L  L  O  E  H  E  W  S  U  I  M  M  S  R  M
N  A  E  T  O  E  S  S  E  O  R  R  A  N  I  S  I  A
L  S  L  L  Y  O  V  U  B  R  I  C  K  S  G  N  A  E
E  L  E  V  A  T  O  R  S  K  E  D  S  R  E  S  A  L
```

AIRPLANES	DISHWASHER	NOTHING	TELEVISION
BATHS	DOMES	PAPER	THAWS
BATTERY	ELECTRIC MOTOR	PASTE	THINKPAD
BEER	ELEVATORS	PLASTICS	TOASTER
BLESSINGS	FIELDWORK	PRINTING PRESS	TWIST TIE
BRICKS	LASERS	PULLEY	VELCRO
BRONZE	LOOM	PYRAMIDS	WALTZ
CAMERA	MACHINES	READOUTS	WHEEL
CD-ROMS	MAGNETS	SIRLOIN	WINDMILLS
CRUSADER	MARIONETTE	SPUMANTE	X-RAYS

ANSWER, PAGE 314

171. Holiday Highlights

Shaped like a Christmas tree, the grid below contains words and phrases associated with Christmas.

```
                              R
                           E  L  T
                        H  M  E  O  B
                     S  W  M  G  N  H  O
                  A  E  O  R  N  T  S  D  W
               D  E  C  O  R  A  T  I  O  N  S
                  R  E  O  P  Y
               E  R  C  U  I  P  P
               D  W  K  C  S  A  R  I  G
            N  R  I  E  R  A  A  E  T  N  X
         O  R  N  A  M  E  N  T  S  R  M  G  A
      D  S  G  G  I  F  C  I  N  E  Z  T  I  L  B
               E  N  S  I  N
            R  S  A  N  T  T  E
         U  E  N  D  R  L  S  I  X
      D  L  T  E  T  E  O  S  T  A  I
   O  L  A  E  W  A  B  R  Y  S  R  T  V
L  C  H  R  I  S  T  M  A  S  E  V  E  H  E
   P  R  I  G  S  E  V  L  E  C  H  I  M  N  E  Y  H
H  G  I  E  L  S  T  S  I  C  A  N  D  Y  C  A  N  E  Z
                           E
                           D
                           E
```

ANGEL	COMET	ELVES	SLEIGH
BLITZEN	CUPID	ORNAMENTS	STOCKING
BOWS	DANCER	PRANCER	TINSEL
CANDY CANE	DASHER	PRESENTS	TREE
CAROL	DECEMBER	REINDEER	VIXEN
CHIMNEY	DECORATIONS	RUDOLPH	WRAPPING
CHRISTMAS EVE	DONDER	SANTA	WREATH

ANSWER, PAGE 315

172. As Good as Cold

Shaped like an ice cube, the grid below contains things that are or may be cold.

```
I G E W T S H O U L D E R
T R U G O Y N E Z O R F A D
R E R N U N G N G N Y M N O N
J F E S S L S S F R E E Z E R I
A R A E A Y N A S C C A R A T C W
C I D C C O M H A Y N T S E R E V E
K G I T S       P   T   L   H   B   R
F E N E O     S N A E C O A T S E F A
R R G N D P A R N T A C S I W R R F
O A U L E   C C O U H K B W G G O F
S T N E M T R A P A D E T A E H N U
T O D H I   E V W E R R T U R A T S
I R Y C W S K A T I N G R I N K T I
  C A V E   I N A T N E O R C D S O
    I I H A R D F A C T S O A M R N
      C L   I D T O M C E O L L A A
        L I Q U I D N I T R O G E N
          E L C I S P O P D S L I Y
```

ANTARCTICA
CAVE
DEEP SPACE
DOG'S NOSE
EVEREST
FREEZER
FRONT
FROZEN YOGURT

FUSION
GLACIER
HARD FACTS
ICEBERG
ICICLE
IGLOO
JACK FROST
LIQUID NITROGEN

MEAT LOCKER
OCEAN
POPSICLE
READING
REFRIGERATOR
SHOULDER
SIBERIA
SKATING RINK

SNOW
SWEAT
TRAIL
TUNDRA
UNHEATED APARTMENT
UNSYMPATHETIC MAN
WIND
WINTERS

ANSWER, PAGE 315

173. The Play's the Thing

```
L A S R A E H E R S S E R D S E P L S W C A S T H
E N E Y R O U D O P I S P H C A L T I K E U S U H
E E N I T A M P O E N A L N E R A E T G H D E O Y
R T O H S I N R K P T Y A O N G Y U M U H I T Y S
A S T A E S D O O G E M Y T E B W T H E A T E R E
E I C N H K T E L U R N B N R C R S L I I I I T G
P B A L C O N Y N O M E I N Y D I R E C T O R N T
S B E A R C A D F A I L L N U S G F K M B N I W G
E R B E O T E R H E S Y L T G H H E F R U A I O N
K C O T S R E M M U S I C A L N T K O O T T Y T O
A U U T S P D N R D I E D R D S U A T R X A S F N
H D W T C R H O P R O P S E A L D M U T Y O A O O
S E U C A A H U R E N S A Y I W I C B N G R B T C
Y D E M O C H E T O N Y A W A R D B L E C E N U M
Y I A R A N D R E W L L O Y D W E B B E R R E O N
```

ACT ONE	CAST	GOOD SEATS	PLAYBILL
ACTORS	CHORUS LINE	HOT TICKET	PLAYWRIGHT
AD LIB	COMEDY	INTERMISSION	PROPS
ANDREW LLOYD WEBBER	COSTUMES	LIGHTING	SCENERY
ASIDE	CUES	MATINEE	SHAKESPEARE
AUDITION	CURTAIN	MUSICAL	STAGE
BACKDROPS	DIRECTOR	OPENING NUMBER	SUMMER STOCK
BALCONY	DRAMA	ORCHESTRA	THEATER
BOX OFFICE	DRESS REHEARSAL	OUT-OF-TOWN TRYOUT	TONY AWARD
BROADWAY	FARCE	PERFORMANCE	UNDERSTUDY

ANSWER, PAGE 316

174. You Wanna Pisa Me?

Shaped like the Leaning Tower of Pisa, the grid below contains references to Italy.

ALPS
AMORE
ARMANI
ARNO
CAESAR
COLOSSEUM
DOGE
"[LA] DOLCE VITA"
DUOMO
ETNA
FASHION
FELLINI
FLORENCE
GELATO
GENOA
GONDOLA
GRAPPA
GRAZIE
ITALIAN
LA SCALA
MICHELANGELO
MILAN
OPERA
PISA
PIZZA
POMPEII
ROMAN EMPIRE
ROME
SAN MARCO
SICILY
TRATTORIA
TREVI FOUNTAIN
UFFIZI
VATICAN
VENICE
WINE

```
                    N W H
                  E I A A A T G
                  N A N C T R E H
                  I T A L I A N E
                  E N M A I T O O
                O P U M Z O T A N
                H I O I Z R O T V
                S R F M I A R F Y
                E F I I P S I A
                U O V C U E A S
              A A R E H E A I H
              F L O R E N C E I
              Y A O T L E S L O
              A C I D A A K E N
              T S V E N I C E A
              I A G M G O S B
              V L A E E P G I
            D E R M I L A N Y
            U C O I A O A L E
            O L M G P M I T G
            M O A I R C F Z O
            O D N A I Z E R D
            M U E S S O L O C
            A O M P I E L M
          W A P P A R G I E
          T I I I E H A N T
          S S N R A R M I E
          A S S E I Z A R G
```

ANSWER, PAGE 316

175. Op-Position

The word list contains 24 pairs of opposites. One item in each pair appears in the arrow pointing left; the other appears in the arrow pointing right. It's up to you to figure out which goes in which position. For good measure, the word OPPOSITES connects the two arrows and appears exactly in the center of the grid.

```
                              C                   I
                          O   L               F   O
                      N   P   U               A   E   P
                  F   E   O   M               G   S   X   I
              I   T   G   S   S               I   E   S   P   A
          D   E   K   A   N   Y               L   P   T   T   E   S
      E   A   R   T   T   A   T               E   P   O   O   R   N   T
  N   N   R   E   C   I   T   N               L   W   H   S   M   O   S   A
T   G   Y   D   I   B   V   D   A             G   Y   T   L   I   U   G   I   R
E   R   I   N   N   O   C   E   N   T         N   O   A   Y   O   T   N   M   V   V
I   Y   O   D   S   I   T   O   H   F   R     I   C   N   I   N   O   I   S   Y   E   I
U   U   S   P   E   L   G   V   W   R   E   O S   I   R   F   E   F   R   V   U   T   C   N
Q H T N E I C N A I O P P O S I T E S U N W A V E R I N G
H   U   E   N   R   C   I   C   S   G   L   M S   O   L   M   G   O   T   P   A   N   E   O
A   G   N   R   Y   O   O   H   A   Y   I     D   F   A   F   N   R   P   Z   T   E   R
E   E   A   U   G   L   Y   E   R   O         E   P   C   L   I   K   Y   R   E   G
M   M   W   T   F   W   H   A   O             H   T   T   V   Z   S   O   H   E
P   I   U   N   A   N   T   P                 T   N   I   C   E   V   H   O
L   O   K   S   A   N   E                     O   A   V   T   E   N   U
O   H   H   S   E   E                         L   S   E   R   R   S
Y   Y   T   D   A                             C   M   T   E   F
E   Y   E   E                                 W   E   D   A
D   S   Y                                     D   O   A
S   W                                         M   E
D                                             O
```

OPPOSITES

ACTIVE	SEDENTARY	GUILTY	INNOCENT
AGILE	CLUMSY	HUGE	TINY
ANCIENT	MODERN	IMPORTANT	TRIVIAL
ANGRY	CALM	INTROVERTED	OUTGOING
BOILING	FREEZING	MARRIED	SINGLE
CHEAP	EXPENSIVE	NASTY	NICE
CLOTHED	NAKED	NEGATIVE	POSITIVE
CONFIDENT	UNSURE	NOISY	QUIET
CRAZY	SANE	PLAYFUL	SERIOUS
EMPLOYED	OUT OF WORK	POOR	RICH
GIVING	SELFISH	SATED	STARVING
GORGEOUS	UGLY	UNWAVERING	WISHY-WASHY

ANSWER, PAGE 317

176. People Who Work Outdoors

```
R R W O R F K F O R E S T R A N G E R I N G O
U E T D R A O O I R T S D I A M R E T E M C R
T T P E A R A L G R U B T A C E O N O F V O L
E N S P T M E P E N E B E O G P U R E T L O U
L I T U A E Y E T O U F W G G H N B F I U R M
A A T D R R T E R O E B I I N G D I A R B E B
V P S O R V T W W E O R E G N E S S E M R P E
G E H I E L E S E Y F C O O H H K N L L I E R
N S E N L C T Y E K C O J D E T E I N T C E J
I U D G A F E E O E S F O R E D E O C R K K A
K O C R H O S N S R I N M R R V P R G A L E C
R H B R W I D M R O T A V A C X E G E C A M K
A A P R O S K I E R N N G R E W R T A L Y A L
P Y T D I T C H D I G G E R A K E I S T E G S
C O N S T R U C T I O N W O R K E R T O R L L
```

BRICKLAYER
CAT BURGLAR
CHIMNEY SWEEP
CONSTRUCTION WORKER
COWBOY
DITCH DIGGER
EXCAVATOR
FARMER

FIREFIGHTER
FISHERMAN
FOREST RANGER
GAMEKEEPER
GARDENER
GROUNDSKEEPER
HOUSE PAINTER
JOCKEY

LUMBERJACK
MESSENGER
METER MAID
MOVER
PARKING VALET
PIT CREW
PRO SKIER
RIGGER

ROOFER
SAILOR
SERF
STEVEDORE
STREET VENDOR
SURVEYOR
TRAPPER
WHALER

ANSWER, PAGE 317

177. Honorable Mention

Shaped like a plaque, the grid below contains references to awards, prizes, and honors.

A TOAST
BLUE RIBBON
BOOBY PRIZE
CERTIFICATE
CITATION
CLIO
CROWN
DIPLOMA
EDGAR
EMMY
FELLOWSHIP
GARLAND
GOLDEN GLOBE
GOLD STAR
GRAMMY
GRANT
HONORARY DEGREE
JACKPOT
KNIGHTHOOD
KUDOS
LOVING CUP

MEDAL
MERIT BADGE
MVP AWARD
NOBEL
OBIE
OSCAR
PALME D'OR
PHI BETA KAPPA KEY
PLAQUE
PULITZER
PURPLE HEART
ROUND OF
    APPLAUSE
SEAL OF APPROVAL
SILVER PLATTER
STANDING OVATION
TITLE
TONY
TROPHY
TWENTY-ONE-GUN
    SALUTE

```
F E L L O W S H I P L K U D O S L
E T T H M T H I S E B E Y R T O A
U U R E O C E R T I F I C A T E V
M L D E O N T Y G B T O N W R K O
P A L M E D O R M O E D E A L N R
L S Y M O N A R Y M I O B P U I P
R N S Y E N L T A N A F O V F G P
P U L I T Z E R G R O R L M R H A
U G E W T S A O T A Y H G E I T F
R E T U H E V P R C C D N B T H O
P N R H Q A S H E S I P E R I O L
L O Z A T A I Y E O T T D G B O A
E Y E I G O L D S T A R L A R D E
H T O N Y D V P R K T I O P B E S
E N B O N O E R A T I H G U R O E
A E N E Z I R P Y B O O B C E C T
R W H E V I P C T O N R I G S R H
  T T E S U A L P P A F O D N U O R
  E T O P K C A J W H O L C I A W D
  N M E R I T B A D G E G V O N
    Y I T A T L T O N B E O A
    B L U E R I B B O N L
    J O R O T H N N R
      D I P L O M A
        S L E A G
        X C E
```

ANSWER, PAGE 318

178. Take It Like a Man

In the man-shaped grid below, every item in the word list contains the letters MAN in consecutive order. When these letters appear in the grid, they have been replaced by a 🚹. We hope you'll 🚹AGE just fine.

ALMANAC
APE-MAN
BALLETOMANE
BATMAN
BEDSIDE MANNER
BEST MAN
CAYMAN ISLANDS
CHAIRMAN
CON MAN
DOBERMAN PINSCHER
DOORMAN
DORMANT
EMANCIPATE
FOREMAN
GENE HACKMAN
GERMANY
HIT MAN
INHUMAN
KATMANDU
MADMAN
MANAGER
MANATEE
MANDOLIN
MANGER
MANGOES
MANIAC
MANILA
MANKIND
MANNEQUIN
MANO A MANO
"MAN OF LA MANCHA"
MANSION
MANTRA
MANUSCRIPT
MICKEY MANTLE
NO-MAN'S-LAND

NORMANDY
ON DEMAND
PAC-MAN
PERFORMANCE
POLICEWOMAN
PORTUGUESE
   MAN-O-WAR
PRAYING MANTIS
REPAIRMAN
ROMANIA
ROMANTIC
SALAMANDER
SPORTSMANSHIP
WOMANIZER
YES-MAN

ANSWER, PAGE 318

179. That Really Hits the Spa

```
I U S T A I H S F M A N I C U R E S Y T O U M
E A N N K R O W P E T S A T O K S E E S E P A
S O U W Y P E I L L I A S T H G I E W T F I L
S A I P P R A M O H T A B D U M C S S R I E D
S B L D A E E M C T H G P E L R R E S E O S S
C Y C I R O U I P T H E I A P U E N O T N E K
I S I N E A A N K E D T A W R B X H A C O B U
B M T C H T C G T I R F H Y O W E R I H U O N
O A S E T R H E C N O I T A T I D E M K A R W
R S I N A L T U H T R T N H E S T E B E E T O
E S L S M M R R O L F I N G X T I E E S R S D
A A O E O E R O P E R S O N A L G R O W T H M
L G H I R V E O R F A C I A L S H R W E A A I
N E O D A E O L O L H O S W E A T S U I T E L
B O D Y A L I G N M E N T L R M S E S S S R S
```

AEROBICS
AROMATHERAPY
BODY ALIGNMENT
CARDIO
DIET
EXERCISE
FACIALS
GET FIT
HOLISTIC
INCENSE

LEOTARDS
LIFT WEIGHTS
MANICURES
MASSAGE
MATS
MEDITATION
MUD BATH
NATURE HIKES
PAMPERING
PEDICURE

PERSONAL GROWTH
REIKI
RELAX
RESORT
ROBES
ROLFING
SAUNA
SEAWEED WRAP
SHIATSU
SLIM DOWN

STEAM ROOM
STEP WORK
STRETCH
SWEAT SUIT
SWIMMING
TAI CHI
TIGHTS
TONE UP
WHIRLPOOL
YOGA

ANSWER, PAGE 319

180. Abbr.-ations

The list below contains abbreviations for common words and phrases that are hidden in the grid. It's up to you to figure what those spelled-out entries are. Two hints: the numbers in parentheses tell you the number of letters in the words; and the list is in alphabetical order based on the spelled-out versions. If you need help, the complete list can be found on page 253.

```
A F M Y I O E S R U N D E R E T S I G E R L G
H S I E R E U O S A R S N M D O T O M B N I N
N O S R E P T N A T R O P M I Y R E V O L M I
E C T O O C M E C E E H U A A O R V O A I I N
P D E M O C R A T E M A O T P G W P R S A T O
P P R D G N O R T R U O H R E P S E L I M E I
O G U L T R A V I O L E T N S A N E Y O A D T
S S A T U U L S G E O T C A E E M D E O I G I
T T I L Q N S E P C V Y O T G I P N T S U H D
E E H D L N O Y K O R E B O T C O O Q G E O N
X L A G T O K A N O S E N T M C B U W A Z Z O
C E J Y I O N I O A G S R S Q U A R E E T J C
H R N A A E O M C A P A I C O L A R N R R U R
A R N D D B W E K C P M O B I H O M E R U N I
N A M N E I N C O T S P O F L R E H S O A I A
G B N O I T A L U D O M Y C N E U Q E R F O N
E D C M E P S E T U N I M R E P S D R O W R O
```

AC (3,12)	ER (9,4)	KO (8)	PX (4,8)
aka (4,5,2)	FM (9,10)	Ltd (7)	R.N. (10,5)
ASAP (2,4,2,8)	gal (6)	mph (5,3,4)	rte (5)
bbl (6)	Gen (7)	Mr (6)	sq (6)
c/o (4,2)	HQ (12)	Mon (6)	tsp (8)
co (7)	Hz (5)	Oct (7)	UV (11)
Dem (8)	HR (4,3)	oz (5)	VIP (4,9,6)
DQ (10)	hp (10)	pkg (7)	vol (6)
Dr (6)	IOU (1,3,3)	pd (4)	wt (6)
doz (5)	Jr (6)	p/t (4,4)	WPM (5,3,6)

ANSWER, PAGE 319

181. It's a Mystery to Me!

Shaped like a keyhole, the grid below contains references to mystery and detective stories.

AGATHA CHRISTIE
ALIBI
BREAK-IN
CAPER
CASE
CLOUSEAU
CLUES
COLD TRAIL
CORPSE
COVER-UP
CRIME
DETECTIVE
EVIDENCE
GUILTY
HERCULE POIROT
HOLMES
"I WAS FRAMED!"
LEADS
MISSING
MOTIVE
MURDER
PLOT
POISON
PRIVATE EYE
SCENE
SECRETS
SLEUTH
SOLVE
SUE GRAFTON
SUSPECT
"THE BUTLER DID IT"
TWISTS
VICTIM
WEAPON
WHODUNIT
WITNESS

```
                S  U  S  P  E  C  T
             I  M  O  T  I  V  E  R  D
          H  W  O  W  R  C  I  R  E  I  O
       R  W  A  I  R  O  W  D  T  I  T  M  R
       C  A  S  E  V  T  S  E  M  L  O  H  E
       E  T  F  E  R  E  C  N  A  D  R  G  P
       S  A  R  M  N  T  R  C  A  P  I  L  A
       S  U  A  L  I  U  A  E  S  U  O  L  C
       P  U  M  V  K  S  O  L  V  E  P  N  Y
       A  N  E  P  A  O  S  E  C  R  E  T  S
          E  D  G  E  D  E  I  I  S  L  E
          V  R  R  V  E  V  N  I  U
          S  I  B  A  A  C  U  G  C
          R  E  C  T  F  G  D  I  R
       T  F  O  E  T  L  T  P  R  E  I
       S  S  E  N  T  I  W  O  N  H  S
       L  Y  M  V  N  A  M  I  N  E  C
    P  E  N  T  U  I  R  N  S  D  A  E  L
    L  U  S  D  G  R  T  T  O  H  S  N  A
    O  T  O  E  E  D  D  E  N  P  T  E  L
 E  T  H  E  B  U  T  L  E  R  D  I  D  I  T
 C  W  T  I  V  E  L  O  O  R  S  T  O  B  R
 Y  A  G  A  T  H  A  C  H  R  I  S  T  I  E
```

ANSWER, PAGE 320

182. Things That Make You Sweat

```
F  G  H  W  A  W  A  I  T  I  N  G  A  V  E  R  D  I  C  T  H  I  F
I  F  N  S  E  B  R  O  W  I  R  I  S  K  Y  B  E  T  O  S  E  E  P
R  W  I  I  E  D  D  M  A  X  E  L  A  N  I  F  B  V  N  T  A  W  U
E  I  N  R  C  E  D  T  H  H  J  T  E  O  N  E  T  S  E  R  V  T  B
F  S  T  W  S  N  E  I  E  A  S  O  T  V  H  E  S  E  P  F  Y  S  L
I  A  E  E  R  T  A  N  N  I  N  G  B  O  O  T  H  S  A  N  L  S  I
G  W  R  R  H  A  D  D  M  G  E  T  E  I  E  T  R  H  L  I  I  E  C
H  T  R  C  U  A  L  A  N  A  N  M  D  L  N  Y  S  O  A  O  F  K  S
T  S  O  L  G  N  I  T  T  E  G  S  A  T  H  T  E  T  J  W  T  Y  P
I  H  G  O  L  E  N  W  O  E  T  A  L  G  N  I  E  B  O  R  I  R  E
N  S  A  U  N  A  E  I  L  D  S  I  N  T  G  D  H  R  E  H  N  R  A
G  F  T  A  C  E  S  F  N  O  R  T  R  O  P  I  C  S  V  H  G  U  K
E  O  I  E  R  A  M  T  H  G  I  N  W  E  S  M  B  N  O  I  D  C  I
T  P  O  C  A  Y  B  R  E  V  O  D  E  L  L  U  P  G  N  I  E  B  N
A  T  N  E  M  S  S  A  R  R  A  B  M  E  N  H  Y  M  T  A  N  W  G
```

AUDIT
AWAITING A VERDICT
BEING LATE
BEING PULLED OVER
   BY A COP
BIG GAME
CURRY
DANCING
DEADLINES

DEBTS
DESERT
DETAILS
EMBARRASSMENT
FEAR
FEVER
FINAL EXAM
FIREFIGHTING
FIRST DATES

GETTING LOST
HEAVY LIFTING
HOT STOVE
HUMIDITY
INTERROGATION
JALAPEÑO
JOB INTERVIEW
MISTAKE

NIGHTMARE
PUBLIC SPEAKING
RISKY BET
RUNNING
SAUNA
TANNING BOOTHS
TROPICS
WEDDING

ANSWER, PAGE 320

183. All Bottled Up

The bottle-shaped grid below contains things found in a bottle.

BBQ SAUCE
BEER
BLEACH
CATSUP
COLOGNE
DISHWASHING LIQUID
DISINFECTANT
GATORADE
GENIE
GLUE
HONEY
JUICE
LIQUOR
MAPLE SYRUP
MESSAGE
MILK
MOUTHWASH
MUSTARD
OLIVE OIL
PERFUME
PILLS
SALAD DRESSING
SHAMPOO
SHIP
SHOE POLISH
SODA
SUNTAN LOTION
VINEGAR
WATER
WINE

```
                    R  S  L
                    E  U  I
                 Y  E  N  O  H
              E  K  B  T  S  E  M
           M  U  S  T  A  R  D  E  A
           N  L  O  W  N  A  N  S  T
           D  G  H  E  L  G  W  S  F
           I  T  R  S  O  E  O  A  M
           U  A  L  L  T  N  S  G  T
        O  Q  L  O  I  I  I  A  E  I  E
     M  L  I  C  O  C  O  V  R  S  T  R  R
     A  P  L  A  N  A  N  E  D  P  I  H  S
     P  E  G  I  D  T  O  G  V  D  S  N  E
     L  A  N  D  Q  S  E  A  S  I  E  K  C
     E  R  I  T  I  U  S  T  L  S  L  L  U
     S  S  H  A  M  P  O  O  A  I  N  O  A
     Y  D  S  E  T  H  P  R  M  N  G  I  S
     R  S  A  H  C  E  E  A  I  F  E  D  Q
     U  D  W  D  O  I  M  D  E  E  N  N  B
     P  Q  H  H  O  U  U  E  O  C  I  L  B
     T  W  S  E  I  S  F  J  S  T  E  A  M
     G  N  I  S  S  E  R  D  D  A  L  A  S
     E  S  D  N  S  A  E  G  C  N  E  I  N
        A  B  O  E  T  P  H  T  T  L  E
```

ANSWER, PAGE 321

184. Making Connections

Help! A gap separates the two sections of the grid! To connect those sections, fill in the gap by writing in letters from the word list that are missing in the grid. When you're done, read those filled-in letters across the gap and you'll find out the name of the connection you've just made.

```
N A E N A R R E T I D E M W S H O E P O
E E N N H U D S O N B A Y I C O L N E I
Z R L U G O M B N I A P R R E I F A R R
T I R S L L A F A R A G A I N U D S S A
G O E D N T I E G C I C R Y M R S F I T
N D O R A T H S I T I C A R I B B E A N
A E R I E E P F H T R B R A O J E C N O
Y L T T C H I E C C A U T H A M E S G S
S A E N O C T R I P H I T R I M O O U P

S L S E A T O A E O R I N O C O E Z F P
E A A S I N T S K C I A M N C A S F O R
T T E S D E G D A I O T F I E E D R F N
A A O S N N M C L O G R T E B L E L A O
R M B O I I A S R U R N A U L E R E L A
H B A R E N T S S E A N N L S E G N A G
P R E P E I N D D L N A G O S E T T S O
U B B U I L D T T H D E C A A E N A K L
E N I E S T L A W R E N C E S E A W A Y
```

ADRIATIC	DANUBE	INDIAN OCEAN	RHINE
AEGEAN	DNIEPER	LAKE MICHIGAN	RIO DE LA PLATA
AMAZON	ELBE	MEDITERRANEAN	RIO GRANDE
ARCTIC	ENGLISH CHANNEL	NIAGARA FALLS	ROSS SEA
ARNO	ERIE	NILE	SEINE
ATLANTIC	EUPHRATES	ONTARIO	ST. LAWRENCE SEAWAY
BARENTS SEA	GANGES	ORINOCO	TAMPA BAY
BERING SEA	GULF OF ALASKA	PACIFIC	THAMES
CARIBBEAN	HUDSON BAY	PERSIAN GULF	TIGRIS
CORAL SEA	HURON	RED SEA	YANGTZE

ANSWER, PAGE 321

185. Taking a Stand

Shaped like a painting held by an easel, the grid below contains references to the world of art.

ABSTRACT ART
AVANT-GARDE
"[THE] BIRTH OF VENUS"
CANVAS
CHAGALL
CHARCOAL
DA VINCI
DADA
DALI
EASEL
FINGER PAINTING
FORGERY
FRESCO
GAUGUIN
GOYA
IMPRESSIONISM
KLEE
"[THE] LAST SUPPER"
LOUVRE
MATISSE
MIRO
"MONA LISA"
MONET
MOULIN ROUGE
MURAL
OILS
PICASSO
PORTRAIT
PRADO
REMBRANDT
RENOIR
"[THE] SCREAM"
SEURAT
SISTINE CHAPEL
SKETCH
SOUP CANS
"[THE] STARRY NIGHT"
VAN GOGH
WATERCOLOR
"WHISTLER'S MOTHER"

```
R  F  I  N  G  E  R  P  A  I  N  T  I  N  G
O  T  H  O  A  E  I  S  T  M  Y  L  E  H  R
L  I  S  S  C  P  O  R  T  R  A  I  T  E  S
O  T  E  E  O  S  N  R  Y  A  N  E  H  D  A
C  L  R  S  U  N  E  V  F  O  H  T  R  I  B
R  H  T  S  T  R  R  R  I  S  O  T  H  C  E
E  L  C  I  P  A  A  M  F  M  L  A  N  K  S
T  R  A  T  C  A  R  T  S  B  A  E  I  A  I
A  P  M  A  E  F  O  R  G  E  R  Y  U  A  M
W  I  O  M  N  K  E  T  Y  I  U  N  G  O  P
G  I  N  M  P  L  S  O  R  N  M  T  U  A  R
A  V  A  N  T  G  A  R  D  E  I  L  A  N  E
T  B  L  S  L  U  T  D  T  O  I  G  G  O  S
C  C  I  R  E  M  B  R  A  N  D  T  H  O  S
B  H  S  E  P  T  R  M  R  V  U  A  U  T  I
W  A  A  V  A  N  G  O  G  H  I  P  R  L  O
Y  G  S  R  H  O  U  N  P  I  C  N  C  P  N
D  A  L  I  C  G  A  E  S  A  P  S  C  D  I
O  L  S  A  E  O  I  T  N  D  I  I  A  I  S
T  L  C  A  N  V  A  S  M  U  C  D  S  T  M
         I        L        A
         T        B        S
      E  S        L        S  E
      X  I        O        O  P
      L  A  S  T  S  U  P  P  E  R  E
      N  L        V           E  I
   G  I           R              L  M
   O  S           E              I  K
   Y                                V
   A                                E
```

ANSWER, PAGE 322

186. Taking It Hard

```
K C I R B T Y O F B U E O H S E S R O H A R R
N E S O N E L L O R R E N N I D D L O K E E W
A A N O T L C H I A Y N G A H P A P L M H V A
R E I D D L G U Y S W I H E C N E E M Y O O U
S C A L C U L U S S S M N N N A A A H T C C L
A H B E S B O O K K I A N G U D H C R E D E L
F I R E H Y D R A N T R E B P E O H B L M L E
E I H T E E A D R U O B T I G A H P E E A O H
T S O S F B N T M C E L P D N S N I T W T H S
Y H A R M O R A A K I E E N I G H T E A B N E
G O U T M U L H M L I L M I X S S N H I S A L
L F T A B L L A B E S A B C O C O N U T R M T
A O I N E D T T E S L E T H B T A H D R A H R
S D R T U E T E R C N O C K S A M E C A F N U
S E S S E R T T A M E M O S Y O N H E L M E T
```

ACORN
ARMOR
BASEBALL BAT
BONE
BOULDER
BOXING PUNCH
BRASS KNUCKLES
BRICK
BULLET

CALCULUS
COCONUT
CONCRETE
DIAMOND
ENAMEL
FACE MASK
FIRE HYDRANT
FRYING PAN
HARD HAT

HELMET
HORSESHOE
LEAD PIPE
MALLET
MANHOLE COVER
MARBLE
NAILS
PEACH PIT
PEARL

SAFETY GLASS
SHIELD
SLEDGEHAMMER
SOME HEADS
SOME MATTRESSES
STEEL DOOR
STONE WALL
TURTLE SHELL
WEEK-OLD DINNER ROLL

ANSWER, PAGE 322

187. Fish Tale

The fish-shaped grid below contains names of fish and ways to prepare or eat them.

```
                    I H N
                  C S C O A
                T I H C M D H         S D
                F E F I E O F     R T M M                         P E
            D F T I E Y E L L A W M U L L E T               G I I S
          S S A L H H P F O E T H O H S E I L Y         P R N R K E
        E T C   H I F A U I E A R O N N L E W T Y G R O P I A E S
      W I L R   I R O N M T L T N A H A N C H O V Y U A T T
        T H O E Y H D R I I R L P S P H L L I D E P A C E I U E D
          D S S E S T B H H P E I E O O C T P E R C H L H N N O
      T A R T A R S A U C E E A A T M A C K E R E L S       W E O A
        T M A E T S S R N O M L A S B O F               B B
            V T H R             E A I I
              O R I T           A S I
                D N L           H S
                  G S
```

ANCHOVY   FILLET   PERCH   STEAM
BONE   FLOUNDER   PIKE   SUSHI
BONITO   GROUPER   POACH   TARTAR SAUCE
BROIL   HALIBUT   PORGY   TILAPIA
CATFISH   HERRING   SALMON   TROUT
CHILEAN SEA BASS   LEMON   SCROD   TUNA
DEEP-FRY   MACKEREL   SKATE   WALLEYE
DILL   MAHI MAHI   SMELT   WHITEFISH
DOVER SOLE   MULLET   SNAPPER   WHITING

ANSWER, PAGE 323

188. Winding Down

Shaped like a stopwatch, the grid below contains references to time.

```
                          Y E A R
                          T T H
                          I O
      I                   U M                           E
            S T       M E R N I E I S       A D
            R E M I T G G E C G P M R E A A
              M G T L T E V C A M I O C R
                P C A H H E E L R I B E N E
            B U S U E C N R O O D D T C T U
            Y S P L I T S E C O N D S N E H
            A F F O U A U R K A I G T O M S
            N U U R N W A N H T G E A L O I
            D G Y S Y L I E I T H K I G N N
            B I L U L A L S A M T L L A O I
            Y T T N B T O M O R R O W W R S
              L P D T I U P I S L I E S H
              B I I E G G R A D N E L A C
                L A R I L B I K K O O Z
                L D D Y L E T A L E
                R I G H T N O W
```

AGES	DECADE	LONG AGO	SPLIT-SECOND
ATOMIC CLOCK	DIGITAL WATCH	MIDNIGHT	SUNDIAL
BIG BEN	EGG TIMER	MINUTE	"TEMPUS FUGIT"
BY-AND-BY	EONS	MONTH	TIMEPIECES
CALENDAR	HOURGLASS	NEVER	TOMORROW
CENTURY	IN A WINK	RIGHT NOW	WEEK
CHRONOMETER	LATELY	SOON	YEAR
DAILY	LITTLE HAND		

ANSWER, PAGE 323

189. Photo Finish

Shaped like a camera with a flash, the grid below contains references to cameras and photography.

APERTURE
BATTERY
BLOW-UP
CANDID
CONTACT SHEET
CROP
DARKROOM
DIGITAL CAMERA
DUPLICATES
EMULSION
EXPOSURE
FILM
FILTER
FLASHCUBE
FOCUS
IMAGE
INSTAMATIC
KODAK
LENS CAP
LOUPE
MATTE
MINOLTA
MODEL
MUG SHOT
NEGATIVE
NIKON
PHOTO
POINT-AND-SHOOT
POLAROIDS
POSE
PRINT
PROCESSING

ROLL
"SAY CHEESE!"
SEPIA
SLIDE
"SMILE!"
SPEED
SPOTLIGHT
STROBE
STUDIO
TINTYPE
TRIPOD
VIEWFINDER
ZOOM

```
                              T  H  S  T  R  E
                           P  L  M  H  O  O  O  M
                        D  T  I  E  I  O  O  U  L  G
                        E  L  R  D  N  H  G  A  I  L
                        E  B  U  C  H  S  A  L  F  P
                        P  T  H  D  H  D  C  O  E  N
                        S  M  O  O  Z  N  S  A  O  N
                        T  R  T  E  B  A  S  K  P  T
                           N  E  G  A  T  I  V  E
                           O  R  T  N  E  T
                                 T  I
                  E                 E  O
            S  P  H                 R  P
   S  O  A  U  E  C  E  L  S  R  P  A  Y  A  Y  S  P  S  T  P
   P  U  Y  O  B  A  U  T  E  E  H  S  T  C  A  T  N  O  C  R
   O  T  C  L  A  N  T  D  T  D  L  E  P  S  R  N  T  R  O
   T  E  H  O  S  D  N  T  A  A  O  P  H  O  T  O  D  I  H  C
   L  M  E  A  F  I  T  W  C  N  M  M  B  L  H  B  A  A  T  E
   I  U  E  T  F  D  I  G  I  T  A  L  C  A  M  E  R  A  R  S
   G  L  S  W  N  T  A  M  L  I  O  S  E  R  E  H  K  A  I  S
   H  S  E  S  L  I  D  E  P  W  E  X  P  O  S  U  R  E  P  I
   T  I  S  A  P  E  R  T  U  R  E  T  L  I  F  I  O  N  O  N
   V  O  D  E  E  E  D  P  D  E  X  K  A  D  O  K  O  I  D  G
   S  N  S  T  E  D  C  I  T  A  M  A  T  S  N  I  M  A  G  E
```

ANSWER, PAGE 324

190. End So It Goes ...

```
T  T  H  O  E  E  I  N  D  O  F  C  A  L  L  I  T  A  D  A  Y  A  L
H  L  I  T  A  I  N  T  O  V  E  R  T  I  L  L  I  T  S  O  V  E  R
A  O  H  I  O  U  A  T  S  I  V  A  L  A  T  S  A  H  R  E  N  A  G
T  H  A  N  K  S  F  O  R  C  O  M  I  N  G  Q  X  P  L  O  L  E  N
S  R  L  I  I  N  A  I  G  E  U  N  O  I  S  U  L  C  N  O  C  N  I
A  W  T  F  C  I  T  L  N  L  P  R  B  E  T  I  O  A  H  R  K  R  D
L  I  E  N  O  G  L  L  A  A  V  P  T  H  A  T  S  A  W  R  A  P  N
L  C  E  O  W  G  A  I  R  H  L  E  A  A  R  T  O  E  I  D  P  W  E
F  E  L  M  N  S  D  T  G  T  A  E  R  C  I  I  T  O  N  N  U  E  Y
O  D  H  O  P  E  Y  O  U  H  A  D  F  U  N  N  A  N  D  E  T  A  P
L  D  L  R  S  S  S  O  G  O  T  E  M  I  T  G  S  S  U  L  D  K  P
K  O  N  E  O  I  I  O  W  T  H  S  E  P  L  T  O  A  P  I  E  P  A
S  C  E  V  F  O  N  L  A  S  T  W  O  R  D  I  R  T  E  A  O  O  H
B  Y  E  B  Y  E  G  G  H  E  F  I  R  U  D  M  S  U  T  T  T  I  O
M  R  E  A  L  L  S  W  E  L  L  T  H  A  T  E  N  D  S  W  E  L  L
```

ADIEU
ADIOS
ALL GONE
ALL'S WELL THAT ENDS
   WELL
ALOHA
BYE-BYE
CALL IT A DAY
CAPPER
CIAO

CLOSING
DONE
[TILL THE] FAT LADY SINGS
FINALE
FINITO
HALT
HAPPY ENDING
HASTA LA VISTA
HOPE YOU HAD FUN
IN CONCLUSION ...

IT AIN'T OVER TILL
   IT'S OVER
IT'S CURTAINS
KAPUT
[THE] LAST WORD
LIGHTS OUT
NO MORE
[THE] PARTY'S OVER
QUITTING TIME

SO LONG
STOP
TAIL-END
THANKS FOR COMING
THAT'S ALL, FOLKS
THAT'S A WRAP
TIME TO GO
TOODLE-OO
WINDUP

ANSWER, PAGE 324

191. Taking Stock

Shaped like a bull, the grid contains words and phrases associated with the stock market. The hidden message is a silly but apt stock market report.

```
I  N  D  E  E  D
            A                                              I     R
      S  C                                          A           N
      E                                             A           R
      E                              S  D  N  E  D  I  V  I  D
      F                           D  M  R  A  L  L  Y  S
         U  A  I  N               B  E  A  R  S  H  S  K  U
      S  P  T  Y  D  S  G  N  I  D  A  R  T  R  E  D  I  S  N  I
      E  E  S  U  T  B  O  N  D  S  N  L  B  G  T  A  L  C  A  L  L
      R  E  K  O  R  B  V  S  B  C  O  U  M  I  P  Q     U  T  R  E
      A  R  C  I  C  E  S  S  D  U  L  O  F  N  W  N        A  N  C
      H  K  D  Y  S  E  S  O  P  L  Y  O  A  E  M
      S  P  C  T  W  A  L  L  S  T  R  E  E  T  G
   O  I  L  O  F  T  R  O  P  E  P  R  N  R  S  R  D  E
   N  E  R        M  N  A  I        D  O  W  J  O  N  E  S
   S  S              I  N           U  L              E  H
   P                 N              O           L  N
   E  C              G  H           A  A     L  N
   C  G              S  E           D  D
```

BEARS	DIVIDENDS	LOSS	PROFIT
BONDS	DOW JONES	MARGIN	RALLY
BROKER	EARNINGS	NASDAQ	RISK
BULLS	FEES	NO-LOAD	SELL
BUYER	FUTURES	NYSE	SHARES
CALL	HEDGE FUND	ON SPEC	STOCKS
CRASH	INSIDER TRADING	PORTFOLIO	WALL STREET
CYCLES	INVESTORS		

ANSWER, PAGE 325

192. The Wheel Thing

Shaped like a bicycle, the grid contains words and phrases associated with a bicycle.

```
            M
            U L O C K                     A S E A T
              H                             K
              A                             A
              I R R R E F L E C T O R
            I N                         A B U
          T R                          E   T E
      G C T E O     E               L I     R L S A W
    O Y G H H U P     I           L N     D U I L E E S
  R C E R G F R U U     N         A     L I S N A I D M V
E L A N G I S D N A H     N         D J E R S E Y T A I N T
E R I C O L N E C B C       A       E U T T E M L E H R R T
S P O K E D T F T H T     P U M P W A T E R B O T T L E E
F F O L L A F R U N A             A G A P I N A U S O D
H A N D L E B A R S P             B I K E L A N E B O N
  I S F A H B N E I               C Y R C L D E R E
  N N I W H C S                     E I W H E E L
    P A I R E                         T K I M T
```

BELL	HANDLEBARS	PUMP	TANDEM
BIKE LANE	HAND SIGNAL	PUNCTURE	TIRE PRESSURE
BRAKE	HEADLIGHT	RACE	TOUR DE FRANCE
CHAIN	HELMET	REFLECTOR	TRIATHLON
CYCLE	HORN	RIDE	TUBE
DERAILLEUR	JERSEY	RIMS	U-LOCK
FALL OFF	PANNIER	SCHWINN	WATER BOTTLE
FLAT	PATCH	SEAT	WHEEL
GEARS	PEDAL	SPOKE	

ANSWER, PAGE 325

193. Under the Big Top

Shaped like a circus tent with flags flying above, the grid contains things associated with a circus.

```
                              S W
                              T H A
                              A
                              B
                        T O D
            R O        E R S              A A
            E K I    C D C S T          U S A
            M        L B A N D          D
            A      Y O I E O H E        I
        S T G    O W T E O I N      G E T
      M U N R A B N O E L E P H A N T S
      S W O R D S W A L L O W E R C R U
      R N I O H F S F A A N S D J E O I
    N I E L I F H A I S B P J U G G L E R
    T C A G N I Y F E D H T A E D T A R E
    W N H R I T S E W S G N I R E E R H T
  E H W O O R T K T S I L A I R E A U A F O
  S I C D I M A R Y P N A M U H R T H Q P E
C R P I F L A M I N G H O O P S T I L T R E R
E O C S E I N O M E R E C F O R E T S A M I Z
U P H S F I R E E A T E R Y D N A C N O T T O C E
```

ACROBATS	CLOWN	HORSE	STILT
AERIALIST	COTTON CANDY	HUMAN PYRAMID	SWORD SWALLOWER
AUDIENCE	DEATH-DEFYING ACT	JUGGLER	TENT
BALLOONS	ELEPHANTS	LION TAMER	THREE RINGS
BAND	FIRE-EATER	MASTER OF CEREMONIES	TIGER
BARNUM	FLAMING HOOPS	POPCORN	TRAPEZE
CIRQUE DU SOLEIL	HIGH WIRE	SAFETY NET	WHIP

ANSWER, PAGE 326

194. Archetypes

In the arch-shaped grid below, every item in the word list contains the letters ARCH in consecutive order. When these letters appear in the grid, they have been replaced by an ∩. So, for example, the word ARCHRIVAL would appear in the grid as ∩RIVAL. We hope you find your footing fast so you won't be needing an ∩ support.

```
                        M O N ∩ Y
                      A Y N ∩ I N ∩
                    ∩ B R I P I D E R
                  M C H E D D ∩ E E S E
                S ∩ H B ∩ ∩       E ∩ S S I
              O A I U P             E I O A H
              S E N N D             H S R F I
            E S K G ∩               E I T M P
            N E U B E               M Y ∩ A ∩
            S R C D A               A D W M A
          ∩ N I ∩ N                 ∩ I V E S
          E ∩ O A D                 T O N N E
        T S E ∩ W                   C ∩ T D G
        ∩ D ∩ L E                   E E ∩ E T
        C R I U L                   S O T M S
        I O P P A                   E L S I I
      B H W E O                     O N ∩ ∩ T
      ∩ T U L P                     G R T N Y
      A O H A ∩                     Y O E A S
      R G T G E                     L C W O U
      T I S O D                     ∩ ∩ A I C
```

ANARCHIST	ARCHIPELAGO	CORN STARCH	PARCHED
ARCHAIC	ARCHITECT	GOTHIC ARCH	PARCHEESI
ARCHDIOCESE	ARCHIVES	HIERARCHY	PARCHMENT
ARCHDUKE	ARCHNESS	IDES OF MARCH	PLUTARCH
ARCHEOLOGY	ARCHWAY	MARCHING BAND	POPULAR CHOICE
ARCHERY	BAR CHART	MATRIARCH	WAR CHEST
ARCHIE BUNKER	CAR CHASE	MONARCHY	WORD SEARCH
ARCHIMEDES	CHEDDAR CHEESE		

ANSWER, PAGE 326

195. Of Thee I Sing

Shaped like a map of the United States, the grid contains words and phrases that appear in the first verses of three patriotic U.S. songs: "America the Beautiful," "America," and "The Star-Spangled Banner."

```
                                                                      T
                                                                   H     T
                                                                E     H     P
         B W G O O D P S O S T I L L T R                   F     G     I
       D U L R S T O U K A M T E L W R G I O T C           I     L A T
       B R O A D S T R I P E S R I E H A E F     S B     L     G E D
       A S U I N T I P E G A L L A N T L Y T     F A   Y   R H E
     U L T W N E D R L S U O I C A P S F E H     I   P L I A T Y
     A C I R E M A O E N S G P N I R M E R E D L R M I I R L
     B Y N H O M E O F T H E B R A V E A C E A A S L U T U G Y
     N I G H T A S E I T S E J A M I Y A R I E P E R N F L T V
       D I E S R A T S T H G I R B A R W N S R D F U I E R A
       T E N P E A C H E R E A E S G N I N I H S O T A E S
         E I W R E N N A B X F O P E T W D N R C U M B I
           E D O O H R E H T O R B E A E N G C A I I R E
             D A R O C K E T S R E D G L A R E N L T O I P
               C F S E V A W R E B M A B G P         N I
                 K S D E S O P                     E G
                     E A M                               K
                     H B
                     S
```

AMBER WAVES	DIED	IN AIR	PROOF
AMERICA	FIGHT	LAND OF THE FREE	PURPLE
BANNER	FLAG	LAST	RAMPARTS
BEAUTIFUL	FRUITED	LET FREEDOM RING	ROCKET'S RED GLARE
BOMBS	GALLANTLY	LIBERTY	SEA TO SHINING SEA
BRIGHT STARS	GLEAMING	MAJESTIES	SHED
BROAD STRIPES	GOOD	NIGHT	SKIES
BROTHERHOOD	GRACE	OF THEE I SING	SPACIOUS
BURSTING	GRAIN	O SAY	STILL
COUNTRY	HAILED	PILGRIMS' PRIDE	SWEET
CROWN	HOME OF THE BRAVE	PLAIN	TWILIGHT'S
DAWN'S EARLY LIGHT			

ANSWER, PAGE 327

196. Hand-Holding

Shaped like a hand, the grid contains things you hold.

```
            T H T
            L I N E E R E
            A A L L M Y C A L L S
              C H O P S T I C K S
    E F I N K R E T W     R E S E R V A T I O N
    O K H S U R B T N I A P     R S I H R O N B
    D S E U G N O T R E N O S I R P O S H T F I U P U
          F E O P F G C L Y T R A P T E W O L
          L O Y B H E R N O O P S C
  S E I N O M E R E C N O I T A U D A R G E G D U R G F
  O B A G O F G R O C E R I E S R E B W V S F A W L E L
  I K C O N V E R S A T I O N S S E N N S O T L A I O O
              H O O E L O C R F D L L J C G
    H P O L I T I C A L O F F I C E T E S S E S R O H
    W O R L D R E C O R D A M L N H R T T B R N D S B
    L O V G N I T E E M E O I R S I I A O N B O O K D
              B C L P F L P L C A M Y E R
        S O F B A T O N C K L L A R O K D U G
        A R E M O T E C O N T R O L M E
        S E N O H P L L E C
```

A JOB	CONVERSATION	[YOUR] HORSES	REMOTE CONTROL
ALL MY CALLS	COURSE	INFLUENCE	RESERVATION
BABY	COURT	KNIFE	SANDWICH
BAG OF GROCERIES	DOLL	[THE] LINE	SHARES OF STOCK
BATON	[YOUR] FIRE	MEETING	SPOON
BELIEF	FORK	OPINION	STILL
BOOK	FORTH	PAINTBRUSH	SWAY
[YOUR] BREATH	GLASS OF MILK	PARTY	[YOUR] TEMPER
CELL PHONE	GOLF CLUB	PENCIL	[YOUR] TONGUE
CHOPSTICKS	GRADUATION CEREMONIES	POLITICAL OFFICE	UMBRELLA
COMB	GRUDGE	PRISONER	WORLD RECORD
CONVENTION			

ANSWER, PAGE 327

137

197. Greenery Scenery

Shaped like a shamrock, the grid contains things that are green.

```
                    E M U S
                  D R A G O N
                E E M S G O N E
                Y M I T S L P G
                R I E E E O A E
                N L G R I N C H
                S S S A O I
          F Y J T   O J O L   T G C C
        U O A H N N   A A   D U R O A V
      E E D S P I N A C H I T R A R C W H
      N E A Y V M E L K C I P T P N T A R
      I E C Y I N C R E D I B L E H U L K
      P G O R F E H T T I M R E K U S E Y
        O V U S A I   Y L   D A S S O M
          A T O B     E O     F E K I
                      L C
                      S C
                    N R O T
                  S S A R G H
                E B L P B A C K
```

ALGAE	GRAPE	LEAF	PICKLE
AVOCADO	GRASS	MASTERS JACKET	PINE
BROCCOLI	GRINCH	MINT	POISON IVY
CACTUS	INCREDIBLE HULK	MOSS	SLIME
CORN HUSK	JADE	PARSLEY	SPINACH
DRAGON	KERMIT THE FROG	PEAS	TURTLE
EMERALD			

ANSWER, PAGE 328

198. Don't Let It Throw You

Shaped like a die, the grid contains things you throw.

```
                        V I C N E P O W O D N I W P
                      T O O K R Y S A G N O ● A I O
                    D N U O R A T H G I E W S E N O
                  E A N S T O ● G O W O L N I L ● L
                C C C O L D W A T E R O N T S L A A
              I O ● T A T H R W H A A S V H G A R R
            D A E R I Y R F U T P U N C H E N B O O
          O T   S   F   R   O   V     T C G A G T F
          U Y L T O Y I S T Y D H O   E R A R N T E
          T R O O P S I N T O A C T I O N U E I E N
          A E F N B S O O L T R T R   C D N M L N O
          R T A E V I S L I N T I N T H E T O W E L
          E T E S H A A D I S W A   I M L O O G S
          M O I U T B ●   P F W S A S T A E B B G M
          A P A R T Y ●   E L R E L   T G T Y A S
          R C G O O D M O N E Y A F T E R B A D
          K S O F F A P U R S U E R   F T O P
          N F E O S S A L S R T H A R N ● I
          Y O U R B A C K O U T O E   O T
          W A G A R B A G E O U T P W C
          A I T A L L A W A Y K Y S H
```

BOOMERANGS	GARBAGE OUT	ONE'S WEIGHT AROUND	SPEAR
BOWLING BALL	GOOD MONEY AFTER BAD	OUT A REMARK	STONES
CAUTION TO THE WIND	HISSY FIT	PARTY	SWITCH
COLD WATER ON	IN THE TOWEL	PASS	TANTRUM
CONFETTI	IT ALL AWAY	PITCH	TROOPS INTO ACTION
DARTS	LASSO	POTTERY	VOICE
DICE	LOOK	PUNCH	WINDOW OPEN
DOWN THE GAUNTLET	OFF A PURSUER	RACE	YOUR BACK OUT
FOOTBALL	ON A COAT	ROTTEN EGGS	YOURSELF INTO YOUR
FRISBEE	ONE FOR A LOOP	SHOE	WORK
GAME			

ANSWER, PAGE 328

199. The X Factor

The X-shaped grid holds words and phrases that contain the letter X. The hidden message spells out two possible alternative titles for this puzzle.

```
T O X I C R                           X P M H A R
  T U X E D O                       S U X E L K
    S A T X X U                   Y D Y X A W
      T E H A O T               X E E A S E
        P L X R R E           O X Y G E N
          O I L O E S     F I V O T O
            S M U L X I M O N A H
              O E X I F X I R P
                B N U P N T O
                  F N O R B L Y
                    L D P O T Y O S S
                  U X U R C X I T R U I
                X X L X A O   I X A A D X
              P M I R N N     O E X X O N
            X I F A N I         U T G S X N
          A X X Y E U             S X D M E E
        X A M I X Q                 T E X M E X
      S M A X E E                     R N X Y N O
```

ANNEX	IMAX	OBNOXIOUS	TOXIC
BORAX	IN A FIX	ONYX	TUXEDO
CRUX	INFLUX	OXYGEN	VOX POPULI
EQUINOX	LEXUS	PIXIE	WAXY
EXAM	LORAX	PRIX FIXE	X-AXIS
EXODUS	LUXURY TAX	RED SOX	XEROX
EXXON	MAXIM	ROUTE SIXTY-SIX	X-MEN
FOXY	MIXED UP	TAXI	X-RAY
HEXAGON	NEXT EXIT ONE MILE	TEX-MEX	XYLOPHONE

ANSWER, PAGE 329

200. Missing in Action

To find the missing word list, look below the grid where it says "Find." There'll you see nine different categories. Identify what words fit those categories and then look for those words in the grid. When you do, you'll see that one of the words in each category does not appear in the grid. Write that word in the blank in the "Missing" column next to the category. For example, if it said "Find 2 of the 3 colors of Olympics medals," you'd say GOLD, SILVER, and BRONZE. However, only two of those colors would appear in the grid. If you were to find SILVER and BRONZE in the grid but not GOLD, you'd then write GOLD in the appropriate blank. After you've filled in all the blanks, read the first letters of the missing words from top to bottom, column by column, to spell out a message that's quite appropriate for a grid shaped like a hand rising out of the ocean. If you're sinking instead of swimming, you can find both the word list and the missing words on page 253.

```
                              M
                        A     T
                        O     S     B
                        T     C     A
                  E     L     O     S
                  T  A  U  R  U  S        S
                  E  R  P  B  U  R
       G              I     K  N  I  F  E           O              E
    L  N  E     D  W  A        O  O  E        T  N  S        E  R  V
    A  I  N  I  M  E  G  A  Q  U  A  R  I  U  S  U  I  R  A  T  T  I  G  A  S
    A  V  B  R  E  S  W  U  T  A  K  T  I  C  A  N  C  E  R  D  T  K  N  C  V
    B  O  R  R  O  W  E  D  O  E  H  H  N  R  O  C  I  R  P  A  C  I  C  I  A
    V  L  E  G  A  E  S  O  N  E  R  T  E  O  D  H  T  U  O  S  L  N  R  A  A
    V  Y  U  J  N  H  T  R  A  E  O  I  W  P  I  S  C  E  S  L  N  G  E  S  J
    S  L  O  E  N  O  T  I  R  A  B  C  F  K  E  R  E  T  A  L  O  C  O  H  C
```

Find	Missing	Find	Missing
11 of the 12 signs of the zodiac	_____	2 of the 3 words in the abbreviation TLC	_____
3 of the 4 traditional "somethings" needed at a wedding	_____	2 of the 3 flavors in Neapolitan ice cream	_____
2 of the 3 most common pieces of silverware	_____	3 of the 4 main directional points on a compass	_____
4 of 5 of the most common voices in a choir	_____	3 of the 4 "elements" that were once thought to compose everything	_____
4 of the 5 cards in a royal flush	_____		

ANSWER, PAGE 329

201. Absolutely Super

Shaped like the shield on Superman's chest, the grid contains words and phrases about the superhero Superman.

```
            I G L E E T S F O N A M F I R
            I N V U L N E R A B L E S U T P E
          D O J E O Y E L L O W B E L T S P R S
        M R A N O C R A E M T N E K K R A L C E C
      E T I H W Y R R E P O R T E R U C P N I N A U
    V S I B T E D H E T H S M A L L V I L L E O R E E
  A L E L A K R R T T L O N H F T N E K A P D N A A M S
  R E F A S T E R T H A N A S P E E D I N G B U L L E T
    O T M T A D F A T V E M C R P L A N E E T E D C O
      E I I S B T H H I B R A H K L T P Z Y X M R M
        N N K O T M G L O E B J I M M Y O L S E N
          O O O A S I L O P O R T E M K U E T H
            I T O I L A T U E M E A F T N I L
            S P B F I H S M I M P H L D O
              I Y C N L S U E I O U E I
              V R I G T T A R L N S
                Y K M I S A C T L
                A L O O I I A
                R E C T N
                  X Y E
                  N
```

CAPE
CHIEF
CLARK KENT
COMIC BOOK
COSTUME
CRIME
FASTER THAN A SPEEDING
   BULLET
FLIGHT
HERO

INVULNERABLE
"IT'S A BIRD!"
"IT'S A PLANE!"
"IT'S SUPERMAN!"
JIMMY OLSEN
JOR-EL
KAL-EL
KRYPTONITE
LARA

LEX LUTHOR
LOIS LANE
MA AND PA KENT
MAN OF STEEL
METROPOLIS
MR. MXYZPTLK
PERRY WHITE
RED BOOTS
REPORTER

RESCUE
SECRET IDENTITY
SMALLVILLE
STRONG
SUPER-BREATH
TELEPHONE BOOTH
VILLAIN
X-RAY VISION
YELLOW BELT

ANSWER, PAGE 330

202. Soft-Spoken

Shaped like a teddy bear, the grid contains things that are always or sometimes soft. The hidden message is an adage made famous by the person for whom the teddy bear is named.

```
            S C P D S
          E I E A A K P
      S S S E R T T A M O S
      O U F T B L A N K E T
      M L E Y A A N L D C A
        T E D D Y B E A R
        R T R E Y C Y A P
        A B F J O B S
    I M T O O F S T I B B A R
  A O G B C B U T T E R S O E T S
  N N I A R I P W O M A N S T O U C H
E R C G K U E R G N I V I L A T C Y O U
Y P I L E O F L E A V E S   W W W O R D S
I O A L     R L D Z G O K       F M F
A L H       R T A W N E H N N
E S       O S E V O L G D I K
        S D O I P A A K R L O
        R I H I B   S N D O E
    R C S L N       O D T O W
    E U L A K       S S I K O
    C O E O S       E V O N L
    W B E C         L N T G
```

ANGORA
BABY'S BOTTOM
BEANBAG
BLANKET
BREEZE
BUTTER
COAL
COTTON
CUSHION
DATA

DRINKS
FOCUS
FUR COAT
GLOW
HAIR
JOBS
KID GLOVES
KISS
LANDING
LIVING

LOTION
MATTRESS
MONEY
MUSIC
PALATE
PILE OF LEAVES
PILLOW
POWDER PUFF
RABBIT'S FOOT
RAIN

SILK
SKIN
SLOPE
SPOT
SUEDE
TEDDY BEAR
VOICE
WATER
WOMAN'S TOUCH
WORDS

ANSWER, PAGE 330

203. Black Hole #4

In this word search, the letters in the center of the grid have been replaced by shaded squares. To solve, do as you usually do but bear this in mind: Several words on the word list cross into the shaded squares and need to have their missing letters filled in. When you're done, read those missing letters in order row by row to finish a joke that begins, "When I asked the clerk at the bookstore to show me the self-help section, she said . . . ." Then find the regular hidden message, which is another joke. Both jokes and more than a dozen items on the word list are related to the theme of books and self-help.

```
A  T  L  E  V  O  N  C  I  H  T  O  G  A  I  L  O  P
B  Y  R  W  H  O  T  O  R  K  N  E  F  N  A  U  O  A
E  S  R  N  B  E  E  H  S  D  I  T  O  D  I  E  A  G
S  I  M  O  N  I  Z  E  E  L  R  N  D  T  T  G  E  E
T  G  D  I  T  R  I  C  I  P  E  E  R  L  O  R  T
S  Y  N  T  T  S  L  H  L  E  N  S  Y  T  F  O  D  U
E  N  O  I  T  C  I  F  I  D  I  D  R  B  I  E  U  R
L  F  S  D  D  I  ■  ■  ■  ■  ■  ■  P  E  N  C  E  N
L  A  N  E  R  A  ■  ■  ■  ■  ■  ■  E  N  S  I  V  E
I  E  B  E  O  B  ■  ■  ■  ■  ■  ■  A  T  E  R  P  R
N  L  S  R  M  V  ■  ■  ■  ■  ■  ■  S  M  E  N  L  E
G  Y  A  W  A  N  ■  ■  ■  ■  ■  ■  I  D  O  N  E  L
A  L  W  R  N  D  R  O  I  R  T  R  M  E  D  A  H  L
U  F  T  B  C  O  O  O  C  T  K  V  C  P  R  A  F  I
T  L  L  E  E  D  S  R  S  N  E  E  U  I  A  T  L  R
H  Y  R  E  D  A  E  R  F  O  O  R  P  O  M  W  E  H
O  U  R  S  E  R  E  V  O  C  T  S  U  D  A  L  S  T
R  E  H  S  I  L  B  U  P  F  T  E  X  T  B  O  O  K
```

ADDENDA	GOTHIC NOVEL	POSEIDON	TEXTBOOK
BEST-SELLING AUTHOR	HEADINGS	PROOFREADER	THEATER
CONTROL	HISTORY	PUBLISHER	THE END
DAILIES	IN-PRINT	ROMANCE	THRILLER
DEFENSIVE	KINETIC	RUNAWAY	TOPICS
DRAMA	LABRADOR	SELF-HELP	TRAVEL
DUST COVER	NOBODY	SIMONIZE	TWOPENCE
EDITION	PAGE-TURNER	SPANNED	URGING
FICTION	PERVERSE	SWAP MEET	UTILIZE
FLYLEAF	POETRY	TAE-BO	WRITER

ANSWER, PAGE 331

204. Quick on the Draw

Shaped like a well you draw water from, the grid contains things you draw.

```
                    P W H A O S T W P W A
                    H A S E R U T A C I R A C
                  C O M I C S T R I P C L A D I
                T O B A T W F L A K H T G L O E R
              E R N E A O S U I W L T U C R O W D C
            K O F C U R T A I N S T N R H E L B C O L
          S S T O L D N T H S E L I T E L B B A R C S E
              U                       S
              S                       E
              I E S T H O P S C O T C H B O A R D
              O           A           N           B E
              N           L           B
              O         T A W         A
              I         E R E         L
              T         N Y T         L
              A                       S
          H W W R B N O S I R A P M O C E B G D T C W
          O A N I S E K E D E T C H A R L F O T E H I
          Y G O P S W A T E R F R O M A W E L L T E B
          S O O S L F I D T A A T E N E M Y F I R E D
          I N T N N A G L O E Y C K C E H C B I E R T
          D P R I S O N S E N T E N C E E N A R P S D
            E A D E D I S A N O S R E P I N L A L D
            C R A E C N E I D U A E G R A L W Y
```

A BEAD ON	[A] CHECK	FLIES	[A] POND
A GUN	CHEERS	[A] GOLF BALL	[A] PRISON SENTENCE
A MAP	[A] CIRCLE	[A] HOPSCOTCH "BOARD"	[A] REPLY
AWAY	[A] COMIC STRIP	INSPIRATION	[A] SALARY
[A] BASE ON BALLS	[A] COMPARISON	[A] LARGE AUDIENCE	SCRABBLE TILES
[A] BATH	[A] CONCLUSION	LOTS	[A] SKETCH
BEER	[A] CROWD	NEARER	STRAWS
[A] BLANK	[THE] CURTAINS	[AN] OUTLINE	[A] SWORD
BLOOD	[UP A] DEED	[A] PERSON ASIDE	[A] WAGON
CARDS	ENEMY FIRE	[A] PICTURE	WATER FROM A WELL
[A] CARICATURE	FLAK	[UP] PLANS	[UP A] WILL
[A] CARTOON			

ANSWER, PAGE 331

205. Two Left Feet

Shaped like two left feet, the grid contains the names of different dances.

```
        D G S C
        O A J A Z Z                          A R O H
        N B N L H C                      I H N G I O I
    W G C M S S S A                  B C O N G A E P E
    T A P D A N C E              R A A P H E N D H D
    N L L R U M B A          C H A R L E S T O N I
    T O R T X O F            C J G A C L W K W U
    W P L A Z R E        T E U N I M A E X N
    O B M I L P          R R D I E T Y S T
    S T O M P        K S F I W U P O
    T A N G O        N L O T S O
    E F M A L        I H W I K
    P O R B K    N   I I E
    F A N D A N G O S   Y Z
            R T W O   N
    H G U B R E T T I J T
    A U G O L C   L M D E
    S R L O I R
        F B A E
```

BALLET	FRUG	JITTERBUG	STOMP
BOLERO	GALOP	LIMBO	SWIM
CANCAN	HIGHLAND FLING	MAMBO	SWING
CHA-CHA	HOEDOWN	MINUET	TANGO
CHARLESTON	HOKEY POKEY	POLKA	TAP DANCE
CLOG	HORA	RUMBA	TWIST
CONGA	HULA	SALSA	TWO-STEP
FANDANGO	JAZZ	SAMBA	WALTZ
FOX TROT	JERK	SHAG	WATUSI

ANSWER, PAGE 332

206. You Can Bed on It

Shaped like a bed, the grid contains words and phrases associated with a bedroom.

```
                                        F
                                        O     R  S
                                        C  R  I  B        O
                                        A  R  G  O  W      N
                                        N  N  O  X  M      E
                                     M  O  A  O  B  R      D
                               H  R  T  P  B  D  E  E      E
    I              E  Y  D  D  E  T  U  D  Y  C  N  L  S   B
    A  L  A  R  M  C  L  O  C  K  O  A  U  F  B  R  P  O  I  D  A  R
    D  L  E  S  O  A  T  I  W  O  D  S  W  O  L  L  I  P  G  A  M  E
    R  T  E  V  U  D  T  L  G  B  S  P  R  E  A  D  A  B  H  R  A  T
    E  E  E  D  H  S  A  T  O  H  A  R  W  E  B  E  T  N  T  C  J  A
    S  R  T  E  O  M  R  A  R  Q  T  E  S  O  L  C  N  I  K  L  A  W
    S  L  I  P  P  E  R  S  U  E  J  S  E  L  D  N  A  C  I  E  P  T
    E     T  B  E  D  T  I  M  E  S  T  O  R  Y  M  A  H  S  H  T  V
    R        A  C  C  L  O  T  H  E  S  N  U  B  O  O  K  S  O  N  S
    E           H  T  H  R  O  W  S  H  E  E  T  S                 E
                E  R  U  T  C  I  P                                T
                S
                T
```

ALARM CLOCK	CRIB	LAMP	SHAM
BEDTIME STORY	DRESSER	"LIGHTS OUT!"	SHEETS
BLANKETS	DUVET	MATTRESS	SLIPPERS
BOOKS	FUTON	PAJAMAS	SPREAD
CANDLES	GOODNIGHT KISS	PICTURE	TEDDY
CANOPY	GOWN	PILLOWS	THROWS
CLOTHES	HEADBOARD	QUILT	TV SET
COVERS	HOPE CHEST	RADIO	WALK-IN CLOSET
CRADLE	JEWELRY BOX	ROBE	WATERBED

ANSWER, PAGE 332

207. Small Wonder

Shaped like an atom, the grid contains things that are tiny or small. The hidden message completes a verse by the poet Hilaire Belloc that begins, "The Microbe is so very small / You cannot make him out at all."

```
                              B U G
                            E T E S M
          F A A             Y N N E P
          L I C E           E D I C E           N S Y
          E T O K E N       O S A O S       N G L U M
          A G R A I N O F S A N D R I L L B I T
            I N G N T E A R E D R S T I T C H E
            S W U P T N E E L I O P P R L
              B A B Y E L F E B H O O
                P Y E N   I G M C
                P C D     N H I
              D T E L A   T I G O H
          S W R U E E E L P M E E H T
        I M A O M N S S H R I M P B R A D
        T R N H S I X T Y F O U R T H N O T E
        F E R O U   A M G P H   H P E A S A
        M G I       P M O T A       K C I T
                    L R C T R       O S L
                    E C O O E
                      I P E
```

ACORNS	EYE OF A NEEDLE	LADYBUG	[ONE] SECOND
ATOM	FINGERNAIL	LENS	SHRIMP
BABY	FLEA	LICE	SIXTY-FOURTH NOTE
BRAD	GENE	MICROCHIP	STAPLE
DICE	GERM	PAWN	STITCH
DRILL BIT	GRAIN OF SAND	PEAS	TEAR[DROP]
DUST MOTE	HUMMINGBIRDS	PENNY	THIMBLE
DWARF	IOTA	PILLS	TICK
ELECTRON	KITTEN	PORE	TOKEN

ANSWER, PAGE 333

208. Petal Pushers

Shaped like a tulip, the grid contains words and phrases about flowers.

```
      A D R         T Y I             S T T
      L I L Y     H E A U N         C H H E
      A B L O S S O M G A R D E N I A S
      I F O R G E T M E N O T N S B G E
        O R C H I D F S F O R T T I T
        O M G C O R J O M P L E E S T
        E Q U E E N A N N E S L A C E
          W I M N T C M H T H T E U
          B E A S T K S U C O R C S
  U           S U L O I D A L G Y T           Y
  O F         R E D N A E L O M             F Y
  L D O       W T F N Y               C N E
  C R A Z     H F S               R O S E
  S O A I N   E O N           D E R N A
    E R N S   P D E           P V S M
    P A N S Y U I I           A E R A S
    U I F C   L L T           Z C R G
    E A E L M P D A       L A Y I E
    S U T O L I S P       P I L U T
    N G O W   T R M       C L E H
      A L T E L O I V I A A
      B R G R A L S L C
```

AMARYLLIS	DAISY	LILAC	PANSY
ASTER	FORGET-ME-NOT	LILY	PEONY
AZALEA	GARDENIA	LOTUS	POSY
BLOOM	GENTIAN	MARIGOLD	QUEEN ANNE'S LACE
BLOSSOM	GLADIOLUS	MUMS	ROSE
CORNFLOWER	HIBISCUS	MYRTLE	THISTLE
CORSAGE	IMPATIENS	NOSEGAY	TULIP
CROCUS	IRIS	OLEANDER	VIOLET
DAFFODIL	JACK-IN-THE-PULPIT	ORCHID	ZINNIA

ANSWER, PAGE 333

209. Listen to This

Shaped like a bell, the grid contains things you listen to or hear.

```
            L  I  C  R  S  R  H
         S  L  O  R  A  C  C  U  T
      B  R  N  E  S  D  T  N  I  M  H
   N  E  C  E  T  N  I  A  L  P  M  O  C
   G  E  N  O  D  P  O  R  L  T  I  N  R
   R  P  M  I  S  N  D  A  E  T  A  K  C
T  N  E  M  E  C  N  U  O  N  N  A  R  O  T
W  I  R  L  O  N  G  C  H  M  O  Y  A  N  Y
I  B  A  E  T  H  H  K  E  T  F  O  S  F  L
N  S  I  S  T  A  U  D  I  O  T  A  P  E  E
D  N  C  E  A  M  O  C  R  E  T  N  I  S  C
C  S  R  E  M  M  A  H  K  C  A  J  U  S  T
H  E  R  E  C  M  E  S  T  F  O  C  R  I  U
M  I  C  P  O  R  L  F  O  F  L  X  F  A  O  R  S
T  M  L  E  A  P  S  I  T  L  E  N  G  I  N  E  I
E  E  E  L  E  H  R  T  C  I  D  R  E  V  R  Y  G
A  S  A  D  O  P  R  J  D  K  O  S  Y  M  C  E  H
E  R  I  U  B  R  S  Y  O  U  R  M  O  T  H  E  R
   L  I  A  M  T  O  G  E  V  U  O  Y  O  N  G  N  I  K  R  A  B
T  S  C  R  E  A  M  N  M  U  H  R  O  T  A  R  E  G  I  R  F  E  R
                  B
                  E
            H  L  E
            R  L  S
```

ANNOUNCEMENT	CRY FOR HELP	LECTURE	SERMON
AUDIOTAPE	DOORBELL	NOISE	SHOUT
BARKING	"DUCK!"	"OOPS!"	SIGH
BEEPER	ENGINE	PLEA	SIREN
CAR ALARM	EXCUSE	RADIO	SPEECH
CAROLS	"FIRE!"	REFRIGERATOR HUM	THUNDER
CLICK	HONK	RUMOR	VERDICT
COMPLAINT	INTERCOM	SALES PITCH	WIND CHIMES
CONCERT	JACKHAMMERS	SAME OLD SONG	YOUR MOTHER
CONFESSION	LAUGHTER	SCREAM	"YOU'VE GOT MAIL!"

ANSWER, PAGE 334

210. Follow Directions

The multi-arrowed grid contains words and phrases, each of which contains at least one directional word: UP, DOWN, RIGHT, or LEFT. These directions have been replaced by appropriate arrows in the grid. For example, LEFT IN THE LURCH would appear as ← INTHELURCH. So get ↓ to work → away. We hope you're ↑ for the challenge.

ACT UP	LEFT BRAIN	"[THE] RIGHT STUFF"	UPPITY
BRIGHTEN UP	LEFT FIELDER	RIGHT-WING	UPRIGHT PIANOS
CHECK UP ON	LEFTOVERS	RING UP	UPROOT
CRACKDOWN	MELTDOWN	"SHE LEFT ME!"	UPSIDE-DOWN
DOWNLOAD	MISTER RIGHT	SIZE UP	CAKE
FRIGHTEN	NO LEFT TURN	TEAR DOWN	UP TO NO GOOD
HOEDOWN	POP-UP	"THAT'S DOWNRIGHT	"UP, UP AND AWAY!"
"IT'S RIGHT UP YOUR	RIGHTEOUS	UNFAIR!"	"WHAT'S UP, DOC?"
ALLEY!"			

ANSWER, PAGE 334

211. Open for Business

Shaped like a can of worms, the grid contains things you open.

```
                                    M
                        O I N   E T A G   E F A S
              D             L   S D         I     E
              E S R U P     D       A     A L       Y
                    A       W       L       E     G E
        T F I G   C       O       B             L
        U   O E L K H T U O M I H K K E S P T A
        N   R L S A V I N G S A C C O U N T S S
        O   E T D G S D D A N O T E B O O K E S
        C   P E R E M A I D L C I H U B I T H E
        O   P K N U R T R A C E W T E S T J C S
        C   A C H E O A T H L E S N Y C A G E C
            R A E O W N L W A O I A S R I Y R A
            W J A E F S O F P W G R S T T B U S
            Y U R O O D P S T N M U C T O I S E
            D F T O N K A A O N I A E X G R A T
            N W L I A L E H P T N T E E E N E A
            A D W A C T H G C E D S E Y N A R R
            C H R I S T M A S P R E S E N T T C
              R E A O K S P U M B R E L L A E
                C E P O L E V N E N
```

BOXES	DOOR	JACKET	PACKAGE
CAGE	DRAWER	JARS	PURSE
CANDY WRAPPER	ENVELOPE	KEGS	RESTAURANT
CAN OF WORMS	[YOUR] EYES	LAPTOP	[A] SAFE
CARD	FILE	LOCK	SAVINGS ACCOUNT
CAR TRUNK	FLASK	[YOUR] MIND	STORE
CHRISTMAS PRESENT	FOLDER	[YOUR] MOUTH	SUITCASE
CLASP	GATE	NEGOTIATIONS	SWITCHBLADE
COCONUT	GIFT	NEWSPAPER	TREASURE CHEST
CRATE	GLASSES CASE	NOTEBOOK	UMBRELLA
DIALOGUE	[YOUR] HEART	[AN] OLD WOUND	WINDOW
			WINE BOTTLE

ANSWER, PAGE 335

212. Read All About It

Shaped like a mailbox, the grid contains things you read.

```
              O  M  E  M
              P  E  A  O
              W  I  L  L
              L
              L
              I
        P  L  E  S  B  R  O  C  H  U  R  E  G  A  S  S  E  M  F  E
        G  A  L  L  E  Y  S  H  E  A  D  L  I  N  E  S  M  S  A  A  F  E
        Y  B  E  D  R  A  C  G  N  I  T  E  E  R  G  O  M  N  L  T  I  Y
     H  I  V  E  A  T  L  L  N  N  I  F  W  E  I  T  S  Z  E  T  H  N  E
     B  O  E  S  T  H  P  O  I  N  I  S  K  Y  W  R  I  T  I  N  G  E  C
     N  G  I  S  G  N  I  K  R  A  P  T  G  W  A  N  T  A  D  S  U  P  H
     B  S  U  A  S  T  O  R  Y  A  T  R  S  I  E  E  W  E  I  V  E  R  A
  P  R  E  P  Y  P  F  E  R  P  K  O  O  B  I  R  R  T  C  A  T  O  I  R
  E  S  E  V  A  E  L  A  E  T  A  D  P  O  N  L  A  U  N  A  M  I  N  T
  W  A  T  C  H  M  P  R  E  P  A  R  E  D  S  T  A  T  E  M  E  N  T
              R  Y  T
              L  L  R
              A  A  U
              U  N  C
              N  G  T
              N  U  I
              A  A  O
              N  G  N
              G  E  S
```

ANNUAL REPORT	FINE PRINT	MAPS	REVIEW
BIBLE	GALLEYS	MEMO	[THE] RIOT ACT
BODY LANGUAGE	GREETING CARD	MENU	SKYWRITING
BOOK	HEADLINES	MESSAGE	STORY
BROCHURE	INSTRUCTIONS	NEWSPAPER	TEA LEAVES
CAPTION	LETTER	NOVELS	TOME
ESSAY	LISTINGS	PARKING SIGN	WANT ADS
EYE CHART	MAIL	PLAYBILL	[YOUR] WATCH
FANZINE	MANUAL	PREPARED STATEMENT	WILL

ANSWER, PAGE 335

213. Go for It

Shaped like a church, the grid contains places and things you go to.

```
                              B   E
                              G   S
                          O   T   O   L
                      T   O   W   N   L   T
                      R   Y   D   G   A   R
                      E   X   T   R   E   M   E   S
                      L   A   E   P   A   N   C   M
              P   E   E   L   S   A   A   D   A   I   N   N   O   A   G
          A   J   T   H   E   A   T   E   R           E   O   V   B   G   O
      R   T   B   A   O   G   L   I   E               C   I   T   A   L   H
  T   E   A   N   E   I   E   H   P   E               A   E   T   D   T   L   O
  Y   F   N   T   E   H   N   L   O   S   E   C       L   A   S   S   C   S   T   A   S
  O   K   N   B   X   G   D   L   R   O   W   Y   E   N   S   I   D   E   B   I   A   L   B
  U   D   I   A   T   N   D   O   G   H   T   R   A   E   E   H   T   F   O   S   D   N   E
  R   O   D   H   L   B   K   C   T   O   T           C   R   H   E   T   P   P   R
  R   E   S   S   E   R   D   R   I   A   H           R   A   I   R   P   O   R   T
  O   I   N   A   V   C   I   P   O   A   L           U   S   U   N   R   O   F   F
  O   I   C   S   E   Z   A   L   B   W   C           H   O   E   U   K   R   A   P
  M   H   E   A   L   T   H   C   L   U   B           C   W   E   D   D   I   N   G
```

[THE] AIRPORT	COURT	[THE] HEALTH CLUB	PIECES
[A] BALL GAME	[THE] DICTIONARY	[THE] HOSPITAL	[A] SHRINK
[THE] BANK	DINNER	JAIL	SLEEP
BATTLE	DISNEY WORLD	[THE] MALL	[THE] STORE
[THE] BEACH	[THE] ENDS OF THE EARTH	[THE] MOVIES	[THE] THEATER
BLAZES	EUROPE	[THE] NEXT LEVEL	TOWN
CHURCH	EXTREMES	[THE] OPERA	[A] WEDDING
COLLEGE	GREAT LENGTHS	[THE] PARK	WORK
[A] CONCERT	[THE] HAIRDRESSER	[A] PARTY	YOUR ROOM

ANSWER, PAGE 336

214. Everything to Lose

Shaped like reading glasses, the grid contains things you might lose.

```
        P  O  W  E  R                                          F  A  I  T  H
     I  A  G  A  P  M  S                                    E  P  E  C  O  L  T
     R  A  T  F  I  G  U  R  E           M  I  N  D         Y  E  P  A  M  R  S  S  M
  G  A  Y  I  L  E  C  A  R  R  N     O        N     E  N  O  T  E  L  C  S  U  M  M
  O  R  M  E  M  O  R  Y  E  S  F  M              U  R  H  N  W  H  O  M  L  R  O  S
  I  C  O  N  F  I  D  E  N  C  E                 O  O  O  W  A  G  E  R  T  N  T
  G  T  H  C  E  A  R  R  I  N  G                 C  R  L  S  G  N  I  R  A  E  B
  I  N  T  E  R  E  S  T  T  T  A                 K  R  G  O  E  G  D  E  M  A  G
     N  R  L  A  W  S  U  I  T                       F  I  R  O  O  M  P  W  W
        I  U  N  N  M  M  I                             C  A  R  K  E  Y  S
           H  T  E  E  T                                   N  H  R  S  G
```

[YOUR] BEARINGS	FOCUS	[A] LAWSUIT	[YOUR] PURSE
[YOUR] CAR KEYS	[A] GAME	[YOUR] LOOKS	[YOUR] TEETH
CONFIDENCE	[YOUR] GRIP	[YOUR] MEMORY	[YOUR] TEMPER
CONTACT	GROUND	[YOUR] MIND	TIME
[AN] EARRING	[YOUR] HAIR	MOMENTUM	TRUST
[YOUR] EDGE	[YOUR] HOMEWORK	MUSCLE TONE	[YOUR] TURN
FAITH	HOPE	PATIENCE	[A] WAGER
[YOUR] FIGURE	INTEREST	POWER	WEIGHT

ANSWER, PAGE 336

215. Movie Editing

Shaped like a drive-in movie screen, the grid contains the titles of 40 famous movies. Well, they were famous until we decided to edit them. In every instance, we changed one letter in the title and created a new plot for the movie, which we briefly describe in the clues below. For example, the clue "Marlon Brando/Al Pacino movie about the head of a New England fish family" would lead to THE CODFATHER. (The original film was, of course, THE GODFATHER.) In this case and similar ones where the word THE or A appears in the title, those little words will be omitted in the grid. When you consider the clues, think of the most famous movie or movies the actors or directors are known for. As an additional hint, we'll tell you that the edited movie titles for the clues below are in alphabetical order. If you need more help, fast-forward to page 254 for the full word list and the original movie titles. When you've completed the puzzle, the hidden message will describe two more movies and their edited titles.

```
N M M S I N K I N I N T H E R A I N I C H P A M R E D I P S C
A A R E G H I G H M O O N C P L A N E T O F T H E A C E S E O
M D G N O K D N I K U B P O R E N G N I D N I F L J E E F V P
O O A X O I W H E N H A R R Y B E T S A L L Y S A K N D L L G
R N A M N I E R D O O R C N T E O R I S Y A W R A T S L N O U
Y B A C S K T O O S T D H F J A B S E S U T C H I N A G O W N
T K U R T F F E K N A S T R R U S T L E R A S F L M I E T H W
T O C O R M I C C E N I W E H T H T I W E N O G E D H N A T S
E N A O U B U B A A S O M E L I K E I T N O T I D R A H G I D
R A B S C D Y I L I Z A R D O F O Z M W O D N I W R A E P W N
P V I W K L L U B G N I G A P U E S T P S N B I G D E S T S O
R C I T S A W O N D E R F U L L I N E K A W A L T S T R E E T
  I           I           M           R           C
  S           N           I           M           N
  U           E           N           A           U
  M           H           K           N           D
```

156

1. Katharine Hepburn/Spencer Tracy movie about a lie told in the Garden of Eden
2. Woody Allen comedy about a suburban shopping center named for a little orphan girl in the comics
3. Alfred Hitchcock thriller about old English poets who terrorize a small California town
4. Michael Keaton movie about a caped superhero who moonlights as a tavern worker
5. Russell Crowe movie about a gorgeous fur coat
6. Jack Nicholson detective movie about a fancy ball dress from Beijing
7. Sylvester Stallone movie about an arrogant boxer
8. Tom Cruise flick about a pilot who uses a policeman's weapon
9. Movie about lions who get a cob vegetable at no cost
10. Bruce Willis action flick about a tough excavation
11. Marx Brothers comedy about what mallards use to do laundry
12. Kevin Costner western about stupid people and animals that run in packs
13. Animated movie about fish who seek a fiddle-playing emperor
14. Harrison Ford/Kelly McGillis movie about an Amish health club
15. Clark Gable/Vivien Leigh drama about a cad who leaves once he's polished off all the Cabernet

16. Cher/Nicolas Cage romantic comedy in which Cher's character falls in love with a hoodlum
17. Rock Hudson/Elizabeth Taylor/James Dean biopic about a Civil War general who works on a Texas ranch
18. Beatles movie about a material used in making rope!
19. Will Smith movie about a female chicken who dresses in a formal color
20. Gary Cooper western about a marshal who fights a duel at night when a light in the sky is at its apex
21. Julie Andrews movie about a dog in an Elvis Presley song
22. James Stewart movie about a terrific come-on for picking up women
23. Steven Spielberg movie about a shark who doesn't bite but simply pokes people
24. Movie about a big but good-hearted ape
25. Judy Garland movie about a gecko in Munchkin land
26. Sean Connery movie about a physician who gives up his practice and becomes a common citizen
27. Robert Preston movie about a guy who sells stereo equipment from a paneled truck

28. Robert De Niro movie about how to beep a matador's opponent
29. James Stewart/Grace Kelly thriller about a guy who sees a crime committed through a fruit-shaped, glass opening in a wall
30. Charlton Heston sci-fi film about a world inhabited solely by World War I combat fliers
31. Julia Roberts/Richard Gere romantic comedy about a cute Italian
32. Dustin Hoffman/Tom Cruise movie about a jockey who's good at controlling horses
33. Paul Newman/Jackie Gleason film about a pool-shark-turned-cattle-thief
34. Alan Ladd western about a gunman who trembles during showdowns
35. Gene Kelly movie about goin' under during thunderstorms
36. Jack Lemmon/Tony Curtis/Marilyn Monroe comedy about a disapproving Yoda
37. Toby Maguire movie about an atlas page that shows where eight-legged insects live
38. George Lucas movie about the lifestyles of celebs in outer space
39. Michael Douglas movie about greed on a Disney World avenue
40. Billy Crystal/Meg Ryan romantic comedy about a wager between a guy and a girl

ANSWER, PAGE 337

216. Land of the Rising Sun

Shaped like the rising sun, the grid contains words and phrases associated with Japan.

```
                                    A
                  I                 L                 I
                  K                 L           N
         I              U   E   M   I   N   A   E           B
            K           B   B   S   O   Z   L   U   D   S       O
               A    K   U   A   U   A   I   D   L   R   H   T   A   T       N
      O            Y   D   R   H   L   Y   K   O   A   U   I   S   Z   M   S           E
         Y            O   D   I   G   S   L   R   N   G   B   K   E   E   N   A   U   D       Y
            K    T   H   J   M   R   I   E   A   A   O   E   P   I   A   I   O   S   R   N   E
   E            O   I   S   E   A   I   E   T   E   B   B   S   K   U   M   G   H   H   A   A   M           K
      O         S   S   T   I   C   G   C   G   T   T   A   T   A   M   I   J   O   W   I   N   P   I   E       I
         S    M   T   F   U   J   I   E   S   R   N   S   S   B   M   E   G   N   H   A   E   V   P   E       M
            I   A   Y   E   C   H   R   Y   S   A   N   T   H   E   M   U   M   T   H   R   O   N   E   O   O
               A   M   A   H   O   K   O   Y   N   I   F   S   E   O   N   A   C   L   O   V   O   R   M   N   R
      O   N   D   A   N   C   I   N   G   C   R   A   N   E   S   E   Y   C   H   E   R   R   Y   B   L   O   S   S   O   M   S
```

ANIME	EMPEROR	KYOTO	SHOGUN
BASEBALL	GEISHA	MIKADO	SONY
BONSAI	GINZA	MISO	SUSHI
BUDDHISM	GODZILLA	MT. FUJI	TATAMI
BULLET TRAIN	HONSHU	ORIGAMI	TEA GARDEN
CARS	IKEBANA	RICE	TERIYAKI
CHERRY BLOSSOMS	IWO JIMA	SAKI	TOKYO
CHRYSANTHEMUM	KABUKI	SAMURAI	VOLCANOES
THRONE	KIMONO	SAPPORO	YOKOHAMA
DANCING CRANES			

ANSWER, PAGE 337

217. Plane and Simple

Shaped like a plane, the grid contains words and phrases associated with airline travel. The hidden message answers the riddle, "Why do they hang mistletoe over the airport baggage center?"

```
                                                              E  E
                        N  C                          S  L  N
                     I  O  O                       G  B  S  O
                  K  C  P  C                    C  A  B  I  N
               C  C  O  A  K                 O  T  T  Y  A  S
            E  U  O  A  S  P  U  C  A  A  Y  N  E  M  I  T  N  O
            H  P  G  K  C  S  I  T  I  R  A  S  T  A  K  E  O  F  F
      M  S  Y  O  C  I  U  R  A  H  E  T  C  A  R  R  Y  O  N  L  C  P
   S  E  A  T  B  E  L  T  U  G  G  N  O  I  T  I  S  O  P  T  H  G  I  R  P  U
   Y  A  L  E  D  G  A  M  O  O  R  G  E  L  T  V  N  E           T  O  L  I  P
      L  G  D  E  P  A  R  T  U  R  E  U  K  C  A  N  S  I
                     R  E  L  G  L  X  O  O  V
                        S  W  I  N  D  O  W
                        D  B  M  Y  E
```

AISLE	COCKPIT	MOVIE	SNACK
ARRIVALS	DELAY	NONSTOP	TAKEOFF
CABIN	DEPARTURE	OCCUPIED	TAXI
CAPTAIN	GATE	ON TIME	TICKET
CARRY-ON	LEGROOM	PASSENGER	TRAY TABLE
CHECK-IN	LUGGAGE	PILOT	UPRIGHT POSITION
COACH	MEAL	SEAT BELT	WINDOW

ANSWER, PAGE 338

218. Hitting Below the Belt

Shaped liked a pair of shorts, the grids contains things that are worn at or below the waist.

```
            M  A  K  E  P  W  E  E  K  C  A  P  Y  N  N  A  F
            S  I  S  T  S  E  L  D  A  P  E  E  N  K  N  A  B
            L  O  N  G  U  N  D  E  R  W  E  A  R  K  G  I  O
         T  A  D  S  Y  Y  O  R  A  U  K  C  D  L  A  A  N  X  B
         S  C  S  F  A  L  Y  I  W  L  H  H  E  O  A  R  P  E  L
         R  K  T  E  T  Y  O  G  O  U  P  B  A  L  M  T  A  R  O
      I  U  S  W  I  M  M  I  N  G  T  R  U  N  K  S  E  N  S  O  K
      E  P  A  B  R  G  O  U  T  S  A  L  S  S  O  I  R  T  N  M  N
      G  H  P  D  B  R  H  E  S  C     S  T  G  H  E  S  Y  E  E  S
   B  U  D  I  A  P  E  R  T  E  T     T  L  N  H  E  E  H  S  R  Y  B
   H  T  O  L  C  N  I  O  L  S        E  O  S  T  R  O  H  S  E  C
   O  V  J  E  R  A  T  E  M  U        L  R  T  I  C  S  T  L  U  D
      S  K  I  R  T  S  E              A  N  K  L  E  T  O
         F  S  H  I                    S  S  N  S
```

ANKLE BRACELET	DIAPER	LOINCLOTH	SARONG
ANKLET	FANNY PACK	LONG UNDERWEAR	SHORTS
APRON	GARTERS	NYLONS	SKIRT
BELT	GIRDLE	PANTS	SLACKS
BLOOMERS	JODHPURS	PANTY HOSE	SOCKS
BOXERS	KHAKIS	PEDAL PUSHERS	SWIMMING TRUNKS
BRIEFS	KILT	PEDOMETER	TIGHTS
BUSTLE	KNEE PAD		

ANSWER, PAGE 338

219. Expense Account

Shaped like a price tag, the grid contains things that are expensive.

```
        S G Y G T G O O D C H A M P A G N E I D
      P V N A I E S T A O C R U F L G M E P L E
    A T O I A M O V I E S T A R S A L A R I E S
    S H M E R L S B O J E S O N V U S X I L L X I
U I I R A D O P O L O P O N Y I I M V E S A U G
O L     N N E L F T I F F A N Y L A M P L W S N
A V     T O S L E C I N F I E A T T R L N Y L E
B E     I M T I D X R I G P W E H V I I L E L R
D R O W Q A A G O L D U K H J I C V T R I R H G
    O A T U I T I O N U I I E A T A P I C A S S O
      T C E D E H E N D E T S C B Y E A S S F I W
      T E V E R E S T E X P E D I T I O N E A N
        I S E S S U P E R B O W L T I C K E T S
```

A PICASSO	EVEREST EXPEDITION	LEXUS	SAFARI
ALIMONY	FUR COATS	MANSION	SILVER
[AN] ANTIQUE	GALAS	MOVIE STAR SALARIES	SPAS
BRACES	GAMBLING HABIT	NOSE JOBS	SUPER BOWL TICKETS
CAVIAR	GOLD	PIANO	TIARA
CRUISE	GOOD CHAMPAGNE	PLASMA TV	TIFFANY LAMP
DESIGNER GOWNS	KIDS	POLO PONY	TUITION
DIAMOND RING	LAWYER'S FEE	PRIVATE JET	VILLA
ESTATE	LEICA	ROLEX	YACHT

ANSWER, PAGE 339

220. Suit to a Tea

In the teacup-shaped grid below, every item in the word list contains the letters TEA in consecutive order. When these letters appear in the grid, they have been replaced by a 🍵. So, for example, the word TEASPOON would appear in the grid as 🍵SPOON. When you're done, the hidden message will complete a quote by former First Lady Nancy Reagan that begins, "A woman is like a 🍵 bag ...."

```
              O N L S P I N Y A N 🍵 T E R Y I D N
                E K A C 🍵 H U 🍵 A H C O T 🍵 B E
                  I W 🍵 🍵 H G I H C O 🍵 A T R E N
        Y L I D 🍵 S N U 🍵 S U O C S E U Q C A J R I
        A       A S M R R K D O O Y S P I A E O A
        R       G 🍵 O 🍵 E U N G L M E N R T R 🍵 T
        T       R D O E L B 🍵 A R 🍵 U S E K T S
          O   🍵 O R A 🍵 L L B L S C M L W E I R
        Z P   F 🍵 E S H I 🍵 E F 🍵 H O B R O 🍵
          R 🍵 D N A R A E W W R S F T O E R L K O
                E C N A D 🍵 D O D N U R E 🍵
                  T B E D S 🍵 D W S 🍵 L T H Y
                  E C S 🍵 M B O A T T G S
                    S M A C U L A L U 🍵
                      🍵 H E P B E I S
```

BEDSTEAD	MACULA LUTEA	TEA CAKE	TEAPOT
BLOW OFF STEAM	PLATEAU	TEA CART	TEAR GAS
BRAINTEASER	RATEABLE	TEACUP	TEARJERKER
CHATEAU	SCENE-STEALER	TEA DANCE	TEAROOM
DRILL TEAM	SCHOOLTEACHER	TEAHOUSE	TEAR-STAINED
FLANK STEAK	SPINY ANTEATER	TEAKETTLE	TEA SET
HIGH TEA	STEALTHY	TEAKWOOD	TEA TRAY
INSTEAD OF	STEAMBOAT	TEAL BLUE	UNSTEADILY
JACQUES COUSTEAU	TEA BAG	TEAMSTER	WEAR AND TEAR

ANSWER, PAGE 339

221. Under Construction

Shaped like a bulldozer, the grid contains words and phrases associated with a construction site.

```
        I                   W E
        N               C E M E N T
        S               R   R W
        P       S       A   E O
        S E F D F H C N U L G A B H N
        A C P O U O O E     N E Y O T A U
T R B   R T B H U M R V S C A F F O L D I R
U S I L D O A I N N P K E G D S O T D R I L L       H
  I K C U R T P M U D S L L E L U R R V L E S     A T
  L O L D F T C E R T A T I B T R G E N E R A T O R
  E D H S E S S A L G Y T E F A S T H M V E   Y   I
  E A W   T S H O R A P L I R T S I B E A M S     D
E R T A   U U B S C T T H C O F F E E U R N     R
S C S     N H K R O W T A N E M I L G       L
```

BAG LUNCH	DRILL	HARD HAT	SAFETY GLASSES
BOLTS	DUMPSTER	HOIST	SAWS
BOULDERS	DUMP TRUCK	I-BEAMS	SCAFFOLD
CEMENT	FOREMAN	INSPECTOR	SHOVEL
COFFEE	FORKLIFT	"MEN AT WORK"	STEEL
CRANE	FOUNDATION	NAILS	TOOL BELT
"DANGER"	GENERATOR	NUTS	TRACTOR
DIRT	GRAVEL	RIVETS	TWO-BY-FOURS

ANSWER, PAGE 340

222. A Hole Lot Going On

Shaped like a button, the grid contains things that always or often have holes in them.

```
                N E E D L E W H
              C D R A O B G E P E N B
            I W O A S Y Y O O G U E S N
          W I F F L E B A L L G A O P I F
        F O O R Y K A E L F O D I B E P I P
        F U E N E D O N U G S R T K N T H O
    E B A M S       I D R E       C G T C R
    S P O U T       O E E A       I O L K E
    W P O T C       A H E R       L Y L E T
    E H O S S E E D C N N W A R T S D S T A
    U R P O B U T T O N S A L T S H A K E R
    S M I C L       M N A K       A I N A G
    B K G T A       P H U O       R L E B W
    E A C S T       A F I T       P D N A A
      S T O O A L A C E U P S H O E S S L
      T C H S K L S T V O N I S C N H T L
        L G T D O F D E P P N R E E D W
          E T U L F I I E A E E R R R
            B I B O S S R I N G L N
              G S C O P C K S
```

BAGEL	FAUCET	LEAKY ROOF	RING
BATHTUB	FLAT TIRE	LOCK	SALT SHAKER
BEADS	FLUTE	NEEDLE	SIEVE
BELT	FUNNEL	OLD SOCKS	SPOOL
BUTTONS	GHOST COSTUME	PEGBOARD	SPOUT
CHEERIOS	GOLF GREENS	PENCIL SHARPENER	STRAW
COLANDER	GRATER	PIERCED EAR	TEA BALL
COMPACT DISC	HOUSE KEY	PIPE	WASHER
DONUT	LACE-UP SHOES	POCKET	WIFFLE BALL

ANSWER, PAGE 340

223. It's a Good Sign

Shaped like a "For Sale" sign, the grid contains words and phrases associated with buying and selling a house.

```
D E V S L M P A S K I N G P R I C E
L D O O H R O B H G I E N E R O R R
O A A Y O O C R T H I Y T I U Q E E
S N S F N L W G T M O V I N G V A N
E I I O G S I W G O R T T L B L W
X T H S A A B A N K A E W I U H E O
A A I G T R I T S G R S Y D S S E
T N E M Y A P N W O D T E E C P T M
G N U R C G H P F I I R E R L A A O
T U P K E E P F A N S D O E R L T H
S E T I M R E T G S W W I L L P E A
Y F O C U R B A P P E A L A W Y E R
              R E
              O C
              P T
              E I
              R O
              T N
              Y R
              I T
```

AGENT	DEED	LISTING	REAL ESTATE
APPRAISAL	DOWN PAYMENT	LOAN	SELLER
ASKING PRICE	EQUITY	MORTGAGE	SHOWING
BANK	ESCROW	MOVING VAN	SOLD
BUYER	GARAGE	NEIGHBORHOOD	TAXES
CLOSING	HOMEOWNER	PROFIT	TERMITES
COUNTEROFFER	INSPECTION	PROPERTY	UPKEEP
CURB APPEAL	LAWYER		

ANSWER, PAGE 341

224. Jnana Banana

Shaped liked the combined letters J and B, the grid contains words, phrases, and names that break into parts starting with J and B.

```
                    N W O R B S E M A J W
                    A A L L A B P M U J O J
                    A Z E G U B E N U J L Z B
                    J A W B O N E S J A B N D
                    J E R R Y B U I L T E J U
                    O J M P R L M E D L O B A
                    H I U I L B L H T A J F
                    A S D N O B S E M A J
                    N E L W K U E T J
                    N E I L B B R
J G J J             E E P B E L O J U
A U O E             S T E S L B U N K T I
C B K W             B J E U N G E C D G J J
K R E E             R N B U B M A L P S A I N
B E B L B       G A N B A E L A N G S Y I N
O T O B J O S E P H I N E B A K E R N B T H
O T O O E J X A O M D U T K A E R B L I A J
T I K X R Y J J B S Z E A B N A O J O R J
    J G R E B S L R A J A N B R A D Y X D
```

JACKBOOT
JAILBREAK
JAMES BOND
JAMES BROWN
JAN BRADY
JAPANESE BEETLE
JARLSBERG
JAWBONES

JAYBIRD
JEB BUSH
JELLYBEAN
JERRY-BUILT
JET-BLACK
JEWEL BOX
JIM BOWIE

JINGLE BELLS
JITTERBUG
JOAN BAEZ
JOE BLOW
JOHANNES BRAHMS
JOHN BULL
JOKEBOOK

JOSEPHINE BAKER
JUG BAND
JUKEBOX
JUMP BALL
JUNE BRIDE
JUNE BUG
JUNK BONDS

ANSWER, PAGE 341

225. Wall-Done

Shaped like a mirror, the grid contains things commonly found on walls. The hidden message is a paraphrase of a quote by the French painter Pierre Auguste Renoir.

```
            P D M
          O Y P E L
        R S H E L V E S E
      D T K C O L C T R I L
      E X I T S I G N S H R
      R E N C I L D T A I P E O
      O C A N W I F R M L O H A
    F R A M E S A C Y A L P S I D
    R R L R C T N P Q A O C I I I
    S I E E R H P U N T O B U N I
    E M N D A G E I P N N G G T S
    M E D I C I N E C A B I N E T
    I L A P K L N E K T E N I R P
    H M R S S N D S R J U L T C O
    C U R T A I N R O D F R X O Y
    O R T N I A P E W U S N E M E
      A T E N O H P T T I L E S
      L B U R G L A R A L A R M
        Y R T S E P A T S S I
        T T O W E L R A C K F
          O R T E L T U O A
            I W A A L
            D W L
```

ARTWORK	DISPLAY CASE	MIRROR	PLAQUE
BURGLAR ALARM	EXIT SIGNS	MURAL	POSTER
CALENDAR	FIRE EXTINGUISHER	NAILS	SCONCE
CHIMES	FLIES	OUTLET	SHELVES
CLOCK	FRAMES	PAINT	SPIDER-MAN
CRACKS	INTERCOM	PEGBOARD	TAPESTRY
CURTAIN ROD	LIGHT SWITCH	PENNANT	TILES
DEER HEAD	MANTEL	PHONE	TOWEL RACK
DIRT	MEDICINE CABINET	PICTURES	WALLPAPER

ANSWER, PAGE 342

In this word search, the letters in the center of the grid have been replaced by shaded squares. To solve, do as you usually do but bear this in mind: Several words on the word list cross into the shaded squares and need to have their missing letters filled in. When you're done, read those missing letters in order row by row to spell out a quip. Then find the regular hidden message, which is another quip. Both quips and some dozen items on the word list are all related to the same theme.

```
F S W M A H G N I T T O N H F N E S
R N S R R O B O H I N P U F A A S T
I O M E S E G T O E N D I T T I H E
A O N E L N L T T H D R O M L R T A
R E O A I K F O D T E W O R R A H L
T E A S W P N M I H P E O B V M W F
U E S R O H ░ ░ ░ ░ ░ ░ O E N D P R
C I C L E N ░ ░ ░ ░ ░ ░ L U M I E O
K C E L L E ░ ░ ░ ░ ░ ░ X Y T A W M
L A N D M A ░ ░ ░ ░ ░ ░ E R D M O T
R O D R D I ░ ░ ░ ░ ░ ░ B A L L S H
E D S N U R ░ ░ ░ ░ ░ ░ Y S S E Y E
H X T H A E Y S R E A N Y O T L H R
C N H O J E L T T I L E H R R B E I
R G K A O E O S T H E T N G E M C C
A E I G L I N E M Y R R E M I I H H
B O R T S E R O F D O O W R E H S H
G I V E T O T H E P O O R R O T O D
```

ARCHER	HOT DISH	ODYSSEY	SHELTER
ARMOR	ICIER	ON A WHIM	SHERIFF
ARROW	KARAOKE	ORIOLE	SHERWOOD FOREST
ASCENDS	KISSING	OTTOMAN	STEAL FROM THE RICH
ELEVATE	LANDMARK	OUTLAW	THANKLESS
EXHALE	LITTLE JOHN	OWNER	THIMBLE
FRIAR TUCK	MAID MARIAN	RERUNS	TOM SELLECK
GIVE TO THE POOR	MERRY MEN	ROBOT	TORTOISE
HIGH NOON	MOTHBALLS	ROSARY	TWINBORN
HOODLUM	NOTTINGHAM	SAWHORSE	WHOOPED

ANSWER, PAGE 342

So You Want To Be A Star

Shaped like a star, the grid contains the names of professions and positions that may lead to becoming famous. The hidden message is a definition of a celebrity.

```
                          A P
                          T T
                          Y E
                          C O
                      P O P E
                      O O E R
                      L N P J
                    S I A U S O
                    N T R C W I
    C I T I R C O M E D I A N T T N R O T C E R I D
      C O M P O S E R S C H O Y O E G A S G E K N
        O O W N E T A I H R V T R L E E I F
        D O X R I A A E E H K I N R
          E P S N N L L F S U E U
            L W T I H E H L R T
            O A S T R O N A U T
            R T A O W A L O G D
          L E O T H M T C D K A N
          O R N O S     S T O N W
        K P E S W       I R C N N
        I V T E           T E T E
        N S N             R S O
      I G S               A S R
```

ACTOR	CRITIC	JURIST	POP SINGER
ACTRESS	DANCER	KING	POPE
ARTIST	DIRECTOR	MODEL	PRO ATHLETE
ASTRONAUT	DOCTOR	NEWSMAN	SAINT
CHEF	EXPLORER	NOVELIST	TALK SHOW HOST
COMEDIAN	GENERAL	POET	TYCOON
COMPOSER	GURU	POLITICIAN	TYRANT
COUTURIER	INVENTOR		

ANSWER, PAGE 343

Shaped like a saguaro cactus, the grid contains things associated with deserts. The hidden message completes a quote about the atom bomb that begins, "Man has ... the power ...."

```
                              B  Y  T  O
                           M  L  U  A  K  E
                           C  A  C  T  U  S              T  A  H
                           E  W  C  T  T  W           D  I  R  A
                           O  R  A  A  R  E           L  O  R  D
               A  D        M  E  S  A  N  E        S  C  E  O  E
            M  R  N        H  N  T  O  R  Y        K  T  T  Y
            O  O  I        S  C  O  R  P  I  O  N  S  S  E  M  O
            J  A  U        L  E  M  A  C  K  B  N  N  K  E  A
            A  L  O  E     H  O  O  D  O  O  S  O  A  T  S
            V  H  D  F  L  A  S  H  F  L  O  O  D  M  N  G  I
            E  E  E  E  S  D  E  S  A  R  A  H  A  S  E  S
               N  B  S  A  G  U  A  R  O  S  L  E
                  U  R  N  T  T  N  A  S  I  L  A
                     D  D  B  H  A  B  G  T  H  D
                           V  I  T  E  S  O
                           A  A  O  K  U  B
                           R  N  L  A  R  E
                           A  A  B  L  B  T
                           C  S  E  T  E  O
                           L  A  U  L  G  Y
                           O  Z  P  A  A  O
                           O  I  M  S  S  C
```

ADOBE	CANYON	HEAT	ROCKS
ALOE	CARAVAN	HOODOOS	SAGEBRUSH
ANASAZI	COYOTE	LAWRENCE OF ARABIA	SAGUAROS
ARID	DEATH VALLEY	MESA	SAHARA
ARROYO	DUNE	MOJAVE	SALT LAKE
BEDOUIN	FLASH FLOOD	OASIS	SAND
BUTTE	GILA MONSTER	PUEBLO	SCORPIONS
CACTUS	GOBI	RATTLESNAKE	YUCCAS
CAMEL			

ANSWER, PAGE 343

229. Cold Comfort

Shaped like a snowman holding a broom, the grid contains words and phrases associated with winter.

```
                        S   O   U   R
                        P   L   O   W
                        T   O   E   B
                B   U   N   D   L   E   U   P
                    W   N   H   L   L   T           F   R   A   C   S   A   D
                    S   B   T   A   O   C               A   T   R   E   E
                    R   L   R   U   W   I                   F   O   L
                    I   I   C   Q   Z   S                           S
                        Z   N   S   E                               S
                    E   Z   E   E   R   F                           C
                S   O   S   A   S   T   O   R   M   W               O
            H   I   B   E   R   N   A   T   E   R   E   N           U
        O       M   O   I   D   O   V   A   K   L   O       I       N
    V           S   O   R   Y   S   S   S   N   S   T           P   T
E           T   R   L   O   I   N   A   N               P   R
    L           S   U   O   R   E   E   G   O                   Y
            S   S   L   B   M   S   T   G   W   I                   S
            C   H   G   F   T   U   K   T   O   M   S   C           K
            O   I   A   L   L   U   I   B   O   E   D               I
            L   V   T   F   D   A   L   M   O   B   R   A           I
            D   E   I   C   E   S   K   A   T   I   N   G           N
            R   B   R   R   R   U   E   F   L   U                   G
                G   U   S   A   M   T   S   E                       T
```

ARCTIC	COLD	ICE SKATING	SHOVEL
BELOW ZERO	CROSS-COUNTRY SKIING	IGLOO	SLED
BLIZZARD	DRIFT	MITTENS	SLEET
BOOTS	FLAKES	MUKLUKS	SLUSH
BRISK	FLURRIES	NIPPY	SNOWMOBILE
"BRRR!"	FLU SEASON	PLOW	SQUALL
BUNDLE UP	FREEZE	SCARF	STORM
COAT	HIBERNATE	SHIVER	TOBOGGAN

ANSWER, PAGE 344

230. Dogging It

Shaped like a bone, the grid contains words and phrases associated with dogs.

```
      O K M                                         G Y D
    O D B R C                                     E M R H R
  M E I S S A L                                 A N A U O F L
  U N F K E T B M A S T I F F P R M I L K B O N E S W B
  C H A S E C A R S D O D U L T L E W A G I T S T A I L
    O D R E H P E H S N A M R E G U I F G Y R B O T B
      P E O A S D I U E Y N C E A P T R P C E E E S
        U W F C A O H P R O H O H S O O R L H S T
      N A T R E P E P O O P E R S C O O P E R T C T
        D L L P I T B U L L V A W I M N T E D Z T F D P E
    I K U L A S S P L T H E E H U S K Y A K L T R I L D S
    T S A T E B C O L L A R L O O H C S E C N E I D E B O
    C O L L I E V                                 G H E P Y I S
      H T O M E                                     O N E S W
        O O R                                         D R K
```

BARK	FLEAS	MILKBONES	SALUKI
BITE	GERMAN SHEPHERD	OBEDIENCE SCHOOL	SETTER
CATCH A FRISBEE	GROWL	PIT BULL	"SIT UP!"
CHASE CARS	HOUND	PLUTO	SNOOPY
CHEW	HUNT	POODLE	SPITZ
COLLAR	HUSKY	POOPER SCOOPER	TERRIER
COLLIE	LASSIE	POUND	TOTO
CORGI	LEASH	PUPPY	WAG ITS TAIL
DOGCATCHER	MAN'S BEST FRIEND	"ROLL OVER!"	WALK
FIDO	MASTIFF	ROVER	YELP

ANSWER, PAGE 344

231. At Loose Ends

The grid is shaped like a cleaver because we've cut off the first or last letter of each item on the list below. It's up to you to figure out which letter to add to which end of each item and then to find that modified word in the grid. For example, given the word DIPLOMA, you'd add a T to the end to form DIPLOMAT, or given AWFUL, you'd add an L to the front to form LAWFUL. Of the 40 items, exactly 20 are missing a letter in front and 20 are missing a letter in back. Also, no letter of the alphabet is used more than once in front nor more than once in back. If you find yourself at loose ends, you can find the complete word list on page 255.

```
        S O M B E S E O L
        H G U O R T Q V E L I O N I Z E D F L A M I N G O F
    K R L Z T R A U Q M S R D W N G A S T R O N O M I C R O
    I F N G N I R I P S A E H T E S M N A E L C E T A R A K
    N A K C H U M P N N H L A E T     Y H I S I N E W C E
    K W H O P P I N G S A Y I E A                   S D
    Y N S A O D P E R R T N R G E
    T V A K A I M O D E M O B I N
  J D A H R L S T L O S I L R O U
  U E L B A T C E L E D F O U M T
  M N L T P A U H I S S L C S W O
  P R E D F S S O N E V A E H E A
  S X Y M R C S H C A R O U S E L
```

ACTORS	CON	KARAT	QUIP
AIRBRUSH	DISCUS	LATE	RAINSTORM
ALIGN	ELECTABLE	LEAN	RANGE
ALLEY	FLAMING	MEN	ROUGH
ANY	FLU	MODE	SCAR
ASPIRIN	HAD	NEATEN	SHE
ASTRONOMIC	HEAVE	OODLES	SINE
CAROUSE	HOPPING	OUTRAN	STEROIDS
CHUM	INKY	PARK	SWAM
COLON	IONIZED	QUART	UMPS

ANSWER, PAGE 345

232. It's Only Money

Shaped like the eagle that appears on the back of a traditional U.S. quarter, the grid contains words and images that are printed on various denominations of United States currency.

```
        Y W                           O G
      I D H           N S E         L R V
    H M E I E         E R       B L E S L
    A U N T M E       R I     E N E A O F
  I M N N E W A S H I N G T O N C T N R N
  O I U E H G S R L E G S I T A I S O A U
  A L S K O T R E Y S O I O G P T E N N L
J W T U H U E A A R P D E A A S N A H K I A
A V O B D S V T I N N W W C W M O L T L N O
C U N I T E D S T A T E S O F A M E R I C A
K N E R S   B H Y M A T R A D E   G E N O I
S C T U A   N T C Y T R E B I L   E A G L E
O E Y L       W S R A U O R S       S L N E
N N Y P         C L O S I N         U T F O
  T N E   J L E G A L T E N D E R   R O N
  S   E                             Y   S
```

ARROWS
CAPITOL
CENTS
DEBTS
EAGLE
E PLURIBUS UNUM
EYES
FLAG

FRANKLIN
GRANT
[THE] GREAT SEAL
HAMILTON
IN GOD WE TRUST
JACKSON
KENNEDY
LEAVES

LEGAL TENDER
LIBERTY
LINCOLN
MONTICELLO
NOTE
PYRAMID
SACAGAWEA
SERIES

STARS
TORCH
TREASURY
UNITED STATES OF
    AMERICA
WASHINGTON
[THE] WHITE HOUSE

ANSWER, PAGE 345

233. Twin Peaks

Shaped like two mountains, the grid contains words and phrases about mountains.

```
                                  F
                              V   O   T
                              R   T   I   A   O
                          S   H   M   L   S   U   E
                  R           R   B   P   M   I   T   K
          L   L   K       S   E   S   N   O   W   C   A   P
      E   E   D   A   K   R   W   L   E   U   B   R   L   R
  S   G   O   V   E   R   L   O   O   K   E   N   O   O   G   I   T
  T   W   A   I   P   I   E   D   L   W   S   T   U   P   C   A   M
N   N   L   S   G   N   T   G   O   F   O   W   A   L   P   H   T   P   B
H   A   H   H   E   O   E   D   E   D   D   I   I   D   I   A   A   I   S
I   N   S   T   E   D   I   V   I   D   L   A   T   N   E   N   I   T   N   O   C
L   C   O   C   P   L   O   T   K   R   F   I   E   C   G   R   G   R   A   N   D   M
L   H   M   A   E   R   T   S   A   O   O   F   W   M   H   O   S   U   L   N   A   T   E   T
E   G   A   I   N   N   E   I   V   S   F   M   Y   A   B   A   S   E   I   K   C   O   R   S   I
P   E   A   A   K   T   E   R   X   E   I   P   A   S   W   A   T   E   R   F   A   L   L   E   E   T
R   O   R   A   J   N   A   M   I   L   I   K   V   O   L   C   A   N   O   T   S   E   R   E   V   E   I
R   E   I   C   A   L   G   E   N   C   E   S   C   E   H   I   K   I   N   G   T   R   A   I   L   S   Y   S
```

ALPS	DOWNHILL	MOUNTAIN GOAT	STREAM
ANDES	ELEVATION	OUTCROPPING	SWITCHBACK
ASCENT	EVEREST	OVERLOOK	TIMBERLINE
AVALANCHE	GAPS	PEAK	TREES
BOULDERS	GLACIER	PINNACLE	VISTA
CHAIRLIFT	HIKING TRAILS	RIDGE	VOLCANO
CLIFF	KILIMANJARO	ROCKIES	WATERFALL
CLIMB	LAKE	SHELTER	WILDFLOWERS
CONTINENTAL DIVIDE	LODGE	SMOKIES	YAKS
CRAG	MEADOW	SNOWCAP	YETI

ANSWER, PAGE 346

234. In the Line of Duty

Shaped like a policeman's badge, the grid contains words and phrases associated with police work. The hidden message is an interesting fact about the creation of the classic TV cop show "Dragnet."

```
            C                 S                 E
        Z H V             E O A             N F O
      U Z A R T P C E F T E R D R A G N E T
    N D U S T F O R F I N G E R P R I N T S T
      H F E F E B I E A E D G D E G E L N U
        M S B F C M E C L T E E H S P A R
        B Q L E U E E R I O A T R T T W F
          U R O F C O P S N S E J A O A
          A L F R E D F N T C C B K I N
          D O L R T I N I D A T S E Y D
          C Y M E D A C A E C I L O P O
          A D I W T K P M H R V A U S R
        C R O R H E P O E F S E E T N D T
        O E T A T N A R R A W H C R A E S
      S C I S N E R O F O B L O T T E R H U
      W D K U D T O N I T O O M R O F I N U
      E R O C A E S S B T A F B E B A D G E
      E R O N R S N U G H A U V T H E P S C
      P A R I U A R S B G E T E E R R Y T O
        W T L T N P I I A L S C S O N
          P E R P E T R A T O R F T
            H O C M E E V R U
            T N S E N
              R
```

ARREST
BADGE
BEAT
BLOTTER
BULLET-PROOF VEST
BUST
CHASE
COFFEE
COPS
CRIME
DETECTIVE
DONUT

DRAGNET
DUST FOR FINGERPRINTS
FORENSICS
FRISK
[THE] FUZZ
GUNS
HANDCUFFS
IN CUSTODY
LAW AND ORDER
MIRANDA RULE
NARC
NIGHTSTICK

NYPD
OFFICER
PATROL
PERPETRATOR
POLICE ACADEMY
PRECINCT
RAID
RAP SHEET
"... RIGHT TO REMAIN
    SILENT"
ROOKIE

SEARCH WARRANT
SIREN
SQUAD CAR
STAKEOUT
STATION
SUSPECT
SWEEP
TICKET
UNDERCOVER
UNIFORM
WIRE

ANSWER, PAGE 346

235. Going Under

Shaped liked a miner's helmet, the grid contains things that are found underground.

```
                        A O U S R D
                      R T I E C A R R O T
                    O C C R F B E N E S U E
                  O I A W R U S E A N K N O T
      I           T N T V A A R F R D B M N A M R
    E L N E L U S P A C E M I T T F E R T E U S E N
    Y A W B U S W C O R I I D H E E L N O L G L W S
    G O H D N U O R G N I T S E T R A E L C U N E E O
    I C N G U M R N E D E C H L R G T R S O K U S P N
    D       B M M R B U R I E D T R E A S U R E I I S
            T O S I S U I S L N L A G A B A T U R P L A
            W L C A S K E T T A N A R A L L E C E N I W
  D O R S D E E S T N A L P E D S T I S O P E D L I O E
  M E T S Y S N O I T A G I R R I R S R E H P O G O L D
```

AIR-RAID SHELTER
BEDROCK
BEETLES
BURIED TREASURE
CARROT
CASKET
CATACOMB
CAVE

COAL
EARTH'S CRUST
GOLD
GOPHERS
GROUNDHOG
IRRIGATION SYSTEM
LAIR
MINERS

MOLE
NUCLEAR TESTING
OIL DEPOSITS
PIPES
PLANT SEEDS
ROOTS
RUTABAGA
SEWER

SPELUNKERS
SUBWAY
TIME CAPSULE
TRUFFLES
TUNNEL
WATER TABLE
WINE CELLAR
WORMS

ANSWER, PAGE 347

236. Chain of Events

This puzzle is literally a chain of events. All the items in the word list are events, and each event links directly to the next. That means that both in the list and in the grid, the letter that ends the first word is the exact letter that begins the second word, the last letter in the second is the exact letter that begins the third and so on, right on through all 40 items. To get you started, we'll tell you the first event, VOLCANIC ERUPTION, is found in the top left corner of the grid. After that, it's up to you to determine what and where the rest of the events are. Each clue in the list gives you the first and last letters of the event, and the total number of letters in the word or phrase. When all of the items have been circled in the grid, they will form a linked chain that ends below the first item. As an added bonus, the hidden message contains two quotes: the first by Samuel Adams, the second by Abraham Lincoln. If you're not up on your current events, you can refer to the full list on page 255.

```
V  O  L  C  A  N  I  C  E  R  U  P  T  I  O  N  Q  G  N  I  T  E  E  M  U
O  E  Q  U  I  N  O  X  Y  O  M  K  I  P  P  U  R  O  T  E  O  N  E  R  W
E  C  A  R  E  C  A  T  N  N  O  T  M  A  K  C  I  I  D  I  T  A  R  O  D
L  N  E  E  E  V  R  E  N  T  S  O  U  R  B  L  O  N  M  U  S  I  N  T  E
V  A  E  W  S  A  H  C  T  A  M  S  I  N  N  E  T  G  S  A  I  S  T  S  A
I  D  O  O  P  I  A  M  P  S  E  K  A  U  Q  A  E  S  R  O  N  V  E  R  T
S  A  T  H  H  I  Y  E  M  U  Q  T  S  E  V  R  A  H  A  K  K  U  N  A  H
S  E  U  S  O  T  R  E  T  N  O  W  O  I  C  T  L  A  I  M  N  O  S  W  T
I  T  T  R  O  H  I  T  N  U  H  G  G  E  R  E  T  S  A  E  A  V  O  T  E
G  C  N  O  O  N  D  T  R  P  A  R  A  D  E  S  R  O  L  R  L  H  E  I  D
H  E  V  E  E  N  E  O  T  S  B  U  T  C  W  T  O  N  F  U  S  E  S  B  S
T  P  L  T  V  X  D  A  I  N  L  Y  T  I  H  A  R  T  E  T  V  E  N  I  T
I  S  H  E  A  E  D  I  L  S  D  U  M  A  V  E  C  I  R  C  O  N  T  H  R
N  O  L  M  O  U  T  B  R  E  A  K  W  A  N  Z  A  A  A  E  L  E  D  X  M
G  R  A  D  U  A  T  I  O  N  E  W  A  L  B  U  M  R  E  L  E  A  S  E  E
```

1. VOLCANIC ERUPTION
2. N _ _ _ _ _ _   _ _ _ T
3. T _ _ _ L
4. L _ _ _ _ _ E
5. E _ _ _ _ _   _ _ _
  _ _ _ T
6. T _ _ P
7. P _ _ _ Y
8. Y _ _   _ _ _ _ _ R
9. R _ _ T

10. T _ _ _ _ _   _ _ _ _ H
11. H _ _ _ _ _ E
12. E _ _ M
13. M _ _ _ _ _   _ _ _ _ _ R
14. R _ _ E
15. E _ _ _ _   _ _ _ _ _ _ _ G
16. G _ _ _ _ _ _ _ _ N
17. N _ _   _ _ _ _ _
  _ _ _ _ _ E
18. E _ _ _ _ _ T
19. T _ _ _ _ _ I

20. I _ _ _ _ _ _ D
21. D _ _ _ H
22. H _ _ _ _ _ _ H
23. H _ _ _ _ _ T
24. T _ _ R
25. R _ _ _ O
26. O _ _ _ _ _ _ K
27. K _ _ _ _ _ A
28. A _ _   _ _ _ W
29. W _ _ S
30. S _ _ _ M

31. M _ _ _ _ _ G
32. G _ _ _ _ S
33. S _ _ _ _ _ _ _ S
34. S _ _ _ P
35. P _ _ _ _ _ S
36. S _ _ M
37. M _ _ _ _ _ _ E
38. E _ _ _ T
39. T _ _   _ _ _ _ E
40. E _ _ _ _ _ X

ANSWER, PAGE 347

237. Are We There Yet?

Shaped like a suitcase, the grid contains words and phrases associated with vacation travel.

```
                    S A P S
                  T         R
                R             I
    W J E T L A G O E A F R E Q U E N T F L Y E R N
    H S G O V E S H R A E R U T R A P E D D S T S O
    S T R A V E L E R S C H E C K S O O V M O U I Y
    U E E S R E M C E H R D S M O T S U C U A I G R
  N R K I H L A R R A T T U E L Y T T C R Y O H H R
A   B C C O C T V B H R I T U N P A C K H T A S T A
R   H I N P H A O M O N E Y E X C H A N G E U L S C
  O T T O P T L A P T O P F L A V I R R A G C I E H
    O T C I I W S A E S K R O N V B D N A B V K E D
    O M O N A S C A L E R E H E R E W U O Y H S I W
    T N E G A L E V A R T E D R A C E N O H P T N N
    S I O P L U G G A G E T A G A B T N E M R A G N
```

ARRIVAL
B AND B
CAMERA
CARRY-ON
CHECK-IN
CONCIERGE
CUSTOMS
DELAY
DEPARTURE

DUTY-FREE
FREQUENT FLYER
GARMENT BAG
HOTEL
JET LAG
LAPTOP
LUGGAGE TAG
MONEY EXCHANGE
OVERBOOKED

PASSPORT
PHONE CARD
POSTCARD
RESERVATIONS
RESORTS
ROOM
SHOPPING
SIGHTSEEING
SOUVENIRS

SPAS
TICKETS
TOOTHBRUSH
TOUR
TRAVEL AGENT
TRAVELER'S CHECKS
UNPACK
VISA
"WISH YOU WERE HERE"

ANSWER, PAGE 348

238. Soccer to Me

Shaped like a soccer ball and cleated soccer shoe, the grid contains words and phrases associated with soccer.

```
        K F S O L              T E A M S
      R I C C N C A            E N O Z H
    E E E D I S F F O          E M A G O
  R L F I W P K S L W G          O R N E W R
  D A E O E Y F Y O A R        P E L K C A T
  W O R L D C U P T L H   S E R E D C A R D O H S
  P H E L B R A Z I L E T T A O H C A O C G E E H
  T T E L S H I N G U A R D S V O Y E S R E J A O
  T O U C H L I N E   N T H S E Y R U J N I D O
  E O I I R K L     I E L L A B D N A H E E T
    F N C K C         P     P     S     R
```

BRAZIL	HALF	PELE	SOCCER MOM
CLEATS	HAND BALL	PENALTY KICK	TACKLE
COACH	HEADER	RED CARD	TEAM
CORNER	INJURY	REFEREE	THROW IN
FIELD	JERSEY	SAVE	TOUCH LINE
FOUL	NIL-NIL	SHIN GUARDS	WALL
GAME	OFFSIDE	SHOOT	WORLD CUP
GOAL	PASS	SHORTS	ZONE

ANSWER, PAGE 348

239. Breakfast Buffet

Shaped like a cereal bowl, the grid contains words and phrases associated with breakfast.

```
S B S T I C K Y B U N S N W O R B H S A H
C T A A P S R R T M O V K L I M E N R D Y
B R I G Y A G E S A D A N I S H E C O O O
  S O R E H C N A R S O V E U H O L G N
  D U I G L S R O M C M L E C L A U E U
  P L C S G E E T A C F O U D F R U I T
  U G R G S K V B L F H K C H T N T R C
  L A E M T A O R A N G E J U I C E O T
    O P B E C N W D G R I E F N T F W
    E I T N R T E E H H F S T F U
      S A U S A G E U N U E
      P T L G E M R B E
```

BACON	DANISH	MARMALADE	SAUSAGE
BAGEL	DONUT	MILK	STICKY BUNS
BUTTER	EGGS	MUFFIN	SYRUP
COFFEE	FRUIT	OATMEAL	TOAST
COLD CEREAL	GRITS	OMELET	TURNOVER
CREAM CHEESE	HASH BROWNS	ORANGE JUICE	WAFFLES
CREPE	HUEVOS RANCHEROS	PANCAKES	YOGURT
CROISSANT	KUCHEN		

ANSWER, PAGE 349

240. The Sound of Music

Shaped like a grand piano, the grid contains the names of musical instruments. The hidden message answers the riddle, "Why did it take Brahms so long to write his famous lullaby?"

```
                        E  T  U  L  F
                     N  R  E  A  I
                     I  U  L  B  F
                  R  M  G  M  E
               U  P  U  I  T  H  C  H  I  M  E  S  L
            E  O  E  B  R  O  K  I  Y  G  O  N  G  L  E  P
      P  T  B  T  F  A  D  T  R  O  M  B  O  N  E  R  Y  L
      R  M  N  A  M  L  S  L  A  G  B  P  Z  B  A  Z
   C  L  A  R  I  N  E  T  S  I  T  N  A  N  A  G  A  I  S  L
   E  T  H  L  L  E  P  O  A  U  I  O  L  N  K  N  A  T  P  T
      N  O  O  S  S  A  B  T  U  B  S           I  H  H
         E  I  I  P  A  A  O  G                 E
            V  V  N                             R
            I  A  J
            N  O
               O
```

BANJO	CLARINET	KAZOO	TIMPANI
BASS DRUM	CYMBALS	LYRE	TROMBONE
BASSOON	FIFE	MARIMBA	TRUMPET
BELL	FLUTE	OBOE	TUBA
BONGO	GONG	ORGAN	VIOLA
BUGLE	GUITAR	PIANO	VIOLIN
CHIMES	HARP	TAMBOURINE	ZITHER

ANSWER, PAGE 349

241. Black Hole #6

In this word search, the letters in the center of the grid have been replaced by shaded squares. To solve, do as you usually do but bear this in mind: Several words on the word list cross into the shaded squares and need to have their missing letters filled in. When you're done, read those missing letters in order row by row to spell out a quip. Then find the regular hidden message, which is another quip. Both quips and more than a dozen items on the word list are related to the same theme.

```
D O W N Y W O O D P E C K E R S T P
H N S T S O L E R E W O H S D L O C
O E S T E W H N O I G O C C T R A E
M E M B E R S W M G R S L P T N T I
N T G E I R N O T N U E U A H A E E
S N W D O O R D D O S D G U G R I T
L A S R A E ▧ ▧ ▧ ▧ ▧ ▧ L I G H T S
E C M O C H ▧ ▧ ▧ ▧ ▧ ▧ T H O U S E
E R N L A U ▧ ▧ ▧ ▧ ▧ ▧ T U P N G I
P A T L H I ▧ ▧ ▧ ▧ ▧ ▧ U N I D S T
I B E R R S ▧ ▧ ▧ ▧ ▧ ▧ T P O S R I
N Y F I T C ▧ ▧ ▧ ▧ ▧ ▧ R O Y N M N
G G E S T E E E S O T I U Q S O M E
B R E Y D N Z G N D A Z E S T Y O M
A E B N E E E U I H N U T T R N E A
G N I S A D D L E H O R S E Y A N O
S E S M A K E A F I R E T S P C E N
R E O P L E E R U T A N O T K C A B
```

BACK TO NATURE
BEARS
BEDROLL
CANTEEN
CANYONS
COLD SHOWER
DELIGHTS
DOWNY WOODPECKERS
ENERGY BAR
FERRETS

GULCH
HAIRPINS
HOEDOWN
IRREGULAR
LAUGHING IT UP
LITIGATE
MAKE A FIRE
MEMBERS
MOCHA
MOSQUITOS

MOTH
NO AMENITIES
OUTHOUSE
PEIGNOIR
PORTAGE
RECTIFY
RED-EYE
REGIONS
REHEARSAL
REINDEER

RIGOROUS
SADDLE HORSE
SEIZURE
SLEEPING BAGS
SOCIETY
SORENESS
TENTS
TWEEZED
VICEROY
"WE'RE LOST!"

ANSWER, PAGE 350

242. Staying Afloat

Shaped like a windsurfer on his sailboard, the grid contains things that float.

```
                              A
                              S  F
                              E  H  P  L
          O  L  A             L  N  S  E  T
          W  I  E  K          D  G  I  I  O  M
          O  L  A             O  E  I  M  F  P  V
             Y           L  O  I  B  C  E  Y  L
       D  A  P  E  L     N  L  I  T  E  C  L  E
       K  N  A  O  L  N  B  E  A  C  H  B  A  L  L
       I  O  D  Y  E     U  R  O  S  A  G  E  P  E
          Y  S  S  R     Y  R  I  H  L  W  E  R  H  J
       B  O  A  T        K  A  L  A  A  N  T  E  G  C
       L  U  U  E        C  B  S  S  G  E  S  W  A  N
       S  B  I  R        U  S  L  U  S  P  O  N  G  E
       E        C        D  R  I  F  T  W  O  O  D
       A        R        R  N  C  L  I  E  K
       L        A        E  E  K  T  H
       T        C        B  E  G
       O  F  K  I        B
    D  E  E  W  A  E  S  D  S  U  R  F  B  O  A  R  D  N  D
    L  I  F  E  P  R  E  S  E  R  V  E  R  S  D  U  O  L  C  O
    L  N  O  I  H  S  U  C  T  A  E  S  E  N  A  L  P  R  I  A  A
```

AIRPLANE SEAT CUSHION
ALGAE
BARREL
BEACH BALL
BOAT
BUOY
CANOE
CLOUDS
CORK

DEBT
DRIFTWOOD
ICEBERG
IDEA
INNER TUBE
JELLYFISH
KAYAK
LIFE PRESERVERS

LILY PADS
LOAN
LOGS
MINE
NOODLES
OIL SLICK
OYSTER CRACKERS
PENGUIN

PEOPLE
RAFT
RUBBER DUCKY
SEAL
SEAWEED
SPONGE
SURFBOARD
SWAN

ANSWER, PAGE 350

243. Six-Pack

Shaped liked the number 6, the grid is packed with six-letter words. For variety, every letter of the alphabet starts at least one word but not more than two. The hidden message spells out the names of three Hollywood movies from the 1990s that contain the word "six" in their titles. Can you guess which movies they are?

```
                    S B E I W X D A
                  L L U N H E G Z
                M O R T A R R N
              E T C E C C S A
              C C U K S T T
            H A O S F S S
          D E H C T E S
          O O K C U C
        R S E O Q P
        A W A R D S
        T A R L J A A T Y I Q
        R I S L A N D O N Z S U I
        A O X D C M N A I L E D A C
        T F E L K C I P A Y D E E R G
        Y F S E A G P S E R V F R A T E
        J I N G L E       U A E B N Z
        V C N I R         C I B N E
        G E T O E         A K Y A E
        H Z S N D         D T U M W
        Y S A S L         E K N S T
        D I N N E R     E D N T E H
          E P U G L I E R E R O I N Y
          S Y O I X D E K N I W G T H
            H A T R E D S S P A H E
            N R C S K I S M E T
              X O V E F U
```

ACCRUE	FIDDLE	MAGNET	STANZA
AWARDS	GLITZY	MORTAR	TARTAR
BLOTCH	GREEDY	NAILED	TWEEZE
BREEZY	HATRED	OCTOPI	UGLIER
CRABBY	ISLAND	OFFICE	UMPIRE
CUCKOO	JACKAL	PICKLE	VESSEL
DINNER	JINGLE	QUARTZ	VISION
DOODAD	KISMET	QUESTS	WHACKS
ENACTS	KNIGHT	REDLEG	WINKED
ETCHED	LEGION	RUCKUS	X-RAYED
FACADE	LOCUST	SALAMI	YES-MAN
			ZIPPER

ANSWER, PAGE 351

244. Do You Believe In Magic?

Shaped like a rabbit in a magician's hat, the grid contains words and phrases associated with magic and the occult.

```
        A Y T     N E Y
        S M A     U C F
          E H     O N
          H A     U A
          C F     I R
          L O F J T
        I A T C A I E
        N C U R S E T
        S R O R R I M
        L T T Y A A D
          W I T C H
          B M T
V A B R A C A D A B R A E P P A S I D A N
      C H W I Z A R D G E D S S
      T A T E K R C C J I N X U
      T R I C K A H C N O C O P
      L M A O G L E V I T A T E
      Y L I D S L I T N W E D R
      B V I S E U O T I L N E N
      H O C U S P O C U S N S A
      C O D G U U L M I C O P T
      O D S N G H A A H R A E U
      N O I T A T N A C N I L R
      J O B L M W N E E E F L A
      U R M O M T R M A G S I L
      R E X E H Y P N O T I Z E
      E R E C N A M O R C E N C
```

ABRACADABRA
ALCHEMY
AMULET
AURA
BLACK ART
CHARM
CONJURE
CURSE
DISAPPEAR
ENCHANT

HEXER
HOCUS-POCUS
HYPNOTIZE
INCANTATION
JINX
LEVITATE
MAGIC
MAGUS
MIRRORS

NECROMANCER
OMEN
OUIJA
POTIONS
PULL A RABBIT OUT OF
    A HAT
SORCERY
SPELL
SUPERNATURAL

TAROT
TRADE PLACES
TRANCE
TRICK
VOODOO
WAND
WICCA
WITCH
WIZARD

ANSWER, PAGE 351

245. "Roll 'Em"

Shaped like a clapboard (the device that's clapped before a movie take), the grid contains words and phrases associated with a movie set. The hidden message is a quote from legendary movie mogul Samuel Goldwyn.

```
                                          S P I C
                                    G N I T H G I L
                              G D R A O B P A L C T
                    H A I R D R E S S E R
            P S R E L I A R T U
    M A K E U P R
    E R
    G W C I N E M A T O G R A P H E R S T S A C A
    L A A R X E F F O W V R R E N N E E T E C C R
    O S F T C T A A A S I E E A N M T E P N T S B
    V T R F R D I R E C T O R S C H A I R O I E E
    E A T M E E D S S R A C E B G N K C R E O I S
    S H C I W R S M S I H M T O U I E L U L N L T
    C T N A O D S O B P U E A D E D L O D I F I B
    E V U B M E R O E T R A C K I N G S H O T A O
    N D E D B E Y Z S S E R T C A A W E C E L D Y
    E S T E I R R O S E L B U O D T N U T S N L U
    S N O N L O C A T I O N I O N S S P R O P S Y
```

"ACTION!"	CLOSEUP	GAFFERS	SCRIPT
ACTOR	COSTUMES	GRIP	STAND-IN
ACTRESS	CRANE	HAIRDRESSER	STAR
BEST BOY	CREW	LIGHTING	STUDIO
BLOOPER	DAILIES	LOVE SCENES	STUNT DOUBLES
CAMERA	DIRECTOR'S CHAIR	MAKEUP	"THAT'S A WRAP!"
CAST	DOLLY	ON LOCATION	TRACKING SHOT
CATERER	EXTRAS	OVER BUDGET	TRAILERS
CINEMATOGRAPHER	FADE-IN	PROPS	WARDROBE
CLAPBOARD	FOCUS	RETAKE	ZOOM

ANSWER, PAGE 352

246. Wedding Party

Shaped like an engagement ring, the grid contains words and phrases associated with weddings.

```
T T L H E N C N O I T P E C E R B R
  E S R O W R O R E T T E B R O F
  E W E I O I O L S A R S A U Y I
    O P I G N M G D E I C Q S F
    V Y H R R Y Y M F H U G H O
      E L O P E O R U E U I E
      M I O T N W R T A E F R
        B M Y O C O R S R T
        B Y F H S O L R I S
        M A N A N D W I F E G D
    M A R O                 N D E E
    Y I Y                   O I R
  U N D                     R R S
  G U O                     R T B
  R R F                     A U E
  L E H                     M X B
  A T O                     T E Y
  W R N                     S D I
    A O L                 T U O
    G R H E             M S J L
      E M A K E A T O A S T A
      A L T A R R N I N I
        R I C E K T
```

ALTAR	ELOPE	HORA	RABBI
BEST MAN	FLOWER GIRL	"JUST MARRIED"	RECEPTION
BOUQUET	"FOR BETTER OR WORSE"	KISS	REGISTRY
BRIDE	GARTER	MAID OF HONOR	RICE
CAKE	GIFTS	MAKE A TOAST	RING
CEREMONY	GOWN	"MAN AND WIFE"	TUXEDO
CHURCH	GROOM	PHOTOS	USHER
COLD FEET	HONEYMOON	PRIEST	VOWS

ANSWER, PAGE 352

247. All Good Things ...

Shaped like a heart, the grid contains things that are good. Here's a wry hidden message about goodness and giving.

```
        W E S A                    H R W E
      H E A L T H                A P E F I L
    L L C H E R R P            Y E E O R P N B
    R O L E M O D E L        E R K E F I O S A
  D M A A K S Y R T N T    H T E O L H E H E R J
  I A E S O L E A S P G    Y N T A S A N O C G U
  P E R S O N A L D A Y T D M T N T P D H O A S
  L R E I B I E R F I U S H S O E S P S O N I T
  O C F C S C W H H A L G T I L D C I D W D N I
  M E U M I E G D E L W O N K E T E N A I C S C
  A C N O H H S B T L M A H I H O E E A N H N E
    I D V T O N E A A P T R G T I R S R D A C
    T S I R U O H C M R A I E G I T S H F N E
      O E A S I H O I C L H H N T A R H A C
      E S I E T C B W R T B S I E O W M L E
        A S H A R E D M O M E N T S O O L
        Y E R C N G R R P E H N E R S O N
          H R A E A S S F E I O R V O
          T V W S I S G M D W O E I
            A N S S E N D N I K T
            P A T C I S U M O
              M K C K N O M
              Y U R W O
                S A R
                P
```

BARGAINS	HELP	NEW CAR	SELF-AWARENESS
BEAUTY	HERO	NICE HOUSE	SHARED MOMENTS
BIRTH	HOLIDAY	NO WAITING	SLEEP
CLASSIC MOVIES	ICE CREAM	PARKING SPOT	STRENGTH
COMPANIONSHIP	JUSTICE	PERSONAL DAY	SUCCESS
DANCE	KINDNESS	PETS	SYMPATHY
DIPLOMA	KNOWLEDGE	PROMOTION	THIS BOOK
FLAT STOMACH	LIFE	RAISE	VACATIONS
FREEDOM	LIGHT	REFUNDS	WARMTH
FRIENDS	LOVE	ROLE MODEL	WEEKENDS
GOOD NEIGHBORS	MASSAGE	ROMANCE	WINDFALL
HAPPINESS	MENTOR	SECOND CHANCE	WINNING THE LOTTERY
HEALTH	MUSIC		

ANSWER, PAGE 353

248. Start Your Day With a Smile

Shaped like a smiley face, the grid contains words and phrases associated with happiness and positive thinking.

```
              T G H   M E R R Y
            T N A L I B U J R E T M
          H A V E A N I C E D A Y S L
        E A T E A S E Y E D E R U S S A
      E C R       S E H P B I       P T C
      M O F       I C H P P N       I A P
    P P I N       S E U S S A       R C I S
    L O O K O N T H E B R I G H T S I D E N
    O W D B U O Y A N T T I O N E T T O V S
    D E J E B U L L I S H P O O S B E N I U
    H R I O S N G F W H E U D I A T D T T N
    O E N   Y A E F L F L I M K E G   W I N
    S D A E   F E U U B A I O B L   R O S Y
    G U T R   I U L N L T I O A S   K R O I
      L N U T   G L P P E W D H   U A R P
      T E C O E     O N D E     H A P Y S
        S E R E N E       D I C A L P
          S F S M I L E Y F A C E L T
            O U D T N E D I F N O C
              L E A G E R O J
```

ASSURED
AT EASE
"BE HAPPY"
BULLISH
BUOYANT
CALM
CHEERY
CONFIDENT
"DON'T WORRY"
EAGER

ELATED
EMPOWERED
GLAD
"[THE] GLASS IS HALF FULL"
GLEEFUL
"HAVE A NICE DAY"
HEARTENING
HOPEFUL
IN A GOOD MOOD

JOLLY
JOYFUL
JUBILANT
"LOOK ON THE BRIGHT SIDE"
MERRY
OPTIMISTIC
PLACID
PLEASED

POSITIVE
ROSY
SECURE
SERENE
SMILEY FACE
SPIRITED
SUNNY
THUMBS-UP
UPBEAT

ANSWER, PAGE 353

249. Boomerangs

In this Australia-themed puzzle, every entry makes a boomerang shape. That is, it needs to make a 90 degree turn halfway through so that the shape ends up looking like a boomerang.

```
B H C D O T N T T N B O O M E W D O Y R A W O E R
R R S H S A H Y D E O J A A R N B T H E L A S T F
U O U U R E G E T Y T S U H A E O R E D N U S M R
S W G O B I S N S S I S P L N O H R R L O N A S O
H D O A C E S O A Y S P S M G C M I T H N W C I N
T S G T R O E T A K D I S R I N E P A H T O U R T
A N D T H T E M C S N E W E S O R S D E D A N I
I L P O S S U M P A Y I E S T B E I T A S R A A E
L R O E A D O U T B D Y T Y B P D M H H L E N O R
M C O W A R R G O I W I K O O N N E W C C I N T S
I A U A S Y T R N A A C C L A O E M I O E A E T S
N D P L A T E A U B O R E T S I N I N H M R A C E
A H N L A B Y R T R A O R B R L I E S A R B K A E
L S Y A W R I A S S C I I S M M S C I I H B R
S U L Z B C E S A R E O E G E A D T T O W D R O T
N C O F N R T A R H A D E N L R N O M A I D N R S
E A C E G U O T R O P I M O A E R I C E N I G I U
E N S E E E D N U D E L S B W Y M E U C A L Y P T
U E H K O O K A B B I L L A H T R I E O P L P Y E
Q T O A D S A Q N E W S O U T N U T K F P L A T S
```

ABORIGINE
AUSSIES
AYERS ROCK
BANDICOOT
BILLABONG
BOOMERANG
BRUSH-TAIL POSSUM
CANE TOADS
CASSOWARY
CHRISTMAS ISLAND
COBBERS
CROCODILE DUNDEE

DIAMOND MINE
DINGO
DOWN UNDER
DUNES
ECHIDNA
EUCALYPTUS TREES
INDIAN OCEAN
IPSWICH
JOEYS
KANGAROOS
KIWIS
KOALA

KOOKABURRAS
MEL GIBSON
NEW SOUTH WALES
NORTHERN TERRITORY
OUTBACK
PERTH
PLATYPI
PRIME MINISTER
QANTAS AIRWAYS
QUEENSLAND PLATEAU
SEAPORT
SHEEP

SHEILAS
SIMPSON DESERT
SUGAR
"THE BUSH"
THE GREAT BARRIER REEF
"THE LAST FRONTIER"
THE SYDNEY OPERA
  HOUSE
TOURISM
WALLABY
WOMBATS

ANSWER, PAGE 354

250. Black Hole #7

In this puzzle, the letters in the center of the grid are missing. Once you've found all the words in the grid, the missing letters will spell out a quote from Bertrand Russell.

```
K O L I V E D N A I N A M S A T C N
E S O X K N F T H P G E S Y R M R P
T O I O A R N O T N I M D A B G I M
S O F L A G O N C A E H N P A P M R
L O K I I A N W U C R C S L H S E I
U A C B N S ■ ■ ■ ■ ■ ■ E R S O F F
S B R O Y O ■ ■ ■ ■ ■ ■ E S A O T R
D E M A K O ■ ■ ■ ■ ■ ■ T D F O H S
N E A P O L ■ ■ ■ ■ ■ ■ A W A N E G
A I L F S H ■ ■ ■ ■ ■ ■ L T R W C H
Y U G E S I ■ ■ ■ ■ ■ ■ I C I L E E
D A B A E L I T A E F T R N J H N A
O R S O N W E L L E S T G O A N T E
B S W R O R O L P K I K N S C T U T
E R R I A N B U L Y I I A M K P R O
P O H S E E R F Y T U D H R E T Y A
A N T R U S H S E W E B S I T E L L
```

AIR DUCT
BADMINTON
BASILISK
BILOXI
BODY AND SOUL
CLASS RING
CRIME OF THE CENTURY
DOMICILE
DUTY-FREE SHOP

FULL TILT
GALLEON
GHOST SHIP
GLAM ROCK
HEARSAY
NEAPOLITAN
NONPAREIL
OAKLAND
ORSON WELLES

PLASMA
PROOF
ROY ORBISON
SAFARI JACKET
SASHIMI
SEWING KIT
SHANGRI-LA
SHREWDEST
SINATRA

SOVEREIGN
STAND-ALONE
TASMANIAN DEVIL
TRANCE
VEERS OFF
WEB SITE
WISE GUY
WOODWORK

ANSWER, PAGE 354

251. You Can Do It

Every item in this word list contains the letters CAN in consecutive order. When in the grid, these letters have been replaced by a 🗑.

AFRICAN
ARCANA
ARSENIC AND OLD LACE
AZTECAN
BUCCANEER
CANADIAN BACON
CANARY ISLANDS
CANBERRA
CANCELS
CANDACE
CANDID CAMERA
CANDLESTICK PARK
CANDY CANE
CANING
CANIS MAJOR

CANNERY ROW
CANNIBAL
CANNOLI
CANONS
CANOPY BED
CANTALOUPES
CANTEEN
CANTILEVER
CANTONESE
CANVAS
CATCH-AS-CATCH-CAN
DECANTED
DOMESTIC ANIMALS
GRAND CANYON

HURRICANES
INCANDESCENT LIGHT
LOOSE CANNON
LOVE CANAL
LUBRICANT
MARC ANTONY
MEXICAN RICE
MOHICANS
NO-CAN-DO
PECAN PIE
PELICAN
PICANTE SAUCE
REPUBLICAN PARTY
SAN FRANCISCAN

SARDINE CAN
SCANDALOUS
SCANDINAVIA
SECANT
SIGNIFICANT
THE CANTERBURY TALES
THE CANUCKS
TIPPECANOE
TRASH CANS
TROPIC OF CANCER
VATICAN CITY
VOLCANIC ASH
WATERING CAN
YOU CAN SAY THAT AGAIN

ANSWER, PAGE 355

252. Everyone Makes Mistakes

While fitting the following mistake-related words into the grid, I accidentally changed one letter from each. These new letters, when read in order, will spell out a quote from Samuel Smiles.

```
I  W  R  I  T  E  O  U  T  H  A  V  R  E  A  S  P  E  Y  P  U  S  F  K  O  G
L  L  I  N  G  C  H  H  S  P  O  O  N  E  R  C  S  M  S  S  E  C  A  K  G  E
D  T  R  T  L  U  E  F  I  T  R  C  A  M  E  W  L  I  T  R  H  M  U  Y  N  P
A  C  Y  I  D  I  S  T  O  R  M  I  O  N  T  O  P  L  A  E  F  I  X  N  I  L
E  Y  C  E  S  Y  M  A  E  R  I  K  F  F  C  I  T  S  R  N  G  A  I  D  O
R  U  N  R  O  R  M  L  L  Y  S  G  R  E  V  U  M  E  E  O  M  I  A  S  N  T
D  A  E  A  K  S  A  S  B  E  C  T  N  E  M  G  D  U  J  N  I  E  S  V  A  L
O  V  T  S  R  E  I  B  O  O  O  O  O  I  C  A  D  N  N  S  O  L  T  S  T  S
O  E  S  A  I  U  I  V  U  L  N  E  R  P  G  I  D  U  H  I  N  B  T  C  S  H
R  I  I  R  S  P  C  O  T  E  E  M  T  H  A  G  L  O  R  M  E  M  W  I  R  R
P  I  E  T  I  M  S  C  S  U  E  C  A  N  A  C  E  R  O  N  I  S  M  E  E  R
Y  L  N  E  Y  O  U  S  A  R  P  P  S  L  E  L  C  B  R  A  S  F  E  W  D  D
C  T  O  O  O  B  A  N  O  N  T  L  I  S  E  T  S  A  E  L  E  T  O  U  N  W
A  T  C  E  R  P  U  P  E  M  I  S  P  R  M  N  T  F  D  D  R  O  F  P  U  Y
L  E  N  C  S  T  I  N  N  I  O  I  T  S  W  E  T  I  H  I  L  G  H  S  S  O
L  M  I  V  O  R  R  I  G  E  N  D  U  M  Y  A  C  H  U  B  L  E  C  K  I  N
A  A  R  R  A  T  A  E  R  L  T  O  L  L  G  E  D  M  L  E  E  L  A  R  A  G
D  T  S  E  W  J  A  N  E  T  N  O  I  T  H  R  R  E  B  A  M  I  O  N  O  R
```

ABERRATION
ANACHRONISM
BLOOPER
BLUNDER
BOOBOO
BUNGLE
CLERICAL ERROR
CORRIGENDUM
DEBUGGING
DIAGNOSTIC
DISTORTION

ERRATA
FALLACY
FAULT
FAUX PAS
FOLLY
FREUDIAN SLIP
FUMBLE
GAFFE
GARBLE
GOOFS UP

HOWLER
INACCURACY
INCONSISTENCY
LAPSE IN JUDGMENT
MISCONCEPTION
MISNOMERS
MISPRINT
MISUNDERSTANDING
MUDDLE
OVERSIGHT

PECCADILLO
PROOFREAD
SCREW-UPS
SOLECISM
SPOONERISMS
STUMBLE
TRESPASS
TYPOS
WHITEOUT
WRONG

ANSWER, PAGE 355

253. Head to Tail

In this puzzle, no word list is given. You begin in the upper left corner with the word START. After that, the next entry to find begins with the final letter of the previous one. This will form a chain of 69 words and phrases in the grid, all at least five letters long. The blanks below are given in order and show the lengths of the words to be found. A list of the words can be found on page 255.

```
S T A R T T N E W S P A P E R R E P O R T E R H E D O I N G
E L E P H A N T S O R O W A C K O E D E E I E H E E L S N R
A K R Y W T M U E L D U E O G N I R Y F A Q J C I T S A L E
A P O I H I P B G N I T T I L P S R A E S L U T R S I M L M
E L A A K E E A O V E O R O P L Y L N R C O V I N I G B C L
S T P A R T Y W O U O F O U U P E I E U L O E W R X M A L I
R N T H H A K E D T R K Y E N O M Y S A E A N T A E W S O N
E A E I A E K L L N E I G H S A A G D I S R A T S E I V O M
V R N N A B C E U R O L N W X L Y R R O N O T N A L R K S N
O R D T I D E R C A R T X E P A A E U N E D E I V C T I M U
E E E E O W N T K P S E E E T E S N O I S I V E L E T I N T
L T C O K S D E C T A R P L N A D E G E N E R G E O L E S C
T H A H E L N M H O W A I R E T N E U R O L O G I S T E L R
E G F A L L A P A R T S S I R K O K S E N I L R I A A S T A
H I E S A M K T R S O P R A N O S K T E O L T A T O T N L C
Y N W I T H C O M I N T C O N D I T I O N A U N C T T T H K
E K N I S N E H C T I K C A T R D A L B P C A E R N O T E E
I N S T E I N I A G A N E H T N E C N A S S I A N N O C E R
```

_ _ _ _ _
_ _ _ _ _ _ _ _ _ _
_ _ _ _ _ _ _ _ _ _ _
_ _ _ _ _ _ _ _ _
_ _ _ _ _ _ _ _ _ _
_ _ _ _ _ _ _ _ _
_ _ _-_ _ _ _ _ _ _
_ _ _ _ _ _ _ _ _ _ _
_ _ _ _ _ _ _ _ _ _ _ _ _
_ _-_ _ _ _ _ _ _
_ _ _ _ _ _ _
_ _ _ _ _ _
_ _ _ _ _ _ _ _ _ _
_ _ _ _ _ _ _ _ _ _ _ _ _ _ _ _ _
_ _ _ _ _ _ _
_ _ _ _ _ _ _ _ _
_ _ _ _ _ _ _ _ _ _

_ _ _ _ _ _ _ _ _
_ _ _ _ _ _ _ _ _ _ _
_ _ _ _ _ _ _ _ _ _ _ _ _
_ _ _ _ _ _
_ _ _ _ _ _ _ _
_ _ _ _ _ _ _
_ _ _ _ _ _ _ _
_ _ _ _ _ _ _
_ _ _ _ _ _ _
_ _ _ _ _ _ _
_ _ _ _ _ _ _ _ _ _ _ _ _
_ _ _ _ _ _
_ _ _ _ _ _ _ _ _ _
_ _ _ _ _ _ _ _ _ _
_ _ _ _ _
_ _ _ _ _ _

_ _ _ _ _
_ _ _ _ _ _ _ _
_ _ _ _ _
_ _ _ _ _ _ _ _
_ _ _ _ _ _ _ _ _ _ _
_ _ _ _ _
_ _ _ _ _ _ _
_ _ _ _ _ _ _
_ _ _ _ _ _ _
_ _ _ _ _ _
_ _ _ _ _
_ _ _ _ _
_ _ _ _ _ _ _ _ _
_ _ _ _ _ _ _ _ _ _
_ _ _ _ _ _ _
_ _ _ _ _ _

_ _ _ _ _
_ _ _ _ _ _
_ _ _ _ _ _
_ _ _ _ _
_ _ _ _ _
_ _ _ _ _ _
_ _ _ _ _ _
_ _ _ _ _ _
_ _ _ _ _ _
_ _ _ _ _
_ _ _ _ _ _ _
_ _ _ _ _ _
_ _ _ _ _ _ _
_ _ _ _ _ _ _
_ _ _ _ _ _
_ _ _ _ _

ANSWER, PAGE 356

195

254. The Sign of Torus

This word search was built on a torus, or doughnut shape. What this means is that some words will go off of one side only to continue on the opposite side. Diagonals can be tricky, so watch out.

```
U L L E R M W N O M E N I S W O P T R R K I N C R
N G W P E I T K C H U R R O E H P T E H E S E A L
U O L F V H O L E S A T T B I M L B O E N A Y R R
M Y I R R I N E F T R A S N C E E D U R C I G N G
O L L I W O L S C U S T A R D U F R O J E L L Y R
L R L E D E S W A N R I P W L A R W K N T E A D T
O M A D M K E T T O H H E B A M I A E Y R I Z I I
C A N O S O L D I D I S E R S F T L E L P E E N R
I N N A M O N B U N L L I E S S T C H E O S G M C
E Y S A I C O K A I G N D N B E E R G D A N I M A
D W O P I W K I N K G T E M A H R A G U S D E R E
E M D O T R U G H N C Z N A U D S E T R S T E H K
V A N I L L A E S U O H O E L D E B U T T E R I E
R S E W I E R V E D H E O R N C E S C S F A L L E
O C O C D E T S A O T D D C O U G H E F B O T U N
Y S I F R O M P C B T H E N O E S N O E L O P A N
D N I D T O R R S O F I S O N L F C O R H Y M A
G T I E O B E I G N E T E T N P A L E A R C O S E
```

APPLE FRITTERS	CHOCOLATE ECLAIR	DUNKIN DONUTS	LEMONY
BAVARIAN	CHURRO	FLOUR	NAPOLEONS
BEAR CLAW	CINNAMON BUN	FROSTING	PASTRIES
BEIGNET	COFFEE	HOLES	POWDERED SUGAR
BLUEBERRY	CREME FILLING	HONEY GLAZE	SPRINKLES
BOSTON CREAM	CRULLER	ICING	STRUDEL
BOW TIE	CUSTARD	JELLY ROLL	TOASTED COCONUT
BUTTER	DEEP-FRIED	KRISPY KREME	VANILLA
CHEESE DANISH	DOZEN		

ANSWER, PAGE 356

255. Wheel of Fortune

All the words and phrases in this puzzle are related to the TV game show "Wheel of Fortune." In the spirit of that show, we've only given you the enumeration and the letters R, S, T, L, N, and E. All entries are given in alphabetical order. A word list can be found on page 256.

```
          V R E M I F I H
        B A N K R U P T A D T O
      S N T U M I M A R C I Z G E
    I N N O I C O N S O N A N T H N
  C A D E V K T F I G G N I T R A P D
  S H R E O N A L T E W H N C E N E N
T H E A W W M A J E J T O O R D G L U E
B E F O R E A N D A F T E R E S M O O S
O N R B A L I H A E S V E T L L A E R A
R D N R C S I E D U I T A N U D N E S Y
S K E E W E G E L L O C A L C I H F U E
T H A T E T E S O C I T O P K C A J N E
N T E T N C G N C D E W E C T O Y N O S
L O S E A T U R N W O V U A L D I B B T
  E S L O M E Y E I E N W S T P I M R
  E P S Y O S U H N A L N H S V E I T
    O B U Y S A T N E N V E L O P E
    E L Z Z U P E H T E V L O S
      V O W E H R L R D A V L
      E W B A F R R Y
```

_ _N_R_ _T	EN_EL_ _E	L_ _ _	T_ _N_
_E_ _RE _N_ _ _TER	E_ENT	_ER_	T_TLE
_ _N_S R_ _N	_REE S_ _N	NE_ _ _R	TR_ _
_ _S_	_ _ESS	_ _RT_N_ _ _ _T	_ _NN_
_ _TE_ _R	_ _N_ _ _N	_ _T S_ _ _ _	_ _ _ELS
_ _ _RL_E _'_ _NNELL	_ _ _ _ _ _T	_L_ _E	_ _EEL_ _T_ _ER
_L_E	_ _N_ _ _RL_	S_LE T_E _ _ _ _LE	_ _NNER
_ _LLE_E _EE_	LETTER_ _ _R	S_N_	_ _R_S
_ _NS_N_NT	L_SE _ T_RN	S_N_ _ _ _TE_	

ANSWER, PAGE 357

256. Passing Zone

Every word in this puzzle passes over one letter from a different entry. That is, every entry in the grid will have an extra letter that is part of another entry.

```
I C A M P I N X G F A L S I G G N A L A H E A D
P O L W I C E O L P A R K A N D R I D R E T E I
H E R O C A R B U S S I N I T U T F H O E N C V
Y R A R L B I L C T O U S N T S R R Y A O W E I
R E N R P I L L A C U S E T U E O E G D I R B D
D P G A E N H A D T O R N F S L O P Z C E P N E
N D A E S O O C T E W N E H W Y R Y E P P I L S
O M E S O E E Y R F O O X N L O A W O L U C L D
I D R L S V E C R E W O T T U W O K O O L N S H
T T S B R W R N I L I L E L A G P D U S L I L I
A O T U U E I E O L A T X W R E U O T E D C M G
M S A O E A N T D H T T O D R A R Y T D E A O H
R C T D P A D G H S P T I F I R S A T A I D S W
O T I O H L E R M C E E T P P E I G T R A R A A
K C O R G N I E L L A F L M S W S R I S D E T Y
F T N E E P N M B Y T R H E E O A E U T E A H O
N L I G H T H E O U S E L E V A R G E S N O O L
I Y R E V A N E B U C K L E U T P H S L D A R R
```

BRIDGE OUT	EMERGENCY CALL BOX	LOOKOUT TOWER	REST AREA
BUCKLE UP	FALLING ROCK	LOOSE GRAVEL	ROAD CLOSED
CAMPING	FIRST AID	MILEPOST	SCHOOL
CURVE	FOOD	NEXT EXIT	SIGNAL AHEAD
DEAD END	FRESH OIL	NO U TURN	SLIPPERY WHEN WET
DEER CROSSING	HILL	PARK AND RIDE	STOP
DETOUR	HOSPITAL	PASS WITH CARE	TELEPHONE
DIESEL	INFORMATION	PICNIC AREA	TOW AWAY ZONE
DIVIDED HIGHWAY	LIBRARY	POLICE	USE LOW GEAR
DOUBLE ARROW	LIGHTHOUSE	RANGER STATION	YIELD

ANSWER, PAGE 357

257. All Mixed Up

None of the words in the list can be found in the grid. Instead, you'll be able to find an anagram of every entry in the grid. The numbers in parentheses tell you the length of all the words in the grid entry. A word list can be found on page 256.

```
R E H T A E W D A B V I C E P R E S I D E N T S T
T H L E B O I A S I C S U P R E M E C O U R T S T
S E O T R S O R T S A O B L F O R R S T E E H T E
N M R D T N A E D R N I R D X N O I T A R E N E G
A P I A U O L N D E L B A R U C E S S T E N R A G
I E S G B S B I A T N T C I I S O U O H D I N D S
R T O N F A N A R N R V K V R E R A C L P G I I C
E N A O T E C R D U Y I E E S E E S G T L N L E E
T E R L C R C T S O S H T R I A D E N R A E L S N
Y M E A E T E G M C S T S S O A N N I I N L P T T
B S N G D N N O U I E L L S A M A M T T E I T I E
S E E N O I T D E L I A R E D N E O A O T V G F R
E L C I T R A S W E N E W A D O M L R R S I R H S
R A D S N C U T H D W S P T P L A N E T I C K E T
P S O H R O R S E O H S K C A R T I P T L N A I A
S P R O U T R P C K W Y R O M E M F O T U O O L G
D G N I K N O I L E H T I C K R I G H T O N C U E
```

ADVERTISERS (6'1,4)
AIRDATE (7)
ARTS AND LEISURE (8,6)
ASSORT (6)
BACKREST (8)
BEARCAT (7)
BRITNEY SPEARS (13)
CANDOR (6)
CENTURIES-OLD (4,8)
CLARET WINES (4,7)
COMPUTER USER (7,5)
DEADLIER (8)
ESCROW (6)

EXONERATING (10,1)
FROM ME TO YOU (3,2,6)
GANGLIONS (9)
IN REGARD TO (3,7)
KEPT IT CLEAN (5,6)
LEANDER (7)
LOCATES (2,5)
LOVE ME TENDER (6,6)
MINERAL SALT (6,5)
NAMELESS (8)
NOISIER (7)
NOTHING LIKE (3,4,4)
PREDICTIVENESS (4-10)

PROGNOSTICATES (9,5)
RAIN DANCES (7,3)
RECEIVING LINE (5,8)
RENAMED (7)
REPLANTED (3,6)
RESHIP (6)
RETOUCHING (5,2,3)
ROMANIANS (3,6)
SACRE BLEU (9)
SECRET AGENT (6,5)
SENATOR (7)
SETTLER (7)
SHORTCAKES (5,5)

STAIDEST (8)
STATESIDE (9)
STOP SIGN (8)
STRANGE (7)
STRUDEL (7)
STUPOR (6)
TASTE BLOOD (4,6)
THE WALTONS (6,4)
THING (5)
UNCRATE (7)
WHEAT BREAD (3,7)
WORRIED (7)

ANSWER, PAGE 358

258. Getting Lost

Everything in the word list is something you can lose. Furthermore, every entry has lost one of its letters before being placed in the grid. No word is allowed to be found completely within another entry.

```
T H A R I N G H E B P R V I L E G E S P R V
Y A O E L I T B B T L E H E R T U T O E S R
M T W P G T I A A T E M A N R U O T U T T E
H I I E R C A L L L N O U T U T S E R E T N
N E W T O E O A L E F T R O H L I P W O T C
Y N T U N L E N E C N E O N N I E P A N F O
O C T S D E L E T A W C E I E S S A Y H S T
R E T D U T I T L A R O H L V B J R U O Y E
M S R N E T A B D U C N S C I O U S N E S S
I N T U C H E C O A A T W M T N E M O M T T
N E E O S R B Y K B Y O L G C K G E I A H C
D C S P I P L A E I N L I N E O N M T G A E
U I E N O D M O Y I N T K Y S R I O I I N P
O E G T E L C O R T C A S E R W T R T B W E
S S H I E S L R C Y E F R E E D O H E E P R
E T O G T O T A O S T E M E P R O A P H O S
P R I A C Y T I A S E I T S E L B A M T W T
K C A B R U O Y F O T R I H S E H T O N E Y
```

ABILITY	DEBATE	MARBLES	SLEEP
ALL FEELING	DIGNITY	MEMORY	STEAM
ALL HOPE	ELECTION	MOMENTUM	STRIPES
ALTITUDE	FAITH	MONEY	TEMPER
APPETITE	FOOTING	NERVE	TEN POUNDS
BABY TEETH	FORTUNE	PATIENCE	THE BIG GAME
BALANCE	FREEDOM	PERSPECTIVE	THE SHIRT OFF YOUR BACK
BATTLE	GROUND	PLACE IN LINE	TITLE
BEARINGS	HEARING	POWER	TOUCH
COMPETITION	HEART	PRIVACY	TOURNAMENT
COMPOSURE	HOUSE KEYS	PRIVILEGES	TRACK
CONSCIOUSNESS	IDENTITY	REMOTE CONTROL	WAGER
CONTACT LENS	INNOCENCE	RESPECT	WALLET
CONTEST	INTEREST	RIGHTS	YOUR COOL
COUNT	LICENSE	SANITY	YOUR JOB
COURT CASE	LUNCH	SENSES	YOUR MIND
		SIGHT	YOUR WAY

ANSWER, PAGE 358

200

259. U-Turns

Every entry makes turn at every U.

```
H A R D W U R E H T N I S R E D R U O R U O T K S
U A L L Y E X C L U R E C L U U M N A L E Q U P O
T T L I U M G U F T S U H B T E T S O T H I E S C
H M U T A O R N U L A I A C H S T U L O N I M B U
E P L R O R H D J U C L V T F U M A S O P U C E U
D O O E P G P G O R U K D E C U M L X E T M E O N
U R E S O U L A U A S F O O M E T E U T L U R U D
R T N E E S G U L P T U H S U H E O R I R A T R S
U U G U H C N A M U S X L T E U U E E D N O U V U
T R M E E S L S R O F L M M U I S E R U N T M E Q
S U E U R U M P U S R E U L O V E H T P U A E U Y
A N S N U T I T S B U Y U P M U S E V P T N S L T
P H E T G T R E N N U T E N A N T U M A I R T U U
O N E E A O C S D U R E A E D S H U H R A N C A D
T S O L S C M N M E N C I D I O E P N U O C E T U
T T T L A U H D U P U R Y L A N U B L A T B P U A
U O T U B M U E P A E G T O S Q A S L E R U S L H
S A P M U G I N A R U Q R E U E W I U A L S U N G
```

ACUPUNCTURE
ALBUQUERQUE
ALDOUS HUXLEY
AUTUMNAL EQUINOX
BEAUTY QUEEN
CULTURE CLUB
CUMULONIMBUS

DUMDUM BULLET
FU MANCHU MUSTACHE
GUNRUNNER
HAUTE COUTURE
KUALA LUMPUR
LAUGH OUT LOUD
LIEUTENANT UHURA
MUTUALLY EXCLUSIVE

PORTUGUESE
PUMP UP THE VOLUME
PUT OUT TO PASTURE
ROMULUS AND REMUS
RUNAROUND SUE
SNUG AS A BUG IN A RUG
SOUP DU JOUR
SUGAR SUBSTITUTE

THE MURDERS IN THE RUE
  MORGUE
THE USUAL SUSPECTS
TOULOUSE-LAUTREC
TRUST FUND
TUMULTUOUS
VESUVIUS
"YOU SAID A MOUTHFUL"

ANSWER, PAGE 359

260. This and That

Each item on the word list is a phrase of the form ____ AND ____. The first word can be found in the word search on the left, and the second word can be found in the one on the right. No word list is given, but there are forty pairs. A word list can be found on page 256.

```
N A B A B I L A I M L N O T B      P O D T H C R O S S B O N E S
I O Y W J H S L N E E D L E O      E A A T E I L U J D A G G E R
C R H D E M R A U E W E Y E O      C A R R Y E O Y U I S A V R E
K H E T K C A R T K I S S W Y      K O O C O R W U D M N E N O T
E C I N Y B T O D N S F Y S P      F C B D E C T S O E I M O T N
L T H E L P S H N A M T A B A      J R I G R L N B T H F A H L E
E A P R L D Y O A E S S L S R      A E N P E A A E T I F K R E C
O R E T T U B T U N A E P H T      F A L I A R G Y L O H E H T S
U C A S D N H U N T S A H O O      D M N L S K T O Y G G U B E E
H S C S S G B N T O G E A R C      L R E T Y R T N N A E P P R C
S L H L D E T O H H M B L T L      E E E A O Y E D W S G I D G N
A O E S R O H A E V O B A D O      I D V F R E L B R E R E T I E
W S S T U N E T Y M O U K C A      F Y E N S L L A B T A E M O I
W H S A C S T R A E O M I L K      Y H D W H E Y I S O U R C O C
K I T H G I R B N S F R O N T      T H R E A D O N F U R I O U S
```

261. Animal Impressions

In this puzzle, no word list is given. You'll need to reconstruct the list of animal-related phrases of the form "as ___ as a(n) ___." Each pair of words that fits will cross on one of their common letters. A word list can be found on page 257.

```
I  N  A  L  D  R  I  B  Y  A  J  N  R  E  G  U  C  B
M  E  N  E  T  S  Y  I  M  W  E  A  K  S  A  I  U  L
E  S  K  R  A  R  E  H  L  T  O  I  M  T  K  G  T  E
S  A  D  E  A  D  O  N  T  S  G  W  S  U  I  N  E  L
N  O  V  K  E  T  E  I  M  L  H  I  L  B  L  S  E  R
P  E  A  C  O  C  K  E  Y  I  A  S  D  B  R  E  B  E
E  R  S  A  C  R  A  I  B  P  E  E  M  O  U  L  A  V
Y  C  O  M  Q  N  N  S  H  P  L  B  H  R  I  U  T  A
T  R  P  U  C  R  S  O  T  E  S  G  E  N  T  L  E  E
V  E  I  N  D  L  O  T  E  R  U  L  D  H  A  I  A  B
N  E  G  A  W  H  A  P  P  Y  O  X  R  M  I  G  G  D
T  S  T  P  H  T  E  M  N  W  I  N  B  B  N  R  L  Y
L  U  E  E  S  N  A  I  L  O  R  C  G  N  G  A  E  L
I  O  S  L  H  P  O  Y  E  R  U  R  A  E  B  C  W  T
A  M  O  N  D  U  M  B  D  M  C  O  D  E  I  E  T  S
D  W  E  S  O  O  G  P  L  A  Y  S  U  B  O  F  A  M
A  E  T  M  E  A  D  T  T  T  H  S  E  W  P  U  L  R
I  O  R  E  T  S  B  O  L  R  E  D  N  U  O  L  F  R
```

ANSWER, PAGE 360

262. Black Hole #8

In this puzzle, the letters in the center of the grid are missing. Once you've found all the words in the grid, the missing letters will spell out a quote from Piet Hein.

```
S P H I L S A O X O F T R E S E D W S O P S C R O L L S A W
E K O J L A C I T C A R P Z H H R E H R S M K E S U E N C S
A T U C M R L T I M A T D E O E A L Y I R F D O R N I Y H N
T D T I H U A L O C A S N E P E C H E A T I N G O N I L U R
T A L R T D R S U E P T E R F H F S E V E C B T L T K C I
L N L T O N S U E H ▓ ▓ ▓ ▓ ▓ ▓ ▓ ▓ ▓ H S K L A T D O K N
E T H E G O O D E A ▓ ▓ ▓ ▓ ▓ ▓ ▓ ▓ ▓ G E R N G I U O J N
M K N M N H O N W I ▓ ▓ ▓ ▓ ▓ ▓ ▓ ▓ ▓ E L P R I N T R O N
A A G O I T P U E T ▓ ▓ ▓ ▓ ▓ ▓ ▓ ▓ ▓ A G L L T G T B N G
R H R E K A E R B E ▓ ▓ ▓ ▓ ▓ ▓ ▓ ▓ ▓ H A L E S U H T E M
I E F G R O T D H L G R L V I D A S I E Z S R U E O F T S O
N M A T O N S S K I A I L A I D S I E G E T O N V D B Y I R
E N I T W L H R O C S P R H E C A C T I O V E R N I G H T D
R E H S E M O C E B H T A E D O L S U P N P I R I E D T H V
S E P A R A P H R A S E I B P N T D U M P I N G G R O U N D
```

A.A. MILNE	DESERT FOX	INVESTIGATORS	SCROLL SAW
BASALT	DIVULGE	LAID SIEGE TO	SEATTLE MARINERS
BASICS	DRACHMAE	METHUSELAH	SHEIKH
BEHAVIOR	DUMPING GROUND	ORPHEUS	SHOP FLOOR
BREEZE	DVD-ROM	OVERNIGHT	STRAIGHT-TO-VIDEO
BROOKLYN	FOOTRACE	PARAPHRASE	TALENTED
CAESAR	GEOMETRIC	PENSACOLA	TALK SHOW
CHEATING ON	GOOD LOOKS	PERIGEE	THE GOOD EARTH
CHEEKBONES	GRETZKY	PET SHOP	TIEBREAKER
CHUCK JONES	HEELPRINT	POND SCUM	TOYOTA
COUNTERTOP	HEN PARTIES	PRACTICAL JOKE	VASSAR
DEATH BECOMES HER	HOLOGRAM	REGATTA	WHITE KNIGHT
DEFEAT	HONDURAS	REWORKING	WRITE-UP

ANSWER, PAGE 360

263. A Star Is Born

The letters STAR in each entry get replaced by a ★ in the grid.

```
T  H  R  E  N  R  O  C  E  H  T  D  N  U  O  ★  U  J  E  W  L  F  A  Y  A
R  B  L  A  C  K  A  ★  T  E  E  A  I  M  P  L  A  Y  D  I  S  I  A  S  A
★  W  L  H  I  O  S  L  E  R  D  M  E  T  A  R  I  ★  E  C  O  R  D  S  E
T  V  L  R  M  D  I  D  ★  N  P  A  ★  G  N  A  G  U  F  E  S  ★  I  T  Y
R  S  E  S  U  A  E  O  ★  R  C  C  E  S  S  T  Y  E  O  B  R  U  M  E
A  A  G  D  E  M  C  R  E  A  U  Y  L  H  A  E  T  V  N  E  U  I  T  H  K
B  E  ★  ★  G  E  R  S  S  ★  D  E  K  A  N  K  ★  S  S  E  E  V  A  T  ★
E  S  E  H  T  R  S  R  D  O  B  S  Y  A  R  ★  A  V  E  U  N  A  N  C  D
C  R  I  C  H  I  O  E  F  I  F  N  N  D  I  I  V  I  L  R  O  L  D  U  R
G  U  L  ★  O  C  A  D  M  L  ★  T  S  I  I  N  C  T  E  H  ★  L  E  T  A
U  E  L  N  W  A  O  ★  R  Y  ★  L  H  N  G  D  B  E  S  U  D  I  T  T  H
E  I  I  R  F  W  T  T  H  B  H  E  O  E  Y  N  D  O  ★  N  E  T  S  H  C
★  ★  W  O  P  E  L  S  U  A  Y  ★  T  O  L  G  I  E  G  L  S  T  S  E  I
T  G  H  C  O  ★  I  C  A  E  A  R  U  T  H  O  E  L  E  C  I  I  L  M  R
I  U  O  B  W  E  K  O  N  P  T  B  E  B  W  O  ★  R  T  T  F  N  H  U  A
S  D  I  D  M  N  E  B  H  C  T  U  H  D  N  A  Y  K  S  ★  A  B  G  ★  E
T  F  E  R  R  A  R  I  T  E  ★  O  S  S  A  R  U  T  ★  H  T  A  E  D  H
```

AMERICA WEST ARENA	CUSTARD	GUEST ARTIST	RICHARD STARKEY
ARISTA RECORDS	CUT THE MUSTARD	IMPRESSIONIST ART	STARFISH
BART STARR	DASTARDS	JUST AROUND THE CORNER	STARK NAKED
BLACK AS TAR	DEATH STAR	LIEUTENANT STARBUCK	STARSKY AND HUTCH
BUENOS TARDES	DEFENSELESS TARGET	PASTA-RONI	STARTLING
BUSTA RHYMES	DOG STAR	RAIDERS OF THE LOST ARK	STARVED
CLARICE STARLING	FERRARI TESTAROSSA	REDSTARTS	TELSTAR
CORNSTARCH	FIRST ARRIVAL	RESIST ARREST	VAST ARRAYS
COSTA RICA	GANGSTA RAP	REST AREA	WILLIE STARGELL
CO-STARRED			

ANSWER, PAGE 361

264. Exchanging Letters

In every one of the mail- and writing-related entries, two letters have been exchanged. For example, EXCHANGING LETTERS could be found in the grid as EXTHANGING LETCERS.

```
E U I V R E S L E C R A P D E T I N C S M Y M S E
S P O O B P X R D E N L E L E S D O I N R S A G U
S X A L I N G W A E P T I D U S M E W M T N V O D
A I B B L Y I T T D U O B P R Y S E M A P G I O E
F L S I G N E T U R A C S O L J D R E U S S L T G
C E P Y E L E L N I R M N I G B O E I U C T A R P
T R D R I R T T W A O R M B O B T H C L E O E T T
S E S E W A O C O R R E S O P N D E N C E T N M S
R C N I E S M A I L N A I L R D P U L T U U N A O
I N P O E A I O Y T H P E M P I L E P R E G E I A
L Y T N T M L B A L E P E R O S S W N G E O L L T
T S R T R I N R D E A D L E T T E R C F F I O E T
X E H A E T P N X W R I O N S G D O A P L N P A E
R B I T P C U C I P Z O D E C D L Y A E C G E R E
S L O S L T H O I N R E V G A A A H M I D L N R E
Y T I O R I R P E W I E N E R P O S T S C R P I T
N I S E P T H Y R E V I S E D L A I C E P L E C P
R E K R O W L A T P O S O S S O H W E V I S U R C
```

AIRMAIL
BAR CODE
CARBON COPY
COMPLIMENTARY CLOSE
CORRESPONDENCE
CURSIVE
DAILY
DEAD-LETTER OFFICE
DEAR JOHN
DEAR SIR OR MADAM
DOCUMENT
DROPBOX

FEDERAL EXPRESS
FIRST-CLASS
MAIL CARRIER
MANILA ENVELOPE
OUTGOING
OVERNIGHT
PAPER
PENCIL
PEN PAL
P.O. BOX
POISON-PEN

POSTAGE DUE
POSTAL WORKER
POSTCARDS
POSTSCRIPT
PRINTS
PRIORITY
RETURN ADDRESS
RETURN TO SENDER
ROUTE
SEALING WAX
SIGNATURE

SINCERELY
SNAIL MAIL
SPECIAL DELIVERY
STAMPS
STATIONERY
STREET NAME
TYPEWRITTEN
UNITED PARCEL SERVICE
U.S.P.S.
WISH YOU WERE HERE
ZIP CODE

ANSWER, PAGE 361

265. Hop, Skip, and Jump

In every entry, one of the letters jumps from its original position to a new position in the word. After the jump, the entry can be found in the grid.

```
T N H E L L A B G N I C U O B E H T W O N L L O F
E R O E A I S N O W O P T R E S O C R A I B E K D
R G O R E P P I K S D M U G U T E D E T O F C A O
L R L O D W F N T O T O D R G A O B N I R P S N A
R A R I V C M R E H H A A T A I G N E O I W E G I
D S T E A U S Y O C O Q C A U N E H A T W S V A D
E H U T D O M K T L A U K L I E T R S H A K E R O
E O Z A I D N O I A G A T P E U I O T H I V A O C
E P L L E U C A G I P T M L B C G U C T T H S T U
E S K D I O F F E E I U R E E O O E N C E K C I B
S P T O S N H P R A X N T Y O T L U G N C C K E L
T E Y P R B O U O J V M G O E E R M R A A H R X E
D R H E T P H A N E T L I O E N T M J S U U A I D
T I A V E L I A M E V E A T P Y O G A U E E C H U
A V E C T O C S O J U A S S T I J F N P L R E Y T
G N I V K I D Y S I T P L B Y N F I D P O D L L H
I N G I E M F L Y N G S Q U I I R R E L N L T H E
I N T M E R E M E D I A T P L E S I T T E S I P S
U O L Y M O P T I K S S M T E T R P E H E N H N A
W K I N B N G E E C O U R D G T A C E D H S A P E
```

ALLEY-OOP	HOPSCOTCH	OBSTACLE COURSE	SKYDIVING
BOUND	HURDLES	PAS DE CHAT	SLAM DUNK
BUNGEE CORD	JUMPING JACKS	POGO STICK	SPRINGBOARD
DOUBLE DUTCH	KANGAROO	POLE VAULT	STEEPLECHASE
FLYING SQUIRREL	LEAPFROG	QUANTUM LEAP	TAE KWON DO
"FOLLOW THE BOUNCING	LUTZ	SACK RACE	TIGGER
BALL"	MEXICAN JUMPING BEAN	SALCHOW	TRACK MEET
GERONIMO	MUDSKIPPER	SKIP ROPE	TRAMPOLINE
GRAND JETE	NORDIC SKIING	"SKIP TO MY LOU"	TRIPLE AXEL
GRASSHOPPER			

ANSWER, PAGE 362

266. Boxing Match

Every entry must be found in the grid in a box shape. It will start in a corner, and then trace out a rectangular path in the grid, ending in a square next to where it started.

```
N A C I S Y A R W H L U B G E N I D B O X I N G A
V A S R U G A R E E L T I N R T E L I S M I E W S
G J O I N O B G B S R A G I S S R R T T I G O N S
S P O E L D W M S N J T D M M E U O Y L E H V O O
N T L E M Y O A E A H C A M R S P W N O I T A I C
E N I M A B L N W E O A A S O A G S B G Y D T S H
G M I J N E F G B I C B F U T U Y R E P H I V I L
A K C O T W O R E G A O I P C C N R E E U Q G T H
E R R O E N O I U G M H T P E R C S N D I S G N I
G I E W Y V L H N O A C H O H A S R S E S E A T R
H E B O X A E V S A E S T H O P P E B E E L R E A
T L I R T E G A S L M E T G H L I F E R N U G S I
L I G H T H V N T M L N E R S N D H R R Y R A P S
E S U R E E T H E O R I A T E O E U G P R H S S
T M P T D O B T B S H O E A B U V U N M R I D N R
E D R B I C H E H A R C L A R T D O A G O N M O E
U N N E Y I H M A R C L L H E L A H L N O G U U N
T E N E G T S O N A I N I X D A Y O C O N P A R T
```

BODY BLOW
CANVAS
CHAMPION
DE LA HOYA
GENE TUNNEY
GENTLEMAN JIM
GLASS JAW
GOLDEN GLOVES
HECTOR "MACHO"
   CAMACHO

HENRY ARMSTRONG
HOLMES
IRON MIKE
JOE LOUIS
LAS VEGAS
LIGHT HEAVYWEIGHT
LISTON
MARCIANO
NEUTRAL CORNERS
ONE-TWO

PUGILISM
PURSES
QUEENSBERRY RULES
RAGING BULL
REFEREES
RINGSIDE SEAT
ROUNDS
SAVED BY THE BELL
SCRAPPER

SPARRING PARTNERS
SUGAR RAY
THE BROWN BOMBER
THE THRILLA IN MANILA
UPPERCUT
USA/ABF
WEIGHT DIVISION
WORLD BOXING
   ASSOCIATION

ANSWER, PAGE 362

267. Trios

They say good things come in threes, and this is no exception. The word list is made of three things that go together like SOLID, LIQUID, and GAS. Every entry in the grid will have at least four letters, however. One element of each set has been given to start you off. The three words do not appear together in the grid. Words are not allowed to be found within other words. A word list can be found on page 257.

```
R A H R R Y M L W R W I N D L I H G D E R E U Q N O C I T E
R E N E E O A E X E C U T I V E O E Y E J H D S N O M I S T
H I K R E M C E D I B T O H V L P V G A U I O N M G S O S N
E A G N I D X K H I R N P L D L E R E E D R I O B A H R E O
B N C N I E E P O B A E N I L G A S Y E G O R U K T R V E O
H Y A A E S R W T I H N O S E L N L A Y E S T E R D A Y N P
A D B K I O M B E L M O N T S T A K E S R C A O K C O T S S
N G E R M I U S N Y S N A E M A P A L R H A P T N L O U I E
D I E A E O N S A N F B Y N T L N E W E R O T O I F L M W S
S H T D S D O E I O L C I H A L G T R A T A T N F I A A C R
O E H T M H Y N R E S N E C N I K N A R F W B H E R E H M O
M S O A T N Y K L O A N E E S O L F M M W O T H A M A I C S
E P V A H E M A C I H C B L O O K E A O A R N S U R I P P S
T H E O D O R E L U C L A I C I D U J D A R A Y I R R D T I
H T N E P E L R A C T T C K K I F O R E N O I T U C E X E C
F I T H N A E P O T I N H J U R Y I H E R M Y A N S T P W S
W A S I I L U L I V W A E M M F W A R D R O B E A I E U A L
K F M C A N D L E S T I C K M A K E R E N T H I N G P E R P
```

ANIMAL	GOLD	LARGE	PLACE
ATHOS	HOOK	LION	PREAKNESS
BAKER	HOPE	LOCK	ROCK
BRAHMS	IGNEOUS	LOUIE	SIMON
DARK	I SAW	MODE	STOP
EXECUTIVE	JURY	PAUL	TODAY
FIRE	KNIFE	PINTA	

ANSWER, PAGE 363

In this puzzle, the letters in the center of the grid are missing. Once you've found all the words in the grid, the missing letters will spell out a quote from Dr. Seuss.

```
I  B  M  I  N  D  Y  O  U  R  M  A  N  N  E  R  S
L  A  R  I  G  R  A  N  D  P  I  A  N  O  K  S  P
E  L  N  O  R  Y  O  N  N  U  S  K  S  E  A  N  O
B  S  S  O  N  E  U  E  D  K  T  I  I  N  S  T  O
G  A  S  G  U  Z  Z  L  E  R  L  C  M  K  E  W  F
N  M  B  A  L  K  E  D  E  M  E  A  H  E  I  S  L
I  F  G  Y  U  A  ■  ■  ■  ■  ■  A  P  D  R  A  O
S  I  N  T  S  R  ■  ■  ■  ■  ■  D  G  N  O  R  W
S  R  I  H  O  I  ■  ■  ■  ■  ■  G  N  A  T  O  E
E  E  G  U  B  K  ■  ■  ■  ■  ■  E  S  R  S  L  R
R  S  N  A  N  B  ■  ■  ■  ■  ■  I  A  R  T  S  G
D  D  I  A  I  I  N  I  A  C  I  E  T  O  S  L  I
D  L  R  O  S  Z  T  S  N  H  E  L  N  C  O  O  R
A  F  B  D  T  A  O  R  I  G  G  J  I  E  H  I  L
L  S  P  U  O  R  G  S  U  C  O  F  E  N  G  E  L
A  A  U  K  A  R  O  D  M  H  R  N  S  E  G  U  D
S  S  T  A  H  E  H  T  N  I  T  A  C  E  H  T  S
```

ANDRE AGASSI
ASKED AROUND
BABYSIT
BALSAM FIR
BIZARRE
BRONZED
CRANIUM
DUTCH DOOR
ELTON JOHN

FLOWER GIRL
FOCUS GROUP
GAS GUZZLER
GHOST STORIES
GLASS CEILING
GRAND PIANO
"I'M SORRY"
ITCHED
KLINGON

L. FRANK BAUM
"MIND YOUR MANNERS"
MISTLETOE
SALAD DRESSING
SAN MATEO
SIDESADDLE
SPOOF
STRAINER

TANGELOS
TECHIES
THE CAT IN THE HAT
TORTOISE
UPBRINGING
WAIKIKI
WRONGDOER
YULE LOGS

ANSWER, PAGE 363

269. Eating Your Words

None of the words in the word list can be found in the grid. That's because they must form pairs, with one of the words being "eaten" by the other. For example, if LAST and PIQUE were in the list, you might find P(LAST)IQUE in the grid. Every word in the word list will be part of exactly one entry in the grid. Grid entries can be phrases. A word list appears on page 257.

```
P U W E R C S Y I F Y O U E T A L P R E P A P B W
O L S O E M O S R E B M U C U A L D B E P U N A N
G A E E R N E D E T I E C N O C E Y E S I G H T E
A E A T B R E B W J U R R P E D O M E T E R E H V
I R S E U F A I A D F A O T F R I T E I S C W R E
I O C S M I N D R E A D E R H O D N E T N I N O R
R P A H T K E H N T W O E N D I T R D A I S A B M
A R P S I G B E T A T E S T E S N A R W C H L E I
E O E R M I T H B W S U N L G T G N L B A W E N
W C S E V A E L R E V O L C I D A A E G C A M S D
S M E T H A A D I D E M B E A R M A R K E T O E U
T N A R E B N G E T I A H O F E R Y E C S R H A C
R R E Y O C H I O S C A L I M O N Y O N H S I D E
O P E R A T E D L C E R L N U S E V E D A I T N M
P H E E S P D E U L A E P T E R E T H U D E N Y E
S R E T N E P R A C A B S E O T I U Q S O M U G N
S R N R O B S L E K I T C H E N R S T S W O U T T
T S O M R E H T E N H E Y D G U E S T H O U S E S
```

ACE	BORE	DINE	INTEND	ONCE	SWEAR
AIL	BORROW	DOME	ITCH	OP-ED	TATE
ALTO	CAD	DREAD	ITEM	PALATE	THERMOS
AN	CARER	EAR	ITO	PENT	THIN
ANGER	CEMENT	EARMARK	JAN	PERP	THOU
ANY	CHIMED	EAU	KEN	PETER	THRO
ARCH	CITED	EIGHT	LACKEY	PORE	TIES
ARES	CLEAVES	ERAS	LARS	PORTS	TINE
ARLO	CLOUT	EWE	LIMO	RAG	UMBERS
ASCAP	COED	FED	LOVER	RATE	VERMIN
BABE	COME	FRANCE	MAPLE	SEE	VET
BAT	CORAL	FREIGHTS	MINER	SHE	VILLA
BE	CREW	GENTRY	MOSQUES	SOW	WANDA
BERG	CURS	GUESSES	NED	SQUAD	WHEAT
BEST	DEED	HAD	NET	STING	WINK
BET	DEGREE	INDUS	NO	SUP	YAP
				SURE	YES

ANSWER, PAGE 364

270. Show of Hands

Every time the letters HAND appear together, they get replaced by a 🖐.

```
T H 🖐 G R E N A D E S R E T S I S R E H 🖐 A N N A H E D O I
D S Y W L D I C O H 🖐 E S K S S E A I R I G H T 🖐 M A N 🖐 W
O S 🖐 T O O K O O L K T I I C V M Y I E T E E D I M A A F A
O G N G I C 🖐 E L I E R 🖐 N O E 🖐 M N E P 🖐 S O F F B T O N
L L I C N A T A Y M R I C 🖐 I C D O S M A S 🖐 G R A B S T T
B N E R A I I G M C C S R A W S 🖐 N A P H S I D C G R 🖐 H T
🖐 D M H O S K E S B H T E L A T P D O C K J D K A E E G O
S C O K 🖐 N 🖐 A F O I R M A D R A C E S X E 🖐 O A T P 🖐 I H
E M C C P T 🖐 C H P E A L I R E O 🖐 A N 🖐 E D O E A V R E O
L E U R A A Y T A S F M A I M C S L E D D L G B N E T E L L
F F I N S 🖐 C T A R C S H E D E 🖐 E E E A 🖐 L 🖐 L S E H S D
F R O D E K C I P 🖐 R 🖐 B A L L H R A W C S L A T O H T E Y
S J A M E S T A 🖐 E R Y T 🖐 I N H G E U A E 🖐 L Y L O O U O
R A W N A I D N I 🖐 C N E R F C 🖐 H O S S S A M V C E E T U
H E S 🖐 A M E S U S T V A R T T M T I T C S 🖐 E G N A H C R
N G N E D I A M 🖐 G O 🖐 B A G S A 🖐 A W H U A T S T H T E 🖐
P I O I N E T B O L 🖐 B C B Y F D T I O R T E 🖐 T A N N I S
🖐 T A L L D A R K A N D 🖐 S O M E C H E R E K U L 🖐 L O O C
```

ALL HANDS ON DECK
BACK-HANDED
CASH AND CARRY
CATCH RED-HANDED
CHANDELIER
CHANGE HANDS
CLOSE AT HAND
COME IN HANDY
COOL HAND LUKE
COWHAND
DISHPAN HANDS
EASIER SAID THAN DONE
FLESH AND BLOOD
FRENCH AND INDIAN WAR

GEORGE HANDEL
HANDBAGS
HANDBALL
HANDCUFF
HAND GRENADE
HANDGUN
HANDICAP
HAND-IN-HAND
HANDKERCHIEF
HANDMADE
HANDMAIDEN
HAND OVER
HANDPICKED
HANDSAW

HAND SOAP
HANDS-OFF
HANDSTAND
HANNAH AND HER SISTERS
IRON HAND
"I WANT TO HOLD YOUR
   HAND"
JONATHAN DEMME
KITH AND KIN
LOVE HANDLES
MERCHANDISE
MLA HANDBOOK
NATHAN DETROIT
ON THE OTHER HAND

OOH AND AAH
RAYMOND CHANDLER
RIGHT-HAND MAN
SCRATCH AND SNIFF
SEARCH AND RESCUE
SHAKING HANDS
SLEIGHT OF HAND
SMASH AND GRAB
TALL, DARK, AND
   HANDSOME
THE PANHANDLE STATE
TOUCH-AND-GO
TRISTRAM SHANDY
W.C. HANDY

ANSWER, PAGE 364

271. Cross Word Puzzle

Each word on the list can either follow or precede the word CROSS to form a new word or phrase. They can all be found in the grid below, along with a second word, with which it is paired. When those pairs are considered, they will have a feature appropriate to this puzzle's theme. A list of the second words can be found on page 258.

```
T N H C O E C O X N R M C E P T S T P T O B E F Y
A T O H F I W E O P E E O C R B P T H L U E X R L
I S R I A H D V D A F I U C O U R T I C G R E E K
N G L N T N T U N A E R E A D O U T K T A H R O G
E E T A I A D I A P R E D N U D H S T H C Y T R E
D R R F S O N R T E E M W E C A E N Q A T H E Y F
E Z A L G G I I N V N A O E T Y E K E U A N I R S
W I D T L H W T M K C E H C O O U R T H I A V N I
S N E E N H G A A A E R H C R O T Y S A S R W S G
O L S O E R D S L A X C U H E S O P R U P G M G E
S S L E T R O U T I N E C S T A L T A C K A O S F
S Y L I P I B S E R I T T T A O N O L Y E Y C T O
N B L E B A T E S D A M I I N R E N R B D I O E N
R O A D S E S C E M S P E C I A L T Y E W A L K S
H E M E E M I T Y A D P B Y L A N P I E C E O E L
A N S R P K A I T A N G O T L U R N I W C K N H E
R B T E R T A O M E I M B E O R O F E D T O H C E
B S R I T I S N H P W A R C P L I A M P B E N T H
```

BEAMS
BILLS
BONES
BREED
BUCKS
CHECK
COUNTRY
COURT

CURRENT
EXAMINATION
FILED
GREEK
HAIRS
HATCH
INDEX
MALTESE

MATCH
PIECE
POLLINATE
PRODUCT
PURPOSE
REFERENCE
ROADS

SECTION
STITCHING
STREETS
TRADE
TRAINER
WALKS
WINDS

ANSWER, PAGE 365

272. Black Hole #10

In this puzzle, the letters in the center of the grid are missing. Once you've found all the words in the grid, the missing letters will spell out a quote from Bern Williams that appeared in *The National Enquirer*.

```
K R J Y D E N N E K F N H O J N O F
W E L E N E D A K G C E I S P O R L
W W A L D O R F A S T O R I A E U A
S O A R B T I O L Q U D L T E C M V
N H T R H H U T N U O I S C E I O O
A S E L K S M P A O U X L R E H R R
F A I L S A ▓ ▓ ▓ ▓ ▓ ▓ N L K M M S
S N T H L E ▓ ▓ ▓ ▓ ▓ ▓ S E W I I T
G E C B H A ▓ ▓ ▓ ▓ ▓ ▓ H T A F L T
Y A G I L D ▓ ▓ ▓ ▓ ▓ ▓ P H V E L S
O L U A P O ▓ ▓ ▓ ▓ ▓ ▓ T S G N I K
J I R N P W ▓ ▓ ▓ ▓ ▓ ▓ B I N G A I
D E L L R W E G T I E N A F A A T P
N N R O H S O N U S A L A D B A R A
O R F I U E A L C N L N G R R A T T
M A I O C A V A L R I E S O O I N R
L C H A L H E N A E T Q U W I R D O
A E E R L O O H C S Y R E S R U N L
```

ALIEN RACE
ALMOND JOY
ANTON CHEKHOV
ARKANSAS
BLOW GUN
CALCUTTA
CAVALRIES
DAGWOOD
DIXIE
EARTHLING

FAILSAFE
FATHOMED
FLAVOR
FORWARD
GADGETS
HONORED
HOUSE-SAT
IN REALITY
JERICHO

JOHN F. KENNEDY JR.
KINGSTON
LUCERNE
MADRID
NURSERY SCHOOL
QUOTA
RUMOR MILL
SALAD BAR
SAO PAULO

SHELLAC
SHOWER
SKI PATROL
SWAN LAKE
SWORDFISH
TIME CLOCK
TRANSPORTATION
WALDORF-ASTORIA
YELLOW PAGES

ANSWER, PAGE 365

273. Letter Perfect

Every word and phrase in this list must be found in the diagram without one of its letters. The missing letter will be one of I, L, M, N, V, W, or Z. This letter will also be the shape that the entry will make in the grid. So, for example, LETTER would be found in the grid as shown below.

```
              E
              T
              T E R
```

```
T L E T N T R G V T E A E R S L O S F C I T I R A
E D R A U E E E A I N U I L R I E F R A R E R E G
E E I I N R G T T H L Z N R Y A G W T R N E E H Y
S T A N S I E A C U E E O T W B N E R H O O D T F
H T L I K H C S A T M R O O T I E G E R E E I A I
R O C E C N K P N A D I N G E R V T E R X P O P P
T B T G E E A E Y T E P L K T D E H I B C I I K R
C S N O J E E R C N E A A L G S R A A U L O N N M
I A I U M C R O O K P O O T I E N A V M A A M E R
E T N M C A B D K A S M I N O O O D A P M I F I O
S Y O D R L L U I C L H E K P M N W U K S C C R S
R K S Y O D N A O T W D A W A O O S D N E A N I E
A C Y S C L T I B Y T E T E R C D E E V I L E M P
F O E O E N Z N I H N T A L A L E L A O T H E M A
A R O D U J E S B A D R E L O V S H U I A E H R T
T N O L S M S S I L I O N Y O D T S I C L C K E H
S O S M U U O L O L D T O L O S N P T O L O R A S
W A L E R G L L G R A P H Y S O Y O E S F O R R O
```

AIRWAVES
AMERICANIZE
ARSENIC AND OLD LACE
BIBLIOGRAPHY
BLINTZES
BOTTLENECKS
BREAKNECK SPEED
BUMPKIN
CITIZENHOOD
CITY HALL
CLAIM CHECK
COMMONSENSICAL
DESTINY
DETROIT

DIDN'T WE ALMOST HAVE
  IT ALL
DRAW A BLANK
ED SULLIVAN
EXCLAIMS
FATS WALLER
FIR TREE
FROM RUSSIA WITH
  LOVE
GET A CLUE
GUN MOLLS
HAVE A COW
HECKLE
HONEYMOON SUITE

HOW TO MARRY A
  MILLIONAIRE
IDENTIFY
INKWELL
JIM CROCE
KILOBYTE
LI'L ABNER
MINIATURE SCHNAUZER
NEGATIVE
NO LONGER
OIL COLOR
PALOMINO
PARALLEL
PERIOD

PRIMROSE PATH
RANGE ROVER
REVENGE OF THE PINK
  PANTHER
ROCKY MOUNTAINS
ROOTIE KAZOOTIE
SIMMER DOWN
TEE SHIRT
THE MARK OF ZORRO
TV DINNER
VATICAN
VAUDEVILLE
VOLUME
WALDEN POND

ANSWER, PAGE 366

274. Split Decisions

Every phrase in the word list starts with one or more words that get repeated later on in the phrase. In the grid, you'll find those repeated words. Adjacent to the end of the word or words, you can find both pieces of the phrase that remains. For example, if the phrase were CLAP ON, CLAP OFF, you would find CLAP in the grid and starting with a letter next to the P you would find both ON and OFF.

```
T O W E S I O N A O Y U R D I P U T S O
A D N S D I E D V F O E I D R G E T D I
U S E E I T N M N Y U S N O O Z E A H W
O D O M V I S A Y L A N R E I R R E M E
Y O O A G O D A O S A N K S D I I T T M
W N L N O O T S K C T T H E O O N E H O
O L I E T S E E H C T A C S T U R A G R
N R K Y A D T A L I V B E H E L T E I E
B D E S O N S L M B Y E A N A K D O S T
H A T F E U A E H A M M S E D N I M F D
M A E L A C T D E E A A L N L T N L H N
R E I M N T O D I M V S F O F E E E A A
U S R E O N H N C Y C O M E E V F Y L E
N D R O S C M E T D H E L A R R O R M R
D O B K R O Y W R O C H E L L E E O R A
E O T A E F G S R G O S T L P S C L O H
E G F E P M O T A H E F I R S T R G O S
P O S A D N O T T E A K E S T U G O N N
```

BRING IN DA NOISE, BRING IN DA FUNK
CATCH AS CATCH CAN
COME ONE, COME ALL
DAY IN, DAY OUT
EASY COME, EASY GO
FIRST COME, FIRST SERVE

LIKE FATHER, LIKE SON
LOVE ME, LOVE MY DOG
NEW ROCHELLE, NEW YORK
NO GUTS, NO GLORY
NOW YOU SEE IT, NOW YOU DON'T

ONE MAN, ONE VOTE
OUT OF SIGHT, OUT OF MIND
PERSON-TO-PERSON CALL
RUN SILENT, RUN DEEP
SAME BAT TIME, SAME BAT CHANNEL

SAY YOU, SAY ME
SHARE AND SHARE ALIKE
SO FAR, SO GOOD
STUPID IS AS STUPID DOES
THE MORE, THE MERRIER
YOU SNOOZE, YOU LOSE

ANSWER, PAGE 366

275. W■rd S■■rch

All of the vowels in the grid have been removed. You'll need to fill them in while solving.

N	■	T	■	R	■	M	■	S	D	■	■	G	P	R	L	N
N	■	L	■	■	M	C	N	G	■	P	B	■	■	■	■
■	R	■	■	N	■	M	■	T	■	■	N	L	P	■	■	S
M	B	V	S	L	S	L	■	N	K	■	P	B	T	R	P	R
T	L	■	■	■	S	C	■	■	F	■	■	■	N	■	■	■
■	G	S	V	S	■	■	■	C	■	■	T	R	■	T	R	D
■	■	■	■	■	N	B	B	T	G	■	G	■	T	L	L	■
B	■	■	■	■	G	■	D	■	■	G	■	■	W	■	■	S
R	■	R	T	T	T	■	■	Q	■	■	■	B	Q	R	H	■
■	L	■	L	T	H	W	D	H	N	■	N	N	■	■	M	B
T	D	R	L	■	■	M	T	■	■	■	V	■	■	■	N	■
■	■	■	■	■	■	B	W	■	C	D	L	R	C	R	S	G	■
W	M	D	G	M	■	■	■	S	■	S	■	■	■	■	T
S	L	■	T	M	■	C	H	■	N	■	C	N	D	G	■	D
■	■	■	K	■	T	N	■	L	L	■	■	N	■	■	R	G
B	T	H	■	W	■	■	■	■	N	G	■	■	T	■	R	■
L	■	T	H	■	■	N	■	■	N	S	■	■	■	S	■	G

ABE VIGODA	CONQUERABLE	IGUANODON	REANIMATION
AERONAUTICS	ERUDITE	LITHUANIA	ROMANIA
AMERICANA	FIGURINE	MISSING THE BOAT	SAO PAULO
ARRAIGN	GASEOUS	OATMEAL	SLOT MACHINE
AS RED AS A BEET	GOOD SAMARITAN	OPINIONATED	THEODORE ROOSEVELT
BASILICA	GRIDIRON	OUAGADOUGOU	ULTERIOR
BOOGIE-WOOGIE	HAWAIIAN GUITAR	QUOTATION	WATER BOATMAN
COCOA BUTTER			

ANSWER, PAGE 367

276. The Eyes Have It

Every item in this word list contains the letters EYE in consecutive order. When in the grid, these letters have been replaced by an 👁.

```
S  T  E  G  N  O  I  T  I  S  O  P  R  O  F  D  👁 K  C  O  J  L  E  S  C  O  P  P  E  S
W  A  D  E  R  V  I  C  S  M  👁 E  N  H  A  V  I  A  O  L  B  L  U  E  👁 S  R  N  G  A
O  A  E  P  D  👁 K  C  A  L  B  S  A  O  R  E  T  L  A  T  K  E  E  P  A  N  👁 O  N  X
R  I  O  N  O  T  S  N  O  T  E  H  I  E  I  S  👁 V  S  I  M  I  L  👁 A  R  D  T  O  E
B  T  W  H  A  P  O  T  T  E  O  E  F  V  👁 T  👁 R  E  H  T  E  W  E  R  A  👁 T  T
👁 H  E  E  T  F  👁 E  👁 L  E  P  P  S  A  R  P  H  H  O  N  S  E  T  O  P  N  T  B  F
E  H  I  E  T  R  O  T  C  O  D  👁 E  W  U  D  A  Y  A  R  K  M  E  D  N  A  M  B  L  O
S  L  V  H  I  N  O  G  H  D  R  I  S  N  I  W  E  T  R  C  A  O  D  👁 N  K  C  A  H  E
I  H  👁 N  T  👁 O  B  J  E  E  👁 F  C  K  T  T  A  C  S  N  T  S  O  P  L  E  L  S
A  A  S  A  G  👁 L  I  V  E  S  L  N  👁 U  E  H  J  T  U  N  K  S  S  W  I  T  T  H  O
R  D  D  H  A  M  U  I  L  T  O  A  P  A  I  T  D  O  U  E  D  👁 E  O  O  F  R  A  N  R
E  R  R  E  T  J  R  D  L  D  E  I  I  S  R  👁 S  U  N  D  B  D  K  R  E  👁 T  T  A  W
S  👁 I  I  L  E  S  L  U  U  E  S  C  L  E  O  K  R  I  E  L  A  Y  C  M  I  T  S  I  O
S  H  B  U  N  R  E  R  S  R  A  👁 K  N  O  D  F  N  N  P  👁 R  R  S  I  O  V  👁 I  L
D  R  U  N  E  S  D  T  C  W  I  X  O  S  U  R  V  👁 D  T  H  O  S  A  B  L  E  K  L  L
L  O  👁 T  S  👁 U  E  👁 M  M  O  O  N  I  N  G  D  N  U  S  U  P  T  O  T  B  C  H  👁
E  H  S  A  👁 L  C  T  N  E  M  E  V  O  M  👁 D  I  P  A  R  N  R  E  I  F  I  U  C  H
C  T  H  👁 O  M  A  N  O  F  T  H  E  G  U  A  R  D  E  B  I  D  E  R  N  C  E  B  P  T
```

AN EYE FOR AN EYE	EYE DOCTOR	MONKEYED AROUND	RUSS MEYER
ARE WE THERE YET?	EYETEETH	OBEYED	SEE EYE TO EYE
BETTE DAVIS EYES	GREYEST	OL' BLUE EYES	SHUTEYE
BLACK-EYED PEA	HACKNEYED	ONE-EYED JACKS	SLEEP WITH ONE EYE OPEN
BIRD'S-EYE VIEW	HAWKEYE PIERCE	OXEYES	SURVEYED
BUCKEYE STATE	JERSEY ELM	POPEYE THE SAILOR	THE YELLOW ROSE OF
CAT'S EYES	JOCKEYED FOR POSITION	PREYED ON	TEXAS
CHEYENNE RIVER	JOURNEYED	PUBLIC-KEY ENCRYPTION	THE YEOMAN OF THE
CROSS-EYED	KEEP AN EYE ON	RAISE EYEBROWS	GUARD
DONKEY EARS	LAMPREY EEL	RAPID EYE MOVEMENT	THOR HEYERDAHL
EVIL EYE	MAN OF THE YEAR	RUDOLF NUREYEV	

ANSWER, PAGE 367

277. Going Too Far

Some of the words in this puzzle go too far. They have one letter sticking outside of the grid. These letters will spell out four phrases, one on each side of the grid.

```
L A F F U B U O H E E E R M G E M A E L
S B A R L R S A R H Q I D A D L S E F A
O E E B C R T R O U B A R N R A I S I N
A K E D A U I O E M R L A D L G H E Y O
A H W C N T N A W A A H E L N T C H E D
A S T S D K T S Y N S T Y O A H A E E C
N I O P E H T E D I S E B H H H M R T M
K H R L A A I S R Z M I T E L B A I R A
H S O S T E P C H I L D L S W L P M C A
O N Y U H O U T E N E I L U B L L Y J K
L A S E G A R A G G C S O O E D E D I A
U Q R V R T K R E O R G O H L N E R T O
U I L D I N G E P O D O N F O O T P A T
A O F A P A R T O E F A U O W S R W R M
E L R U S Y E S K A C P M C T N A R T N
P L L O E R S A E I N E E S H T T L S A
U O R E P B N S F R M O R L E O E E E A
E P L I R E T I U E E I U R B R M W H I
E I L L U B T D N B F I S I E B C A C H
T O C A O O M T A I E K D O L V U L R E
```

AAA BATTERIES
ANOUILH
APOLLO
AUSTIN
BARN-RAISING
BELOW THE BELT
BEQUEATH
BESIDE THE POINT
BUBBLE
BUFFALO
BUILDING
BULLIED
CACHE
DEBUSSY

DEHUMANIZING
DISASTER
EL CID
ENSEMBLE
ENTRANT
EUREKA
FAIR SHAKE
FAKED
FIRST STRIKE
FOOTPATH
GARAGE SALE
GARLANDS
GROUCHO MARX
HELICOPTER PILOT

HOARD
HOI POLLOI
HOUSEHOLD NAME
ICIER
KIT CARSON
KOBE BRYANT
LAREDO
MACHISMO
MCDONALD
MEMENTO
NAKED
NASALLY
NOT IF I CAN HELP IT
ODYSSEY

ORCHESTRA
OUR TOWN
POKE FUN AT
RAIDED
SHISH KEBAB
SIBERIA
STATUS QUO
STEPCHILD
TAJ MAHAL
UMBRELLA
VARIABLE
VULCAN DEATH GRIP
WATER-SKI
WHIG

ANSWER, PAGE 368

278. K Turns

Every entry makes turn at every K.

```
K O O H Y O U L K I L S K R A M R B M K E Y O R K
L A L K N U J E L K E Y O S K A R O P E R L A I O
I N I F K E A E O I M R O E R O A O S M D U N S M
N E T O E L R P F A K D L U O C S K E H E G T R S
E W O O A G Y E R I U S E D N G O H K T B K I K O
A Y H D E E N K K A N L D I S O P E J A C K L S W
N O Y J K O H A A T H K U L E E Y R M R A O A T
D R K U K D E T R N H E D F Y P L R E S T B C E D
S K T N E A I H K O D H I E E E O K M A R K T N
I A R K I E C C I R K T K R P L K H C T A L I E A
N E E L W C U L K N R K H C S T D C A K S T O C K
K R K A A M K V O K O U C E O R E N L P I C K H N
S K R W L S A A A C W L L A F J S U B T H P E N T
I I I Y K N M S E E K A R I M U K B T K O U T I C
A E M K D L R J K I N G C R A B N Y E C C R H C O
L S S Y E O I N N G F E A K R O F K K F O O L A Y
U E K Y K L A K E A N E G Y P T I A N C I N N L K
K A L A S K K N I W L L U B D N A Y K H A N U K G
```

A CLOCKWORK ORANGE
ALASKAN KING CRAB
ANTILOCK BRAKES
BLACK MARKET
BOOKKEEPER
DESK JOCKEY
DICK VAN DYKE
DUDE LOOKS LIKE A LADY
HANUKKAH

HOKEY POKEY
HOOK, LINE, AND SINKER
IF LOOKS COULD KILL
JACK KEMP
JUNK FOOD JUNKIE
LATCH-KEY KID
LOCK STOCK AND TWO
   SMOKING BARRELS

LUKE SKYWALKER
MACK THE KNIFE
MARKY MARK AND THE
   FUNKY BUNCH
MUCKRAKER
NEW YORK KNICKS
PICKPOCKET
RIMSKY-KORSAKOV

ROCKY AND BULLWINKLE
SNORKELS
TALK TURKEY
TECHNICAL KNOCKOUT
TREKKIES
WACKY
WALK LIKE AN EGYPTIAN

ANSWER, PAGE 368

In this puzzle, the letters in the center of the grid are missing. Once you've found all the words in the grid, the missing letters will spell out a quote from Stephen Fry.

```
P A S P D N O M A I D S G E L R R O F E A
E A D S S I O S R W U B I N F I R E U P D
E D R A G T N A V A C S E E I O E L X I L
W N A K E E W O D I K H T D O L T T E O I
E A Y L E K S A S T S R E L L E T K N A B
E Y R D A R T X E A O I N E R A A R S O R
S I E M X N P E O N U N W I E F M E A O A
B D B L A I S             P U K C I T S
I E M W S S L             V I R T U E S
G I U S E P P             Y L A E E K B
A S L P W N H             O R D E N A A
D T T E V O L             R O T O N I N
V N H U D T B             E N W N N Q D
E E U E O E T             E H H R A O B
N V D I W W U O F N N G C H O A O R O P B
T M I B L O E I S O A A O W S R S W Z N I
U U O S R R L B E N O M R O H H T W O R G
R C O G E T R F N E S I E E F F H S T L Y
E R E N E H C I M T M I L L I S E C O N D
H I E R L Y D I F A E E O R T F R V R A N
P C O E C L O A K A N D D A G G E R P T A
```

ADHESIVE	DRIFTWOOD	LEGS DIAMOND	PARKER POSEY
AD LIB	DUCK SOUP	LET GO OF	PEE-WEE'S BIG ADVENTURE
ANDY GIBB	EL NORTE	LUMBERYARDS	PROTOZOAN
AS NEEDED	EXTRA DRY	LYLE LOVETT	RENFIELD
AVANT GARDE	FAKE ID	MICHENER	SEROTONIN
BANK TELLERS	FIRE UP	MILLISECOND	STARTLING
BEDLAM	GEAR RATIO	NED ROREM	STICK UP FOR
BOXER	GIUSEPPE VERDI	NEWBIE	THE WOLF MAN
BRASS BAND	GLOVE	NOTEWORTHY	TUNA MELT
CIRCUMVENTS	GROUCHY	OCTET	ULTERIOR
CLOAK AND DAGGER	GROWTH HORMONE	OF SORTS	VIRTUE
COBWEB	HELEN	OIL FILTER	WAIT AND SEE
DARK MATTER	HELIX	ORIGAMI	WANT AD
DINOSAURS	KNOW-HOW	ORWELL	WHO'S THERE
		PANTRY	WRONG

ANSWER, PAGE 369

280. Getting Directions

Every country, republic, etc. in the list will have one or two letters removed before it can be found in the grid. The letters removed will be either N, S, E, W, N and E, S and W, S and E, or N and W. The letters removed will tell you the direction that the word heads in the grid (north is up).

```
H I T H A V G R N A D A I R L A N D
O E C H I L A N Z E A A X U I I S T
N A O E B N T I Y J I A L T N L N M
D L M N P A L T I A U K N A I A O P
U E O I A A H A T E R G H U E A A S
R U R T N D B A D Y R O R A B Z B O
A Z O D H R A E M A U B A V R B E E
B E L I Z O N R N A I A T H O E L N
R E N A E A G W R I O R I T R E A T
M V T I I A L A M I I E A N D A R K
L I L O U H A V T E R N R I A T U A
C O C M E G D Z D O A I G A L A P Z
A L G R I A E B A B M I Z A O R A A
I A N O O R H A S A N I D O P R I K
E M T C L N E V U G A U R E N O N H
M O Z A M B I Q U P S M W A T D R T
R A N O K N Y A R H A I G S L A H A
A D N M A R K T T C A P E V R D E N
```

ALGERIA	CAMEROON	KAZAKHSTAN	RWANDA
ANDORRA	CAPE VERDE	KENYA	SAMOA
ARMENIA	CHILE	KUWAIT	SAN MARINO
ARGENTINA	COMOROS	LEBANON	SINGAPORE
AZERBAIJAN	DENMARK	LESOTHO	SPAIN
BANGLADESH	ERITREA	MALAWI	SWAZILAND
BELARUS	ESTONIA	MICRONESIA	SWEDEN
BELIZE	GABON	MONACO	SWITZERLAND
BENIN	GHANA	MOZAMBIQUE	TAIWAN
BOTSWANA	GRENADA	NEPAL	THE BAHAMAS
BRUNEI	HONDURAS	NEW ZEALAND	THE SUDAN
	IRELAND	NORWAY	VANUATU
	ISRAEL	PAPUA NEW GUINEA	VENEZUELA
		POLAND	ZIMBABWE

ANSWER, PAGE 369

281. Right and Left

Every entry makes a right turn at every R and a left turn at every L.

```
R A O R L Y L B E L Q U A R R I P D R R P A R L A N O N R S
T O M D K O I U E B S C H T D A O F I O L O T C I N D E R A
X I I I J N A F U S D O I B A C H E L E I Y O H S V L E A
E E U N L L D E C O T L A L E S K E S T L O N H E E D S L L
S M A A Y T Y O D D U E M O E L A K R I N O A O O E S R E L
A R O I O I R G R L G V H C R C L S T T T E P L I C S T L I
T U E R L R E N O R S E R A N A A I D R I G M R S T E E R A
L S S E L G D G U O E S A O T R C N O H R L H E I T R A I M
Y B S Y T A N C N H H O C A F A U C D E E L B W G R L T N K
U S R L B N U O D A L O E R L T Y I C L D U P O E N F A G C
C T I A U L I A R J E R O N A L E T T N M E D P Y O A U R A
I B D A O R U M A E A K D E T E T K H A E C R W O R L R B L
R B A F D O V F E H E E O B O D B F R Y O O A U T K N O I L
R E D N A L L I T F S R E R O N E I D E T L L E S E X T I L
H O G R I E L E L S N P A I K I I E D R O M L M S R A P A R
L D A R S V E R P E I R A N K L L M R D F I L L U T I H E K
C L U O G E A R A R A F M S I E A I A C T F S O T U R S N E
L B O R C L F E M L T T A E A R S L L W I T L R E S U O H R
```

A FISTFUL OF DOLLARS	CLEVELAND	GOLDEN OLDIES	PARKER HOUSE ROLLS
ALERT	DOUBLE-BLIND	HARD-BOILED	POLITICALLY CORRECT
ALL ROADS LEAD TO ROME	DOUBTLESSLY	HELD UP	POWER STEERING
ALOE VERA	DRIP-DRIES	HORSERACE	PRERINSE
BACHELOR PARTY	ED MARINARO	KILLJOY	QUARTILES
BEAR FRUIT	EXTRAORDINAIRE	MAPLE LEAF	SEXTILLION
BLACKMAILERS	FABRIC	MARKET FORCES	SHARON GLESS
BLUE-COLLAR WORKERS	FLOURISH	MILLARD FILLMORE	SLOT RACERS
BURGLAR ALARM	FRANKLIN DELANO	NONALCOHOLICS	TEARJERKERS
CANDLELIT	ROOSEVELT	ORCHESTRAL	UNDERGROUND RAILROAD
CINDERELLA	GERBILS	ARRANGEMENT	WALLET

ANSWER, PAGE 370

282. Snake Pit

In the grid below, all entries can be found in a snakelike shape in the grid. This means that it won't be found in a straight line. Instead, it must be turning at each step. In addition, no two entries can cross paths.

```
K K T H R E C F R L E R H I A I A C
T C R N A A T E I H E P H A D U S N
A A S T E K A R S T P N O O B K N H
B I T N E A A K M S O E G W A E A M
A D G N E H S E G I S E T N S R S
N K I A C R T C F R N A K S I T L E
O M G A R O G E A A D E C A E T P Y
O A E T B A K D U U S A D N R T O I
I R E O E R A N S C N U S P I R V T
D S L R P M E N O C E C O L A I O C
N C O A A A R S N T A N I P R T N G
W A F T C T R W A A E R A P E M A N
K A T F U I S E D R H S E H B T E M
E D N S P R S A N M E L O T A N R S
D O P B T U D E E I O A I P I O A E
E C T Y N D I T W O C D A S E N J T
D R A T A O E S N I M C I N N A L T
B O O N H M Y V E M N D O A R E U S
```

ANACONDA
BOA CONSTRICTOR
BUSHMASTER
CADUCEUS
CLEOPATRA
COPPERHEAD
CORAL SNAKE
DIAMONDBACK

FANGS
GARTER SNAKE
GREEN SNAKE
HOGNOSE SNAKE
INDIANA JONES
KING COBRA
KRAIT

MAMBA
MEDUSA
OPHIDIAN
PIT VIPER
PUFF ADDER
PYTHON
RACER

RATTLER
REPTILE
SIDEWINDER
SLITHERING
SNAKE CHARMER
VENOM
WATER MOCCASIN

ANSWER, PAGE 370

283. Lost in Translation

Every language on the list must be altered before being found in the grid. The first letter has been translated, that is, moved ahead, some number of spaces. The letters that get "pushed off" the end are placed at the beginning. For example, ENGLISH could be found as HENGLIS, SHENGLI, ISHENGL, etc.

```
C S H S P A N I A M A N T E I V E S E F
H T S O N E R R K A A Q H D U T C L R E
E L P G E W A H E R N Y U O J A H S U R
C C E I A N H A W A I O M E E L E A E B
O R R S A R I I G C H T S A B N T Z D E
M O A I L N W C I I N E S L O A A E T H
A O N I A A T A I A N H O A W I S C M W
N E T M A N N Y P A E U E T N I S H D A
M O O P L H E A P S N L S A P S C C E N
I R E R U U D A M A I P J C K T H H D E
N S T N A I R O M C E I L N A A F A N U
I G G U U K E P S A A E R O K N R O G H
A A E E G R V C L B E N W R H I E P E T
R N M T C U O C T A W C H I N H N T D I
K B A E E T E Y W S C H P M L E A I R L
U K L T T H H S E S W N A A A A Y C M N
N E I I L S I R E E K G E A N H T C G A
A U S A N L G E L P R U S V S D N I H I
S H O E I E L S I L O P H I O L H O N N
G B A H G L A T I N P I D N R A C I B A
```

AMESLAN
ARABIC
ARAMAIC
ARMENIAN
AZERBAIJANI
BASQUE
CATALAN
CHOCTAW
COMANCHE
COPTIC
CREOLE
CZECH

DANISH
DUTCH
ESPERANTO
ETRUSCAN
FRENCH
GERMAN
GREEK
HAWAIIAN
HEBREW
HINDI
HUNGARIAN
ITALIAN
JAPANESE

KOREAN
LATVIAN
LINEAR B
LITHUANIAN
MANDARIN
MAORI
NORSE
PHOENICIAN
PIG LATIN
POLISH
PORTUGUESE
PROVENCAL
ROMANIAN

SANSKRIT
SCOTTISH
GAELIC
SOMALI
SPANISH
SWAHILI
THAI
TURKISH
UKRAINIAN
URDU
VIETNAMESE
WELSH
YIDDISH

ANSWER, PAGE 371

284. Cubism

The diagram below can be folded up into the surface of a 7 x 7 x 7 cube. All entries involve cubes in some way, and many of them are games. All words are to be found on the surface of this cube and may travel from one side to another adjacent side. Orientation of the letters on the cube doesn't matter.

```
                          G O T D N O H
                          O I T O N O R
                          O L Y P L T A
                          S H A K E Y S
                          D I C S E H E
                          E A U L S O H
                          S O O M S E E
  T I M N G E S M T N H E P L R O C W S S A T H H C L E D
  I C S N A K E E Y E S Y O I E F W R A H E P S I R L E T
  H E U O Y R C A N I N A O T P A Y D A Y B E P S E O M E
  N D S M T T Y E P H D H N E N C R H A P W N A T U R A L
  K I N M G I O N E E I T N D S E T E I N S Q R M U O H T
  O X C A R S U E D O I Z C E D S E I R O V I C O A N J B
  N O T G B E L S I C E E V L E R T H A T V G O N D P O L
                          A R N Y E A B
                          S D U I B C M
                          E W B P Y I A
                          K C A B L G G
                          T G H T O A H
                          E G C N P O I
                          S N S M O O S
```

BACKGAMMON	FACES	MOUSETRAP	ROLL
BALDERDASH	GAMBLED	NATURAL	SHAKE
BOXCARS	IVORIES	PARCHEESI	SNAKE EYES
BUNCO	LOADED	PAYDAY	TRIVIAL PURSUIT
CRAPSHOOT	MAH-JONGG	PICTIONARY	YAHTZEE
DUNGEONS AND DRAGONS	MONOPOLY	PIPS	

ANSWER, PAGE 371

285. Bar Code

Every time BAR appears in an entry, it is replaced by a — in the grid.

```
J W S S A R — M E U K O T — A L E B — — — Y C O A S T S L R
T O R E K — E V I L C B H D E C Z A B U S A E Y — O U R E E
E R — S E K L I W V D O U I E A C E E E R O M Y R — W E R D
E — R B E A C H E E E M S N U D H R O — E G S A T S I — N
A L L F I W A S H L Y A — Z R W C O L U N N N D G T E B D E
H E E P W Z A O C C B R I G I T T E — D O T I I E R A — N T
L E D D T N O I A H A — D R E S L M B D W O K R D J E S A —
T H E — T — T N T N R P E T M O E — A L — — H L — N Y K C
H W R A B — N O S U A Y Y R M D E G W I N S E U E R A T C —
R O — H U U A U U C — N S — W A N O V A F O D — E H T G O C
E — S S H E H K M N H I D L A B I T C R N B S B N E A Q T A
A — D N C H N R — E A O T D E — O L N I A O L P Y E U T S L
D O L T I I H E E E V E O O N R E D O M N F L I M E P C K O
— T O E F M H I L H Z E — L N S L F E O R N M E E I A O C U
E R H N Y N U R D E T N A H P E L E E H T — A B C B S W O N
L L O D E I B — N S I O B R O A R D — A L L E — — — C T L G
A T N S T E R M A E M D M — R A C K S O W A R D D R M U — E
— R E D N U W J H K — R R O K W C O N A N T H E — — I A N R
```

BABAR THE ELEPHANT
BARBADOS
BARBARELLA
BARBARY COAST
BARBECUED
BARBED WIRE
BARBER
BARBIE DOLL
BARBIZON SCHOOL
BARCALOUNGER
BARCELONA
BARISTAS
BARITONE
BARLEY
BAR MITZVAH

BARNACLES
BARN OWL
BAROQUE
BARRACKS
BARRAGE
BARTENDER
BARTON FINK
BART SIMPSON
BELA BARTOK
BRIGITTE BARDOT
CABARET
CAPYBARA
CAROLE LOMBARD
CHRYSLER LEBARON
CINNABAR

CLIVE BARKER
CONAN THE BARBARIAN
DEBARKING
DREW BARRYMORE
EL DEBARGE
EMBARGO
EMBARRASS
GABARDINE
HANDLEBAR MUSTACHE
HOSNI MUBARAK
J.M. BARRIE
KAREEM ABDUL-JABBAR
LOCK, STOCK, AND BARREL
MOTHER HUBBARD

NO HOLDS BARRED
OPEN BAR
P.T. BARNUM
RHUBARB PIE
SANTA BARBARA
SCABBARD
SUBARTICLE
THE BARD OF AVON
THREADBARE
THUMB A RIDE
WHEELBARROW
WILKES-BARRE
WUNDERBAR
ZANZIBAR

ANSWER, PAGE 372

286. Do-It-Yourself Word Search

In this word search variation, you must make the word search grid. To do this, place all the words in the word list into the grid, one letter per gray square. Any square that is used as the first letter of one of the words is given to you. Any black squares in the grid will not be used.

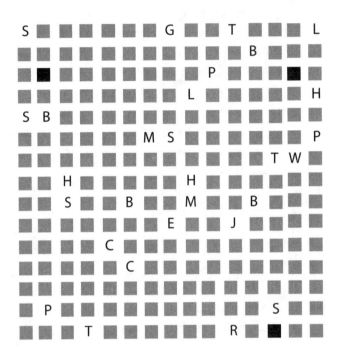

BASICS	ERRORS	MIRROR	SPANNER
BOLSTER	GLUE	MR. FIX-IT	SPROCKET
BOLTS	HAMMER	PAPER	STAIN
BOOKSHELF	HANDSAW	PEEN	STAIRS
BOX	HARD HAT	PILASTERED	STEEL
BRASSY	HOES	PLANE	SWISS ARMY KNIFE
BRIDLE JOINT	JACKS	PLASTER	TACK
CARPENTER	LADDER	PLUMBER	TAPE MEASURE
CHEST	LAMINATE	REPRO	TILES
CREEL	LATHE	RULER	TOOL BELT
CROSS	LEDGE	SANDING	T-SQUARE
CUT	LIGHTING	SCREWDRIVER	WORKBENCH

ANSWER, PAGE 372

287. Take Your Best Shot

The word search below is shaped like a pool table. It's also filled with words related to either billiards or pool. There are also two special rules that apply here. Some of the diagonally hidden words will ricochet off the sides of the table, at ninety degree angles. Other words will end up in the pockets, shown as gray squares, and their final letter will need to be entered in that square. When read in the appropriate order, they will tell you how to recognize the winning team.

```
■ E S V L G R A P H I T E E R ■ Y R G V D R A W S H O T S R ■
T T H E K U L F C L E A N T E S G L E E E R E Y A L P O M E E
O A A N P L L K L A M A R K E R E R W E Y R S B H I L N P K L
O T R F G B R I D G E L C D B A L K L I N E S A B R E A K I T
H L K A A I B S E C R O F A R R D S A B L E L E U T S T B R S
S E M F N T O S M E P O Y E N O M F O R O L O C E H T U N T U
E E R E I W O C U E S T I C K R O H A O P B I L A N Y R S S H
B I L N L I S D A R D S T O E R M Y O W A E E L S G A L G I
F A S T E D D I E F E L S O N N A S A E K T B N M N O L I M G
M E O N B R S T L N E H C T A R C S T L K L I A R O N E I M A
I H A N A W F O K K N A B R M O E O A I V O R Y C O S R P S R
S E S Z L I O C U S H I O N S C H H M D E O R N I K T C S O H
C K A F L T A L T H E J M U N S C I A B T P E T D E S E O S T
U H C A R R T E L S F T U H P O M A W S I J A E S R F P F N E
■ R W I L L I E H O P P E M S ■ U T E S O N N D N O M A I D ■
```

BACKSPIN	DRAW SHOTS	LEATHER	REVERSE ENGLISH
BALKLINE	EIGHT BALL	KISS	SCRATCH
BANK	EWA MATAYA	MARKER	SETUP
BILLIARD ROOM	FAST EDDIE FELSON	MASSE	SHARK
BREAK	FELT	MINNESOTA FATS	SHOOT
BRIDGE	FLUKE	MISCUE	SIDE POCKET
CALL GAME	FOLLOW	NATURAL	SNOOKER
CAROM	FORCE	NINE-BALL	STRIKER
CHALK	GRAPHITE	PLAYER	STROKE
COMBINATION	GREEN	POOL HALL	THE COLOR OF MONEY
CORNER	HAZARD	POOL TABLE	TRICK SHOT
CUE STICK	HUSTLER	RACK	WILLIE HOPPE
CUSHIONS	IVORY	RAIL	WILLIE MOSCONI
DIAMOND	JUMP SHOT	RAKES	

ANSWER, PAGE 373

288. Black Hole #12

In this puzzle, the letters in the center of the grid are missing. Once you've found all the words in the grid, the missing letters will spell out a quote from G.K. Chesterton.

```
N O I T I N G O C E R P T B H O U T S I D E
S E F S S I M R O I N U J A R T E G T N S S
A I A T N A O O X F A O T L M I G R A T E R
S G T G O G M I O K O U O O D E C L N R O E
S E H S L T L U S N C F I N R G T A D B I L
E A E O I E N ░ ░ ░ ░ ░ ░ ░ ░ O S A B E I L
M B R A I N C ░ ░ ░ ░ ░ ░ ░ ░ S W E Y R H U
B D B E T E O ░ ░ ░ ░ ░ ░ ░ ░ D R U S B A C
L L R H N E H ░ ░ ░ ░ ░ ░ ░ ░ S P A N A R C
Y O O I Y S E ░ ░ ░ ░ ░ ░ ░ ░ N E S E K A M
L F W W E L C ░ ░ ░ ░ ░ ░ ░ ░ O I U C L A N
I F N N F N I I J N O O A L V E I K L A T O
N A I Q U I T O D O K O R E E A F T L V B S
E C O F U T S R O I R P I D I R H F T A G R
S S E R T N U H K P C L C H H A O E O S W A
T D E R T Y J O U N V A N I T Y P L A T E C
```

ABSURDIST
ACIDIC
ALL THAT
ASSEMBLY LINE
BAKLAVA
BALONEY
BLOWFISH
BRAIN CORAL
BRIC-A-BRAC
CARSON MCCULLERS
CODE WORD
DEFUNCT
EASTER EGGS

ELIXIR
ETHEL
FATHER BROWN
FIFTY
FLANNEL
GINGHAM
HOOPLA
HUNTRESS
JUNIOR MISS
JUSTICE
KEMO SABE
LORELEI
MAKE SENSE

MIGRATE
MOONLIT
NET GAIN
NO ONE
OUTSIDE
PIONEERS
PRECOGNITION
PRIORS
QUITO
ROBBERS
SAMURAI
SCAFFOLD
SCOTLAND

SHORTCUT
SITS IN ON
STANDBY
TALKIE
THIEVES
TIN EAR
TOFFEE
UPROARS
VANITY PLATE
WALKING STICK
WELCOME
WINE CASK
WINGSPAN

ANSWER, PAGE 373

289. Getting a Clue

The following puzzle is based on the board game Clue. Once you have solved it, you should know who killed Mr. Boddy, where it was done, and with what weapon.

```
L E P I P D A E L I T S A M A D T T
E L P R O F L O E I M R G R E E N T
F E O A F B U S U S P E C T S T E E
M O O R G N I N I D A R E D E E A L
D W N T G H N L O W T C H A C M B R
T R S E C N H E L S T T S E U G O A
D E A E O A O K C I T S E L D N A C
N N D T N E I T V H A A P V E T R S
E C E A S L E E I F R E M D I D S
H H A D E U E M R B O D D Y L N G S
C I Y F R C M N E S O P K R A U A I
T H I R V C N L S A A O E S O D M M
I N M R A A S E E S W V K H I O E T
K E Y R T R F I S N O P A E W H M N
T H D E O O B A N L O I N E T W E E
N S U E R I G I V B A L L R O O M G
H T T P Y E Y E L F I V O E M O V I
E C S L S U R M R S P E A C O C K E
```

ACCUSE
BALLROOM
BILLIARD ROOM
BOARD GAME
CANDLESTICK
CARDS
CASE
COLONEL MUSTARD
CONSERVATORY

DEDUCE
DETECTIVE
DINING ROOM
GUEST
HALL
KITCHEN
KNIFE
LEAD PIPE
LIBRARY

LOUNGE
MISS SCARLET
MR. BODDY
MR. GREEN
MRS. PEACOCK
MRS. WHITE
NOTEBOOK
PASSAGES
PROFESSOR PLUM

REVOLVER
ROLL
ROPE
SNOOP
STUDY
SUSPECTS
WEAPONS
WHODUNIT
WRENCH

ANSWER, PAGE 374

290. Stop and Go

In this rebus, every gray circle either stands for the letters STOP or the letters GO. Each circle will stand for only one or the other and not both. Thus, the ones representing STOP could be colored red and the ones representing GO could be colored green.

AIMS TO PLEASE
ANGORA CAT
ARISTOPHANES
ASIAGO
BLOWING ONE'S TOP
BOGOTA
BONGOS
BURST OPEN
CHICAGO
CHRISTOPHER WALKEN
COMES TO PASS
CONGO
DOORSTOP
DYING OUT

DYSTOPIAN
EGO TRIPS
EVONNE GOOLAGONG
FALLS TO PIECES
GOBBLEDYGOOK
GOBLIN
GODSEND
GOES TO PRESS
GOETHE
GO-GO GIRLS
GOLGOTHA
GOOD LOOKS
GOOGOLPLEX

GOOSE THAT LAID THE
   GOLDEN EGGS
GORGONZOLA
GORILLA
GOTHS
"I GOT RHYTHM"
INDIGO
LOG ON
LOST OPPORTUNITY
MCGOVERN
MEPHISTOPHELES
OINGO BOINGO
ORGAN STOP

PAYS TOP DOLLAR
POINTS TO PONDER
POST-OPERATIVE
SHORTSTOPS
STOPLIGHT
STOP SIGN
STOPWATCH
THE GONG SHOW
THE GOONIES
TOM STOPPARD
TRUCK STOP
VERTIGO
WHISTLE-STOP

ANSWER, PAGE 374

291. Treasure Hunt

The grid below represents a map of a square island somewhere in the South Pacific where the pirate Captain Margaid has buried his treasure chest. It is known that one of the letters in the grid is the location where the chest is buried but this word search is the only clue left. Can you discover where the treasure is hidden?

```
T K O C A O N T R E L W A R C T H G I N
T S A O C T S A E I N F U E A T A K I E
A A L L O O T F T N I H E W O T R H D S
I M N T I E E H D A O L R E V O C E L I
S A Y T P A C N H D W C R I T R E H E T
K D E I A H H R I V E R M O U T H T E M
A P L A T O N I C Y E M A A B A A C O T
N O L K W A I R L L D S E T E G H L E I
G N O P L A Q C E L T S B H I R L E M G
A I W B N A U L O A U P A V H U C A B H
R E F T M I E U E U C M A A S B L E O T
O H O R D A T E U S R N I K A S N A C L
O D O R E L B U P U A D S N S Y O V F I
C N R S A T U N H G U O D O A T F E T P
O H E W P E I R O C F I R R S T T S L P
U E H W T I T E R R N T S T H E I D I E
R S T W A I T L I L A A G I V G E R Y D
T O T U T Y H A A B E F M P I R T O G E
W E I V E R I N L A L I N U S T R P U C
T I H O N B M A L L A I C I F I R C A S
```

ABEAM	EUPHORIA	MOLLUSKS	RIVER MOUTH
ALBATROSS	FU MANCHU	NAVIGATE	SACRIFICIAL LAMB
BAMBOO	GETTYSBURG	NIGHT CRAWLER	SEA URCHIN
DAMASK	HAIFA	ONE-WAY	TAPIOCA
DOUGHNUT	HIT THE ROOF	OUTLAW	TECHNIQUE
EAST COAST	HOSPITAL	OVERLOAD	TIGHT-LIPPED
EAVESDROP	ICE CREAM CONE	PLATONIC	USUALLY
EGO TRIP	ILLUMINATI	RATCHET	YELLOW
EPILOG	KANGAROO COURT	REVIEW	

ANSWER, PAGE 375

292. Black Hole #13

In this puzzle, the letters in the center of the grid are missing. Once you've found all the words in the grid, the missing letters will spell out a quote from Igor Stravinsky.

```
B T S U E H P R O Y S I T T I N G D U C K
R O O U C M A N A A Y N P S I E C C M C E
E V E R G L A D E S R E D A E R F O O R P
A S A H O A R I F H M Z M A E R C R U O S
K T U S O I R N I T C O R S K F A I N E N
S O H C A P Z ■ ■ ■ ■ ■ ■ ■ N M I H T S D
T I Y H H I T ■ ■ ■ ■ ■ ■ ■ A P M O C H R
H D D A T H O ■ ■ ■ ■ ■ ■ ■ Y S N O A U I
E A L D W S O ■ ■ ■ ■ ■ ■ ■ E Y T Z R N B
B R L V G D A ■ ■ ■ ■ ■ ■ ■ E T E B M E E
A M U A B N E N N A T M E K A L I F E T R
N F E N K E R T T D H O P E N E I H L E I
K M O C T I S M I N O T A U R N I N W D F
I A I E G R N R O N R S T T R V R A E B V
I N N D S F T G K B U S H L E A G U E Y E
```

ADVANCED
A LA KING
AM/FM RADIO
ASPARAGUS
BAD HAIR DAY
BEEHIVE
BREAKS THE BANK
BUCHAREST
BUSH LEAGUE
COMPADRES
CRESCENTS

DOZEN
EAT DIRT
E.B. WHITE
EVERGLADES
FIREBIRD
FRIENDSHIP
GAZPACHO
HAZELNUTS
HOP TO IT
"I AM A ROCK"
IN A MOMENT

KEYNOTE
MINOTAUR
MOUNT CARMEL
NICKNAME
ORPHEUS
PROOFREADER
ROAST BEEF
SITCOM
SITTING DUCK
SOOTHSAY

SOUR CREAM
STARCH
TANNENBAUM
TELEPATH
TEMPURA
TESLA
TOE THE LINE
TOMATO
UNITED WAY
YANKEE

ANSWER, PAGE 375

293. Antimatter

Twenty letters of the alphabet have been grouped into ten pairs in this puzzle. Whenever such a pair meets in the word list, the two letters cancel each other out and the entry must be found in the grid without either of them. Every letter pair will be canceled out three times total in the puzzle. The six letters that are not paired can be anagrammed to form an appropriate word.

```
W A L L S T R E E T U R N A L S
S O A N N Y A O E T E B R U T R
E N O S E W G Q H L O I N S N E
O T O I L T U S R H A T O V C V
W L M K N I S E E D I R B I Y O
E L Q S E D D U P M A I D T N E
R A T N I L E E E N I T N A Z L
E E T U I T R A P O U N D M U M
W L I U T O E G S R H U E I O Q
R L D S D Y O A A H E O N A W
S O C E K D P N M N O C T B U A
B V N R S C D I O E E C T C R S
S R T V A O I S T D O A D O I L
B R O A A Y M U S I C A L L R O
T A N N I E L J Q S Y T N E W T
P I H S N I T I C S B O H X R H
```

ACCOUNTING	EQUIPMENT	POWDERED SUGAR	TWENTY-SIX
BODYBUILDER	EZRA POUND	QUADRANGLE	VITAMIN B COMPLEX
BROADWAY MUSICAL	JUMPS IN	QUICKSILVER	VOLLEYBALL
BRONZE	LEFTOVERS	SLIDE PROJECTOR	WALL STREET JOURNAL
BYZANTINE	LUNCHTIME	STOMACHS	WASHCLOTH
CITIZENSHIP	MAGNETISM	TOXINS	WEREWOLVES
CRAFTY	PAVLOV'S DOG	TURBOJET	WOODWIND
DECEITFUL	PEROXIDE		

ANSWER, PAGE 376

294. Looking Sharp

When finding the words in this puzzle, you'll have to look sharp since all of them make a single sharp (or 45 degree) turn at some point.

```
L H E L W S A A E V A E L C S A W Y W L
I L S A N R L W W R A Y S P H H O E S M
R O B C O O C U S G N A O T E U R K H I
D N G I I S T O A N P I D A H C R H S W
P O L S T S I E F R N T D A S S A C S O
H T H U M B I N E G H U T K R O C D A R
E I M M T E A G L E E C S E P F A U L D
R H E A L R N F D Y H E T I R O A N T D
K I C N A U T A E H E P N E R E N R D H
N K E T H W G G E R B I E B C C E C A M
I E I B U S A S N L O P S O R N E R U E
F M I C S B E S G N N X T A E E B E G R
E D W I R E F W N O C R A P F R E N H N
P B E W H T D A I I H E O K S E I I K A
I A R C S R H A A R A R P I C F T P O I
E P R A Z O R B L G E D L P C F I Y O L
R A L I B T R C E T C A E H A I T S H S
D D E H C E E N T B N N C I L D E R H G
```

ARROWHEAD
BARBED WIRE
BROADSWORD
BUTCHER KNIFE
CHAINSAW
CHEDDAR CHEESE
CHURCH KEY
CLAWS
CLEAVER
CORKSCREW

CORNER
CUTLASS
DAGGER
DAPPER DAN
DIFFERENCE OF OPINION
DRILL BIT
EAGLE EYE
FINGERNAILS
FISHHOOK

FOCUS
HATCHET
HUNGER PANGS
LANCE
LETTER OPENER
MUSICAL NOTE
PENCIL
PICKAX
PIPE CUTTER

POINT
RAPIER
RAZORBLADE
RETORT
SAFETY PIN
SCIMITAR
SCISSORS
SEWING NEEDLE
THUMBTACK

ANSWER, PAGE 376

295. Every Which Way

In the grid below are a number of arrows. Whenever a word reaches an arrow, it must continue in that direction until it either ends or hits another arrow. Also, none of the entries are given. As a hint, all of them are things associated with or that have arrows and the enumerations have been given in alphabetical order. A word list can be found on page 258.

```
→ L E R E H ←→ R D I D ↙ G I S N ←
  L E A S A E A R E G D N → A S S O R
  O   R E ↗ W → L L I A ↓ P ↘ C A T U
  R F O T R A I Q P L R M M O R E T T
  T T R ↗ ↑ O W ↗ U C E T ↑ T N B U W
  N ↑ S A F S R E ← I S ↖ B A U T ↑ T
  ↑ H U V M A ↘ H E ↙ V R ↗ V R E H ←
  E O I H A S T L T Y M E R E O B E T
  Y ↓ C A B A R ↙ E S O B ↑ ↑ L E R A
  S D F E ↗ W O T A ↑ N F O O ↘ A D E
  U E P ↓ M O S T ↘ O L H I L ↗ T T W
  I → O G A ↖ R A E Y E ↘ I C S H B I
  ↑ S T I H S U T K A B B I E B D ↘ ↓
  O R W T ↖ C ↑ T R O F O I N ↙ O C A
  ↓ D A T R E ↙ ↑ E E N R A M H O W L
  E R P ↖ T A E A ↑ E L I P ↓ S ↑ O L
  M A U M S B I T W T L U L R F L ↑ F
  ↗ M O ↘ ↑ Y A ← Y E ↘ R S D L E I ←
```

‾ ‾ ‾ ‾ ‾ ‾   ‾ ‾ ‾ ‾ ‾ ‾ ‾   ‾ ‾ ‾ ‾ ‾   ‾ ‾ ‾ ‾ ‾ ‾ ‾ ‾ ‾

‾ ‾ ‾ ‾ ‾ ‾ ‾ ‾ ‾ ‾ ‾ ‾ ‾ ‾ ‾ ‾ ‾   ‾ ‾ ‾ ‾ ‾ ‾ ‾ ‾   ‾ ‾ ‾ ‾ ‾ ‾ ‾ ‾ ‾ ‾

‾ ‾ ‾ ‾ ‾   ‾ ‾ ‾ ‾ ‾ ‾ ‾ ‾ ‾ ‾ ‾   ‾ ‾ ‾ ‾ ‾ ‾ ‾ ‾ ‾ ‾   ‾ ‾ ‾ ‾ ‾ ‾ ‾ ‾ ‾ ‾

‾ ‾ ‾ ‾ ‾   ‾ ‾ ‾ ‾ ‾ ‾ ‾ ‾ ‾   ‾ ‾ ‾ ‾ ‾ ‾ ‾ ‾ ‾ ‾   ‾ ‾ ‾ ‾ ‾ ‾ ‾ ‾ ‾

‾ ‾ ‾ ‾ ‾ ‾ ‾ ‾ ‾ ‾ ‾ ‾   " ‾ ‾ ‾ ‾ " ‾ ‾ ‾ ‾ ‾ ‾ ‾   ‾ ‾ ‾ ‾ ‾ ‾ ‾ ‾ ‾ ‾   ‾ ‾ ‾ ‾ ‾ ‾ ‾ ‾ ‾ ‾

‾ ‾ ‾ ‾ ‾ ‾ ‾ ‾ ‾ ‾ ‾ ‾   ‾ ‾ ‾ - ‾ ‾ ‾ ‾ ‾ ‾ ‾ ‾ ‾

296. Sea Search

Every item in this word list contains the letters SEA in consecutive order. When in the grid, these letters have been replaced by a ≈.

```
T O L A I R E T A M H C R ≈ E R A I ≈ S T I N K S E L I M ≈
H P A E O N L R Y G R E A C S H T R ≈ I H T F O T O N U T S
H E N R I R O U S ≈ U Q N U R L A L I A F A I C D ≈ I A T M
S N O I O ≈ E X P E N ≈ C C O U N T Z N L F O ≈ E G L J R ≈
B ≈ S O N E D S A L T S N T H E H O R ≈ N D C A R R I A G E
I S R N N G E P D B U T U L ≈ T V N L A C O T O ≈ T C M N H
H O E E O E F H A U E ≈ A D E ≈ O A O F W L B S N E ≈ E T T
≈ N P H V T E ≈ E N T K ≈ A V N R Y I N S ≈ O L A B N ≈ T T
T G D H A O N T P E L C S C I M N A H B E M V ≈ P E A R R A
T Y N I A G ≈ I R L L A H S H T U O S E H T N D T M I L U G
L C ≈ I L H T S L A A B O E T E U ≈ N R M D D E E H B J ≈ N
E D O E H W T L A C W N R R L ≈ S D R N D ≈ T N C A A O R I
≈ R L S O C O N I R ≈ I E S R M H T P E U B U I ≈ L R N I T
H C C H A ≈ R O U N D L S R O F D F S ≈ S I O A C I A E D S
A I P ≈ T A N ≈ R S R O E B U C K I L L L T B R N A T S N R
W D U U I L E V E L ≈ S F H O R S I ≈ P R O ≈ T E D M R E U
K E R R L W Y O R D T O F T C T O H E S A D O S M I A D O B
S N R F O O T L O O ≈ N D F A N C Y F R E E N A Y L ≈ T Y M
```

AD NAUSEAM
ARABIAN SEA
AZOV SEA
BACKSEATS
BASE ANGLE
BERNESE ALPS
BURSTING AT THE SEAMS
CEASE AND DESIST
CHASE AROUND
CHELSEA CLINTON
CLOSE AT HAND
DEFENSE ATTORNEY
DUTCH ELM DISEASE
EXPENSE ACCOUNT
FALSE ALARM

FOOTLOOSE AND
    FANCY-FREE
HENRI ROUSSEAU
HORSE AND CARRIAGE
HOUSE ARREST
JAMES EARL JONES
LOSE A TURN
LOTUS-EATERS
MORTISE AND TENON
NOSE ABOUT
NOT OF THIS EARTH
OPEN SEASON
OVERSEAS
PAN-SEARED
RAISE A STINK

RED SEA
RESEARCH MATERIAL
RESTS EASY
ROSEANNE
ROSEATE
SEABORGIUM
SEA CHESTS
SEA COW
SEAHORSE
SEALAB
SEALANT
SEA LEVEL
SEA LION
SEA MILES

SEANCE
SEAN LENNON
SEAPLANE
SEARCHING
SEARS ROEBUCK
SEASHORES
SEASONED SALT
SEATTLE SEAHAWKS
SEAWALL
"THE SOUTH SHALL RISE
    AGAIN"
TRAINED SEALS
UP CLOSE AND PERSONAL
WISEACRE

ANSWER, PAGE 377

297. Patchwork Quilt

The grid below can be divided into disjointed sections, each containing one of the words from the list below. In each section, the word will be read from left to right and top to bottom. For example:

```
        P
      U Z
      Z L E
```

```
S  I  N  G  R  P  A  F  R  P  I  E  R  E
E  C  Z  O  E  T  C  H  A  C  T  C  G  I
C  T  O  N  D  I  E  W  O  U  C  E  O  O
O  R  N  E  S  N  T  R  R  E  M  P  N  O
T  I  T  U  E  T  E  K  F  R  N  E  N  T
P  R  S  L  N  T  R  R  I  A  D  C  H  I
S  E  C  I  C  T  O  R  G  M  V  I  P  I
E  I  N  E  D  Y  E  N  T  I  S  I  O  N
G  M  C  T  S  T  R  I  C  T  S  E  C  T
A  E  N  F  I  E  P  O  P  A  R  I  S  O
R  T  L  L  O  D  R  T  I  O  T  S  C  N
E  A  C  A  L  I  T  R  A  N  P  R  A  P
E  L  T  E  C  Y  U  T  C  T  A  R  S  H
M  E  N  T  T  I  N  G  C  E  L  R  E  D
```

AREA	FIELD	PATCHWORK	SECTOR
CHIP	FRACTURE	PIECE	SEGMENT
COMPONENT	FRAGMENT	PORTION	SHRED
CONSTITUENT	INGREDIENT	PRECINCT	SLICE
CUTTING	LOCALITY	REGION	TERRITORY
DISTRICT	PARCEL	SCRAP	TRACT
DIVISION	PARTS	SECTION	ZONE
ELEMENT			

ANSWER, PAGE 378

298. Bridging the Gap

In the grid below, a number of words must bridge the gap that separates the two sections of this word search. This will require you to place letters in the gap in order for them to cross. When you read these letters from left to right, you will find out the name of that gap.

```
P F Y A B E K A E P A S E H C O S L I T
B F T H I N C P I A E N P S W A T E R N
H U C A C G R G O L D E N G A T E R E E
T R N T H I E E C R D S A M A E E A L M
A G L G E N F I V E T H T O O B L L O T
P S O L E E H F S E V A M J E T W A Y U
D T B E R E R T A L T U R T S O H E B
Y A P R V R R U O R C I M T I S R E T A
C O O O B I U I T U T B T L H N K D S A


B Y R N L G I A T C U R D L A G R E O E
K L S V E I I R N L W R K H E C R I O S
C L S L E V A R T E L O T E A S T P T E
H I A R E V I R T A O O H S C E Y I N Y
A B R W E C O V E R E D R E R L X I O S
S S U R T S N O B A R I V T O E E R P E
M N S I W A S H I N G T O N S K P A I N
T A E T E R C N O C A K S H S R N U U A
L S H C N O I S N E P S U S H S E V S L
```

ABUTMENT
ACROSS
ARCH
BILLY GOATS GRUFF
BROOKLYN
BUNGEE
CABLE
CANTILEVER
CATWALK
CHASM
CHESAPEAKE BAY

CLEARANCE
CONCRETE
COVERED
EAST
ENGINEERING
EXITS
GOLDEN GATE
I-BAR
JETWAY
LANES
MOAT

PATH
PEDESTRIANS
PONTOONS
PORT AUTHORITY
PYLONS
RAILROAD
RIVER
SPANS
STEELWORK
STRUT
SUPERSTRUCTURE

SUSPENSION
TOLLBOOTH
TRAFFIC
TRAVELS
TRAVERSAL
TROLL
TRUSS
VEHICLES
VIADUCT
WASHINGTON
WATER

ANSWER, PAGE 378

299. Roundabout

Each word in the grid must be found in a circular shape like the word CIRCULAR below.

```
          R  C
       A        I
       L        R
          U  C
```

The word can start in any part of the circle and can go either clockwise or counterclockwise.

```
A  I  A  I  B  C  S  S  I  R  Z  I  N  D  C  L
D  E  R  M  S  U  I  S  F  U  T  A  N  L  N  H
R  E  T  E  R  N  O  R  O  C  I  S  I  L  O  I
O  E  T  L  A  B  R  O  D  C  C  H  E  Y  N  F
G  I  S  G  C  A  E  H  A  E  N  S  B  U  O  T
C  P  D  I  N  M  L  Y  K  L  C  U  Q  I  S  T
E  A  T  O  I  A  A  E  O  L  U  N  T  G  A  I
N  D  N  W  D  N  I  V  A  P  S  H  E  N  E  R
Y  C  E  A  R  L  E  T  H  T  O  P  L  O  R  G
J  T  B  D  E  C  H  Y  O  O  O  O  A  Y  O  K
E  I  M  N  S  T  E  L  F  T  O  D  D  A  O  R
A  E  L  E  A  M  A  G  L  N  E  S  R  W  O  B
W  R  E  L  I  P  R  B  E  U  O  P  D  W  O  Y
E  O  I  D  I  U  L  E  G  L  N  E  N  K  E  D
L  N  O  T  T  O  R  O  T  M  L  H  S  N  L
T  I  C  O  A  M  P  O  T  P  A  R  H  I  L  D
```

AGE GROUP	ETERNITY	MERIDIAN	TOOL BELT
BANISTER	FLARE GUN	MID-LEVEL	TRIBUNAL
CAROUSEL	GARGOYLE	NEW DELHI	UNSPOKEN
CRABMEAT	HULA HOOP	OPEN ROAD	VALHALLA
DECISION	ICE CUBES	PHOTO OPS	WELL-DONE
DERELICT	IN LIEU OF	QUOTIENT	WINGSPAN
DIAMETER	JIM DANDY	ROADWORK	YES AND NO
DIPLOMAT	KEYBOARD	SOUL FOOD	ZUCCHINI
DOWNHILL	LABOR DAY	SUNROOFS	

ANSWER, PAGE 379

300. Buddy System

In each of the blank spaces in the grid, there are two letters that belong there. Any word that goes through that space will use both of them in left-to-right order. When you are finished, those missing letters will spell out a quote from Honore de Balzac.

```
D  I  F  I  D  D  L  E  F  A  D  D  L  E  L  S  M  O  T  M  O  T  D  O  P
E  N  O  E  T  B  C  E  A  U  S  O  L  I  E  A  V  R  E  I  T  H  B  L  M
K  A  ■  S  R  ■  L  O  ■  O  G  T  ■  J  U  N  ■  E  R  ■  F  R  ■  I  I
C  L  E  N  P  D  S  E  O  A  O  I  F  P  R  L  E  C  U  E  O  T  E  N  L
A  E  C  O  R  E  R  S  F  S  D  A  R  R  I  I  L  S  N  D  E  V  M  Y  K
P  T  ■  H  E  ■  P  E  ■  P  T  E  ■  C  O  L  ■  S  T  ■  N  G  ■  C  Y
M  A  A  E  A  P  S  D  A  L  O  E  A  Y  O  U  S  U  N  L  P  I  T  I  W
U  I  N  D  X  K  L  O  J  S  H  T  S  D  N  B  E  G  A  B  R  I  E  L  A
U  C  ■  A  B  ■  S  E  ■  T  E  E  ■  D  E  B  ■  S  B  ■  T  T  ■  H  Y
C  E  H  H  C  N  B  I  T  O  E  Y  A  O  Y  N  R  A  E  S  L  M  T  S  K
A  N  E  A  I  I  J  I  A  S  N  E  J  R  E  A  D  L  V  V  Y  L  E  N  T
V  T  ■  H  E  ■  H  P  ■  S  E  E  ■  O  T  M  ■  S  E  ■  O  P  ■  O  L
S  U  K  E  I  T  W  C  I  H  G  T  Z  O  O  G  S  D  O  L  R  B  S  O  C
J  R  E  H  T  M  T  H  E  A  E  T  T  U  R  E  P  F  O  I  E  R  K  H  G
S  I  ■  G  R  ■  E  L  ■  D  L  O  ■  O  P  N  ■  L  I  ■  I  C  ■  P  T
S  O  F  A  B  E  D  V  H  A  P  E  E  T  P  E  H  R  N  U  A  S  Y  T
I  N  N  O  S  S  A  N  W  O  D  K  C  A  M  S  C  O  B  O  B  C  A  T  V
```

ALFRED	CHICANA	JUNIPER	SLUSH FUND
AND THE LIKE	DEAD ENDS	MID-THIGH	SMACKDOWN
ASTERISK	DUNDERHEAD	MILKY WAY	SOAP DISH
AVERAGE JOE	EXHIBITS	MISLED	SOFA BED
BADMOUTHED	FIDDLE-FADDLE	NIGHT MOVES	SPOT TEST
BASEMENT	FRACAS	NEOLITHIC	STRINGENCY
BASS VIOL	GABRIEL	NONKOSHER	TOM-TOMS
BEDSHEET	GONDOLIERS	ON THE BRINK	TOUPEES
BEHAVIOR	GORILLAS	PLASTERING	TRIPLICATE
BOBCAT	GROVEL	POTHOLDER	TWO-PIECE
CATHODE RAY	HIGH JINKS	PRINCIPAL	TYPHOONS
CENTURION	HOT DOGS	SATYRS	VACUUM-PACKED
CHEOPS	JANE FONDA	SLIPSHOD	WALTZ
CHERUB	JULIA CHILD	SLOVENIA	WHERE IT'S AT

ANSWER, PAGE 379

301. Pangram

The word search grid below is a pangram, which means that it contains all 26 letters of the alphabet. In fact, the top 26 shaded squares and the bottom 26 shaded squares both consist of exactly one copy of each of the letters in the alphabet. It's your job to figure out which letters go where.

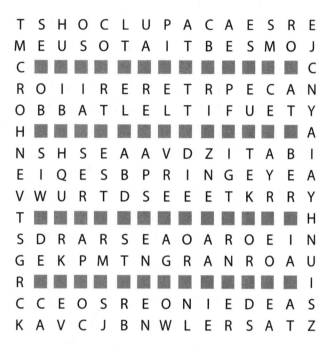

ABRUPT	DISTURB	JOKES	QUARK
ACAPULCO	DWARVES	LOKI	RAGTIME
ACHED	ERSATZ	LOOT	ROCKET FUEL
ACTRESS	FANJET	NEWSPAPER	SNOOZE
CABLE TV	GERBIL	PAY RAISE	SQUEEGEE
COBWEBS	GLOW	PECAN	TO DIE FOR
COMPADRES	GO STEADY	PIXEL	VORTEX
COURT JESTER	IQ TEST	POETRY	WISHBONES
CRAYON	JACUZZI		

ANSWER, PAGE 380

302. Wedding Bells

There are 40 words and phrases hidden in the grid below. Each item is either something old, something new, something borrowed, or something blue. There are ten items in each category. Enumerations for the words are given in alphabetical order. A word list can be found on page 258.

```
S N W O D E M D N A H R Y T C U P O F S U G A R O
Y P O L A J K E H E P Y E O D U L R M A R N R I A
L G O E B R F I I N M M N N I A N E L B U O R T R
G E W R I T G R H L O O O V T E E I I N T S H O E
W E F D T H D I E N G B M E C A D R U P E T B W S
S H E T F S F O S S I L B N P E L E B Y V I E R K
Y N O L O U S R E W H R E I A R O T E Y N H N G O
O A A M O V I E P R E M I E R E D S U S D M I D O
C M E E T E E I C A I T A E E E A W E X H L A E B
E L G N J S E R K T V E R N N R C G S J R F O Y Y
A B A B Y A O I S U I I R E T R G A A M T I G M R
N H N S T V N S U H H O U A S T U Y L S U P O G A
W D I E S G N S N P A S N H C U B R E P O R T E R
A I O N S N N M P A G I R R A I I T A G T E F L B
T I C T N I O A E S S R N O R T A E S O F S A S I
E T O U U M S T D E N T A D C L E A R S K Y R H L
R R U R S F I N E W I N E D O O W D E R T N A I G
Y N N E P Y N I H S B A N M E T H U S E L A H D F
```

Something Old	Something New	Something Borrowed	Something Blue
____ ____	____	_____ _____	_____ ___
_____	_____	___ __ _____	_____ _____
_____ _____	___ _____ ___	____	_____
____-__-____	_____	_____ _____	____ _____
_____	___ ____	_____ _____	_____
_____	____-_____	_____ , ___	_____
_____	_____	_____ ___	_____ , _____
____ ____	_____ ___	_____ _____	_____ ___
_____ _____	_____ _____	_____	_____
_____	_____ _____	_____	_____ , ____
	_____		_____

ANSWER, PAGE 380

244

303. Repeat Performances

All of the words in the list need to be altered before being found in the grid. In each of them, there is one letter that used to appear at least twice but every occurrence of that letter has been removed before being placed on the list. So, for example, if the word BOO was on the list you might have to find BOWWOW in the grid. The entries in the grid can be phrases. A word list can be found on page 259.

```
G N I L I A M S S A M I N S E R T S
U N D O C A R B O M B S T E R N E A
S T H N X R T L H I Y R E N I R A M
C U T I C L E S O A N D S O A S R F
S L M B A P U S D B B Y E X V I C S
E A T M L E S R C R O C U S E S H E
L R I A I S U S P E N D O R R E E C
O P C B I T A L S C N S E S A E R G
H S A A A N L E B C E T N R G E S O
K R S S M E L A T E A S E T E O S U
C S L E S S Y H N N U D N G A C T K
A W O F N P S C H T S R I A A S O B
L O R O R I O L E E E R T I E A L A
B R C T F L R R D R E R E T R L E S
C L O T M C P I T P E N N A N T C S
O D A S E E V R A S O O S L C A O I
R L T S E I R E E H C O M I N O U S
F Y L E D E D I L L O C V C A N T T
```

ACHES
AMINO
ASSAILING
ASSORTS
AXIAL
BACKHOES
BAIT
CAROMS
CELTS
CHANT
CHRIST

CLANS
CLIPS
COLLIE
CONES
EASE
GRASS
HARNESS
INERT
IVIES
LATER
LATISH

MAINE
MINUS
PEAT
PRIG
REENTER
RESENT
RILE
ROUSES
SALLY
SANDS

SCAPE
SHARD
STURDY
SUIT
TALC
TREBLE
UPEND
UTILE
VERGE
WORDY

ANSWER, PAGE 381

304. Missing L-i-n-k-s

The missing links in the grid below are the letters L, I, N, K, and S. Every one of those letters has gone missing and it's up to you to find them. To do so, you'll need the list of words that appear in the grid, given below.

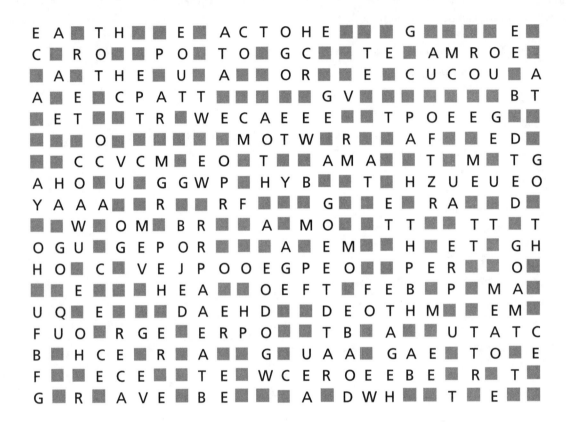

ALGONQUINS	ILLINOIS	PENKNIFE	TAKE NO PRISONERS
BELLS AND WHISTLES	INSIDE JOB	POINT BLANK	THE SUN ALSO RISES
BUSINESSWOMAN	KERPLUNK	SEA LIONS	TRIVIAL
CIVILIZATION	KINFOLK	SELLING LIKE HOTCAKES	UNHOLY ALLIANCE
CLOSE RANKS	LEGALLY	SKATING ON THIN ICE	WALK THE PLANK
ESSENCE	LOUNGE SUIT	SKEPTICISM	WEAKLING
HEADLINES	LUCKIEST	SOCIAL SCIENCES	WIND INSTRUMENT
HEAT-SEEKING MISSILE	MULTIMILLIONAIRE	STUMBLING BLOCK	

ANSWER, PAGE 381

305. What's Next?

There are a number of places in the grid with gray boxes. When filled in properly using the words on the list, they will reveal a sequence that should be very familiar.

```
P E L U D E H C S W K E E P S A K E
E U I D O C L N L Y C G T N W A P G
S N R P H I D I N G A E G A S G O D
Y ■ T E Y F ■ T F K P ■ O I G D ■ O
A B E A W L C M C L X K M N F T L O
D S T D O O F A I A I F L A G D A Y
E N O O W P O F N S A T R G T M T
H A D M O E R K O R T H N E I O W L
T ■ W E R R ■ W P H E ■ A M N T ■ U
T T C A L E N D A R S O E O V H G D
N O C O E W F O E R O L Y P O L Y A
U R R J N W H D A R I O R F U D R G
O A O B A C K B O N E T F T C C A N
C ■ R C L I ■ B E U T ■ E R H D ■ U
H C N I P A N I Q U A R R I E S I O
T O Z D I O A N O Q U A V U D A S Y
J D N A B P P L A N N E R Y T L D E
```

ARCHIVE
BACKBONE
BIPLANE
CALENDARS
CARE PACKAGE
CHEESE
CONCOCTION
COUNT THE DAYS
DOG'S AGE
FLAG DAY
GAMMA RAYS

GODFATHERED
HIDING
IN A PINCH
JANE DOE
JOSEPH
JUNK FAX
KEEPSAKE
LAUGH OFF
LIFEBLOOD
MALAPROP
MAYANS

MINT JULEP
NAIL FILE
P B AND J
PLANNER
POMERANIAN
POPCORN
POWER UP
PROOFREAD
QUARRIES
ROLY-POLY

SCHEDULE
SHOOFLY PIE
SIDECAR
SIX-PACK
TIMELINE
TURNOVER
VOUCHED
WEREWOLF
YOUNG ADULT
ZILCH

ANSWER, PAGE 382

306. Meandering

Starting in the upper left corner, all of the words in the list below can be found along one continuous trail, roaming throughout the grid. This trail can make turns at any time but never crosses itself.

```
C O W H I L L Y D D A O L A Y O R O
U W N H O N D P E L R M U T T H B Y
T S U P A T S E T T O B R A R I V E
I L L A N O I M R N H G D W D O E S
N T O T T O O A H I E T C L A P C Y
O I U U I S B E R P O K E A B T I H
H N K I N G R C A G O F C T H H A E
K L E T O B E H T E T I S C T Y T R
C O T U A T W L W W A T Y T S T A R
K A R E R A Y K O A U R I W S R U S
P O E T L O F C W L O I S S T D H Y
O A U U T O I H K E L A R E I G E A
S M O T D N T I P L W P H E D I R G
C C I N A S H N A S M E T T N A Y O
U P H T W I G C C O A N D T E R I N
G A G I O S R E P R D N E V R E A E
R R O P A T T E Y O E U A R L I H D
E E L S S E D S O C R A W L T E M S
```

AMBULATORY
BIRDWATCHER
COMPASS
CONSTITUTIONAL
FOOTHOLD
GRADIENT

HIKING BOOTS
MARCH
OUTDOOR TRACK
PACE
PEDESTRIAN

PERIPATETIC
STROLL
SWITCHBACK
TOPOGRAPHIC MAP
TREADMILL

TRUDGE
UPHILL
WALKING STICK
WANDER
WATER BOTTLE

ANSWER, PAGE 382

307. The End

In this puzzle, each of the words in the grid have a little something extra at the end—an extra letter that is not given on the list. If you read these letters in the order that the original words appear on the list, you will get a quote by Evan Davis.

```
T Y H N P U P A R W U T M O S T P E
E E N D M A I Y T K O R A N G A R J
U S E E T A M I T L U S T I I F Y T
B O U N D C M H E W M E A U E N I S
A L D O S I T B Y T I M E R T X E L
L C C E L O R E N E C N E G A S N T
C H E X N R E E R O E P D I S O I U
L S O P M O S L M M P M D U I E L T
I H A I I N U P Y A I E O T P A R F
N G T R H A L E C A S N A C N I E N
C S T A M E T J M T D M U I T U D O
H S N T T A T T R E M S F S I U R I
E F I I H E G U S U N T M G E H O S
R E O O A S C E S S A T I O N G B U
U N E N N T I D D Q U O S L O T A L
S T I T I O R N N D P E R I O D E C
P A Y O F F G U I B O Y S P O T S N
A G N I D N E L C F E N O E N T R O
O H T S K Y I N O I T A N I M L U C
```

ARMAGEDDON
BORDERLINE
BOUND
CAPPER
CESSATION
CLINCHER
CLOSE
COMPLETION
CONCLUSION

CULMINATION
CURTAINS
CODA
DENOUEMENT
DESTRUCTION
DOOMSDAY
ENDING
EPILOG
EXPIRATION

EXTREMITY
FINAL
FINISH
LIMIT
OUTCOME
PAYOFF
PERIOD
RAGNAROK
RESULT

RUIN
STOP
SUMMATION
TERMINUS
ULTIMATE
UTMOST
WINDUP
WRAP-UP

ANSWER, PAGE 383

Word Lists

90. Currency Exchange

YEN
RAND
KRONE
POUND
MARK
SUCRE
REAL
DINAR
BAHT
LIRA
SHILLING
FRANC

118. Word Ladders

Underlined words are not in the grid.

STALE
shale
shall
shell
swell
swill
twill
trill
trial
triad
tread
BREAD

WHITE
while
whole
whose
chose
chore
shore
share
stare
stars
sears

seats
beats
belts
bells
balls
bales
pales
PAGES

GRASS
brass
brash
brush
crush
crust
cruet
cruel
creel
creek
cheek
check
chick
thick
trick
track
crack
crank
prank
plank
plant
plait
plain
slain
STAIN

136. Bad Ideas for Movie Sequels

NINE MEN OUT
  ("Eight Men Out")
SIXTH ELEMENT
  ("The Fifth Element")
SIX EASY PIECES
  ("Five Easy Pieces")
FORTY-NINE HRS
  ("48HRS.")

FORTY-THIRD STREET
  ("42nd Street")
FIVE WEDDINGS AND
  TWO FUNERALS
  ("Four Weddings and a Funeral")
FRIDAY THE FOURTEENTH
  ("Friday the 13th")
MAGNIFICENT EIGHT
  ("The Magnificent Seven")
NINE AND THREE-QUARTERS
  WEEKS ("Nine ^{1}/$_2$ Weeks")
TEN TO SIX ("9 to 5")
OCEAN'S TWELVE
  ("Ocean's Eleven")
TWO-EYED JACKS
  ("One-Eyed Jacks")
ONE MILLION AND ONE B.C.
  ("One Million B.C.")
EIGHTH SEAL
  ("The Seventh Seal")
EIGHT YEAR ITCH
  ("The Seven Year Itch")
SEVEN DAYS EIGHT NIGHTS
  ("Six Days Seven Nights")
SEVENTEEN CANDLES
  ("Sixteen Candles")
SEVENTH SENSE
  ("The Sixth Sense")
ELEVEN COMMANDMENTS
  ("The Ten Commandments")
FOURTH MAN ("The Third Man")
FORTY STEPS
  ("The 39 Steps")
FOUR AMIGOS
  ("¡Three Amigos!")
FOUR FACES OF EVE
  ("The Three Faces of Eve")
FOUR MEN AND TWO BABIES
  ("3 Men and a Baby")
THIRTEEN ANGRY MEN
  ("12 Angry Men")
ONE O'CLOCK HIGH
  ("Twelve O'Clock High")
THREE FOR THE ROAD
  ("Two for the Road")

148. **What A Beast!**

AMULET
BATHING SUIT
BEARDED
BOOKWORM
BOWLER
BULLET
CANTER
COMMANDEER
CROWN JEWELS
DANDELION
EXCLAMATION POINT
FLAMBÉ
FOX TROT
FROGMAN
GOATEE
GUACAMOLE
HAS-BEEN
HOT DOG
INTRAVENOUS
JAY LENO
LEAVE IT TO BEAVER
LOTTERY
POOL SHARK
SAWHORSE
SCATTER
SCOWL
SEALING WAX
SHARES
SIGN UP
SPIGOT
SPREAD-EAGLE
STIFFLY
TIGER LILY
TOADSTOOL
VIDEOTAPE
WRATH

162. **Wordy Gurdy**

1. ALL FALL
2. BAD AD
3. CHOSE FOES
4. CLAW LAW
5. DEAR EAR
6. EYES PRIZE
7. FETCHES SKETCHES
8. FREE TEA
9. GET NET
10. GRAY DAY
11. HEAT SUITE
12. I LIE
13. JAGGER'S DAGGERS
14. KEEP JEEP
15. LANCE'S DANCES
16. MAID STAYED
17. NEW CUE
18. NO SNOW
19. ON SWAN77
20. PEER FEAR
21. PRETTY CITY
22. QUEEN'S JEANS
23. RARE PAIR
24. REFERENCE PREFERENCE
25. SPIN PIN
26. TOP COP
27. TRYING SPYING
28. USHER RUSHER
29. VINDICATION INDICATION
30. WAX SAX
31. YELLOW CELLO
32. ZOO CREW

180. **Abbr.-ations**

AIR CONDITIONING
ALSO KNOWN AS
AS SOON AS POSSIBLE
BARREL
CARE OF
COMPANY
DEMOCRAT
DISQUALIFY
DOCTOR
DOZEN
EMERGENCY ROOM
FREQUENCY MODULATION
GALLON
GENERAL
HEADQUARTERS
HERTZ
HOME RUN
HORSEPOWER
I OWE YOU
JUNIOR
KNOCKOUT
LIMITED
MILES PER HOUR
MISTER
MONDAY
OCTOBER
OUNCE
PACKAGE
PAID
PART TIME
POST EXCHANGE
REGISTERED NURSE
ROUTE
SQUARE
TEASPOON
ULTRAVIOLET
VERY IMPORTANT PERSON
VOLUME
WEIGHT
WORDS PER MINUTE

200. **Missing in Action**

Word List By Category

Zodiac Signs
CAPRICORN
AQUARIUS
PISCES
ARIES
TAURUS
GEMINI
CANCER

VIRGO
LIBRA
SCORPIO
SAGITTARIUS

Bridal "Somethings"
NEW
BORROWED
BLUE

Silverware
FORK
KNIFE

Choir Voices
SOPRANO
ALTO
BARITONE
BASS

Royal Flush
KING
QUEEN
JACK
TEN

TLC Abbreviation
LOVING
CARE

Neapolitan Ice Cream
CHOCOLATE
VANILLA

Compass Points
NORTH
SOUTH
WEST

Elements
EARTH
FIRE
WATER

Missing Words From Categories

Zodiac Signs: LEO
Bridal "Somethings": OLD
Silverware: SPOON
Choir Voices: TENOR
Royal Flush: ACE
TLC Abbreviation: TENDER
Neapolitan Ice Cream:
    STRAWBERRY
Compass Points: EAST
Elements: AIR

When read in order, the first letters of these missing words spell out the appropriate message "Lost at sea."

215. Movie Editing

Word List & Original Movie Titles

1. ADAM'S FIB [Adam's Rib]
2. ANNIE MALL [Annie Hall]
3. [THE] BARDS [The Birds]
4. BARMAN [Batman]
5. [A] BEAUTIFUL MINK [A Beautiful Mind]
6. CHINAGOWN [Chinatown]
7. COCKY [Rocky]
8. COP GUN [Top Gun]
9. CORN FREE [Born Free]
10. DIG HARD [Die Hard]
11. DUCK SOAP [Duck Soup]
12. DUNCES WITH WOLVES [Dances With Wolves]
13. FINDING NERO [Finding Nemo]
14. FITNESS [Witness]
15. GONE WITH THE WINE [Gone With the Wind]
16. GOONSTRUCK [Moonstruck]
17. GRANT [Giant]
18. HEMP! [Help!]
19. HEN IN BLACK [Men in Black]
20. HIGH MOON [High Noon]
21. [THE] HOUND OF MUSIC [The Sound of Music]
22. IT'S A WONDERFUL LINE [It's a Wonderful Life]
23. JABS [Jaws]
24. KIND KONG [King Kong]
25. [THE] LIZARD OF OZ [The Wizard of Oz]
26. MR. NO [Dr. No]
27. [THE] MUSIC VAN [The Music Man]
28. PAGING BULL [Raging Bull]
29. PEAR WINDOW [Rear Window]
30. PLANET OF THE ACES [Planet of the Apes]
31. PRETTY ROMAN [Pretty Woman]
32. REIN MAN [Rain Man]
33. [THE] RUSTLER [The Hustler]
34. SHAKE [Shane]
35. SINKIN' IN THE RAIN [Singin' in the Rain]
36. SOME LIKE IT NOT [Some Like It Hot]
37. SPIDER-MAP [Spider-Man]
38. STAR WAYS [Star Wars]
39. WALT STREET [Wall Street]
40. WHEN HARRY BET SALLY ... [When Harry Met Sally ...]

231. At Loose Ends

Word List

(F)ACTORS
(H)AIRBRUSH
(M)ALIGN
(V)ALLEY
(Z)ANY
ASPIRIN(G)
(G)ASTRONOMIC
CAROUSE(L)
CHUM(P)
COLON(Y)
(I)CON
DISCUS(S)
(D)ELECTABLE
FLAMING(O)
FLU(B)
HAD(J)
HEAVE(N)
(W)HOPPING
(K)INKY
(L)IONIZED
KARAT(E)
LATE(X)
(C)LEAN
MEN(U)
MODE(M)
(U)NEATEN
(P)OODLES
OUTRAN(K)
PARK(A)
QUART(Z)
(E)QUIP
(B)RAINSTORM
(O)RANGE
(T)ROUGH
SCAR(F)
SHE(D)
SINE(W)
(A)STEROIDS
SWAM(I)
(J)UMPS

236. Chain Of Events

Word List

1. VOLCANIC ERUPTION
2. NUCLEAR TEST
3. TRIAL
4. LECTURE
5. EASTER EGG HUNT
6. TRIP
7. PARTY
8. YOM KIPPUR
9. RIOT
10. TENNIS MATCH
11. HAYRIDE
12. EXAM
13. METEOR SHOWER
14. RACE
15. ELVIS SIGHTING
16. GRADUATION
17. NEW ALBUM RELEASE
18. EXHIBIT
19. TSUNAMI
20. IDITAROD
21. DEATH
22. HANUKKAH
23. HARVEST
24. TOUR
25. RODEO
26. OUTBREAK
27. KWANZAA
28. ART SHOW
29. WARS
30. STORM
31. MEETING
32. GOINGS
33. SEAQUAKES
34. SUNUP
35. PARADES
36. SWIM
37. MUDSLIDE
38. EVENT
39. TEA DANCE
40. EQUINOX

253. Head to Tail

START
TAMBOURINE
EXTRA CREDIT
TAE KWON DO
OUT OF KILTER
REEXAMINE
EAR-SPLITTING
GOOD LUCK CHARM
MINT CONDITION
NO-NONSENSE
EASY MONEY
YUPPIE
EYE CONTACT
TELEVISION SET
TANK TOP
PATRIOTISM
MOVIE STARS
SOUNDTRACK
KITCHEN SINK
KNIGHT ERRANT
TAIWAN
NEWSPAPER REPORTER
REJUVENATE
ENSEMBLE
ELASTIC
CRIMSON
NUTCRACKER
RECONNAISSANCE
EDISON
NEUROLOGIST
TATTOO
ON CALL
LILACS
SANTA
AIRLINES
SKIRT
THEN AGAIN
NECK AND NECK
KARAOKE
ELEPHANTS
SUPERHERO
OVERSEA

ALPHABET
TEMPT
TALKED
DECAF
FALL APART
TAPE PLAYER
REFER
REQUIRE
EXISTED
DOING
GREMLIN
NO SWEAT
TWITCH
HEELS
SAMBAS
SILVER
RENEGE
ENERGY
YELLOW
WACKO
ONLOOKER
RAPTORS
SOPRANOS
SKELETON
NEIGHS
SLANG
GOURD

255. Wheel of Fortune

BANKRUPT
BEFORE AND AFTER
BONUS ROUND
CASH
CATEGORY
CHARLIE O'DONNELL
CLUE
COLLEGE WEEK
CONSONANT
ENVELOPE
EVENT
FREE SPIN
GUESS

HANGMAN
JACKPOT
KINGWORLD
LETTERBOARD
LOSE A TURN
LUCK
MERV
NEW CAR
PARTING GIFT
PAT SAJAK
PLACE
SOLVE THE PUZZLE
SONY
SYNDICATED
THING
TITLE
TRIP
VANNA
VOWELS
WHEELWATCHER
WINNER
WORDS

257. All Mixed Up

DRIVER'S SEAT
RADIATE
TREASURE ISLAND
ASTROS
BRACKETS
CABARET
PRESBYTERIANS
DACRON
DELI COUNTERS
NEWS ARTICLE
SUPREME COURT
DERAILED
COWERS
GENERATION X
OUT OF MEMORY
SINGALONG
DOG TRAINER
PLANE TICKET

LEARNED
TO SCALE
DENVER OMELET
SILENT ALARM
SALESMEN
IRONIES
THE LION KING
VICE-PRESIDENTS
OPERATING COSTS
SARDINE CAN
CIVIL ENGINEER
MEANDER
RED PLANET
PERISH
RIGHT ON CUE
SAN MARINO
SECURABLE
CENTER STAGE
TREASON
LETTERS
TRACK SHOES
DISTASTE
STEADIEST
POSTINGS
GARNETS
RUSTLED
SPROUT
SODA BOTTLE
TALENT SHOW
NIGHT
CENTAUR
BAD WEATHER
WORDIER

260. This and That

ABOVE & BEYOND
ALI BABA & THE FORTY THIEVES
ALPHA & OMEGA
ARMED & DANGEROUS
ARTS & SCIENCES
BACK & FORTH
BATMAN & ROBIN

BERT & ERNIE
BONNIE & CLYDE
BRIGHT & EARLY
CASH & CARRY
CLOAK & DAGGER
COPS & ROBBERS
CURDS & WHEY
DUNGEONS & DRAGONS
FAST & FURIOUS
FRONT & CENTER
HANSEL & GRETEL
HUNT & PECK
HORSE & BUGGY
JEKYLL & HYDE
KISS & MAKE UP
LEWIS & CLARK
MONTY PYTHON &
   THE HOLY GRAIL
NEEDLE & THREAD
NICE & EASY
NICKEL & DIME
PART & PARCEL
PEACHES & CREAM
PEANUT BUTTER & JELLY
ROMEO & JULIET
SCRATCH & SNIFF
SHORT & SWEET
SHOW & TELL
SKULL & CROSSBONES
SPAGHETTI & MEATBALLS
STARS & STRIPES
SWEET & SOUR
TRACK & FIELD
WASH & WEAR

261. Animal Impressions

BALD AS AN EAGLE
BLIND AS A BAT
BUSY AS A BEE
CROSS AS A BEAR
CURIOUS AS A CAT
CUTE AS A BUG

DEAD AS A MACKEREL
DUMB AS A DODO
EAGER AS A BEAVER
FLAT AS A FLOUNDER
GENTLE AS A LAMB
GRACEFUL AS A SWAN
HAIRY AS AN APE
HAPPY AS A CLAM
HEALTHY AS A HORSE
LOOSE AS A GOOSE
LOWLY AS A WORM
MEAN AS A SNAKE
NAKED AS A JAYBIRD
PROUD AS A PEACOCK
QUIET AS A MOUSE
RED AS A LOBSTER
SLIPPERY AS AN EEL
SLOW AS A SNAIL
STRONG AS AN OX
STUBBORN AS A MULE
WEAK AS A KITTEN
WISE AS AN OWL

267. Trios

ANIMAL, VEGETABLE, MINERAL
ATHOS, PORTHOS, ARAMIS
BUTCHER, BAKER,
   CANDLESTICKMAKER
BACH, BEETHOVEN, BRAHMS
TALL, DARK, HANDSOME
EXECUTIVE, LEGISLATIVE,
   JUDICIAL
EARTH, WIND, FIRE
GOLD, FRANKINCENSE, MYRRH
HOOK, LINE, SINKER
FAITH, HOPE, CHARITY
IGNEOUS, SEDIMENTARY,
   METAMORPHIC
I CAME, I SAW, I CONQUERED
JUDGE, JURY, EXECUTIONER
FORK, SPOON, KNIFE
SMALL, MEDIUM, LARGE

LION, WITCH, WARDROBE
LOCK, STOCK, BARREL
HUEY, DEWEY, LOUIE
MEAN, MEDIAN, MODE
PETER, PAUL, MARY
NINA, PINTA, SANTA MARIA
PERSON, PLACE, THING
KENTUCKY DERBY, PREAKNESS,
   BELMONT STAKES
ROCK, PAPER, SCISSORS
ALVIN, SIMON, THEODORE
STOP, LOOK, LISTEN
YESTERDAY, TODAY, TOMORROW

269. Eating Your Words

AC(CURS)E
A(LIMO)NY
AR(CHIMED)ES
BA(THRO)BE
B(EAR MARK)ET
BER(THIN)G
BE(TA TE)ST
B(LACK EY)E
BO(W AND A)RROW
C(ARLO)AD
CAR(PENT)ER
CL(EAR) OUT
C(LOVER)LEAVES
C(ONCE)ITED
COR(PORE)AL
CO(VET)ED
C(UMBERS)OME
DE(BAT)ED
DI(AL TO)NE
ERA(SURE)S
E(YES)IGHT
F(AIL)ED
F(RAG)RANCE
FRE(E WE)IGHTS
GEN(E AU)TRY
GUES(T HOU)SES
INDU(CEMENT)S

JA(DE GREE)N
K(ITCH)EN
LA(BORE)RS
MA(YAP)PLE
MIN(D READ)ER
MOSQU(ITO)ES
NE(THERMOS)T
NE(VER MIN)D
N(INTEND)O
OPE(RATE)D
PA(PER P)LATE
PE(DOME)TER
S(CREW) UP
SE(ASCAP)E
S(HAD)OW
S(PORTS)WEAR
SQUA(SHE)D
ST(ARCH)ING
T(ANGER)INE
T(WINK)IES
V(AN)ILLA
WH(ITE M)EAT

271. Cross Word Puzzle

APACE
NYLON
WENCH
WHEEL
YACHT
CREAM
PENNANT
DOUBT
COMRADE
MEANINGLESS
SALSA
EXERT
CHINA
TOTED
AUDIO
ROUTINE
ANTIC

DWEEB
SPECIALTY
READOUT
KRYPTON
UNDERPAID
SMALL
DAYTIME
TREACHERY
NAKEDLY
GLAZE
SQUIRMS
COLON
TANGO

Note: The word pairs form cross-shapes; that is, the two words cross at right angles on their center letters.

295. Every Which Way

COMPASS
COMPUTER KEYBOARD
CUPID
CURSOR
ELEVATOR BUTTON
FAST FORWARD
FEATHERS
FLOW CHART
FOOTBALL FIELD
HEART TATTOO
"MALE" SYMBOL
ONE-WAY STREET
QUIVER
ROBIN HOOD
SAGITTARIUS
TREASURE MAP
TURN SIGNAL
VIDEO GAME CONTROLLER
WEATHER VANE
WILLIAM TELL
YOU ARE HERE

302. Wedding Bells

Something Old
FINE WINE
FOSSIL
GIANT REDWOOD
HAND-ME-DOWNS
JALOPY
LEFTOVERS
METHUSELAH
MING VASE
MOLDY BREAD
RUINS

Something New
BABY
COINAGE
CUB REPORTER
FRESHMAN
HIT SONG
LATE-BREAKING STORY
LATEST FAD
MOVIE PREMIERE
SHINY PENNY
UPGRADE

Something Borrowed
CLASS NOTES
CUP OF SUGAR
IDEA
LIBRARY BOOKS
MONEY
PARENT'S CAR
RENTAL TUX
SPORTS SECTION
TIME
TROUBLE

Something Blue
CLEAR SKY
FIRST PLACE RIBBON

HIGH FLAME
JAYBIRD
JEANS
OCEAN WATER
ROBIN'S EGG
SAPPHIRE
SINATRA'S EYES
SMURF

303. Repeat Performances

ARCHERS
BAMBINO
MASS MAILING
PASSPORTS
MAXIMAL
BLACK HOLES

BASSIST
CAR BOMBS
OCELOTS
CHIANTI
CHEERIEST
CLEANSE
ECLIPSE
COLLIDED
CONTEST
TEA SET
GREASES
HAIRINESS
INSERTS
DIVIDES
LANTERN
FLATFISH
MARINER
OMINOUS

PENNANT
PERIGEE
REC CENTER
CRESCENT
ORIOLE
CROCUSES
USUALLY
SO-AND-SO
SCALPEL
SHEARED
SATURDAY
SUMMIT
ITALIC
TRUE BLUE
SUSPEND
CUTICLE
AVERAGE
WORLDLY

ANSWERS

1. Things To Do While Sitting

"I shall sit here, on and off, for days and days," said one "Alice in Wonderland" character…not in a loo.

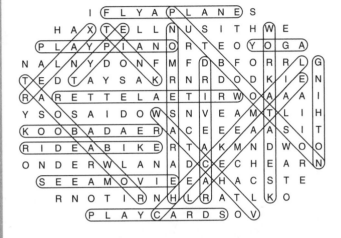

2. Famous Johns, Johnnys, and Jons

A few other notable Johnnys are Carson, Weissmuller, Cash, Miller, Bench, on-the-spot, and come-lately.

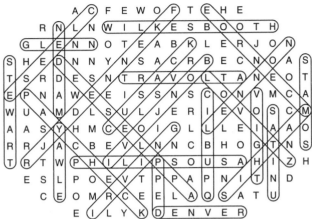

3. Signs On Doors

A sign tacked onto the door of a dog obedience school read, "Back in five minutes. Sit! Stay!"

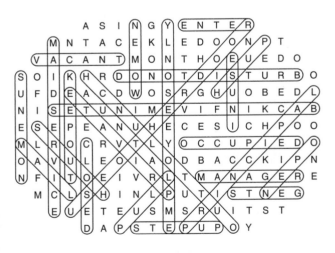

4. Vowel Play

Some common words that contain all five vowels, each used once, are sequoia, facetious, subcontinental, and uncomplimentary.

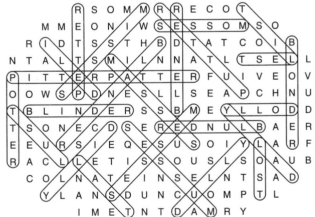

5. Car Pool

Hmm...if people away from home too long can get homesick, do people away from their cars too long get carsick?

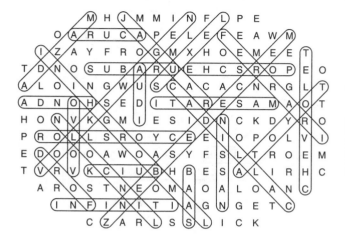

6. Royal Flush

A dead man's hand has two aces and two eights. It is named for what Wild Bill Hickok held when he was shot in the back.

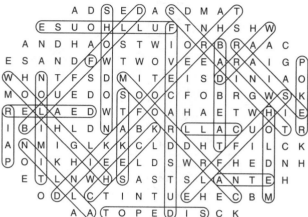

7. Off on a Cruise

Though film star Tom Cruise has had a phenomenal movie career, next to his mirror he keeps a piece of paper that reads, "Relax."

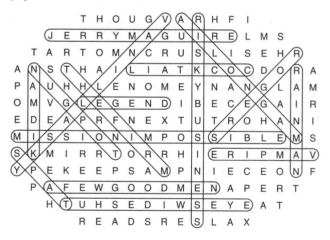

8. Things That Come in Pairs

"If you should find romance, you'll pant and pant once more, and that's a pair of pants."—by Allan Sherman [from his song, "One Hippopotami"]

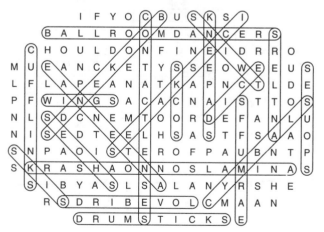

9. Just Desserts

Robinson Crusoe would have been much happier if he'd been stranded on a dessert island.

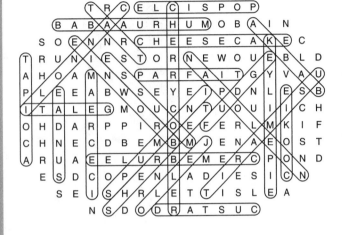

10. Body Language

Let's face it. Body parts show up in tons of everyday phrases…and that's saying quite a mouthful.

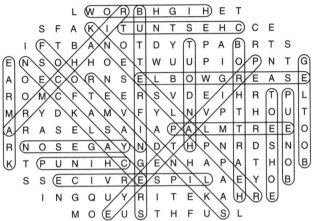

11. Sitting on the Throne

The patriotic song "America" copies the tune of the U.K.'s anthem "God Save the Queen."

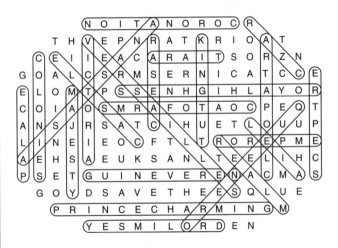

12. The Doctor Is In

Creator of "Jurassic Park" and TV's "ER," Michael Crichton graduated from Harvard Med School.

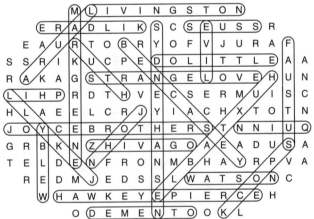

13. There Is Superstition

Purple horseshoes and green clovers are some Lucky Charms to find in a box of that cereal.

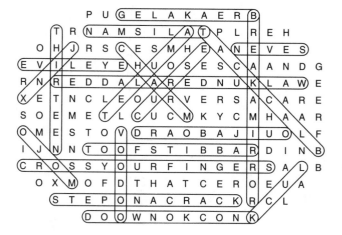

14. One for the $

We want you to get your money's worth, so this grid comes with a money-back guarantee.

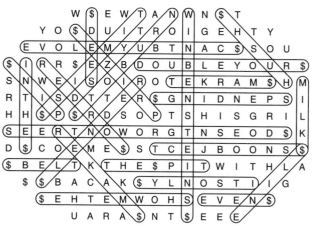

15. Things Found in the Bathroom

The thing that you are most likely to find in the bathroom is other family members.

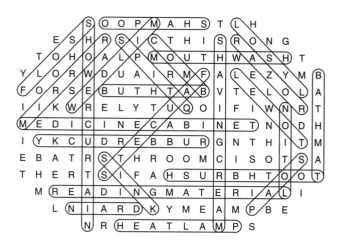

16. Road Trip

A few years back, a guy named Rob made a sixty-seven day road trip to see games at all thirty MLB stadiums. (His baseball odyssey was posted for awhile on a web site.)

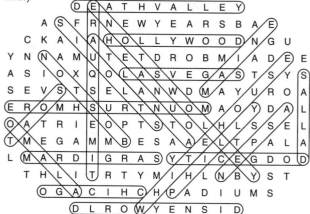

17. An Awarding Experience

The Cesar is the French version of the Oscar. Rotten Tomatoes are given to the worst movies of the year.

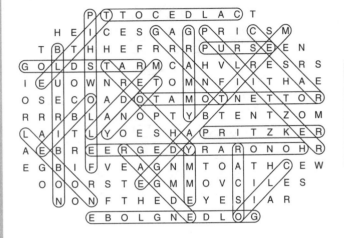

18. Things with Strings

Don't accept a deal from a guy who says he'll sell you his harp with no strings attached.

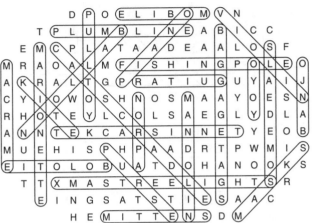

19. I'd Like to Be a Rich and Famous...

Did you ever notice that the old saying, "I'd rather be rich than famous" is usually said by people who are neither?

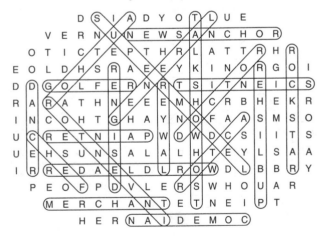

20. W.C.

According to popular legend, the water closet, or W.C. for short, was invented by a plumber named Thomas Crapper.

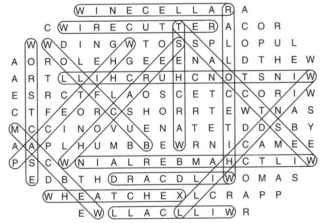

21. "& So It Goes …"

If Andy Garcia and Barbra Streisand walked hand-in-hand, would it cause a scandal or just be jim-dandy?

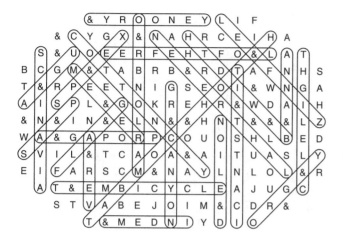

22. Wooden It Be Nice?

Paper is normally made from wood, but to save trees, paper could also be made from cotton, flax, and even banana stalks.

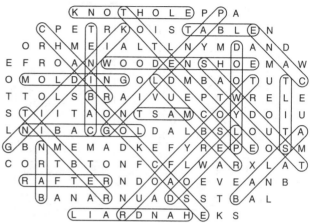

23. #1 Or #2?

Full of fables and good advice, Aesop once said, "Be content with your lot; one cannot be first in everything."

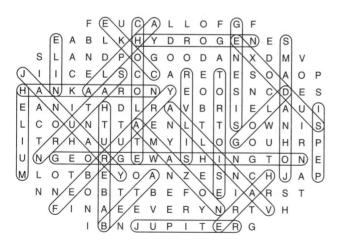

24. Go for the Green

There's a joke that golf is like taxes: you drive as hard as you can to get to the green, only to end up in the hole.

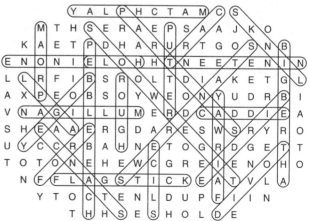

25. With Ease

Sheets are lines that hold a ship's sails. If they are loose, the ship is out of control. Hence "three sheets to the wind."

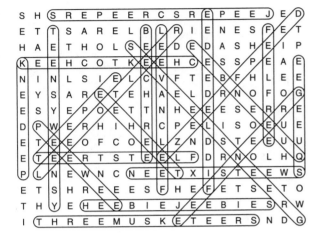

26. A Quick Workout

I have never taken any exercise, except sleeping and resting, and I never intend to take any. —Mark Twain, at age seventy

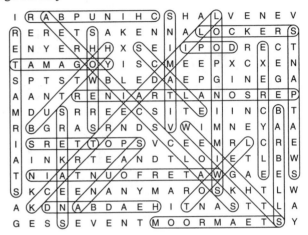

27. Careful!

Trappist monks take a vow of silence, but this doesn't mean they don't communicate. They use sign language instead.

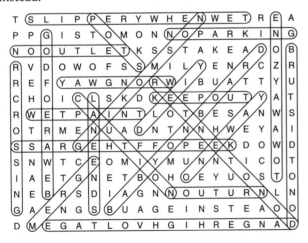

28. That's About the Size of It

The largest living thing on earth is a giant underground fungus that covers more than two thousand acres.

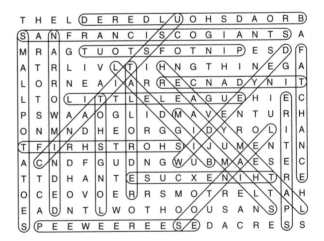

29. In Fashion

Fashion is something barbarous, for it produces innovation without reason and imitation without benefit.
—G. Santayana

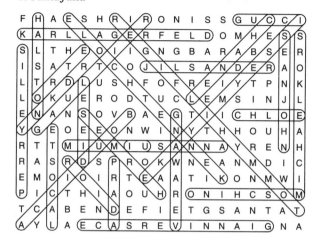

30. Spy Game

Love is whatever you can still betray. Betrayal can only happen if you love. —from *A Perfect Spy* by le Carré

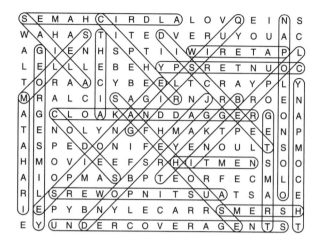

31. Sound Effects

Foley artists create sound effects for radio and film—for example, shaking metal sheets to make the sound of thunder.

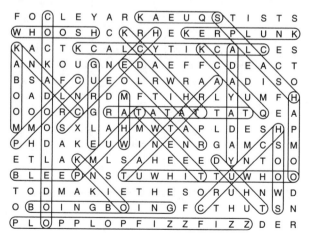

32. Look Out Above!

Frogs have been known to fall out of the sky. The most likely explanation is that they have been caught up in a waterspout and blown far away.

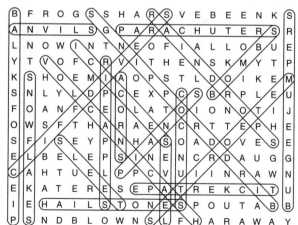

33. Why?

They throw the ball, I hit it. They hit the ball, I catch it. — Willie Mays, alias the Say Hey Kid, on his secret to success

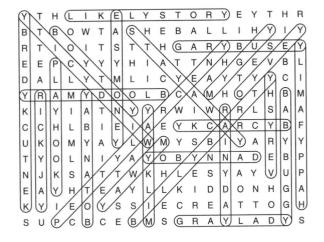

34. Keeping a Clear Head

Time to turn back and descend the stair, / With a bald spot in the middle of my hair— / (They will say: "How his hair is growing thin!") —by T.S. Eliot

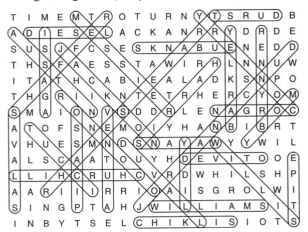

35. Not Keeping a Clear Head

He was impatient of topcoats and hats, preferring to be exposed. —E.B. White, writing about John F. Kennedy

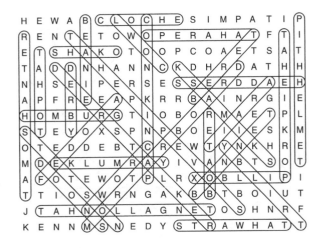

36. Doubling Up

Double Indemnity author James M. Cain liked the plot twists in the movie so much he said he'd have used them if he'd thought of them.

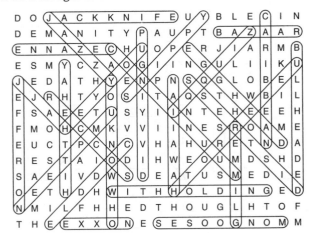

37. Let's Stick Together

I believe that truth is the glue that holds government together. —from President Gerald R. Ford's inauguration speech

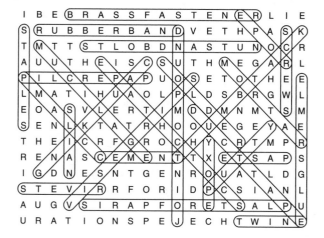

38. Springfield Is in the Air

The Simpsons are named after Matt Groening's family—except for Bart, whose name is an anagram of "brat."

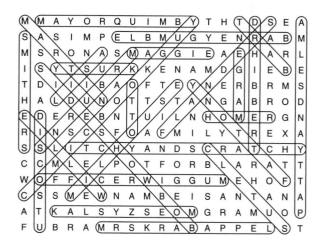

39. Musical Numbers

If you sang "99 Bottles of Beer on the Wall" and counted all the numbers mentioned throughout the entire song, it would add up to 14,850.

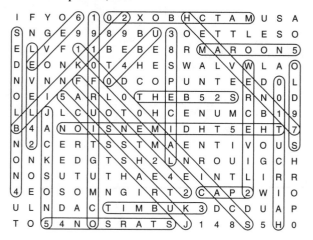

40. Foul Play

Football combines the two worst things about America: it is violence punctuated by committee meetings. —political pundit George Will

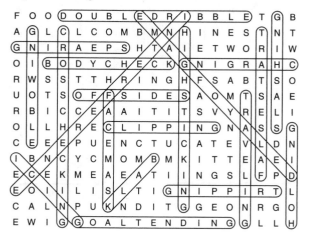

41. Some Stuff

The writer is either a practicing recluse or a delinquent, guilt-ridden one; or both. Usually both. —Susan Sontag

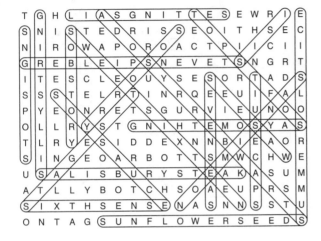

42. Let's Dance

I don't want to be the oldest performer in captivity. I don't want to look like a little old man dancing out there. —Fred Astaire

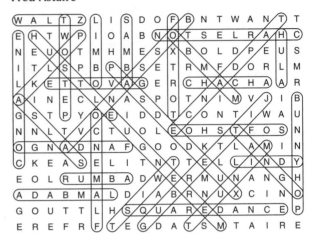

43. Secret Identities

Superman has been involved with four women: Lana Lang, Lois Lane, Lyla Lerrol, and Lori Lemaris (a mermaid). What's with the L's, dude?

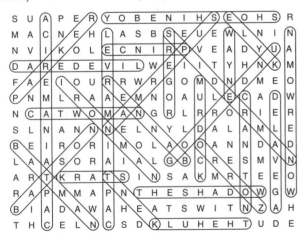

44. Rare Antonyms

It's our experience that political leaders don't always mean the opposite of what they say. —Abba Eban

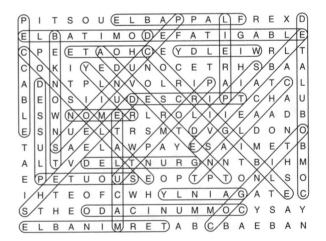

45. Aye, 'Tis a Word Search About Pirates, It Is

Johnny Depp based his *Pirates of the Caribbean* character on Keith Richards—who played his father in the sequel.

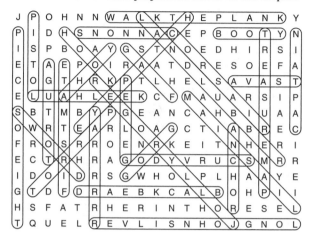

46. Hot ...

I'd like to sup with my baby tonight / Refill the cup with my baby tonight / But I ain't up to my baby tonight / 'Cause it's too darn hot. (Cole Porter)

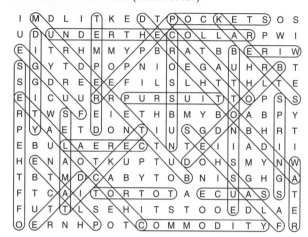

47. Higher Education

Education is the art of making man ethical. —Georg Hegel

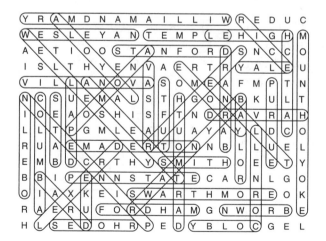

48. Wild Kingdom

All animals, except man, know that the principal business of life is to enjoy it. —author Samuel Butler

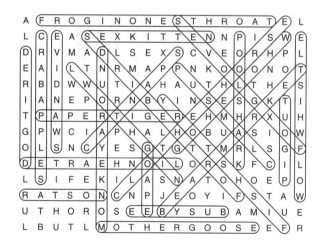

49. Wilder Kingdom

What a chimera then is man. What a novelty! What a monster, …what a contradiction, what a prodigy. —B. Pascal

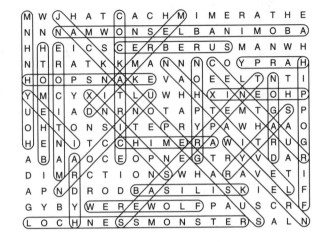

50. The Things We Carried

But what has it got in its pocketses, eh? Not string, precious, but not nothing. —Gollum, from *The Hobbit*

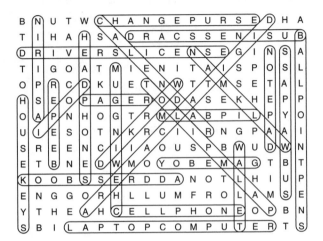

51. Rise and Shine

Cindy Crawford once said, "Even I don't wake up looking like Cindy Crawford."

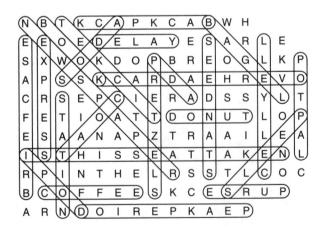

52. On the Train and Bus

Where do brokers sit on a train? The stock car.

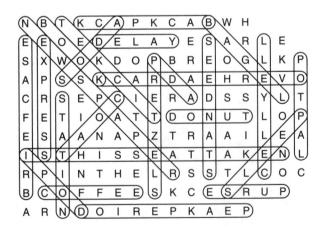

53. Java Jive

Teddy Roosevelt dubbed Maxwell House "Good to the last drop."

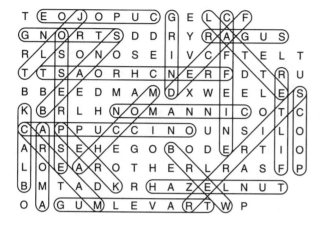

54. Beatles' "A Day in the Life"

The massive final note of the song took three pianos and lasts over forty seconds.

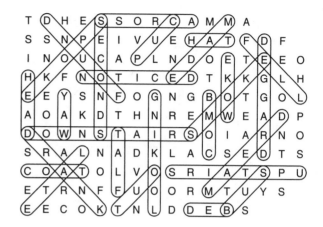

55. Work, Work, Work

"Hard work never killed anybody, but why take a chance?"—Edgar Bergen

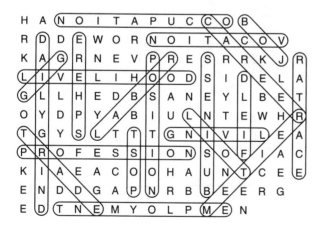

56. All the News That Fits

The first crossword was in the *New York World* in nineteen thirteen.

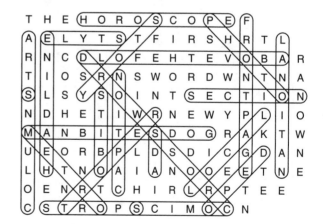

57. Car Talk

"Traffic signals in New York are just rough guidelines."
—[David] Letterman

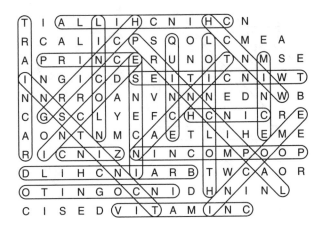

58. Think "Inc."

Inc. also means "engraved by," from the word "incised."

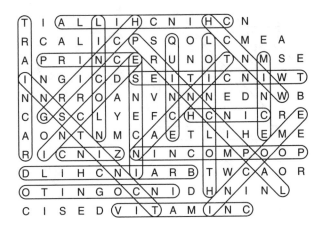

59. Working Scripts

"I can sit…and do nothing as good as anyone."
—Clockwatchers quote

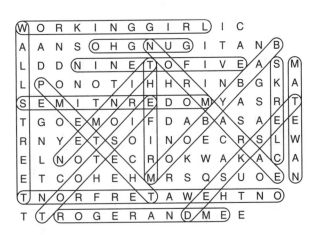

60. Bagel Break

"Protect your bagels, put lox on them."—shop sign

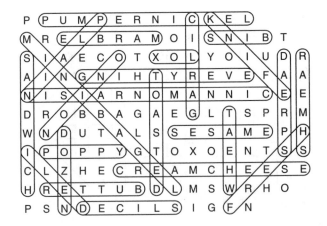

276

61. At the Train Station

Every day, half a million people pass through Grand Central.

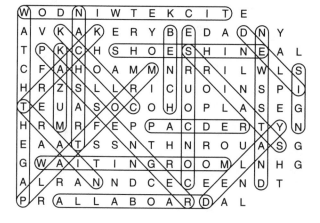

62. Why We Do It

"Run for your life from any man who tells you that money is evil."—[Ayn] Rand

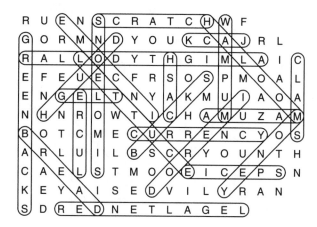

63. RR Crossings

Rex Reed played Myra Breckinridge pre-sex change.

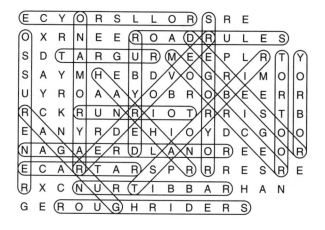

64. "Sorry I'm Late"

Neat excuse: The dog ate my keys. We are hitchhiking to the vet.

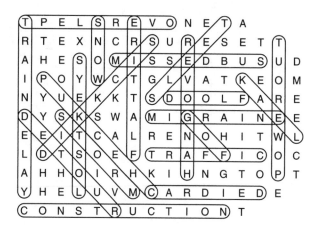

65. TV Working Stiffs

TV dud *Working Stiffs* had Jim Belushi and Michael Keaton.

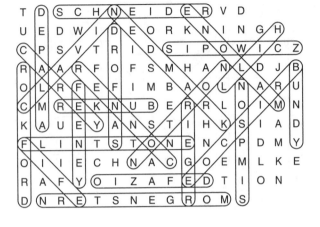

66. Subway Stop

A baby born on the tube was named Thelma Ursula Beatrice Eleanor.

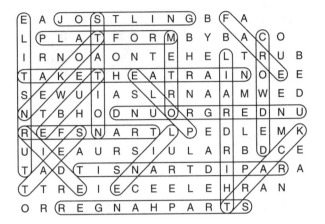

67. Office Seeking

Dilbert says, "Everything can be filed under 'miscellaneous.'"

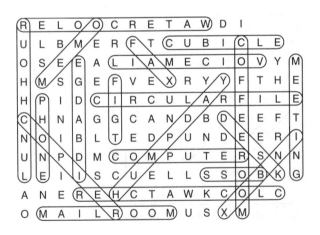

68. Time Sheet

Earth is slowing, so leap year won't be needed eons from now.

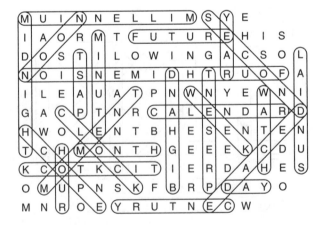

69. Cell Out Crowd

The first cell call was made to the inventor's rival.

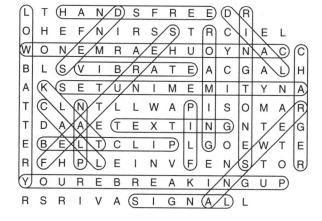

70. "Bus" Depot

Hope you are going gangbusters on this commuter omnibus.

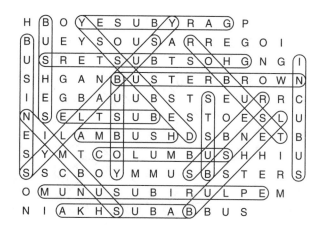

71. The Fortune 100

Sam Walton said, "Capital isn't scarce; vision is."

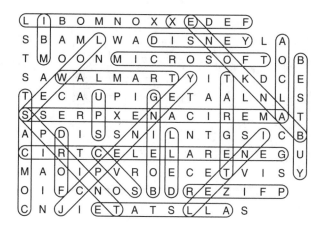

72. I've Been Working on the RR

Some think Dinah is a train, not a woman. The name might even come from "diner."

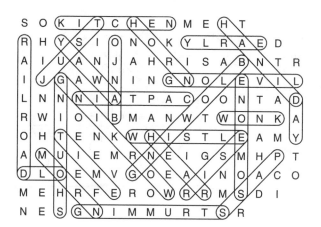

73. The Telecommute

"If Al Gore invented the Internet, I invented spell check."
—[Dan] Quayle

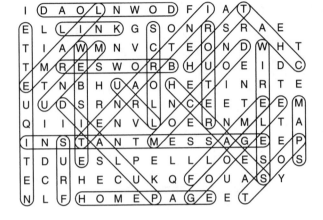

74. Weekend Planner

"Only Robinson Crusoe had everything done by Friday."
—speaker unknown

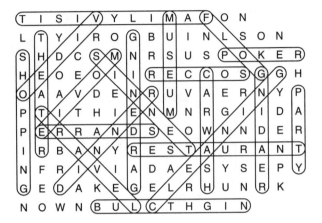

75. Welcome Aboard

Thomas Edison introduced "hello" as the telephone greeting. Alexander Graham Bell said "ahoy" instead.

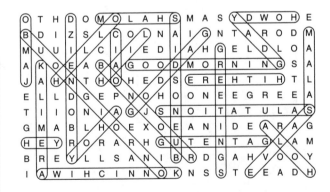

76. "Bon" Voyage

Did our bona fide bon mots bonanza drive you truly bonkers?

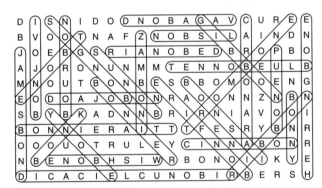

77. I Packed My Suitcase ...

The world's longest baggage moving system, at Kuala Lumpur's airport, runs over twenty miles.

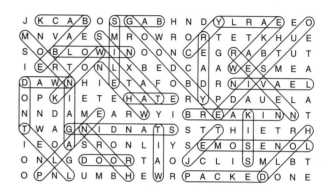

78. Leaving on a Jet Plane

John Denver wrote the song, but it became a hit for Peter, Paul and Mary. It was the trio's only song to climb to number one.

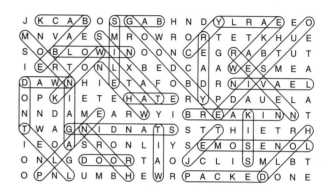

79. Anchors Aweigh!

Two Titanic survivors, who were infants when it sank, are living at this writing.

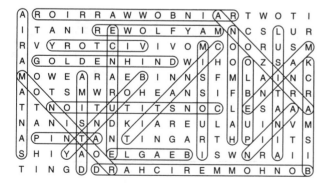

80. Travel Log

The word "travel" is from "travail," perhaps because travel used to be so hard.

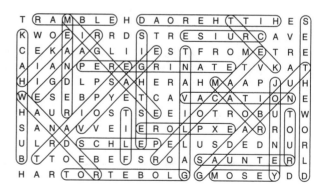

81. Wise Guides

The first *Red Guide* by Michelin on a location outside Europe is the new guide to New York City.

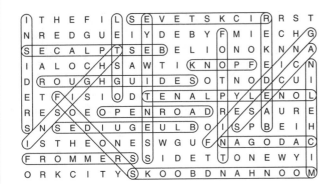

82. Cruise Control

Some luxury cruise ships sell condos to super-rich people who want to live onboard.

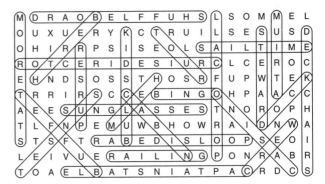

83. Island Hopping

When *Survivor* was new, a *New Yorker* cartoon showed animals voting the unicorn off the island.

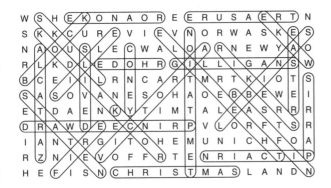

84. Circling at the Airport

The man who inspired *The Terminal* still lives at De Gaulle.

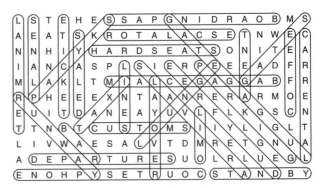

85. Travelers of Yore

Ponce de Leon was really not looking for the fountain of youth when he discovered Florida.

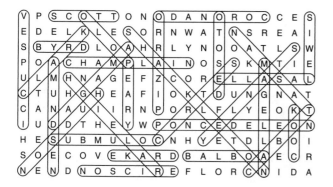

86. Fictional Millionaires

The Monopoly guy's name was Rich Uncle Pennybags, but is now officially Mr. Monopoly.

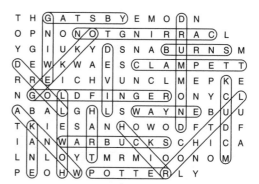

87. Berlitz Blitz

Actual sign at a Bangkok dry cleaner's: Drop your trousers here for best results.

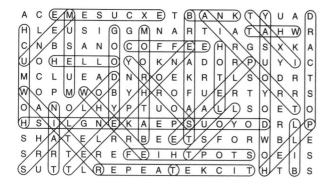

88. Amtrak Meet

The first passenger train to offer full-view dome cars was the California Zephyr.

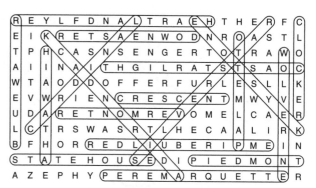

89. Get a Room

Las Vegas is home to sixteen of the twenty largest hotels in the world.

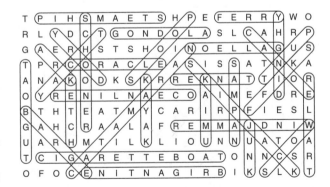

90. Currency Exchange

There's a series of six coins from Somalia all in the shapes of famous electric guitars.

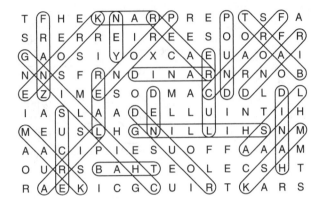

91. Shipping Department

The world's largest ship is a tanker that carries half a million tons of oil.

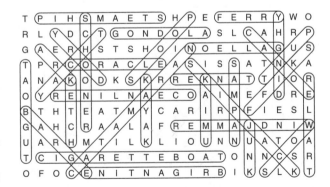

92. Plane Speaking

The smallest jet plane in the world is just twelve feet long.

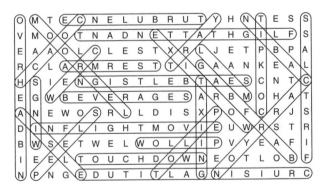

93. Lost: The Trip from Hell

The original script had Jack die early on.

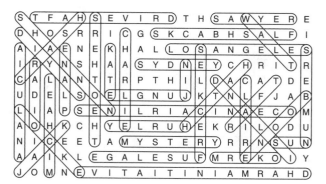

94. Wonders of the World— Natural Department

Theodore Roosevelt named Devils Tower the country's first national monument.

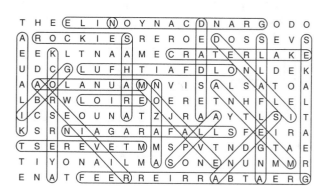

95. Wonders of the World— Man-Made Department

The Empire State Building still has zeppelin mooring gear, though the idea never worked.

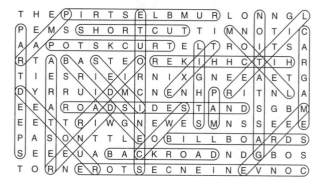

96. Road Trip

The longest interstate is I-Ninety, running between Seattle and Boston.

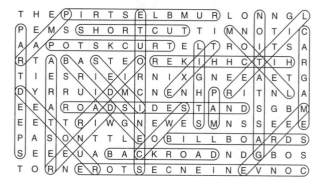

97. Frame-Up Job

Author Peter de Vries once said, "Murals in restaurants are on a par with the food in museums."

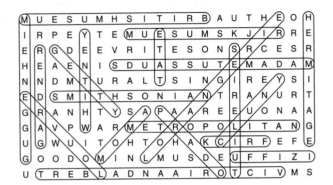

98. S.S. Wordloop

Strong search solvers surely sidestepped sticky situations, simply said.

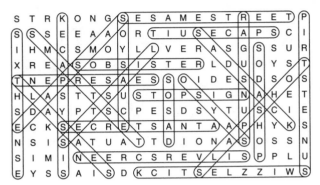

99. Jet Set

When showing *Rain Man*, most airlines except Qantas cut Ray saying Qantas is safest.

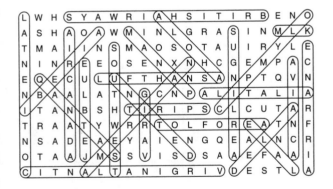

100. Souvenir Shop

The office of the Los Angeles county coroner actually has a souvenir store.

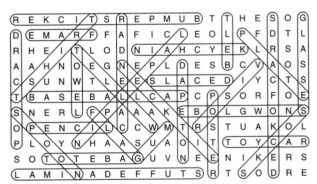

101. "Oh, Heavens!"

Want to fly to Never Land? Then take the "second star to the right and straight on till morning." [—from "Peter Pan"]

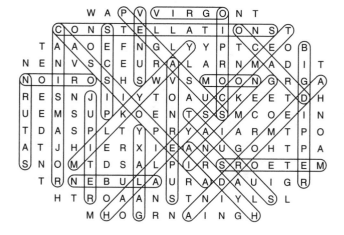

102. Rave Reviews

"Wow, that was totally mind-boggling, absolutely astounding, truly sensational!"…"Uh-huh, but was it any good?"

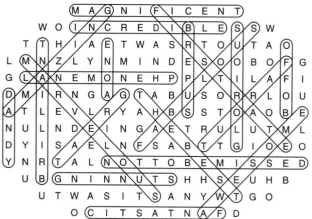

103. Electronic Marvels

"I shall make electricity so cheap that only the rich can afford to burn candles." —Thomas A. Edison

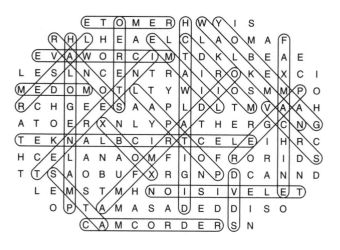

104. Nature Calls

Don't be a birdbrain. If you have to, make a beeline for the answers, and you'll be the cat's pajamas.

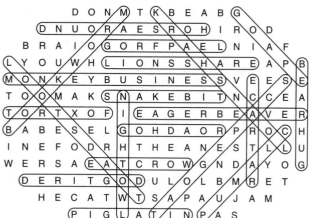

105. Down Under

Aussies love to eat Vegemite, a yeast extract they'll spread on bread and other foods.

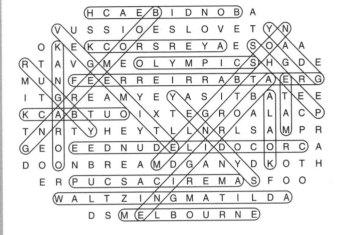

106. Broadway Blockbusters

Investing in a Broadway show is risky. The odds of recouping one's money are only about one in ten.

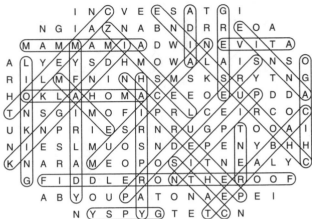

107. Weather or Not

In "Poor Richard's Almanac," Ben Franklin said, "Some are weatherwise; some are other-wise."

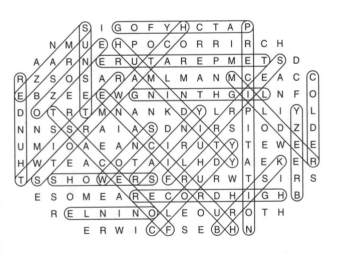

108. Gardener's Delight

To keep Bambi-like animals out of the garden, there's a brand of repellent spray called "Not Tonight Deer!"

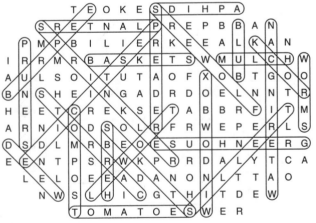

109. Cup o' Joe

Joe Yule Jr. adopted the name Mickey Rooney after fame hit.

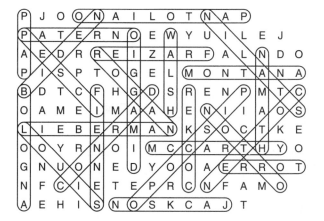

110. Business Trip

American Airlines had the first frequent flyer miles.

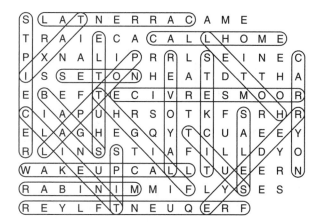

111. The S&P

Square pegs sent packing shouldn't pooh-pooh severance pay.

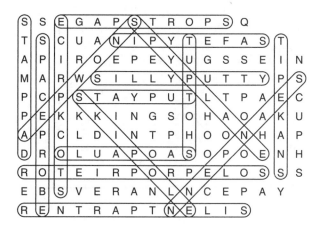

112. Working Dogs

Dogs are color blind, so guide dogs look at traffic rather than lights.

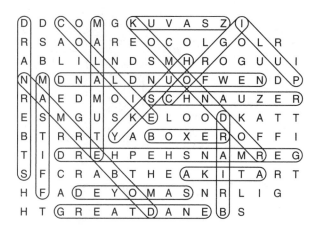

289

113. Happy Hour

The zombie was invented to be a cure for hangovers.

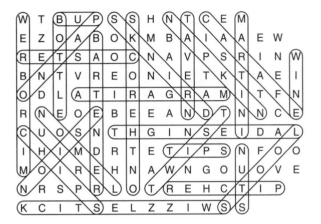

114. Rails in America

The hobo world in their slang was hobohemia.

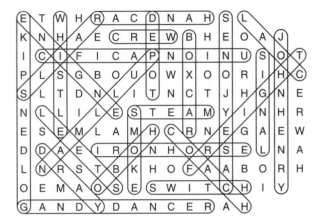

115. The Great Outdoors

Camping is nature's way of promoting the motel business. —humor writer Dave Barry

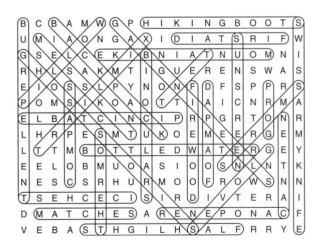

116. Dept. of Redundancy Dept.

Football is an incredible game. Sometimes it's so incredible, it's unbelievable. —famed Dallas coach Tom Landry

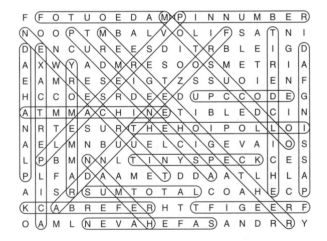

117. The Periodical Table

They didn't want it good, they wanted it Wednesday.
—Robert Heinlein on writing sci-fi for pulp magazines

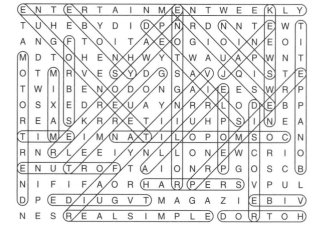

118. Word Ladders

You will see that it is easier to go down the social ladder than to climb it. —from *Caligula* by Albert Camus

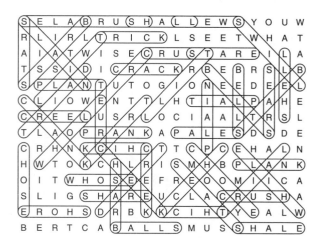

119. A Concerted Effort

When I was twenty, I couldn't imagine still doing this at thirty. —Sir Paul McCartney on aging and rock and roll

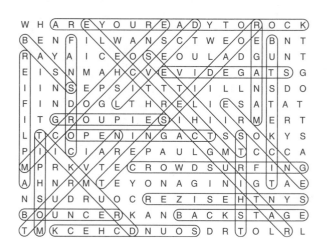

120. Form Letters

A woman's best love letters are always written to the man she is betraying. —Lawrence Durrell

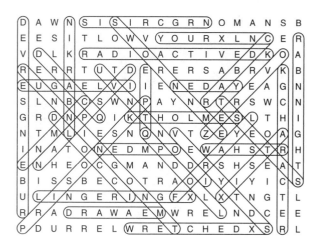

121. Um ... Um ...

It's the small doubts of timid souls that accomplish their ruin. It's the narrow vision, the fear and trembling hesitation, that constitute defeat. —A. MacDougall

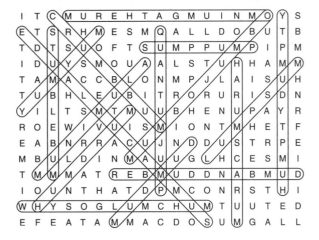

122. Vacation Reading

The Valley of the Dolls is widely thought to be the best-selling novel of all time.

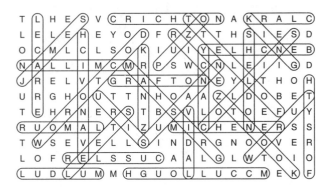

123. Avast Conspiracy

The scuttlebutt was originally a ship's water cask—the watercooler.

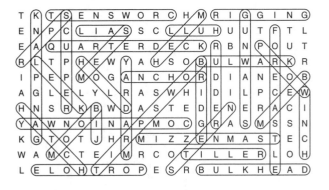

124. The Inn Crowd

There are real hotels constructed of snow and ice that are rebuilt every year after they melt.

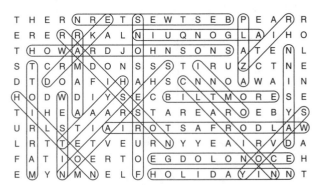

125. The Love Boat

Desperate housewife Teri Hatcher started her career as a singing, dancing *Love Boat* Mermaid.

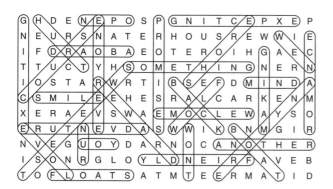

126. Round Trip

Boxing rings are officially square but were originally circular.

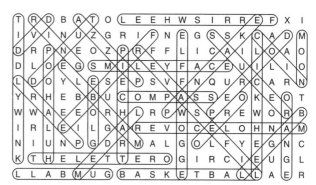

127. Touchdown!

"Airplane travel is nature's way of making you look like your passport photo." —remark from Al Gore

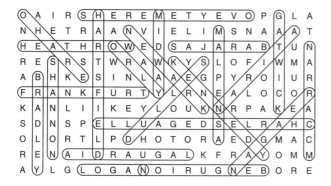

128. Travel and Vacation Flicks

Planes, Trains and Automobiles is said to be Steve Martin's favorite of his films.

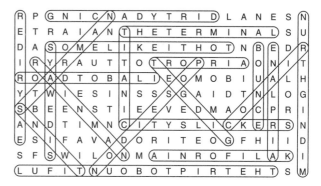

129. Captains Courageous

Captain Kangaroo and *The Mickey Mouse Club* both had their TV debuts on the same day.

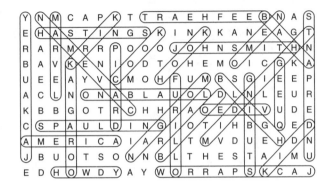

130. It's Good to Be Home

The humorist George Ade once said, "The time to enjoy a European trip is about three weeks after unpacking."

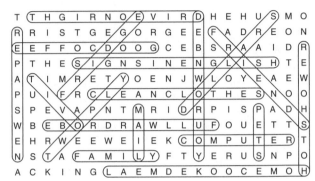

131. Rarin' to Go

"Where shall I begin, your Majesty?" the White Rabbit asked. "Begin at the beginning," the King said gravely, "and go on till you come to the end; then stop." —*Alice in Wonderland*

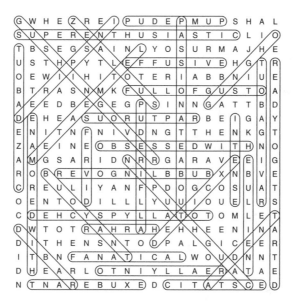

132. So How Sharp Are You?

If you're keenly observant, highly sarcastic, very fashionable, and good with a gun, you're a sharp-eyed, sharp-tongued sharp dresser who's a sharpshooter.

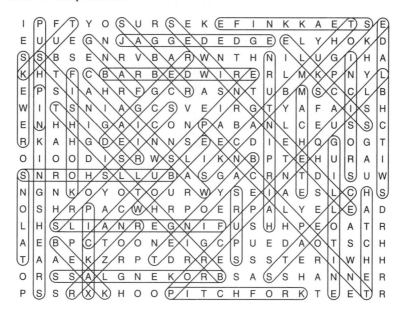

133. Off and Running

I bet on a horse at ten to one. It came in at half-past five. [paraphrase of a quip by Henny Youngman]

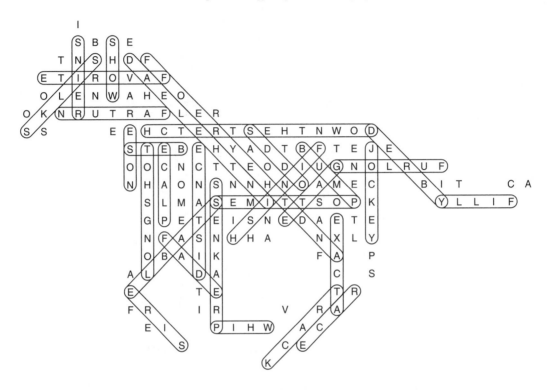

134. Gossip Columns

"Show me someone who never gossips, and I'll show you someone who isn't interested in people." —[Barbara] Walters

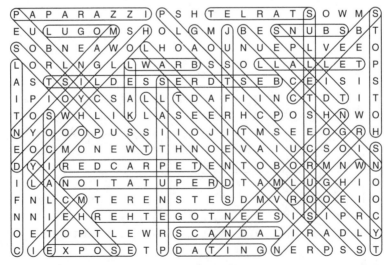

135. It's in the Cards

A sleight-of-hand artist who likes to play his cards close to the vest may—in a snap!—have an ace up his sleeve.

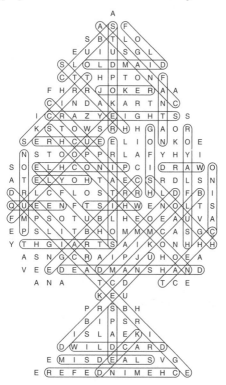

136. Bad Ideas for Movie Sequels

And be sure you miss "Two Flew Over the Cuckoo's Nest," "Four Coins in the Fountain," "Snow White and the Eight Dwarfs," and "Around the World in Eighty-One Days."

137. Give Me a Break!

"The morning cup of coffee has an exhilaration about it which ... the afternoon or evening cup of tea cannot be expected to reproduce." [—Oliver Wendell Holmes, Sr.]

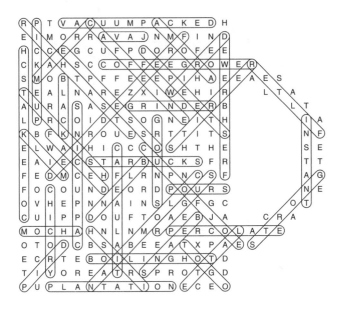

138. Car Pool

I asked a friend, "How often do you rotate your tires?" He said, "Every time I drive."

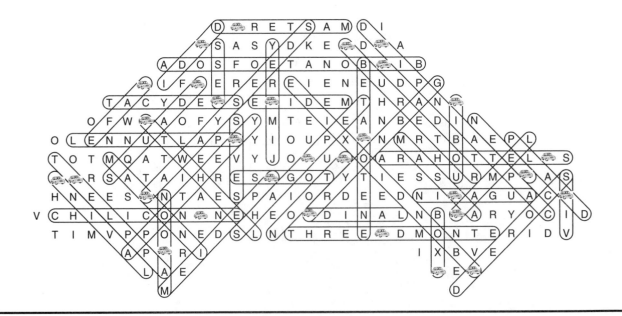

139. Let's Celebrate

If something easy is a piece of cake, but you can't have your cake and eat it too, does that mean nothing is ever easy?

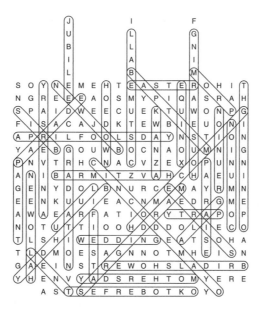

140. White on Schedule

With no snow in the forecast, the ski lodge owner said to his guests, "Don't worry … everything'll turn out all white."

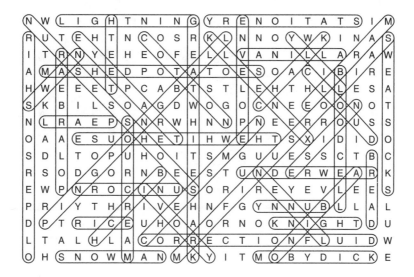

141. Start the Music

"Music is your own experience, your thoughts, your wisdom. If you don't live it, it won't come out of your horn." — [Charlie] Parker

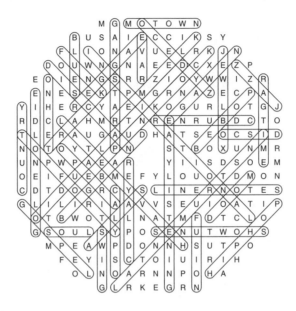

142. Black Hole #1

Center quote: The best cure for insomnia is to get lots of sleep.
Other quotes: "Sleeping is no mean art: for its sake one must stay awake all day." —Nietzsche ... "Life is something to do when you can't get to sleep." —[Fran] Lebowitz

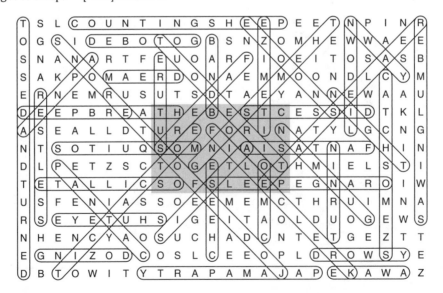

143. It's a Shoe Thing

It is [totally] impossible to be well dressed in cheap shoes. [—couturier Hardy Amies]

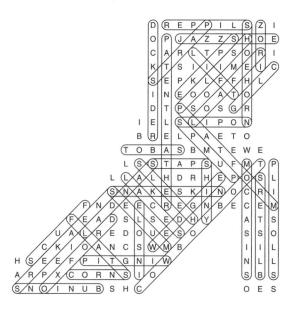

144. Give It the Old College Try

Singer Pete Seeger said, "Education is when you read the fine print; experience is what you get when you don't."

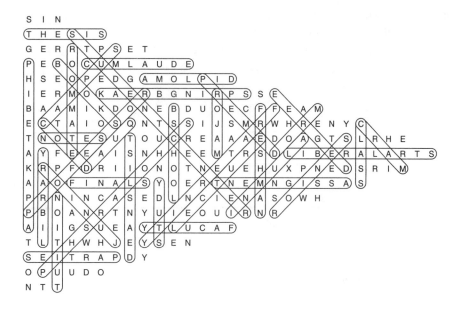

145. Just Add Water

Every entry in this grid contains two aitches and an O, or H2O, the chemical formula for water.

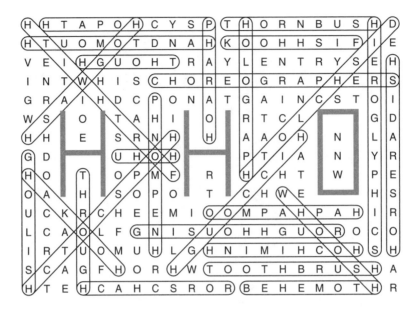

146. Smell It Like It Is

The movie "Polyester" originally came out in Odorama—a gimmick in which audiences could smell various odors in the movie by using scratch-and-sniff cards at noted moments.

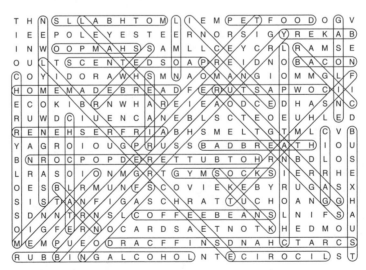

147. Tennis, Anyone?

Know why you shouldn't go out with a tennis player? To him, love means nothing.

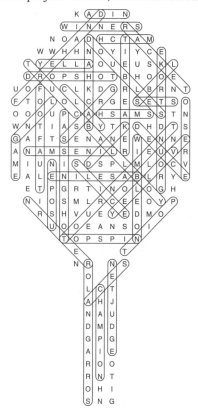

148. What a Beast!

"The desire to take medicine is perhaps the greatest feature which distinguishes man from animals." —Doctor William Osler

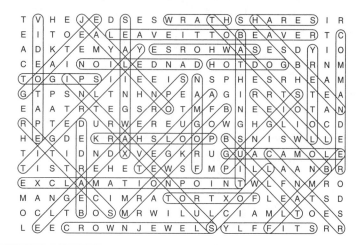

149. Up in the Air

When it comes to predicting the weather, it seems that the likelihood of any forecast being right is completely up in the air.

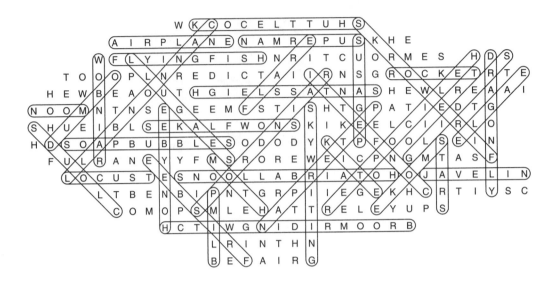

150. Think Big

"If the government is big enough to give you everything you want, it is big enough to take away everything you have." —Gerald Ford

151. Gridlock and Key

If Heather Locklear and Sandra Bullock did a cockeyed Keystone Kops comedy with Mickey Rooney, would it turn out to be a "schlock-key" movie?

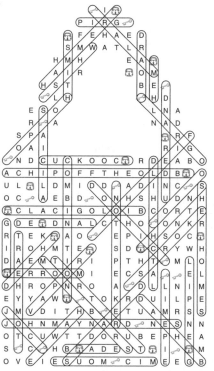

152. Don't Touch Me!

Since all words on the list deal with separateness, no words in the grid connect with each other.

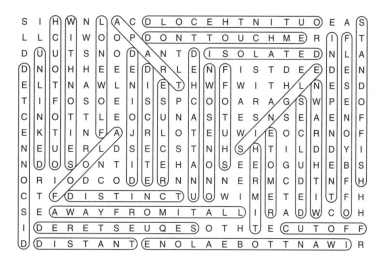

153. Hair Apparent

On its closing day, a hair salon that was shutting its doors for good put up a sign that said, "Hair Today, Gone Tomorrow."

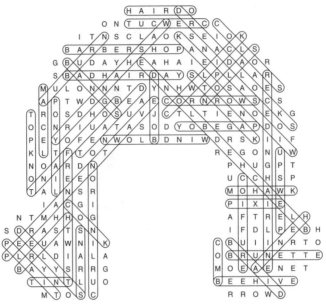

154. On a Roll

"Looking out upon the future ... I could not stop it if I wished .... Like the Mississippi, it just keeps rolling along." — [Winston] Churchill

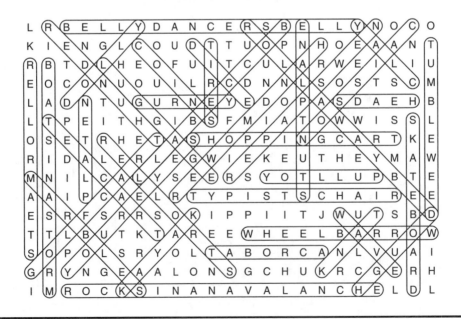

155. What's on TV

Reading helps to make a person well-rounded. So does sitting in front of the TV gobbling snacks.

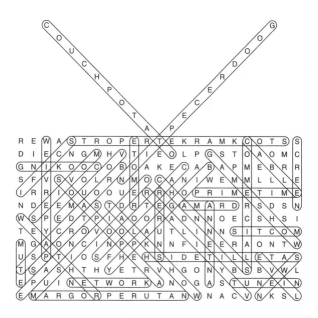

156. Black Hole #2

Center quote: "I can resist everything except temptation."
Regular quote: "Experience is the name everyone gives to their mistakes."
—from the play "Lady Windermere's Fan" by Oscar Wilde

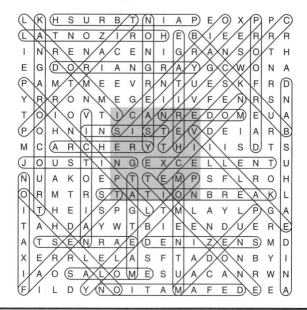

157. It's a Shore Thing

When you see shells on the shore, are you shore that they're seashells?

158. We're in the Money

I've got enough money to last me for the rest of my life ... just as long as I don't have to buy anything.

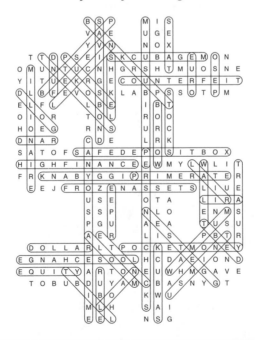

159. Cover Letter

"You don't write because you want to say something; you write because you've got something to say."
—[F. Scott] Fitzgerald

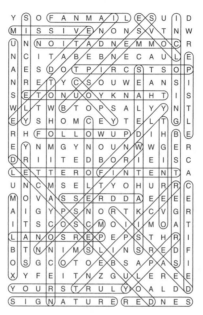

160. Today's To-Do List

"Never put off to tomorrow what you can put off to the day after tomorrow." "Procrastination is the art of keeping up with yesterday."

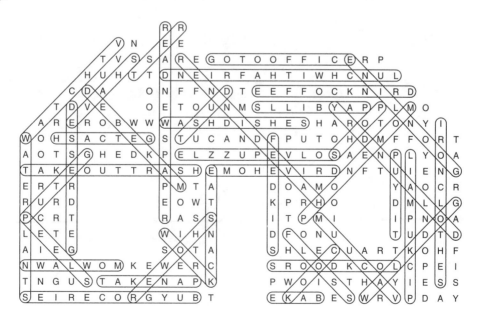

161. At the Pharmacy

Rx stands for the Latin word for recipe. So a prescription is a recipe for mixing ingredients to make a drug.

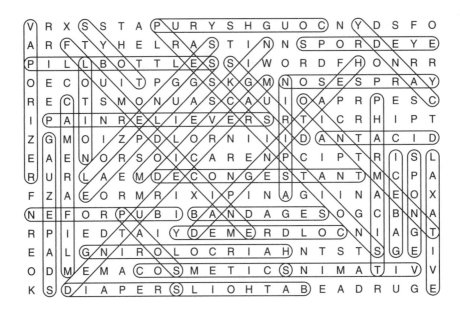

162. Wordy Gurdy

Make my letter better or give my story glory and I'll be crediting editing, but make a verse worse and you commit a rhyme crime.

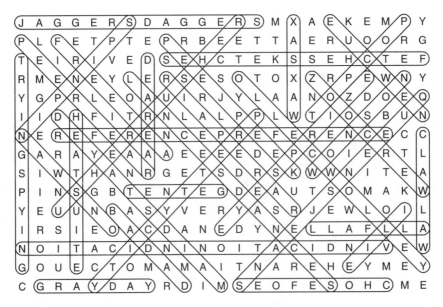

163. Give Me a Ring

"Oh! how many torments lie in the small circle of a wedding-ring!" [—dramatist Colley Cibber]

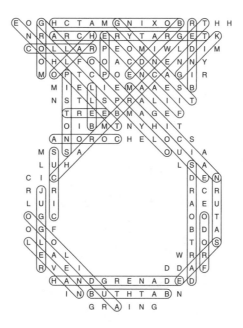

164. In the Papers

Napoleon Bonaparte said, "Four hostile newspapers are more to be feared than a thousand bayonets."

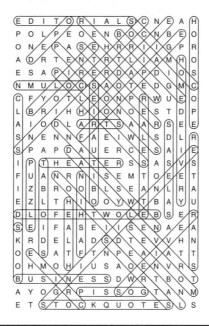

165. Solar Eclipse

When the moon dims the sun during an eclipse, you could say it's a form of natural sunblock.

166. Picture Perfect

Some well-known PP's are Pablo Picasso, Priscilla Presley, Patti Page, Peter Piper, Porky Pig, and the Pink Panther.

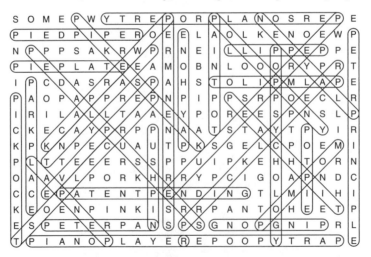

167. Changing Direction

If, like most people, you don't like change, change your attitude about change and you might enjoy change for a change.

168. Things You Make

"Use it up, wear it out; make it do, or do without." "The man who makes no mistakes does not usually make anything." —[Edward John] Phelps

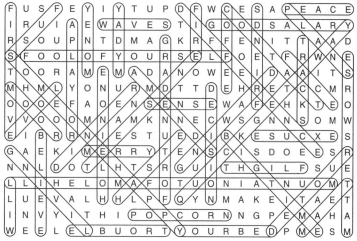

169. Road Signs

While driving, I saw a sign that said, "Ten Years at the Same Location." Now most businesses would be proud of that achievement, but this was a road crew.

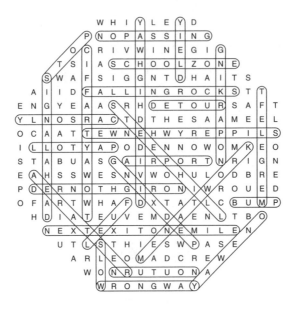

170. Black Hole #3

Center quote: What was the best thing before sliced bread?
Regular quote: "Inventing is a combination of brains and materials. The more brains you use, the less materials you need." [—Charles F. Kettering]

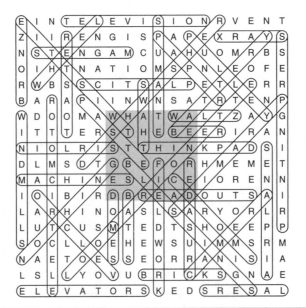

171. Holiday Highlights

Money is a great Xmas gift. It's always the right size.

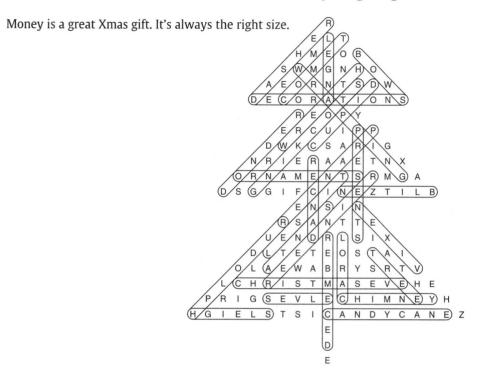

172. As Good as Cold

"I get a runny nose, a scratchy throat and an awful cough every winter," said Tom coldly.

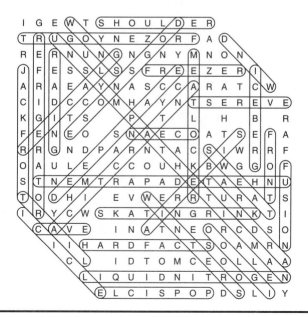

173. The Play's the Thing

"When you do Shakespeare, they think you must be intelligent because they think you understand what you're saying." —Helen Mirren

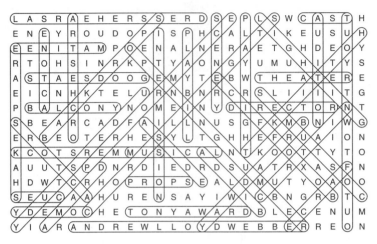

174. You Wanna Pisa Me?

When the moon hits your eye like a big pizza pie, that's a mess. [—to be sung to the tune of "That's Amore."]

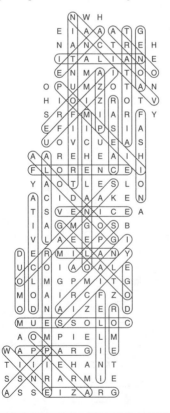

175. Op-Position

If opposites attract, why do most of us prefer the company of people who think the same way as we do?

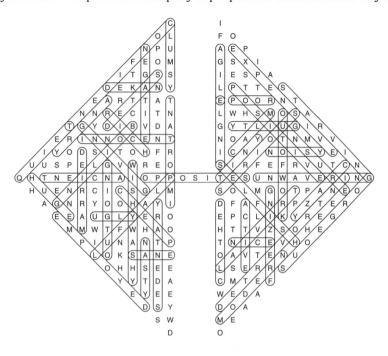

176. People Who Work Outdoors

Working outdoors can often be pretty tough, but doing so while collecting fees for crossing a bridge can really take its toll.

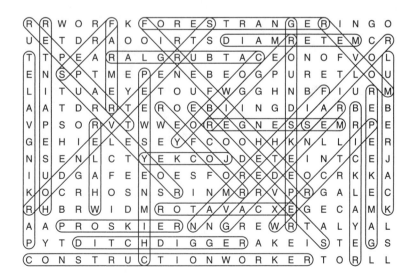

177. Honorable Mention

"Let this be your motto—Rely on yourself! For, whether the prize be a ribbon or throne, The victor is he who can go it alone!" —John Saxe

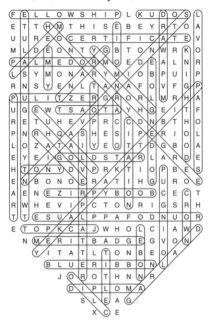

178. Take It Like a Man

As in the grid, show me a man who has both feet planted firmly on the ground, and I'll show you a man who can't get his pants on.

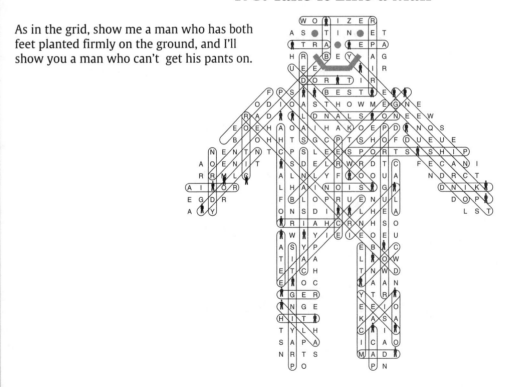

179. That Really Hits the Spa

"If you mean to keep as well as possible, the less you think about your health the better." —Oliver Wendell Holmes, Sr.

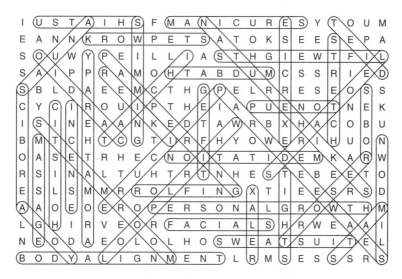

180. Abbr.-ations

FYI, here's an M.O. to become a V.I.P. ASAP: go to a St. U., get a deg. in econ.; then get an M.B.A., join a co. and become its pres. and CEO.

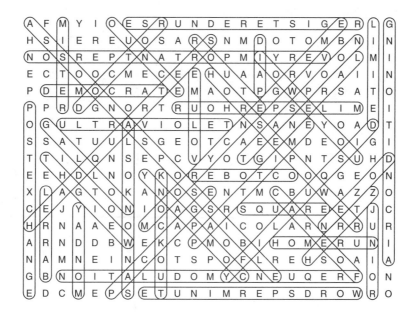

181. It's a Mystery to Me!

Horror writer Edgar Allan Poe deserves credit for inventing the detective story.

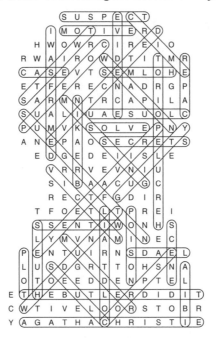

182. Things That Make You Sweat

"His brow is wet with honest sweat, He earns whate'er he can, And looks the whole world in the face, For he owes not any man." [from "The Village Blacksmith" by Longfellow]

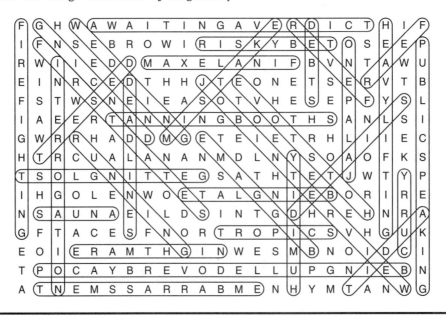

183. All Bottled Up

Like a note from a sailor stranded on a desert island, this hidden quote is a message in a bottle.

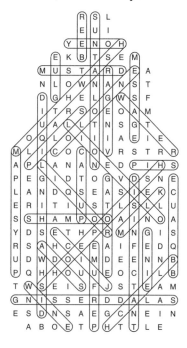

184. Making Connections

When Colombia refused terms for the project, the U.S. sent troops to Panama, freed it from Colombia's rule, and got to build the canal.

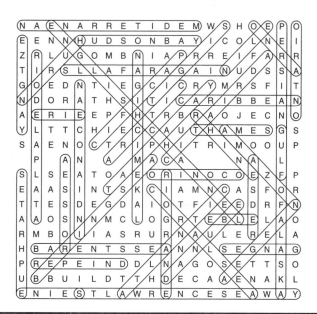

185. Taking a Stand

The style, history, and artist help make a painting important, but to be truly so, Picasso said, it must be expensive. [Just kidding.]

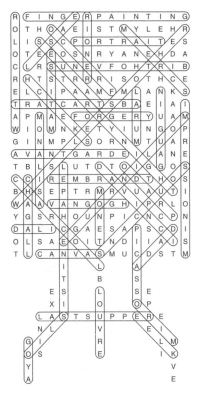

186. Taking It Hard

"You are snatching a hard guy when you snatch Bookie Bob .... I hear the softest thing about him is his front teeth." — [Damon] Runyon

187. Fish Tale

I catch deformed fish. They're the ones with their heads too close to their tails.

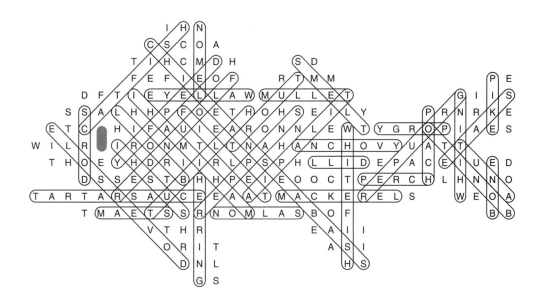

188. Winding Down

"Time is a great teacher, but unfortunately it kills all its pupils." —[Hector] Berlioz

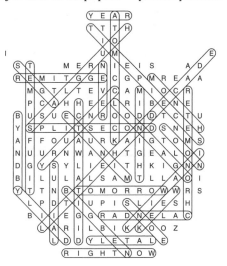

189. Photo Finish

The photograph doesn't restore the past but attests that what I see has indeed existed. [paraphrase of a line by Roland Barthes]

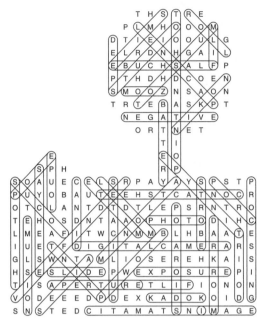

190. End So It Goes ...

"The end of all our exploring will be to arrive where we started and know the place for the first time." [—T.S. Eliot]

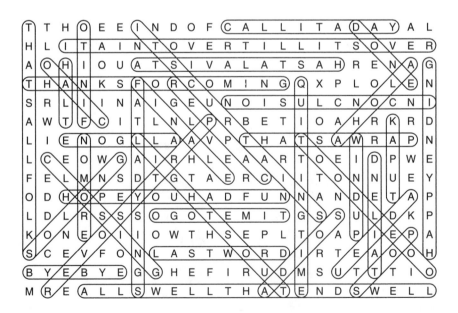

191. Taking Stock

Indeed, Air Canada is up, Dell Computer is down, and Pampers remain unchanged.

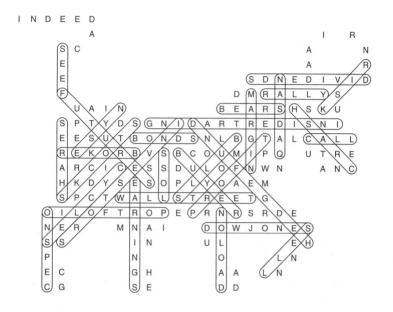

192. The Wheel Thing

"Marriage is a wonderful invention; but, then again, so is a bicycle repair kit." [—Scottish comedian Billy Connolly]

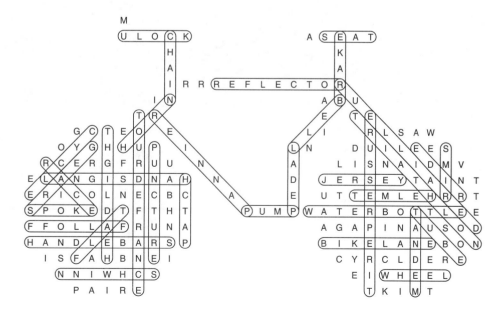

193. Under the Big Top

What does a kid say he's going to run off and join if his parents work for the circus?

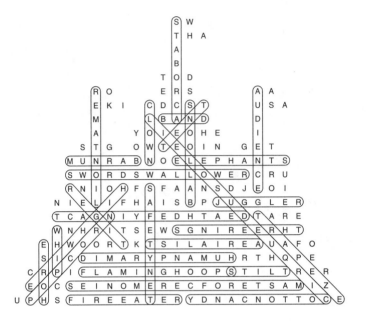

194. Archetypes

An archbishop and his archenemy saw an archangel at the St. Louis Arch.

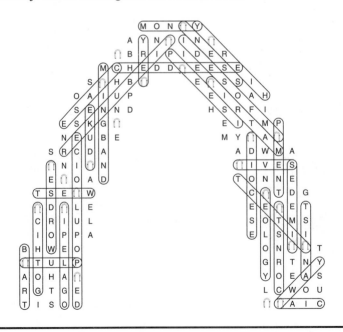

195. Of Thee I Sing

The words to "America the Beautiful" were inspired by a view a teacher experienced atop Pikes Peak.

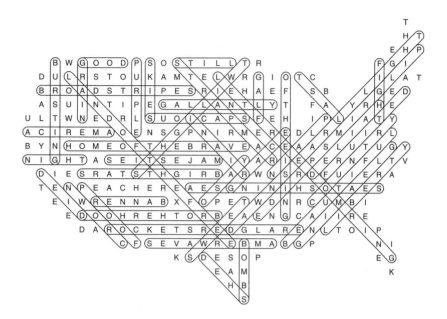

196. Hand-Holding

There are two kinds of people who like to hold hands: lovers, and players of card games.

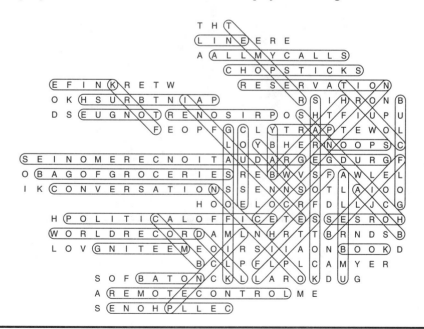

197. Greenery Scenery

U.S. money is green, so if you have it, why are you said to be in the black?

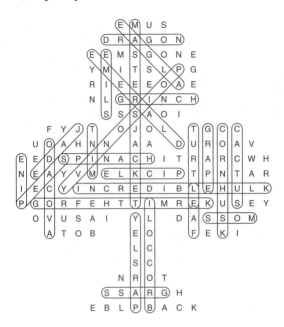

198. Don't Let It Throw You

Victory against Goliath was very close for David as it was merely a stone's throw away.

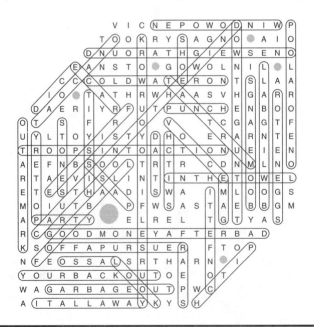

199. The X Factor

X Marks the Spot and X-Games

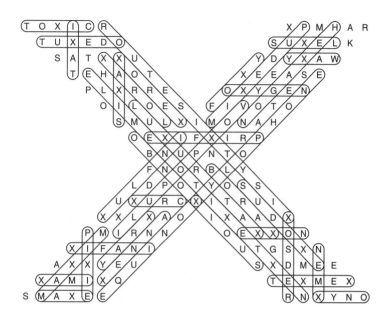

200. Missing in Action

The first letters of the missing words spell out "Lost at sea."
Regular hidden message: Mates buried at sea are said to have gone to Davy Jones's locker.

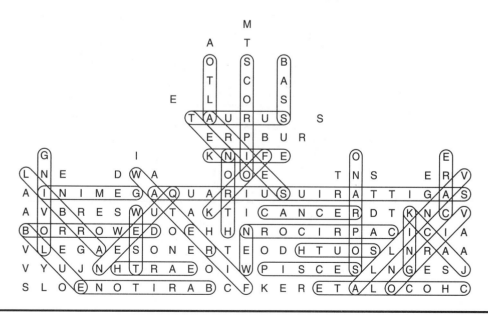

201. Absolutely Super

If Superman came uninvited to Earth from a far planet, does than make him an illegal alien?

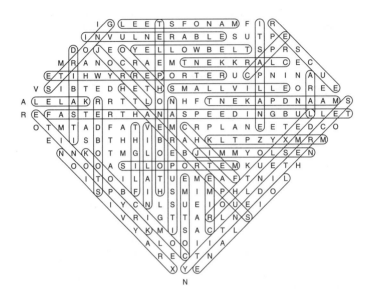

202. Soft-Spoken

"Speak softly and carry a big stick; you will go far." —Theodore Roosevelt

203. Black Hole #4

Center quip: "If I did, that would defeat the whole purpose."
Regular hidden message: A tailor who refused to alter clothes for businessmen wrote a book called "Suit Yourself."

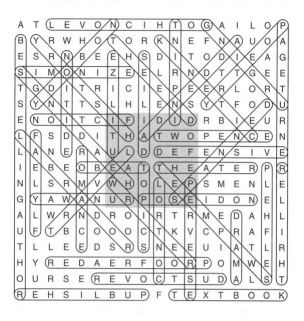

204. Quick on the Draw

What was the result of the contest between the two sketch artists? Fittingly, it ended in a draw.

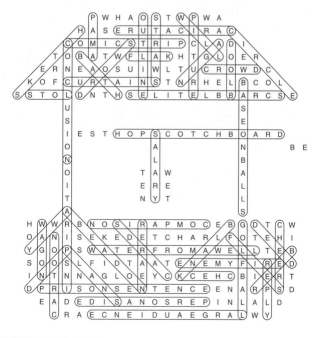

205. Two Left Feet

Dancing is "a perpendicular expression of a horizontal desire." [—George Bernard Shaw]

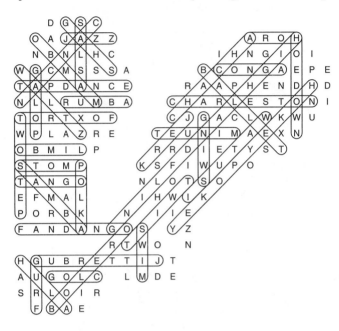

206. You Can Bed on It

For some married couples, two beds are better than one.

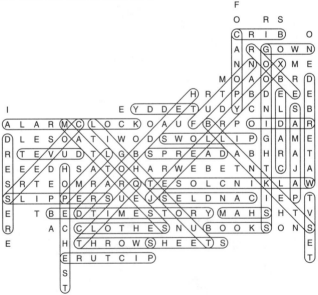

207. Small Wonder

"But many sanguine people hope / To see him through a microscope."

208. Petal Pushers

"Art is the unceasing effort to compete with the beauty of flowers—and never succeeding." —[Marc] Chagall

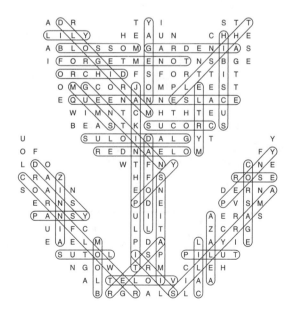

209. Listen to This

"Listening, not imitation, may be the sincerest form of flattery." —Dr. Joyce Brothers

210. Follow Directions

Time's up! Put down your pencil right now!

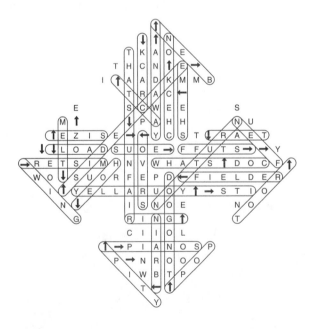

211. Open for Business

"Minds are like parachutes. They only function when they are open." [—Scottish physicist James Dewar]

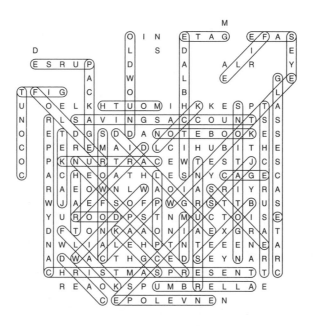

212. Read All About It

"People say that life is the thing, but I prefer reading." [—Logan Pearsall Smith]

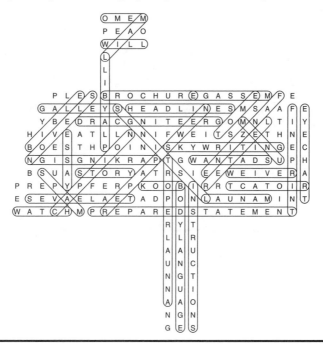

213. Go for It

Be good and go to the head of the class; be bad and go to the principal's office.

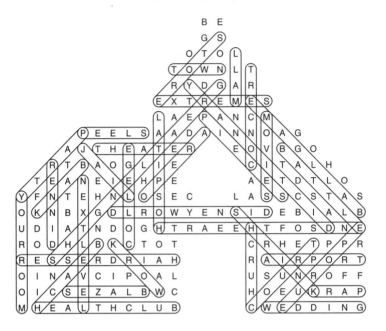

214. Everything to Lose

Game players may learn more from losing than from winning.

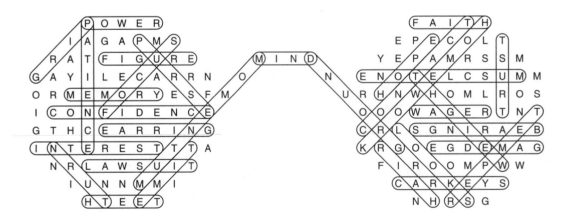

215. Movie Editing

Michael J. Fox is a doctor in "Back to the Suture." Natalie Wood has a baby in "West Side Stork."

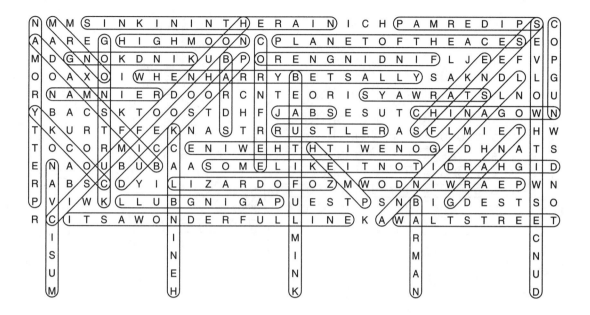

216. Land of the Rising Sun

Is it true greedy Japanese businessmen have a yen for money?

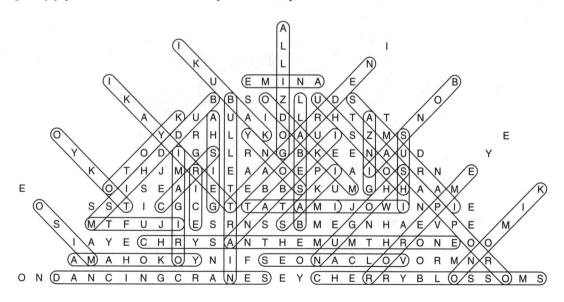

217. Plane and Simple

So you can kiss your luggage good-bye.

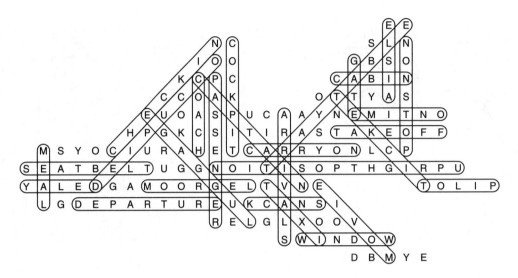

218. Hitting Below the Belt

Mae West said, "You can say what you like about long dresses, but they cover a multitude of shins."

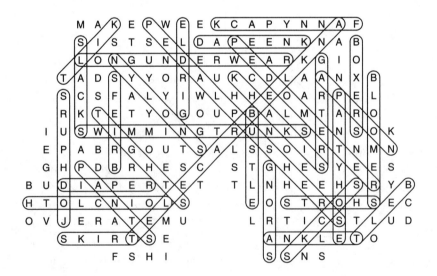

219. Expense Account

"Give me the luxuries of life, and I will [willingly] do without the necessities." [—Frank Lloyd Wright]

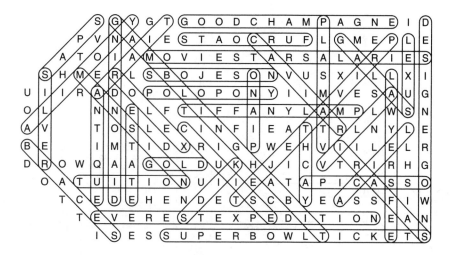

220. Suit to a Tea

"... only in hot water do you realize how strong she is."

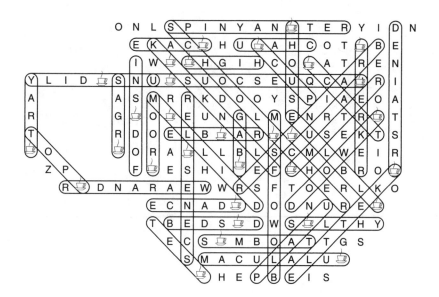

221. Under Construction

"We shape our buildings; thereafter they shape us." —[Winston] Churchill

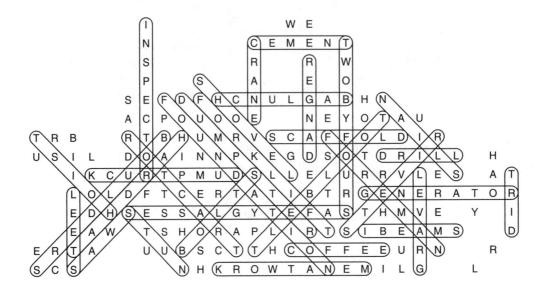

222. A Hole Lot Going On

"When I was young, I found out [that] the big toe always ends up making a hole in a sock. So I stopped wearing socks." [—Albert Einstein]

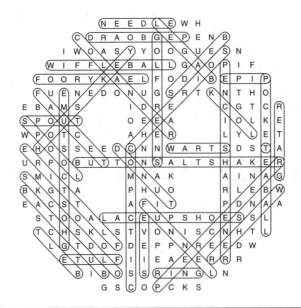

223. It's a Good Sign

"Everything is worth what its purchaser will pay for it." [—Publilius Syrus]

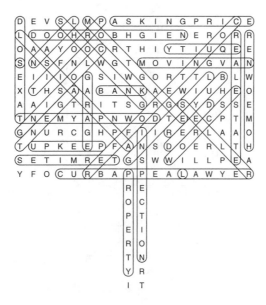

224. Jnana Banana

A jazz band jumped bail after putting jumping beans in the jury box.

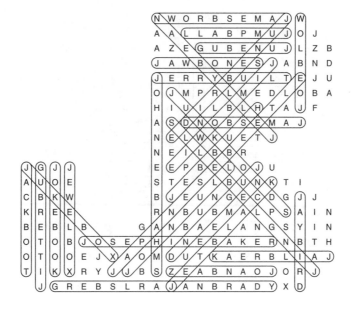

225. Wall-Done

"My predilection for painting lends joyousness to a wall."

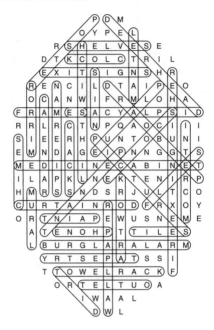

226. Black Hole #5

Center quip: Was Robin Hood's mother known as Mother Hood?
Regular hidden message: When Robin passed the home of the people next door, did they say, "There goes the neighbor Hood!"?

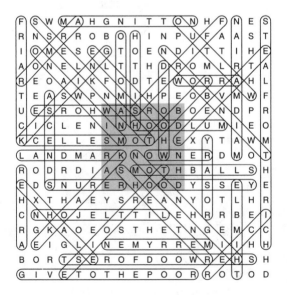

227. So You Want To Be A Star

A person who's known for his well-knownness. [—Daniel J. Boorstin]

228. Just Deserts

"… to make the world a desert or to make the deserts bloom." [—Adlai Stevenson]

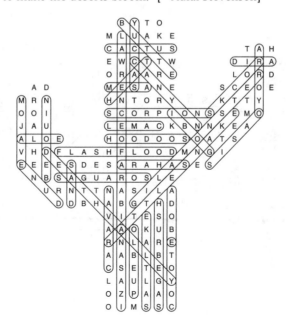

229. Cold Comfort

Our town has a terrific snow removal system. It's called August.

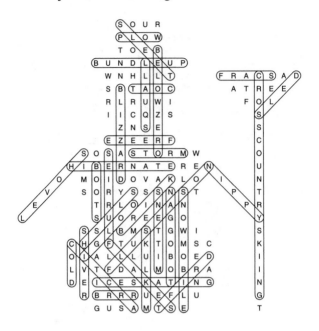

230. Dogging It

My doberman flunked out of obedience school. He claimed the kids ate his homework.

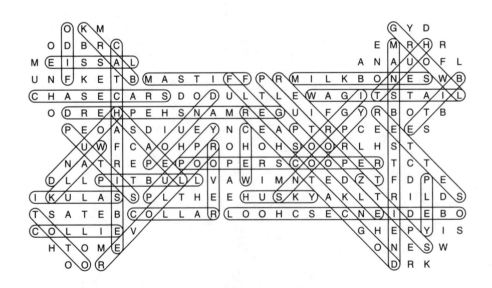

231. At Loose Ends

Some solvers won't make heads or tails of this word search.

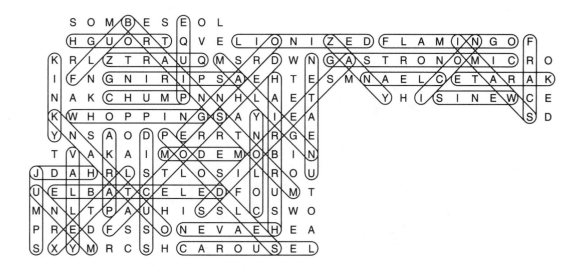

232. It's Only Money

"I never been in no situation where havin' money made it any worse." —Clinton Jones

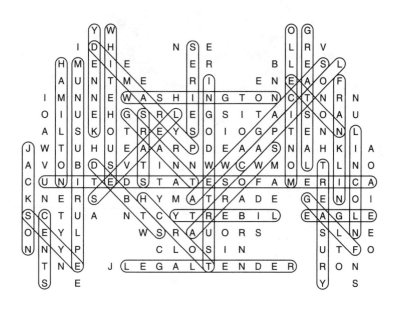

233. Twin Peaks

For thrill seekers, getting to the top of a mountain is a peak experience.

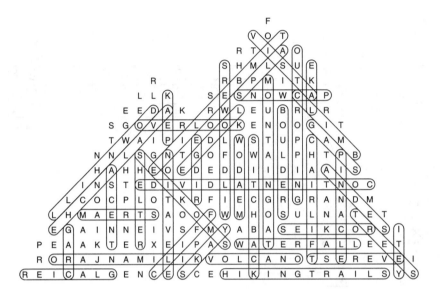

234. In the Line of Duty

Seven Fourteen, the badge number of Joe Friday, was chosen to honor Babe Ruth's career total of home runs.

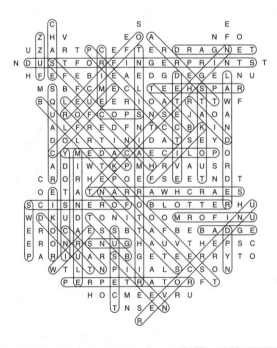

235. Going Under

"Our defense is not in armaments ... nor in going underground. It is in law and order." [—Albert Einstein]

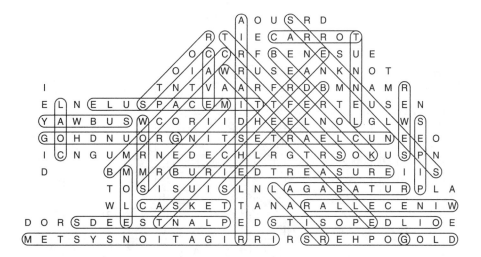

236. Chain of Events

Quote one: "We cannot make events. Our business is [wisely] to improve them." Quote two: "I claim not to have controlled events, but confess plainly that events have controlled me."

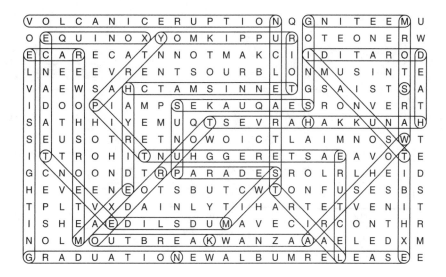

237. Are We There Yet?

We've had so much rain lately that I thought I was on vacation.

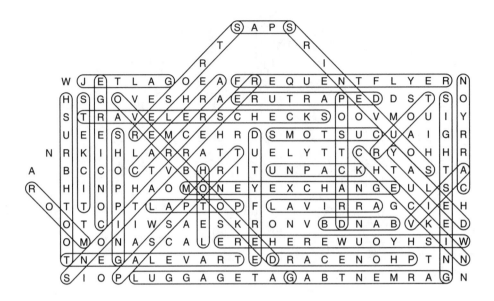

238. Soccer to Me

Soccer is one way for people to get their kicks.

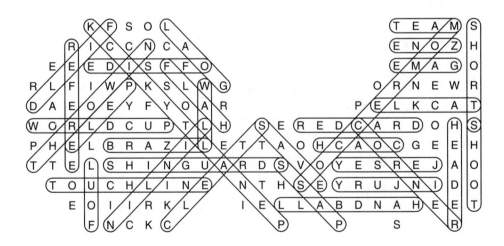

239. Breakfast Buffet

A [French] proverb: A good meal ought to begin with hunger.

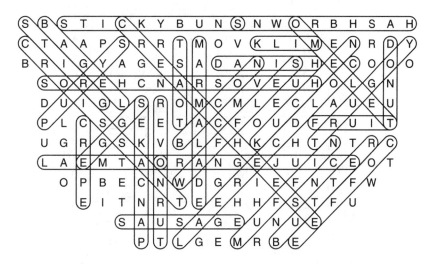

240. The Sound of Music

He kept falling asleep at the piano.

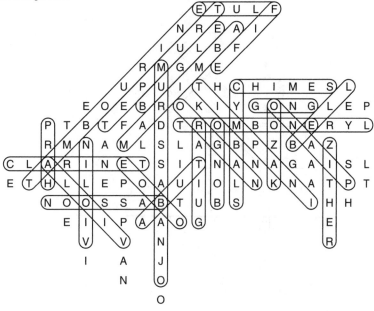

241. Black Hole #6

Center quip: Her idea of roughing it is slow room service.
Regular hidden message: Those who go camping in the woods during thunderstorms tend to be in-tents people.

242. Staying Afloat

"Afloat. We move: Delicious! Ah, / What else is like the gondola?" [—English poet Arthur Hugh Clough]

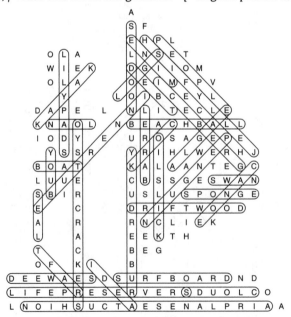

243. Six-Pack

"Six Degrees of Separation," "Six Days Seven Nights," and "The Sixth Sense."

244. Do You Believe In Magic?

"Any sufficiently advanced technology is indistinguishable from magic." [—Arthur C. Clarke]

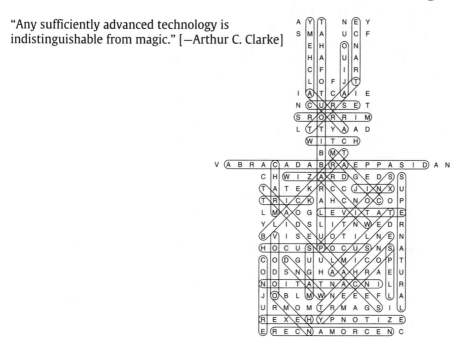

245. "Roll 'Em"

"Pictures are for entertainment; messages should be delivered by Western Union."

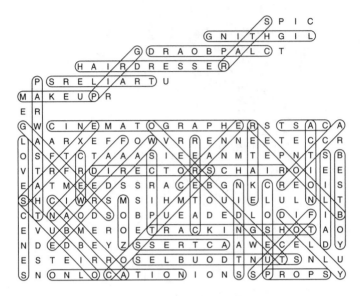

246. Wedding Party

There is a saying, "If you marry for money, you surely will earn it."

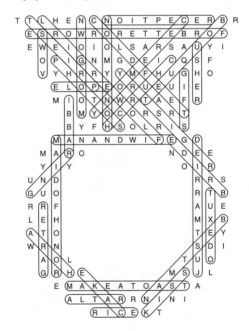

247. All Good Things ...

"We are all here on earth to help others; what on earth the others are here for I don't know." [—W.H. Auden]

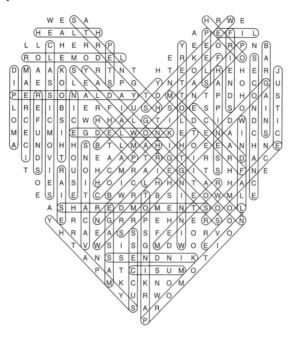

248. Start Your Day With a Smile

"The secret of happiness is not in doing what one likes, but in liking what one has to do." [—James M. Barrie]

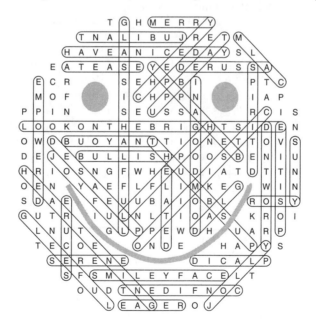

249. Boomerangs

"Don't worry about the world coming to an end to day, it's already tomorrow in Australia." —Charles M. Schulz, creator of the comic strip "Peanuts"

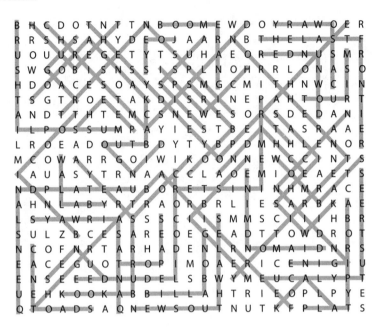

250. Black Hole #7

Center quip: A proverb is one man's wit and all men's wisdom.
Regular hidden message: "One of the symptoms of an approaching nervous breakdown is the belief that one's work is terribly important." —[Bertrand] Russell

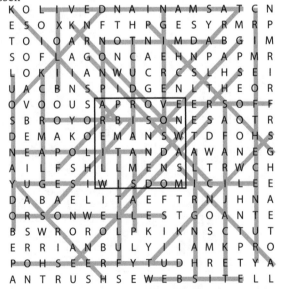

251. You Can Do It

Politics is not a bad profession; if you succeed there are many rewards, if you disgrace yourself, you can always write a book. —President Ronald Reagan

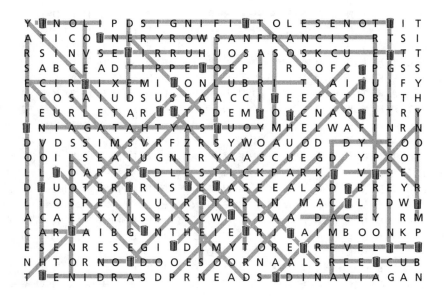

252. Everyone Makes Mistakes

Regular hidden message: "I have a spelling checker it came with my pc. It plainly marks four my revue mistakes. I cannot sea. Ive run this poem threw it. I'm sure your pleased too no its letter perfect in its weigh, my checker tolled me sew." —Janet Minor

Extra Quip: He who never made a mistake, never made a discovery. —Samuel Smiles

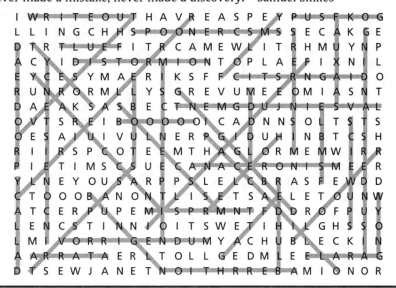

253. Head to Tail

"The ordinary telegraph is like a very long cat—you pull the tail in New York and it meows in Los Angeles. The wireless is the same only without the cat." —Albert Einstein

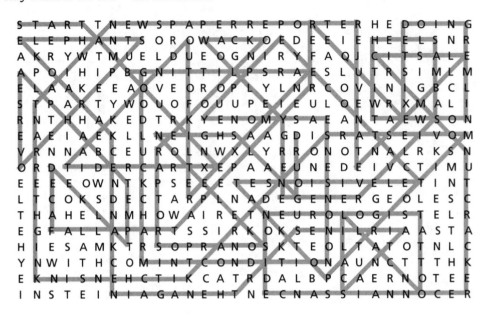

254. The Sign of Torus

"Women working with the Salvation Army in France during World War I wanted to make the American soldiers feel less homesick and began making them doughnuts, the soldiers were hence called dough boys." —from the editors of *Information Please*.

255. Wheel of Fortune

"If I had to summarize in one sentence the major lesson I have learned in life, that sentence would be sometimes you have to buy a vowel." —Dave Barry

256. Passing Zone

"If all the cars in the country were placed end to end some fool would still pull out and try to pass them." —Epigram written by the author Evan Esar

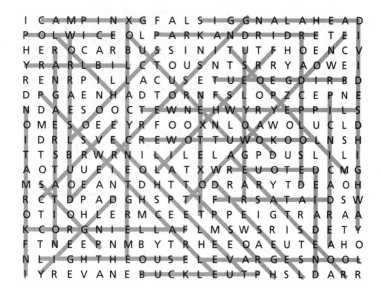

257. All Mixed Up

"The basic tool for the manipulation of reality is the manipulation of words." —Philip K Dick

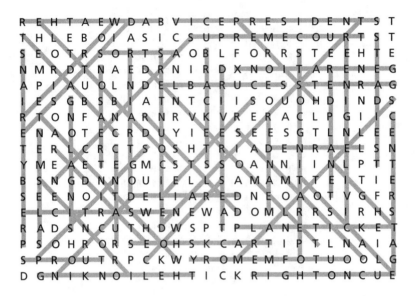

258. Getting Lost

The problem with an unwritten law is that you don't know where to go to erase it.

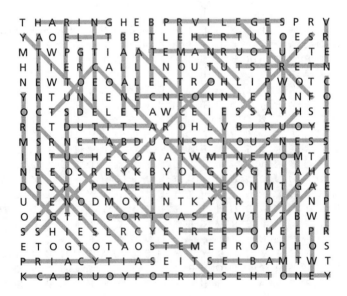

259. U-Turns

"Hardwork spotlights the character of people: some turn up their sleeves, some turn up their noses, and some don't turn up at all." —Sam Ewing

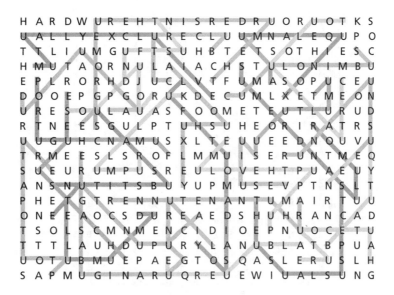

260. This and That

"I'm nobody! Who are you? Are you nobody, too? Then there's a pair of us—don't tell! They'd advertise you know." —Emily Dickinson [quote modified slightly]

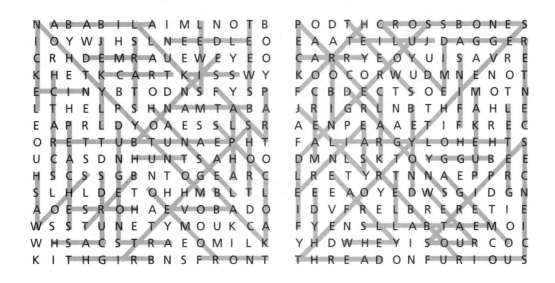

261. Animal Impressions

In argument, similes are like songs in love; they describe much but prove nothing. —Written by English poet and diplomat Matthew Prior.

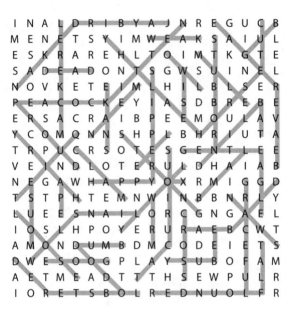

262. Black Hole #8

Center quip: Problems worthy of attack prove their worth by hitting back.
Regular hidden message: "Philosophers must ultimately find their true perfection in knowing all the follies of mankind—by introspection." —Piet Hein

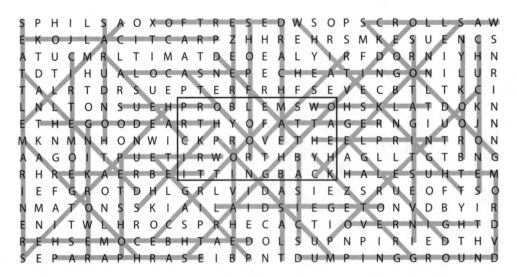

263. A Star is Born

"The way a team plays as a whole determines its success. You may have the greatest bunch of individual stars in the world but if they don't play together, the club won't be worth a dime." —Babe Ruth

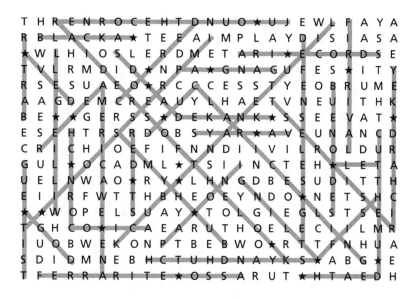

264. Exchanging Letters

"My spelling is wobbly. It's good spelling but it wobbles and the letters get in the wrong places." —A.A. Milne, *Winnie the Pooh*

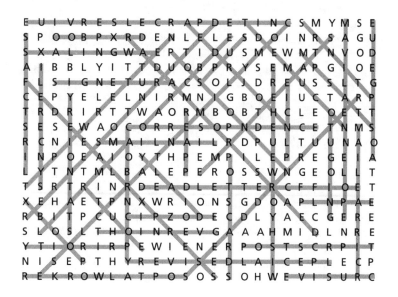

265. Hop, Skip, and Jump

"There is no prescribed route to follow to arrive at a new idea. You have to make the intuitive leap but the difference is that once you've made that intuitive leap, you have to justify it by filling in the intermediate steps." —Stephen Hawking

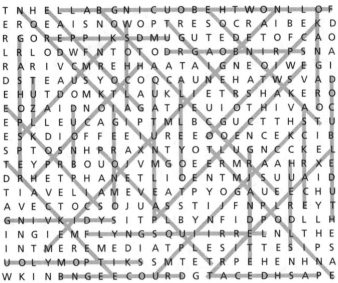

266. Boxing Match

"When I retire I'm going to spend my evenings by the fireplace going through those boxes. There are things in there that ought to be burned." —Richard Milhous Nixon

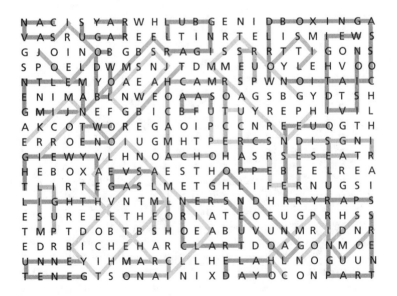

267. Trios

"A writer needs three things: experience, observation, and imagination. Any two of which, at times any one of which, can supply the lack of the others." —William F. Aulkner

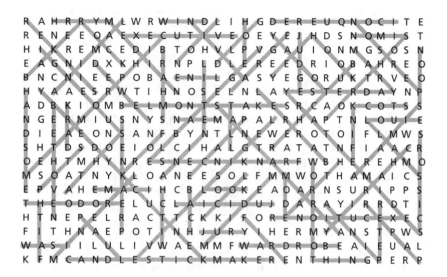

268. Black Hole #9

Center quip: Adults are obsolete children.
Regular hidden message: I like nonsense; it wakes up the brain cells. —Theodor Geisel, a.k.a. Dr. Seuss

269. Eating Your Words

"If you would be pungent, be brief, for it is with words as with sunbeams—the more they are condensed, the deeper they burn." —Robert Southey

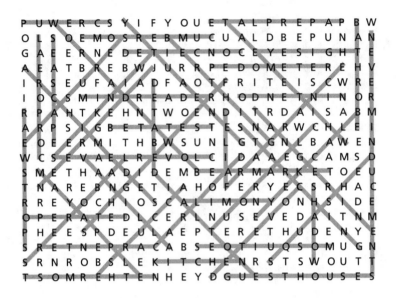

270. Show of Hands

"The old chess is too limited. Imagine playing cards, black jack for example, and every time the dealer has the same starting hand, you have the same starting hand. What's the point?" —Bobby Fischer

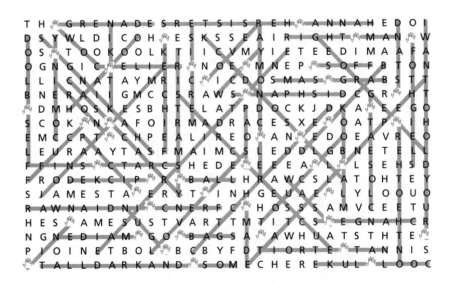

271. Cross Word Puzzle

"The concept of two people living together for twenty-five years without having a cross word suggests a lack of spirit only to be admired in sheep." By Alan Patrick Herbert, member of the British Parliament

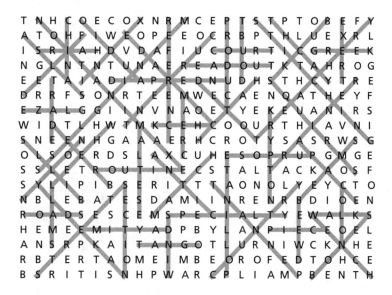

272. Black Hole #10

Center quip: Few things are as democratic as a snowstorm.
Regular hidden message: "Knowledge is power but enthusiasm pulls the switch." —Ivern Ball in the *National Enquirer*

273. Letter Perfect

"Letters are largely written to get things out of your system." —John Dos Passos

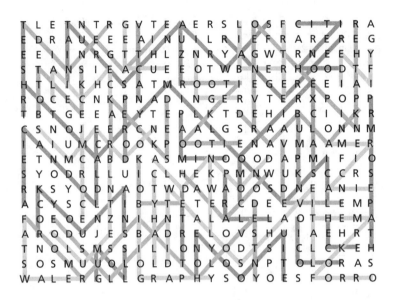

274. Split Decisions

"Two roads diverged in a wood and I—I took the one less traveled by, and that has made all the difference." From the Robert Frost poem "The Road Not Taken."

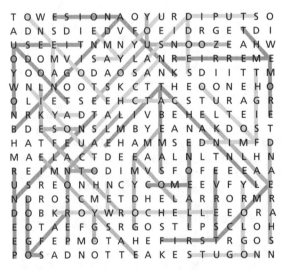

275. W■rd S■■rch

"Playing bop is like playing Scrabble with all the vowels missing." —Duke Ellington

276. The Eyes Have It

"Telescope. A device having a relation to the eyes, similar to that of the telephone to the ear, enabling distant objects to plague us with a multitude of needless details. Luckily it is unprovided with a bell summoning us to the sacrifice." —[Ambrose] Bierce

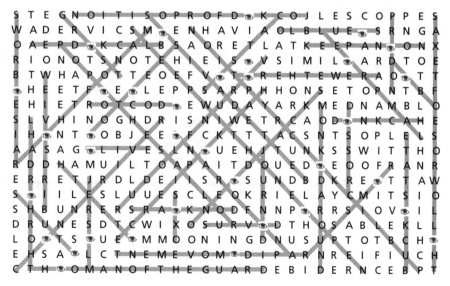

277. Going Too Far

"Here's a riddle for our age: When the sky's the limit, how can you tell you've gone too far?" —Former U.S. Poet Laureate Rita Dove

Phrases: (Starting at the top and going clockwise)
Above and Beyond
Go Over the Edge
Think Outside the Box
Off the Board

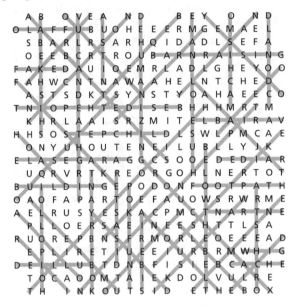

278. K Turns

"Your morals are like roads through the Alps; they make these hairpin turns all the time." —Erica Jong, *Fear of Flying*

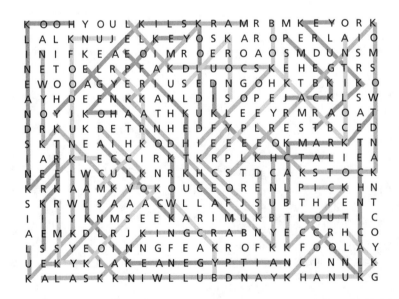

279. Black Hole #11

Center quip: "Old professors never die; they merely lose their faculties." — [Stephen Fry]
Regular hidden message: "A professor is one who talks in someone else's sleep." —W.H. Auden, quoted in Charles Osborne's *The Life of a Poet*

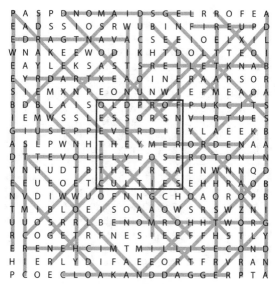

280. Getting Directions

"I have an existential map. It has 'you are here' written all over it." —Comedian Steven Wright

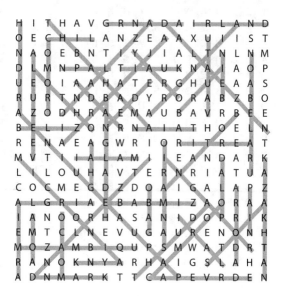

281. Right and Left

"So much of life is luck. One day you make a right turn and get hit by a car. Turn left and you meet the love of your life. I think I made the correct turn." —Loretta Swit

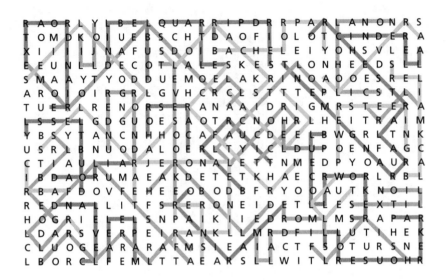

282. Snake Pit

"The fact that a snake wags its tail at you doesn't mean it wants to be petted." —anonymous

283. Lost in Translation

"After all, when you come right down to it, how many people speak the same language even when they speak the same language?" —Russell Hoban

284. Cubism

"God not only plays dice, he also sometimes throws the dice where they cannot be seen." —Stephen Hawking on Einstein's quote "I cannot believe that god plays dice with the cosmos."

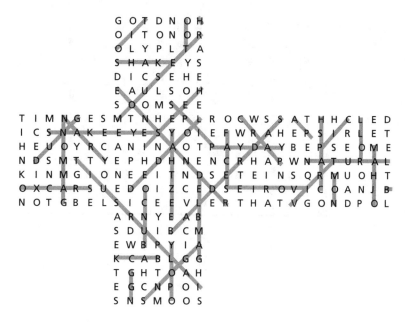

285. Bar Code

"Just because your voice reaches halfway around the world doesn't mean you are wiser than when it reached only to the end of the bar." —Former news broadcaster Edward R. Murrow

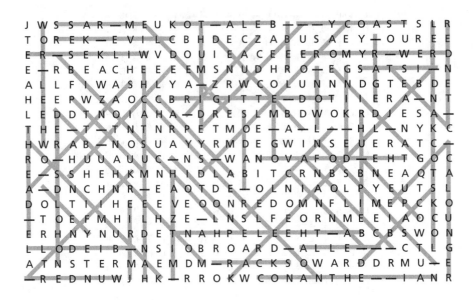

286. Do-It-Yourself Word Search

Other answers may be possible.

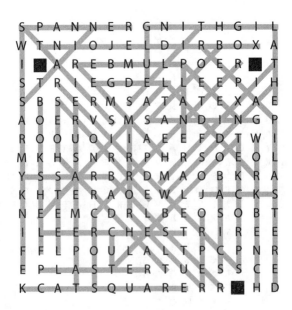

287. Take Your Best Shot

"Every gentleman plays billiards but someone who plays billiards too well is no gentleman." —former President of the United States, Thomas Jefferson
Winning Team: STRIPE

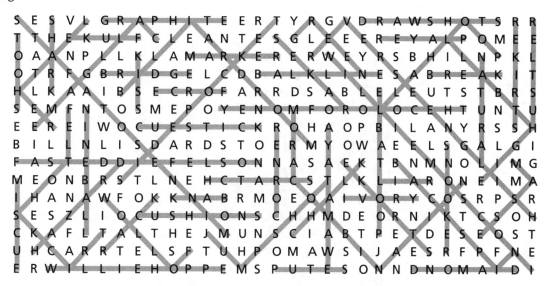

288. Black Hole #12

Center quip: Art, like morality, consists of drawing the line somewhere.
Regular hidden message: "The test of a good religion is whether you can joke about it." —G. K. Chesterton

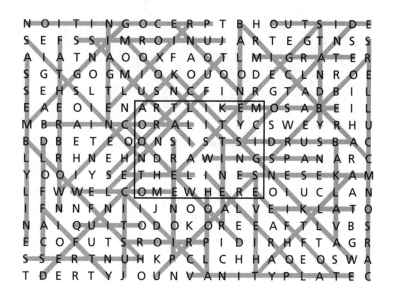

289. Getting a Clue

"It's a matter of life after death, now that he's dead I have a life." —Madeline Kahn as Mrs. White in the nineteen–eighty five movie *Clue*.
Mrs. White, hall, rope (the words on the list that don't appear in the grid)

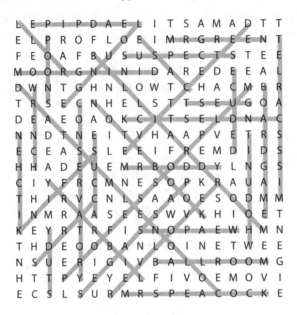

290. Stop and Go

"Natives who beat drums to drive off evil spirits are objects of scorn to smart Americans who blow horns to break up traffic jams." —Mary Ellen Kelly

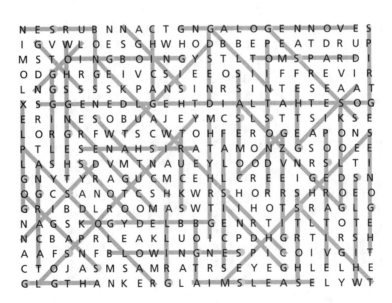

291. Treasure Hunt

Regular hidden message: "To continue, take all of the words in the list and write them backwards. Then place them in alphabetical order and read off their first letters. This will give you the final instruction."

After doing that, you get: "The spot in the grid has been marked for you."

The correct square is the U in Euphoria (there is an X shape made up of nine U's with that one in the center.

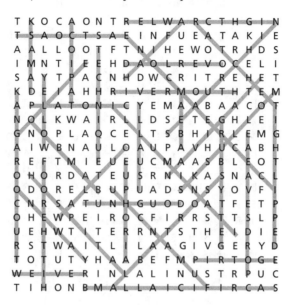

292. Black Hole #13

Center quip: "A good composer does not imitate; he steals." —Igor Stravinsky
Regular hidden message: "Too many pieces of music finish too long after the end." —Igor Stravinsky

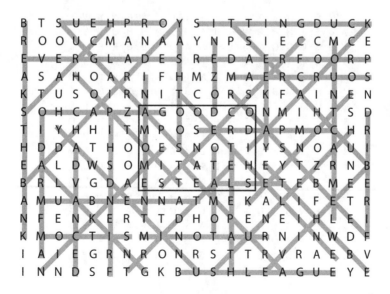

293. Antimatter

"Anyone who is not shocked by quantum theory has not understood it." —Niels Bohr
Letters that aren't part of pairs: QUARKS

294. Looking Sharp

"He was always smoothing and polishing himself, and in the end he became blunt before he was sharp."
—G.C. Lichtenberg

295. Every Which Way

"Ideas are great arrows, but there has to be a bow. And politics is the bow of idealism." —Bill Moyer

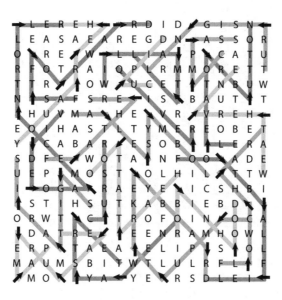

296. Sea Search

"The only great qualification for being put at the head of the Navy is that I am very much at sea." —Edward Carson, Irish public official and former Lord of the Admiralty

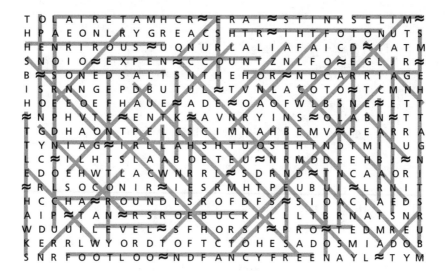

297. Patchwork Quilt

```
S I N G R P A F R P I E R E
E C Z O E T C H A C T C G I
C T O N D I E W O U C E O O
O R N E S N T R R E M P N O
T I T U E T E K F R N E N T
P R S L N T R R I A D C H I
S E C I T O R G M V I P I
E I N E D Y E N T I S I O N
G M C T S T R I C T S E C T
A E N F I E P O P A R I S O
R T L L O D R T I O T S C N
E A C A L I T R A N P R A P
E L T E C Y U T C T A R S H
M E N T T I N G C E L R E D
```

298. Bridging the Gap

"Politicians are the same all over. They promise to build a bridge even where there is no river." —Nikita Krushchev
Letters in gap: Grand Canyon

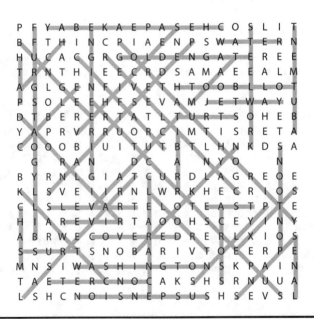

```
P F Y A B E K A E P A S E H C O S L I T
B F T H I N C P I A E N P S W A T E R N
H U C A C G R G O L D E N G A T E R E E
T R N T H I E E C R D S A M A E E A L M
A G L G E N F I V E T H T O O B L L O T
P S O L E E H F S E V A M J E T W A Y U
D T B E R E R T A T L T U R T S O H E B
Y A P R V R R U O R C M T I S R E T A
C O O O B I U I T U T B T L H N K D S A
G   R A N   D C   A   N Y O   N
B Y R N L G I A T C U R D L A G R E O E
K L S V E I R N L W R K H E C R I O S
C L S L E V A R T E L O T E A S T P T E
H I A R E V I R T A O O H S C E Y I N Y
A B R W E C O V E R E D R E R L X I O S
S S U R T S N O B A R I V T O E E R P E
M N S I W A S H I N G T O N S K P A I N
T A E T E R C N O C A K S H S R N U U A
L S H C N O I S N E P S U S H S E V S L
```

299. Roundabout

"A circle is the longest distance to the same point." —Tom Stoppard

300. Buddy System

"I do not believe that friends are necessarily the people you like best, they are merely the people who got there first."
—Peter Ustinov
Missing Letters quote: "Friendships last when each friend thinks he has a slight superiority over the other."
—[Honore de Balzac]

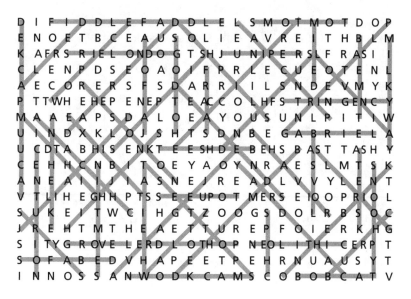

301. Pangram

"There must be more to life than having everything." —Maurice Sendak

302. Wedding Bells

"To keep your marriage brimming with love in the wedding cup whenever you're wrong, admit it; whenever you're right, shut up." —Ogden Nash in, "Marriage Lines: Notes of a Student Husband"

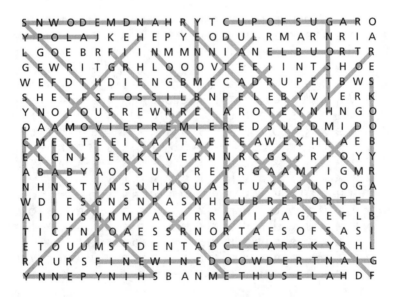

303. Repeat Performances

"Underneath this flabby exterior is an enormous lack of character." —Composer Oscar Levant

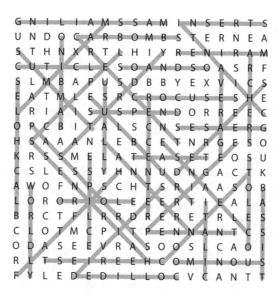

304. Missing L-i-n-ks

"Anthropologists are a connecting link between poets and scientists though their field work among primitive peoples has often made them forget the language of science." —Robert Graves

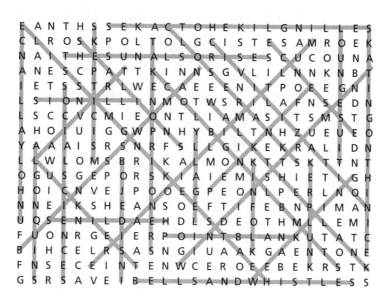

305. What's Next?

"We don't want to go back to tomorrow. We want to go forward." —Attributed to Dan Quayle
The gray boxes have the abbreviations of the months in order.

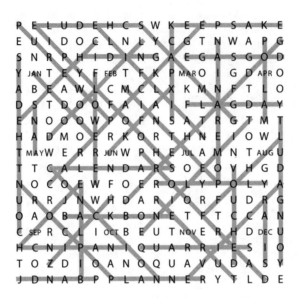

306. Meandering

"Why do you wonder that traveling does not help you, seeing that you always take yourself with you, the reason which set you wondering is ever at your heels." —Socrates

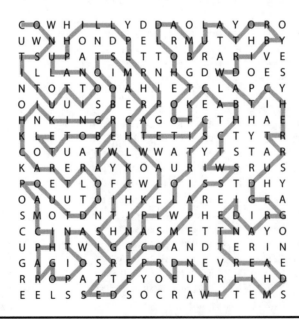

307. The End

Regular hidden message: "The end may justify the means as long as there is something that justifies the end."
—Quotation by Leon Trotsky
Extra letter message: Nice guys finish last, but we get to sleep in.

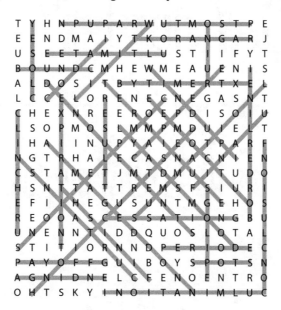